PEOPLE OF THE EARTH

An Indian couple eating, painted by John White in the late sixteenth century. Thomas Hariot wrote of the Indians ''They are verye sober in their eating and trinkinge, and consequently verye longe lived because they doe not oppress nature. . . . I would to God we would followe their exemple.''

THIRD EDITION

PEOPLE OF THE EARTH

An Introduction to World Prehistory

Brian M. Fagan

University of California, *Santa Barbara*

Little, Brown and Company   BOSTON   TORONTO

CREDITS

Frontispiece. Courtesy of the Trustees of the British Museum.

CHAPTER 1
Figure 1.3: From *Invitation to Archeology* by James Deetz. Illustrated by Eric Engstrom. Copyright © 1967 by James Deetz. Reprinted by permission of Doubleday & Company, Inc. *Figure 1.5:* Courtesy of the Society of Antiquaries of London. *Figure 1.6:* From *Invitation to Archeology* by James Deetz. Illustrated by Eric Engstrom. Copyright © 1967 by James Deetz. Reprinted by permission of Doubleday & Company, Inc.

CHAPTER 3
Table 3.1: Adapted from *Glacial and Quaternary Geology* by R. F. Flint, © 1971, by permission of John Wiley & Sons, Inc. *Figure 3.1:* Adapted, with permission, from Karl W. Butzer *Environment and Archeology* (New York: Aldine Publishing Company). Copyright © 1971 by Karl W. Butzer. *Figure 3.2:* Adapted from *Glacial and Quaternary Geology* by R. F. Flint, © 1971, by permission of John Wiley & Sons, Inc.

CHAPTER 4
Figure 4.2: By permission of Elwyn L. Simons, Yale Peabody Museum, New Haven, Connecticut. *Figure 4.3:* Photograph by Baron Hugo Van Lawick. © National Geographic Society. *Figure 4.4:* (a) and (b): Redrawn with permission of Macmillan Publishing Co., Inc. from *The Ascent of Man* by David Philbeam. Copyright © 1972, David Philbeam. (c): Redrawn with permission of Bantam Books, Inc. from *Monkeys and Apes* by Prudence Napier, copyright © 1972. All rights reserved. *Figure 4.5:* Courtesy of Transvaal Museum. *Figure 4.6:* Courtesy of Alun R. Hughes, University of the Witwatersrand. *Figure 4.8:* Peter Jones, © National Geographic Society. *Figure 4.9:* Courtesy of the Trustees of the National Museums of Kenya. *Table 4.3:* Adapted by permission from Mark L. Weiss and Alan E. Mann, *Human Biology and Behavior: An Anthropological Perspective,* 2nd Ed. Copyright © 1978, 1975 by Little, Brown and Company (Inc.). *Figure 4.10:* From Mark L. Weiss and Alan E. Mann, *Human Biology and Behavior: An Anthropological* (Credits continue on page 399.)

TO

- All the dozens of archaeologists and students who have read and used this book in its various editions and sent me their comments and criticisms. This is the only way I can thank them all and expose them for what they are — honest and unmerciful critics. I am deeply grateful.
- All the people at Little, Brown who have worked on this manuscript and invariably managed to produce an attractive book out of it. I am grateful for their cheerful help, and above all for their friendship, which is much cherished.
- And, lastly, and as usual, to our cats, who disapprove of authors in general and my writing efforts in particular. Their contribution was to tread on the manuscript — with muddy paws, of course.

TO THE READER

People of the Earth is an attempt at a straightforward narrative of human history from the origins of humankind up to the beginnings of literate civilization. To make the book accessible to those who have not previously studied archaeology, I keep technical terms to a minimum and define them where they do occur.

Anyone who takes on a task having the magnitude of a world prehistory must make several difficult decisions. One such decision was to gloss over many heated archaeological controversies and sometimes to give only one side of an academic argument. But each chapter has notes at the back of the book that are designed to lead you into the more technical literature and the morass of agreement and disagreement that characterizes world prehistory.

The structure of *People of the Earth* is comparatively straightforward. Part 1 deals with general principles of archaeology, theoretical views of the past, and with the climatic background. The remainder of the book is devoted to the story of human prehistory. Chronological tables are provided at the beginning of most chapters, putting cultural names, sites, dates, and other subdivisions of prehistory into a framework. Key dates and terms appear in the margins to give you a sense of chronological direction throughout the text. Special notes about dates appear on pages xix and 235. A table for calibrating radiocarbon dates is given on page 173 (Table 10.1). All measurements are given in both metric and nonmetric units. Metric equivalents are used as the primary unit except in the case of miles/kilometers. More readers conceive of long distances in miles, so it seemed logical to use them first.

TO THE INSTRUCTOR

People of the Earth has now flourished through two editions, serving as a text in courses as varied as introductory anthropology, physical anthropology and archaeology, archaeology, and, of course, world prehistory. Having begun the book with considerable reluctance, I am now very glad that I stuck with it, for I have learned a great deal of archaeology along the way. The experiences of instructors and students, including my own experience teaching from the book, have justified some of my initial decisions and caused me to make major changes in the book as well. I think it is worth sharing some of my decisions with you.

Undoubtedly the biggest problem in preparing this book is the huge flood of literature that now surrounds world prehistory. It is impossible for me, or anyone, to keep pace with all the material from every corner of the world. Like most archaeologists, I am not a linguistic genius. Unlike Heinrich Schliemann, who mastered at least eight languages, and Arthur Evans, who spoke a minimum of six, my expertise is limited to English and French with a smattering of German and Swahili. Thus, my reading has necessarily been selective, especially in regions like central Europe, where a knowledge of German is essential. In these and other areas, I have had to rely heavily on secondary and tertiary sources. For these reasons, I have undoubtedly missed some key references and misled readers with some wrong information. I hope that you will update readers from your own knowledge, and, if you find oversights, drop me a line to tell me about them. I am deeply grateful to those of you who have taken the time to send me reprints, corrections, or information on references. Your efforts are valuable and deeply appreciated. It is now almost a full-time job to keep up with world prehistory, because the days of the specialist, and the subspecialist, are truly with us.

Almost all users have supported the broad geographical coverage of this book, so it remains a feature of the third edition. Ethnocentric prehistories are a thing of the past, for insights from less well-known areas can often illuminate problems nearer home. One need only look at the research on shell middens being carried out in New Zealand or the living archaeology from the Kalahari desert in southern Africa to get the point. If I have sometimes skimped on detailed coverage of well-known areas, I am unrepentant. It is well worth it in the interest of balanced coverage.

In response to the specific requests of users of the second edition, I have expanded coverage of method and theory, ancient Egypt, and food production, while trimming the sections on the origins of humankind and hunters and gatherers. In the interests of updating the coverage, I have added some sites and omitted others. I have also made a conscious effort to correlate illustrations, especially tables and maps, more closely with the text, so that students can use them as tools for gaining chronological and spatial perspectives on world prehistory. Several illustrations are new, and the ones dealing with sites are amplified. On the assumption that typological details are best filled in at a later stage, I have avoided including too many pictures of artifacts.

Everyone working with students who are new to the field has to balance strict scientific accuracy and terminological precision against the dangers of misinformation and overstatement. I have tried to avoid a catalog and have deliberately erred on the side of overstatement. After all, the objective in a first course is to introduce students to a fascinating and complex subject. The overstatement is more likely to be remembered and to stick in their minds. It can always be qualified at a more advanced level, leaving the complexities of academic debate to more specialized syntheses and to advanced courses. The important truth that students should learn early is that science deals not with absolute truth, but with successive approximations of the truth. Half a truth is better than no truth at all.

Anyone writing a world prehistory is poised on the horns of a sharp pointed academic dilemma. Should one write a book that is heavy on theory, perhaps encased in a specific theoretical framework? Or is it better to compile a basic culture history of the world with relatively little emphasis on theory? *People of the Earth* has evolved to the point where it balances relatively meaty discussions of data with some treatment of theory. Data are, after all, what all archaeologists depend on to verify their basic hypotheses. I have written *People of the Earth* without an overriding theoretical framework, and with plenty of descriptive passages, in the knowledge that different instructors use the book in their own ways. If there is a pervasive theme, it is the gradual progress of humankind as a member of the world ecological community. Both the ecological approach and systems models offer exciting possibilities for the future study of world prehistory.

I would like to thank the dozens of colleagues and students who have provided feedback on *People of the Earth*. Professors Richard E. W. Adams at the University of Texas, San Antonio, Kwang-Chih Chang at Harvard University, and Albert Spaulding at the University of California, Santa Barbara, advised on specific chapters, as did Sylvia Hallam of the University of Western Australia. I benefited greatly from the advice and criticisms of Elizabeth B. Goerke at the College of Marin, Dennis L. Heskel at the University of Utah, Timothy Roufs and his colleagues at the University of Minnesota, Duluth, William Sumner at Ohio State University, H. David Tuggle at the University of Hawaii, and William Turnbaugh at the University of Rhode Island. My final debt is to Jane Aaron, Jan Welch, and Tina Schwinder of Little, Brown and Company, whose friendship and support made the revision of this book a (comparative) pleasure.

Contents

Chapter Twenty-Two

EARLY CIVILIZATION IN PERU

NOTE ON CHRONOLOGICAL TABLES

A chronological table appears at the beginning of most chapters, which covers the sites and cultures mentioned in the narrative. These sites and cultures, and their dates, are also listed in the margins opposite the place where they are mentioned. *Only sites and cultures listed in the margins are in the tables.*

In addition to being keyed to the text, the chronological tables are labeled A, B, C, and are cross-referenced at the beginning of the chapter. They form an interlocking sequence; the beginning and end of each chart are keyed to earlier and later chapters.

The following key is used throughout the tables:

————————	A continuous line means that the chronology is firmly established.
————————→	A line terminating in an arrow means the time span continues beyond the arrow.
————————⊣	A line terminating with a horizontal bar means the limit of chronology is firmly established.
- - - - - - -	A broken line means the chronology is doubtful.
? Omo	A question mark beside a site name means its date is not firmly established.
Omo	A name in italics is an archaeological site, normally named after the locality at which it occurs.
ACHEULIAN	A name in capital letters is an archaeological culture, usually named after a type site which in turn is labeled after a geographical location. For instance, the Acheulian culture is named after the French town of St. Acheul, near which many Acheulian sites are found.

PART ONE
PREHISTORY

"We are concerned here with methodical digging for
systematic information, not with the upturning of earth in
a hunt for the bones of saints and giants or the armory of
heroes, or just plainly for treasure."
— Sir Mortimer Wheeler

Part 1 contains the essential background about the study of archaeology
needed for any examination of human prehistory. We make no attempt to give a
comprehensive summary of all the methods and theoretical approaches used by
archaeologists. Rather, Part 1 touches some of the high points and basic principles
behind archaeologists' excavations and laboratory research. Our narrative is, in the
final analysis, based on the systematic application of these principles. Chapter 3
gives some all-important background on the great climatic changes that form the
backdrop to human prehistory.

Chapter One

ARCHAEOLOGY

PREVIEW

❧ The systematic study of world prehistory began in the late nineteenth century as anthropologists began to study human diversity. At the same time biologists and social scientists were exploring the implications of biological and social evolution.

❧ Archaeology is the study of human societies in the past and is an integral part of anthropology. Archaeologists have three objectives: the construction of culture history, reconstructing past lifeways, and the study of the processes of culture change.

❧ Culture is a theoretical concept formulated by anthropologists to define the adaptive systems unique to humanity, for culture is the means by which we humans adapt to the challenges of the world's diverse environments.

❧ A culture is a complex system, a set of interacting variables that serve to maintain the population in equilibrium with its environment. No cultural system is ever static. It is always changing in ways that can be studied in the archaeological record.

❧ The archaeological record is the data amassed from archaeological survey and excavation. Preservation factors play an important part in the amount of information that can be obtained from the archaeological record.

❧ Every archaeological find has a context in space and time, be it an artifact, a site, or food remains. The study of patterns of artifacts in space depends on the Law of Association, the notion that an object is contemporary with the other objects found in the same archaeological level.

❧ Relative chronology is based on the Law of Superposition, which holds that the lowest occupation level on a site is older than those that have accumulated on top of it. Chronometric chronology involves dates in years and is developed by a number of methods: potassium argon dating, radio carbon dating, dendrochronology, and cross-dating using objects of known age.

▸ Archaeological survey and excavation are carried out using carefully formulated research designs. Excavation methods vary with the type of site being investigated.

▸ Archaeologists have developed sophisticated classification methods to describe artifacts and other finds; the classifications provide the basis for theorizing about archaeological cultures and for studying cultural process (the mechanisms by which cultures change).

People have long been curious about their origins, and have manifested their curiosity in legend, folklore, and systematic inquiry.[1]* The study of early human history is nothing new, but only really came into its own during the nineteenth century when human frontiers were expanding rapidly. While ardent European rulers dispatched explorers and merchants to every part of the globe, amateur diggers were uncovering the long lost civilizations of the Near East and the Americas. The astonishing diversity of humankind was fully revealed for the first time.[2]

Once nineteenth-century scholars became aware of this diversity they began to study other societies and to speculate on the reasons why some peoples had attained urban civilization while others had remained as simple hunter-gatherers. From these studies came the academic disciplines of archaeology and anthropology, which combine with the study of historical events to write the long chronicle of early human experience in these pages.

ANTHROPOLOGY

Anthropology encompasses the whole range of human cultures, both Western and non-Western.[3] As the study of humanity, anthropology is a holistic discipline that uses comparative methods to study the ramifications of economic, political, religious, and other institutions and customs throughout every human society. Anthropologists are interested in comparisons between different cultures, and in biological and cultural evolution. The comparative and evolutionary aspects of anthropology make it unique among the social sciences.

Archaeology is the study of the lives and cultures of ancient peoples. Archaeologists study and interpret the material evidence of past human activity. The archaeologist is a special type of anthropologist who has three basic objectives: the study of culture history, reconstruction of past lifeways, and explanation of cultural process. There are many types of archaeologist, each having distinctive objectives, methods, techniques, and theoretical approaches. *Classical archaeologists* study Greek and Roman civilization; *historical archaeol-*

Anthropology

Archaeology

* See pages 369–370 for notes to Chapter 1.

ogists study relatively recent sites such as Colonial American towns or medieval cities. *Anthropological archaeologists* are concerned with sites of all ages, but they tend to concentrate their research efforts primarily on prehistoric settlements.

Physical anthropology

Physical anthropologists study the emergence and later evolution of humankind, and the reasons why human populations vary one from another.[4] Early human evolution is documented by fossil human and prehuman remains found in archaeological sites and geological levels. Physical anthropologists are deeply involved in modern human biology, trying to find out why different human populations have adapted physically to widely differing natural environments. *Primatologists* are physical anthropologists who are experts on ape and monkey behavior. Their work provides information relevant to the study of early human behavior.

History

History is the study of our past through written records; such records only extend back 5,000 years. *Prehistory*, the millennia before documentary history, goes back at least four million.

HUMAN CULTURE

Culture is a term we will use again and again in these pages.[5] Anthropologists study human cultures and all of us live within a culture. Most cultural descriptions can be qualified by one or more labels like "middle-class," "American," mountain-dwelling, or "Masai." This qualification often becomes associated in our minds with certain behavior patterns or features that are typical of the culture so labeled. One such attribute for "middle-class Americans," for example, might be the hamburger.

Culture

Culture is an entirely theoretical concept developed by anthropologists to describe the distinctive adaptive system used by human beings. Culture is our primary means of adapting to our environment. Until the emergence of humanity, all animals adapted to their environments through biological evolution. If an animal was well adapted to its environment, it prospered. If it was not, it either evolved into a new species, moved away, or became extinct. The forces of biological evolution gave the polar bear a thick coat and layers of fat to protect it from the arctic cold. But the Eskimo, the human occupants of the Arctic, do not possess layers of fur. They wear warm clothing and make snow houses to protect themselves from the environment. Their tools and dwellings are part of their culture — their adaptive system that coincides to the polar bear's fur.

When animals die, their experience dies with them. But with humans, once biological evolution had led to the development of speech, they were able to communicate their feelings and experience from one generation to the next. They could share ideas, which in turn became behavior patterns that were repeated again and again. We see abundant traces of this throughout prehistory, when the same types of tools and sites are found, almost unchanged, over millennia of prehistory. A good example of this phenomenon is the stone hand ax, a multipurpose tool that remained in use for more than a million years (Figure 5.3).

Human beings use the symbolic system which is language to transmit ideas and their culture. Culture is learned by intentional teaching as well as trial and error or simple imitation. Since people share ideas by teaching, the same artifacts and behavior continue from one generation to the next. Culture is an ongoing phenomenon which changes gradually over time.

It follows that the diversity of human languages has served to accentuate the differences between cultures, simply because people cannot understand one another.

Unlike biological adaptation, culture is nongenetic — and provides a much quicker way to share ideas that enable people to cope with their environment. It is the adaptive nature of culture that allows archaeologists to assume that artifacts found in archaeological sites are patterned adaptations to the environment.

A culture is a complex system, a set of interacting variables — tools, burial customs, ways of getting food, religious beliefs, social organization, and so on — that function to maintain a community in a state of equilibrium with its environment. When one element in the system changes, say hunting practices as a result of a prolonged drought, then reacting adjustments will occur in many other elements, so that the system stays in a state as closely approximating the original system as possible. It follows that no cultural system is ever static. It is always changing in big and small ways that can be studied in archaeological sites.

Cultural system

Cultural changes take place through time, most being gradual and cumulative. Inventions and design improvements result in dozens of minor alterations in the ways people live. Generally, culture evolution was gradual in prehistoric times, although there are cases of sudden change, like the Roman conquest of Gaul. Dramatic cultural modification can result from the diffusion from neighboring areas of a new idea or invention, such as the plow (Chapter 2). Culture change is proceeding at a dizzying pace in our own society, to the extent that we have problems adjusting to constant social change.

The cumulative effects of long-term culture change are easily seen. Compare the simple flaked stone tools of the earliest humans with the sophisticated contents of the Egyptian pharaoh Tutankhamun's tomb to understand the power of cumulative change over thousands of years.

Modern archaeology swirls with controversy about the goals of research. Earlier archaeologists were often content just to collect and classify their finds into long sequences of human cultures. They described changing cultures but made no effort to explain why change took place and what changes meant. Today's archaeologist is concerned with explanation as well as description of ancient cultures, with processes of cultural change through time. The term process is used in archaeology to refer to mechanisms by which cultures change. These processes are studied by looking at variables in cultural systems that could lead to cultural change (Chapter 2).

Archaeologists study human cultures of the past and have to be content, for the most part, with the surviving, more durable evidence of prehistoric culture.[6] Any excavator is like a detective piecing together events from fragmentary clues.

What we can find out about the past is severely limited by soil conditions. Stone and baked clay are among the most lasting substances, surviving under almost all conditions. Wood, bone, leather, and metals are much less durable and seldom remain for the archaeologist to find. In the Arctic, however, whole sites have been found frozen, preserving highly perishable wooden tools or, in Siberia, complete carcasses of extinct mammoths.[7] Waterlogged bogs in Denmark have preserved long-dead victims of human sacrifice, and wooden tools survive well there too. Everyone has heard of the remarkable tomb of Egyptian Pharaoh Tutankhamun, whose astonishing treasure survived almost intact in the dry climate of the Nile Valley for more than three thousand years.[8] But most archaeological sites are found where only a few durable materials survive, and reconstructing the past from these finds is often a difficult riddle to solve.

Archaeological record

The archaeological record is the data amassed from survey and excavation; we might think of the archaeological record as the archival raw materials of world prehistory.

The inevitable result of having only durable remains to study is that many prehistoric cultures are interpreted solely on the basis of such imperishable tools as stone axes or clay potsherds, which are almost indestructible. The only way archaeologists can combat this emphasis on the durable and material elements of a culture is by meticulous study of sites where preservation conditions are outstanding; through careful examination of the patterns of artifacts in the soil, archaeologists can discover a clue as to the activities or social status of the artifacts' owners.

One way the archaeologist can overcome the restrictions of differential preservation conditions is by accepting the assistance of scholars from other disciplines. Botanists and zoologists can identify seeds and bone fragments from ancient living sites to reconstruct prehistoric diets. Geologists study lake beds, gravels, and caves for their many tools from early millennia. Paleontologists and paleobotanists specialize in the evolution of mammals and plants, studying bones from extinct animals and pollens from long-vanished plants. They help reconstruct ancient climates, which have fluctuated greatly through our long history. Chemists and physicists have radioactive methods of dating for use on volcanic rocks and organic substances such as bone and charcoal. These techniques have produced a rough chronological framework for more than two million years of human life. Modern archaeology is truly a multidisciplinary team effort, depending on scientists from many fields of inquiry. In one afternoon, an excavator may call on a glass expert, an authority on seashells, an earthworm specialist, and a soil scientist. Each has a piece to fit into the archaeological puzzle.

Prehistory

ARTIFACTS, SITES, AND CONTEXT

World prehistory is recorded in thousands of archaeological sites and artifacts, each of which has a precise place in space and time, its context. Some understanding of the ways in which archaeologists study the dimensions of space and time is essential to an understanding of prehistory.[9]

Archaeological Context is the culturally significant location of a find spot of any object found in an archaeological site.[10] *Cultural context* is a subcategory — the position of an object; was it found in a pit, in a room, on a surface? Metric data is used to define the position of the object uniquely. The time component of the context is the date of the object in years, or its position in the layers of an archaeological site relative to other artifacts and layers. The time and space context of an archaeological find provides the basis for building up long sequences of archaeological sites in time and space.

Artifacts are "anything which exhibits any physical attributes that can be assumed to be the <u>results of human activity</u>."[11] The term *artifact* covers every form of archaeological find — from stone axes to clay pots, butchered animal bones, and manifestations of human behavior found in archaeological sites.

Archaeological Sites are places where traces of ancient human activity are to be found. The Great Pyramid of Gizeh is an archaeological site; so is a tiny scatter of hunter-gatherer artifacts found on the surface of the Utah desert. There are millions of sites in the world, many still undiscovered. They are limited in number and variety only by preservation conditions and the activities of the people who lived on them. Some, like the early campsites at Olduvai Gorge, Tanzania, were occupied for only a few short days.[12] Others, like the great Mesopotamian city mounds or *tells*, like Ur of the Chaldees, were occupied for thousands of years.[13] Archaeological sites are often classified according to the activities that took place upon them — living sites, kill sites, burial sites, art sites, and so on. Many archaeological sites contain evidence for different activities: those of individual households, of entire communities, perhaps even of a single craftsperson like a potter, whose artifacts lie in a pattern as they were abandoned.

(margin notes: Context / Artifact / Site)

SPACE

The archaeological context of space can run from a simple spatial relationship between two artifacts, to the distance between several households, or even to the relationships between an entire regional network of communities.[14]

Context in space is closely tied to cultural behavior. Archaeologists infer behavior from artifacts and their associations, from the patterning (spatial arrangement) of tools around, say, an abandoned bison carcass. A single projectile head dug up out of context at this particular site would allow you nothing more than the reasonable inference that it was part of a weapon. But the patterning of many such weapon heads in association with the butchered remains of the bison can tell us much about how the animal was killed and cut up. The relationships between the carcass and the tools in the ground are our primary source of information on human behavior there.

The *Law of Association* is based on the principle that an object is contemporary with the other objects found in the precise archaeological level in which it is found (Figure 1.1). The study of space is the study of associations between artifacts within their archaeological cultures. It also involves the study of the distribution of human settlements against a background of the ancient environment in which they flourished.

TIME

World prehistory extends through at least four million years of gradually accelerating cultural change. The measurement of this enormous timescale has been a preoccupation of archaeologists for years.

Figure 1.1 The Law of Association: (a) a skeleton associated with a single dagger, (b) a pot and a stone ax, separated by a stratigraphic break, which are not in association; (c) two contemporary household clusters associated with one another; (d) an association of two communities that are contemporary.

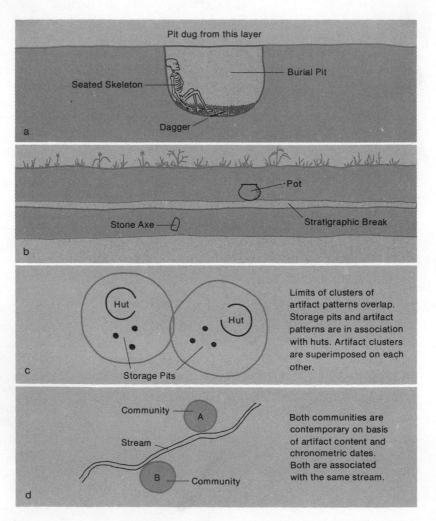

Relative Chronology

At the end of the eighteenth century people began to realize that the earth's rocks were stratified, or laid down in layers, one after another. The notion of geological stratification was soon applied to archaeological sites, and is now a cornerstone of *relative chronology, the correlation of prehistoric sites or cultures with one another by their relative age.*

Stratification is based on the *Law of Superposition, which says that the lowest occupation level on a site is older than those accumulated on top of it.* The principle can be readily understood by placing a book on a flat surface. Then place a second book on top of the first. Obviously, the first book was put on the table earlier than the second that lies upon it. Unless you took a stopwatch and timed the exact interval in minutes and seconds between the time you placed the first and second books on the surface, you have no idea how much time separated the two events. All you know is that the second book was placed on the first at *a relatively later* moment. Figure 1.2 illustrates the principle of superposition in archaeological practice.

Superposition

Superpositions are established by careful excavation and observation of archaeological layers. These layers are excavated with great care, and the artifacts associated with them carefully studied relative to the stratigraphy of the site. We have stated that artifact styles change slowly through time. Every artifact style, however elaborate or simple, has a period of maximum popularity. This can be a few short months in the case of a dress fashion, or tens of thousands of years for a stone tool. By careful study of artifacts such as pottery found in the successive layers of several archaeological sites in a single region, it is possible to develop a relative chronology of changing artifact styles that is based on the assumption that the period of maximum popularity of a particular pottery type, or series, is the one when it is most frequently found (see Figure 1.3). By using these plots of artifact frequencies, one can develop a relative chronology that can later be used to place isolated sites into the sequence on the basis of their artifact content. This type of ordered or *seriated* relative chronology is not expressed in years unless it can be checked by some dating method that provides dates in years.[15]

Seriation

These ordered sequences of sites and layers can be expanded very effectively by a technique known as *cross-dating*. This requires a well-studied sequence of different artifacts whose development through time has been established by excavation, seriation of the artifacts, and stratigraphic observations. In the Tehuacán Valley in Mexico Richard MacNeish was able to assign a relative date to isolated settlements by careful analysis of their pottery.[16] The counts of different vessel forms and decorations then provided a means of inserting the isolated site into its proper place in the relative chronology. Cross-dating like this has been used over wide areas of Mexico to compare sites in different valleys and environments.

Cross-dating

Another type of cross-dating has proved useful in Europe and later American sites. The early civilizations of the Near East traded extensively with the Minoan and Mycenaean civilizations of Greece and Crete as well as with Barbarian Europe.[17] They exchanged luxuries such as semiprecious stones and

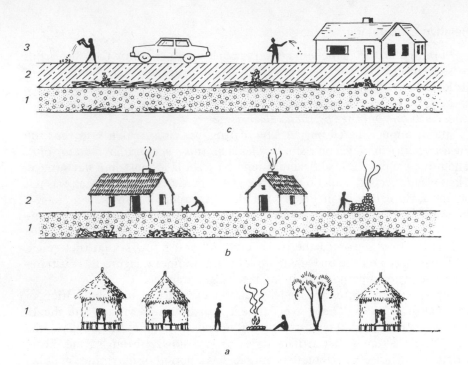

Figure 1.2 Superposition and stratigraphy:

a. A farming village built on virgin subsoil. After a time, the village is abandoned and the huts fall into disrepair. Their ruins are covered by accumulating soil and vegetation.

b. After an interval, a second village is built on the same site, with different architectural styles. This in turn is abandoned; the houses collapse into piles of rubble and are covered by accumulating soil.

c. Twentieth-century people park their cars on top of both village sites and drop litter and coins which, when uncovered, reveal to the archaeologist that the top layer is modern.

An archaeologist digging this site would find that the modern layer is underlain by two prehistoric occupation levels, that square houses were in use in the upper of the two, which is the later (law of superposition), and that round huts are stratigraphically earlier than square ones here. Therefore, village 1 is earlier than village 2, but when either was occupied or how many years separate village 1 from 2 cannot be known without further data.

ornaments with the illiterate Europeans in exchange for copper, salt, and other raw materials. Some of these luxuries can be dated very precisely in their home countries, so much so that their discovery on an archaeological site in Central Europe enables one to say that the level in which the dated foreign object was found dates to the time of the import or later. Since the date of the artifact is known at source, the settlement in which it is found can be relatively dated to a period contemporary with, or younger than, the exotic object of known age. For instance, a Roman coin of 55 B.C. found in an undated French village would date that settlement to a date no earlier than 55 B.C.

Chronometric (Absolute) Chronology

Chronometric dates are dates in calendar years. Prehistoric chronologies cover long periods of time, millennia and centuries as opposed to days or minutes. Some idea of the scale of prehistoric time can be gained by piling up a hundred quarters. If the whole pile represents the entire time that humans and their culture have been on earth, the length of time covered by historical records would equal considerably less than the thickness of one quarter.

How do we date the past in years? Numerous chronometric dating techniques have been tried over the years, but only a few have survived the test of continual use (Table 1.1).[18]

Potassium argon dating

TIME SPAN: From the origins of humankind down to about 400,000 years ago.

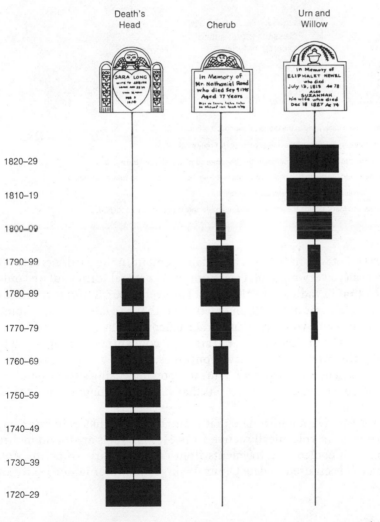

Figure 1.3 Seriation. The changing styles of New England gravestones from Stoneham, Massachusetts, between 1720 and 1829, seriated in three different styles. Notice how each style rises to a peak of maximum popularity and then declines as another comes into fashion.

Table 1.1 Methods of dating in prehistory.

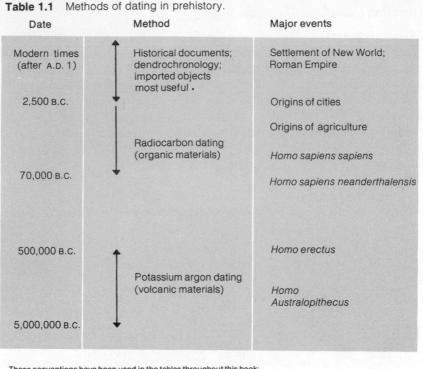

Date	Method	Major events
Modern times (after A.D. 1)	Historical documents; dendrochronology; imported objects most useful ·	Settlement of New World; Roman Empire
2,500 B.C.		Origins of cities
		Origins of agriculture
	Radiocarbon dating (organic materials)	*Homo sapiens sapiens*
70,000 B.C.		*Homo sapiens neanderthalensis*
500,000 B.C.		*Homo erectus*
	Potassium argon dating (volcanic materials)	*Homo Australopithecus*
5,000,000 B.C.		

These conventions have been used in the tables throughout this book:

———————— A continuous line means that the chronology is firmly established.

————————▶ A line terminating in an arrow means the time span continues beyond the arrow.

————————| A line terminating with a horizontal bar means the limit of chronology is firmly established.

– – – – – – A broken line means the chronology is doubtful.

?Escale A question mark beside the name of a site means its date is not firmly established.

PRINCIPLES: Potassium (K) is an abundant element in the earth's crust and is present in nearly every mineral. Potassium in its natural form contains only a small proportion of radioactive ^{40}K atoms. For every 100 ^{40}K atoms that decay, eleven percent become argon 40, an inactive gas that can easily escape from its material by diffusion when lava and other igneous rocks are formed. As volcanic rock forms by crystallization, the argon 40 concentration drops to almost nothing. But the process of ^{40}K decay continues, and eleven percent of every 100 ^{40}K atoms will become argon 40. Thus it is possible, using a spectrometer, to measure the concentration of argon 40 that has accumulated since the volcanic rock formed.

APPLICATIONS: We are fortunate that many of the world's earliest archaeological sites occur in volcanically active areas. Human tools are found in direct association with cooled lava fragments from contemporary eruptions. Potassium argon has been used to date Olduvai Gorge and other famous early sites (Chapter 4).[19]

Radiocarbon dating (C14)

TIME SPAN: about 70,000 years ago to A.D. 1500.

PRINCIPLES: The radiocarbon (C14) dating method, developed by physicists J. R. Arnold and W. F. Libby in 1949, puts to use the knowledge that living organisms build up their own organic matter by photosynthesis and by using atmospheric carbon dioxide. The percentage of radiocarbon in the organism is equal to that in the atmosphere. When the organism dies, the carbon 14 (C14) atoms begin to disintegrate at a known rate. It is possible then to calculate the age of an organic object by measuring the amount of C14 left in the sample. The initial quantity in a sample is low, so that the limit of detectability is soon reached, although efforts are being made to extend the limit beyond 70,000 years.

Radiocarbon dating is most effective for sites dating between 50,000 and 2,000 years before the present (B.P.). Dates can be taken from many types of organic material, including charcoal, shell, wood, or hair. When a date is received from a C14 dating laboratory it bears a statistical plus or minus factor; for example, 3,621 ± 180 years (180 years represents one standard deviation), meaning that chances are 2 out of 3 that the reading is between the span of 3,441 and 3,801. If we double the deviation, chances are 19 out of 20 that the span (3,261 to 3,981) is correct. Most dates in this book are derived from C14 dated samples and should be recognized for what they are — statistical approximations.[20]

CALIBRATION: Radiocarbon dating was at first hailed as the solution to the archaeologist's dating problems. Later research has shown this enthusiasm to be a little too optimistic.[21] Unfortunately, the rate at which C14 is produced in the atmosphere has fluctuated considerably because of changes in the strength of the earth's magnetic field and alterations in solar activity. By working with tree-ring chronologies from the California bristlecone pine, several C14 laboratories have produced correction curves for C14 dates between about 1850 B.C. and the earliest pine tree dates of about 6000 B.C. Calibrated dates have not yet come into wide use because the calibration tables are provisional, but standardized correction charts are likely to alter all C14 chronologies radically within the next decade (see Figure 1.4).

APPLICATIONS: Radiocarbon dating has been used to establish most of the chronologies described in this book for sites dating to the period between 70,000 B.P. and A.D. 1500. It has been used to date early agriculture in both the New and Old Worlds, the beginnings of metallurgy, and the first settlement of the Americas. Without C14 dates, world prehistory would be almost undated.

Dendrochronology

TIME SPAN: Present day to 59 B.C. in the American Southwest.

PRINCIPLES: Many years ago Dr. A. E. Douglass of the University of Arizona used the annual growth rings of trees in the southwestern United States to develop a chronology for this area that extends back 8,200 years.[22] Douglass used the sequoia and other slow growing trees to develop a long master series of annual rings that he used to date fragments of wooden beams found in Indian pueblos. By using cycles of rings from dry and wet series of years he was able to set up an archaeological chronology for the Southwest that extends back to 59 B.C. Tree rings produce a highly accurate chronology, for the long sequence of annual growth is connected to present day trees. Dendrochronology is most effective in areas like the Southwest where there is marked seasonal tree growth.

APPLICATIONS: The chronology of Southwestern archaeology described in Chapter 13 is developed from dendrochronology. Tree rings have been used to date Roman sites in Germany, even the oak boards that formed the backings for Dutch old master paintings!

Historical records (Present day to 5,000 years ago)   Historical records can be used to date the past only as far back as the beginnings of writing and written records. The Sumerian King Lists of Mesopotamia are some of the first attempts to record past events.[23] Many areas of the world, like New Guinea or Tropical Africa, only entered the realms of recorded history in the last century, while continual historical documentation began in the Americas with Christopher Columbus.

Experimental methods   A number of newly developed dating methods promise to amplify both potassium argon and radiocarbon techniques. *Fission track dating* uses the principle that minerals and natural glasses contain uranium atoms that decay by spontaneous fission.[24] The decay rate can be measured in volcanic rocks and has been used to date some samples from Olduvai

Figure 1.4   The difference between C14 dates and actual dates between modern times and 4500 B.C.

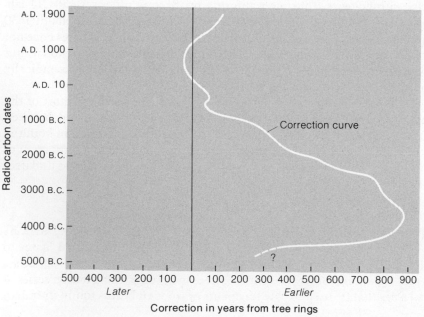

Prehistory

Gorge. Fission track dating may have applications for sites between a million and 100,000 years old.

Amino Acid Racemization may emerge as a method for dating fossil bones between 100,000 and 5,000 years old. Racemization dating is based on the fact that the amino acids, which make collagen in bones, slowly change their character. The rate of change can be measured, a technique that has been used with interesting results on early American Indian skeletons in California; some specimens have been dated as early as 40,000 years (Chapter 7).[25]

Thermoluminescence dating involves measuring the radioactive properties of baked clay vessels. Sudden and violent heating of the vessel allows the scientist to study stored energy and radioactive impurities in the clay. Thermoluminescence may one day provide a means of dating clay vessels as old as 10,000 years, but the method is still under development.

None of these experimental methods has yet played a major part in the development of the chronology of world prehistory.

However effective and accurate a chronometric method, it is useless unless the dated sample — be it a fragment of a wooden beam, a handful of charcoal, or a lump of cooled lava — is interpreted correctly. For instance, a lump of lava associated with an early stone tool does not date the tool, it dates the moment at which the lava cooled. It is up to the archaeologist to establish that the tool is contemporary with the lava. Beams may be used years after their parent tree was cut down, buildings burnt down centuries after they were built. All these factors have to be taken into account when interpreting chronometric dates.

ARCHAEOLOGICAL SURVEY AND EXCAVATION

How do archaeologists find sites? Many large sites like the pyramids of Gizeh in Egypt, or Teotihuacán in Mexico, have been known for centuries. Evidence for less conspicuous sites may be accidentally exposed by water or wind erosion, earthquakes, and other natural phenomena. Burrowing animals may bring bones or stone tools to the surface on ancient settlements. Farmers plow up thousands of finds. Road makers and land developers move massive quantities of earth and destroy sites wholesale. Treasure hunters and collectors have done irreparable damage to many more locations.

Most archaeological sites are discovered as a result of careful field survey and thorough examination of the countryside for both conspicuous and inconspicuous traces of the past.[26] A survey can cover a single city lot or an entire river basin, a reconnaissance that could extend over several years. The theoretical ideal is to locate all sites in the survey area. But this is impossible, for many sites leave few traces above ground, and the best one can hope for is a sample of what is in the area. The most intensive surveys are made on foot, with fieldworkers spaced out at regular intervals so that as little as possible is missed. Aerial photography is often used to plot more conspicuous sites, a technique used with success in the Virú Valley in Peru and in many parts of Europe.[27] Surface finds from newly discovered sites can provide a clue as to the identity of the occupants, although even scientifically collected surface finds are no substitute for excavation. By no means every site found is excavated. Many surveys are undertaken to establish prehistoric *settlement patterns, the distribution of human occupation on the landscape.*

Excavation

Settlement pattern

Archaeological excavation has developed from a form of treasure hunting into an exact and precise discipline. The fundamental premise of excavation is that all digging is destruction, even that done by the experts. The archaeologist's primary responsibility, therefore, is to record a site for posterity as it is dug because there are no second chances.

Every excavation is undertaken to answer specific questions, according to a

Research design

formal *research design* that is worked out beforehand. The research design can ask questions about the chronology of the site, the layout of the settlement it contains, or about changing artifact styles within the levels to be excavated.[28] By meticulous digging and careful sampling of the archaeological deposits, the excavator implements his research design and digs up and records the data that is used to test the hypotheses developed as part of that research design. Most archaeologists distinguish between two basic excavation methods (Figure 1.5):[29]

Area excavation

1. *Area or horizontal excavation,* where the objective is to uncover large areas of ground in search of houses or entire settlement layouts. This type of digging is on a relatively large scale, and is designed to uncover household and other activities that are normally discoverable only by digging over an extensive area.

Vertical excavation

2. *Vertical excavation,* designed to uncover stratigraphic information or a sequence of occupation layers on a small scale. This type of excavation is often practiced when chronology or artifact samples are a primary concern.

The numerous archaeological sites described in this book fall into several broad categories, each of which presents special excavation problems. The

Living sites

most common are *living sites,* the places where people have lived and carried out a multitude of activities.

Much of our knowledge of the earliest hunters and gatherers is found by excavating abandoned living sites. They favored lakeside camps or convenient rock overhangs for protection from predators and the weather, abundant water, and ready access to herds of game and vegetable foods. Olduvai Gorge in Tanzania is renowned for its prehistoric settlements, small lakeside campsites occupied by early humans for a few days or weeks before they moved on in their constant search for game, vegetable foods, and fish (Figure 4.7).[30]

Fortunately for archaeologists, these people abandoned food bones and tools where they were dropped. Crude windbreaks were left and might be burned down by the next brush fire or blown away by the wind. In Olduvai, the gently rising waters of a prehistoric lake slowly covered the living floors and preserved them for posterity with the tools lying where they were dropped. Other people lived by the banks of large rivers. Their tools are found in profusion in river

Figure 1.5 Vertical and horizontal excavations at Maiden Castle, Dorset, England. Although archaeologists excavate in many ways and sometimes use sampling techniques, there is a basic distinction between vertical (a) (photo at left) and horizontal (b) methods.

a. A vertical excavation shows how a narrow trench is cut through successive layers of an earth rampart. Notice that only a small portion of the layers in the trench walls has been exposed by the vertical cutting. The objective of this excavation was to obtain information on the sequence of layers on the outer edge of the earthwork and in the ditch that originally lay on its exterior side. Only a narrow trench was needed to record layers, the finds from them, and the dating evidence.

b. In contrast, this excavation is a grid of square trenches laid out with unexcavated soil between them. The grid method is designed to expose large segments of ground on a site so that buildings and even layouts of entire settlements can be traced over much larger areas than those uncovered in a vertical excavation. Horizontal excavation is widely used when budget is no big problem and the archaeologist is looking for settlement patterns. The photo at the right is a classic example of horizontal excavation, carried out at Maiden Castle in 1938.

gravels that were subsequently jumbled and re-sorted by floodwater, leaving a confused mass of tools, not undisturbed living floors, for the archaeologist to uncover.[31]

Caves already occupied more than half a million years ago were reoccupied again and again as people returned to preferred spots. Many natural caves and rock shelters contain deep occupation deposits that can be removed by meticulous excavation with dental pick, trowel, and brush. The sequence of occupation layers can be uncovered almost undisturbed from the day of abandonment.[32]

In contrast, farmers usually live in larger settlements than hunters, for they are tied to their herds and gardens and move less often. Higher population densities and more lasting settlements left more conspicuous archaeological sites from later millennia of human history. In the Near East and many parts of the New World, farming sites were occupied time after time over several thousand years, forming deep mounds of refuse, house foundations, and other occupation debris. These *tells* require large excavations and extensive earth-moving if anything is to be understood about how towns and settlements were laid out.

Kill sites are places where hunter-gatherers killed large mammals, then camped around the carcass for several days as they butchered their prey. The most famous kill sites come from the Great Plains, where entire bison herds have been found trapped in narrow defiles where they were driven to their death (Figure 7.5).[33] The stone projectile heads, scraping tools and butchering artifacts used by the hunters have been found around the carcasses. *Ceremonial sites* may or may not be part of a living site.[34] Mesopotamian temples formed the focus of a city, while Maya ceremonial centers like Tikal in Guatemala were an integral part of a scattered settlement pattern of towns and villages in the countryside (Figure 21.8). Some structures, like the pyramids of Egypt or Stonehenge in England (Figures 16.3 and 19.6), were isolated sites that served the religious needs of a king or of a wider community around them.

Burial sites can yield important data from periods later than 70,000 years ago, the time when the first deliberate burials were made.[35] Skeletons and their accompanying grave goods give us a rather one-sided view of the past — funerary rites (Figure 16.5). Among the most famous prehistoric burials are those of the royal kings depostied at Ur of the Chaldees in Mesopotamia during the second millennium B.C. (Chapter 15),[36] as well as the Shang graves in China, into which the royal dead were accompanied by their charioteers and many retainers (Figure 20.4).[37] The celebrated mounds of Pazyryk in Siberia show us other spectacular burial customs (Chapter 6).[38] Important people were buried with their chariots and steeds, the latter wearing elaborate harness trappings preserved by ice that formed when water entered the tombs and froze.

Studying the Finds

Archaeological finds take many forms: they may include fragmentary bones from game or domesticated animals. Vegetable foods such as edible nuts or cultivated seeds are sometimes found in archaeological sites where preservation conditions are good. Pottery, stone implements, iron artifacts, and, occasionally, bone and wooden tools all build up a picture of early technical achievements.

Archaeologists have developed elaborate classification systems that set down certain criteria for their finds. They also apply sophisticated analytic techniques for both classifying and comparing human artifacts.[39] They use collections of stone tools, pottery, or other artifacts like swords and brooches for studying human culture and its development. Whatever the classificatory techniques used, however, the objective of analyzing bones, pottery, and other material remains is the study of prehistoric culture and of cultural change in the past. We classify the remains into arbitrary groups either by their shape or

Function	The flat round shape of the tray is determined by its function, for such trays were used to roast seeds by tossing them with embers in the tray. The function of a tray normally cannot be inferred from its shape, but identical modern versions have been found that are used for parching. We employ the technique of analogy, inferring that the archaeological find had the same function.
Context	The archaeological context of the tray is defined by its position in a site and what it is associated with, level, square, etc.; its relationship to other features, such as houses, is also recorded. Unless this information is known, the tray is an isolated specimen devoid of a cultural context or even a date. Context cannot be inferred from an artifact alone.
Construction and materials	The tray was made of reed, its red-brown color determined by the reed, known from modern observations to be the best material available. The steplike decoration on the tray was dictated by sewing and weaving techniques of basketry. The diamond patterns were probably added as a personal touch by the craftsman who made it. The shape and decoration of the tray are repeated in many others that have been found and are evidently part of a well-established Chumash basketry tradition. More information about an artifact's construction and materials can be learned than about any other category of inference.
Behavior	The parching tray reveals something about the cooking techniques of the Chumash, but again only by analogy.

Figure 1.6 Inference from an artifact. The Chumash Indian parching tray from Southern California shows how inferences can be made from an archaeological find. Clearly, the range of inferences that can be made from artifacts alone is limited, especially when the find has no context in a site.

design or by their use, the latter a difficult task (Figure 1.6). We fit them together to form a picture of a human culture.

From time to time we shall refer to archaeological groupings like the Acheulian culture or the Magdalenian culture, which consist of the material remains of human culture preserved at a specific space and time at several sites; these finds are the concrete expressions of the common social traditions that bind a culture. When we speak of the Magdalenian culture, we mean the *archaeological culture representing a prehistoric social system, defined in a context of time and space, which has come down to us in the form of tools or other durable objects.* The description "Magdalenian" is quite arbitrary, derived from the cave site at La Madeleine, France, where the tools of the culture were first discovered. Such labels as Magdalenian are devised by archaeologists for their convenience.

Archaeological culture

The geographic extent or content of any archaeological culture is also defined somewhat arbitrarily, but as precisely as possible, so that an archaeological word has an exact implication for other scholars. Much of the archaeological data summarized in this book consists of carefully compiled chronological sequences of archaeological cultures often extending over thousands of prehistoric years. The workings of archaeological research compare one collection of artifacts with assemblages from different layers in the same sites or other sites near or far away from the original find. Our record of human activity consists of innumerable classified and cataloged archaeological finds whose relationships determined much of the story of human culture that follows in these pages.

EXPLANATION AND INTERPRETATION

Anthropological archaeology is much more than inference and induction from the archaeological record, for our ultimate aim is to explain the past, not simply describe it. Until recently, most archaeologists concentrated on descriptions of sites and artifacts. They accumulated the minute chronological and spatial frameworks of archaeological data that provide a basis for observing *how* particular cultures changed and evolved through prehistoric times. Many scholars felt constrained by poor preservation conditions from making inferences about anything other than the material remains of ancient human behavior. They were unable to explain *why* the cultures they had studied had changed.

Recent years have seen a rapid change in archaeological approaches, often identified with the emergence of a "new archaeology" whose concern is explaining why human cultures reached various stages of cultural evolution.[40] Using both advanced methods of data collection and new theoretical models, some archaeologists of the 1970s are seeking to apply the theories of anthropology to archaeological evidence to arrive at general laws of cultural progress. Others are primarily after the history of culture, viewing each society as a unique phenomenon.[41] These new attempts to explain the major developments of world prehistory are a logical outcome of over a century of speculation about world prehistory. We review them in Chapter 2.

Chapter Two

APPROACHES TO WORLD PREHISTORY

PREVIEW

⚘ Although biological evolution resulted in the emergence of humankind, cultural evolution assumed the dominant role in our prehistory. It became humankind's unique means of adapting to the natural environment.

⚘ Early archaeologists confronted with the problem of classifying and dating the past were at a loss until Christian Jurgensen Thomsen developed the Three Age subdivision for prehistory. This scheme was verified by excavation and widely adopted during the nineteenth century.

⚘ The social scientist Herbert Spencer developed the notion of social evolution. Along with Edward Tylor and Lewis Morgan, Spencer believed in unilinear cultural evolution, under which all humankind progressed from a state of simple savagery to civilization.

⚘ Later scholars showed that these schemes were too simplistic when tested against data from archaeological excavations. We describe the basic cultural processes: invention, diffusion, and migration, and give examples of their application.

⚘ Franz Boas and V. Gordon Childe fostered detailed studies of sites, peoples, and artifacts that placed scientific archaeology on a new footing. Childe believed in cultural evolution in which technology played a major role. He ignored the importance of environmental adaptation in world prehistory.

⚘ Anthropologists Julian Steward and Leslie White played an important role in showing cultural evolution to be a major cornerstone of world prehistory. Steward demonstrated that all human cultures interacted with their natural environments and stressed the importance of constantly changing adaptations. Leslie White conceived of cultures as complex systems whose various parts interacted with each other, and with the natural environment.

⚘ From these researches developed two concepts, those of cultural ecology and of multilinear cultural evolution — both based on the notion that each human culture evolved independently, and as a result of changing adaptations to its ever changing environment.

- Elman Service, Morton Fried, and Marshall Sahlins developed four stages of sociopolitical evolution, which are widely used to classify groups: bands, tribes, chiefdoms, and state-organized societies.
- The 1960s and 1970s have seen a trend toward rigorous scientific methods in archaeology, methods that use models based on the principles of general systems theory. We use the example of early agriculture in highland Mexico to illustrate applications of systems models.
- Our narrative of world prehistory is based on gradual, multilinear cultural evolution and on increasingly effective adaptations to the natural environment that have led to the dangerous overexploitation of resources commonplace today.

The theory of evolution and natural selection provides an explanation for the biological evolution of humankind. We modern people do differ from our predecessors; we have adapted successfully to the world's many environments as a result of our superior intelligence, gradually acquired during biological evolution.[1]* The evolutionary process of *adaptive radiation*, whereby animal species branch off from a common ancestral form, has led to an order of primates, and a family of *Hominidae*, of which modern people (*Homo sapiens* — the wise human being) are only one member and the sole survivors. Space restrictions prevent us from describing the basic principles of biological evolution here; the interested reader is referred to the many standard textbooks on the subject.[2]

Humankind is unique in its use of culture as a means of adapting to the natural environment, and our culture has evolved to great levels of complexity since the appearance of the first human beings over three million years ago. The study of world prehistory is the study not only of biological evolution, but primarily of cultural evolution and the ways in which people have adapted to their natural environment. The cultural diversity of humankind is truly amazing, and extremely difficult to explain. Ever since scholars first began to study world prehistory, they have tried to explain this diversity, and to account for its origins, and for the reasons why some societies achieved a much greater cultural complexity than others. Why, for instance, did the Australian aborigines never take up agriculture, but develop a highly complex social life? Why did their contemporaries the Ancient Egyptians enjoy a literate civilization that lasted for thousands of years? The explanations for cultural diversity must come from anthropological archaeology, the primary source of data on early human history.

In Chapter 1 we described the three basic objectives of anthropological archaeology:

Constructing culture history, a descriptive process that involved studying archaeological sites and artifacts in time and space,

* See pages 370–371 for notes to Chapter 2.

Studying ancient lifeways, ways in which people adapted to, and exploited, their natural environment,

Studying cultural process, how human cultures have changed in the past, and explaining these changes.

Much of the prehistory in these pages is basic culture history — based on hundreds of sites, cultural sequences, and thousands of individual artifacts. These culture histories from all areas of the world have been constructed using the basic principles mentioned in Chapter 1. But culture history alone does not serve to explain culture change, nor does it provide information on the ways in which people have adapted to the natural environment or exploited it. It is only in recent years that archaeologists have attacked the complex problems of reconstructing past lifeways and studying cultural process — with the aid of digital computers, sophisticated statistical methods, and enormous new bodies of excavated data from all over the world.[3]

Today's theoretical models and methodology for studying world prehistory cannot be considered in isolation from earlier attempts at explaining past lifeways and culture change. Our approaches to the past are cumulative in the sense that they are based on the contributions of many earlier scholars, who were working with inadequate data and much less sophisticated methods than are available in the 1980s. We must remember that the debt we owe our predecessors is enormous.

ACCOUNTING FOR CULTURAL DEVELOPMENT

The early excavators of the eighteenth century dug into burial mounds and ancient settlements with such frenzy that they acquired an enormous mass of miscellaneous artifacts that defied classification into any semblance of chronological order. Then, in 1807, Christian Jurgensen Thomsen, Curator of Denmark's National Museum in Copenhagen, rearranged the prehistory galleries to represent three periods of development: a Stone Age when metals were unknown, a Bronze Age, and an Iron Age. Thomsen's Three Ages were strictly technological stages. They were soon widely adopted throughout Europe, and their broad labels are still used as convenient terms today (Table 5.1).[4]

Thomsen's Three Ages

In 1838 Danish zoologist Sven Nilsson invented an economic model for the past, arguing that humankind had developed through a series of stages — from a state of savagery, to one of herdsman-agriculturalist, and a fourth phase, civilization. Nilsson based his economic model on both archaeological and anthropological observations. Nilsson's model was not in conflict with Thomsen's; it merely addressed a different aspect of the fact of evolution. Thomsen concerned himself with how the level of technology affected the evolution of cultures, while Nilsson concentrated instead on how in different societies lifeways always seemed to change in the same direction.

Nilsson's economic model

The essential (that is, demonstrable) validity of Thomsen's Three Age theory of cultural development was proved not long after he proposed it by excavations all over Europe. But these early nineteenth-century excavations raised a whole set of new questions about the Three Ages.

Spencer's cultural evolution

The economic and technological frameworks of the early archaeologists were developed at a time of intense interest in human origins and progress. Pioneer social scientists like Herbert Spencer (1820–1903) began to develop theories of human progress that saw Victorian civilization as the pinnacle of human achievement, a state to which all humankind aspired.[5] Spencer, indeed, was the first person to use the term *survival of the fit*, but in a social context. The Three Age system implied that all humankind had passed through comparable broad stages of technological development. It was logical for Herbert Spencer and others to think of prehistory as an extension of biological evolution. Had human culture evolved just as our bodies had?

CULTURAL EVOLUTIONISTS

Two anthropologists had a strong influence on the development of an evolutionary approach to world prehistory: Edward Tylor and Lewis Morgan.

Edward Tylor

Sir Edward Tylor (1832–1917) was a gentleman of leisure who became interested in anthropology as a result of a visit to Mexico in the 1850s.[6] He devoted the rest of his life to the study of non-Western societies and their institutions. Tylor was the first person to attempt a chronicle of the full extent of human diversity. He argued that the cultures of humankind were governed by laws of evolutionary change somewhat similar to those in biological evolution. Human beings, said Tylor, had behaved in a common sense and rational way since the earliest times. This rational behavior had led to cultural evolution over time, during which processes of selection, like those of natural selection in biological evolution, had made human institutions more efficient and more complex. Tylor was an ardent believer in human progress and argued that the institutions of Western civilization had their origins in those of what he called "ruder" peoples.

Tylor's evolutionist view of human society was, of course, far too simple to reflect reality, and his beliefs that some human races had greater intellectual and moral powers than others are no longer accepted. He went as far as to propose three broad stages of human development: savagery, barbarism, and civilization. Few societies occupied the civilization rung of Tylor's ladder. Despite his prejudices, this fine scholar made two lasting methodological contributions to anthropological archaeology: (1) He studied prehistoric cultures by examining surviving peoples at the same broad level of development; *ethnographic analogy* has become one of the cornerstones of modern archaeology. (2) He developed a technique for sampling the culture of dozens of different peoples, a method that developed into the *comparative method* of study which is used extensively by anthropological archaeologists today.

Lewis Morgan

Lewis Morgan (1818–1881) was a pioneer American anthropologist and ardent social evolutionist who thought that social evolution occurred as a result of human societies adapting to the stresses of their various environments.[7] Morgan identified no less than seven stages of social evolution in his classic book *Ancient Society* (1877). His "Lower Status of Savagery" was a stage of simple food gathering, while the ultimate rung of his evolutionary ladder was "Civilization," which he considered to be attained when a society developed writing. Both Tylor and Morgan believed that all human societies had passed through evolutionary stages on their way to civilization. But neither of their schemes could stand up against the actual complexity of human cultural diversity revealed by later fieldworkers. The most lasting contribution of these, and other pioneer evolutionists, was this basic assumption: Human cultural change has, in general, proceeded from the simple to the complex.

INVENTION, DIFFUSION, AND MIGRATION

Spencer, Tylor, and Morgan believed in human progress, in universal schemes of cultural evolution that were soon shown to have little substance in reality. Even before Tylor started work on his universal schemes, the Danish anthropologist J. J. A. Worsaae had pondered the ways in which cultures changed:[8] How, for example, did humankind acquire bronze weapons? Did one people invent metal tools and then spread their innovation to other parts of the world? Or did metallurgy come into being in many areas? Worsaae raised one of the fundamental questions of archaeology: By what processes did culture change take place? Did it result from the invention of the same idea in many different places, through gradual parallel evolutions? Or did it result from the diffusion of ideas, or from actual migrations of people carrying new cultures with them? The study of prehistoric culture change is still concerned with these basic questions, albeit in a much more sophisticated form.

The refinement of research methods used by the pioneer evolutionists enabled scientists to study what were soon recognized as *primary cultural processes* in prehistory: invention, diffusion, and migration. Both the comparative method and ethnographic analogy played an important part in the refinement of the study of these processes.[9]

Invention involves creating a new idea and transforming it — in archaeological contexts — into an artifact or other tangible innovation that has survived. An invention implies either modifying an old idea or series of ideas or a completely new concept. It can be made by accident or by intentional research. Inventions are adopted by others if they are useful; if sufficiently important, they spread very rapidly. The transistor, for example, is in almost universal use because it is an effective advance in electronic technology.

There is a tendency to think of inventions as dramatic discoveries, the products of a moment of inspiration. But in practice most inventions in prehistory were the result of prolonged experimentation, a logical extension of use of, and refinement of, an existing technology, or else a response to changes in the surrounding environment.

For instance, people once searched for the site where the first solitary genius planted grain and invented agriculture. Today's archaeologists are still investigating the origins of food production, but they are finding dozens of major and minor changes in peoples' lifeways that cumulatively resulted in a shift from hunting and gathering to agriculture and animal domestication. The toolkits and subsistence activities that archaeologists have found show evidence of changes over a long period. In the Tehuacán Valley of Mexico, for example, people experimented for thousands of years with maize cultivation, and their toolkits reflect an increasing dependence on cereal agriculture.[10] But the old hunter-gatherer tools and practices still appear in the archaeological record long after maize cultivation had become commonplace.

Culture change is cumulative — that is, people learn the behavior patterns of their society. Inevitably some minor differences in learned behavior will appear from generation to generation; minor in themselves, they do accumulate over a long time, especially among isolated populations. This snowballing effect of slow moving cultural evolution can be detected in dozens of prehistoric societies, among them the coastal peoples of Peru, who relied heavily on fishing and maritime resources and gradually developed complex societies based largely on fishing and gathering.[11]

Diffusion is the label for those processes by which new ideas or cultural traits spread from one person to another, or from one group to another, often over long distances. These ideas are socially transmitted from individual to individual and ultimately from group to group, but the physical movement of many people is not involved. Instances of diffusion are legion in prehistory — cases where ideas or technologies have spread widely from their place of origin. A well-documented instance is the spread of the religious beliefs of the Adena and Hopewell peoples of the American Midwest, whose beliefs about death spread far beyond the relatively narrow confines of their homeland some two thousand years ago.[12] These religious beliefs were embodied in distinctive rituals which involved extensive earthwork and mound building. Such monuments are found far outside the Adena and Hopewell heartlands, as are the cult objects associated with Hopewell ritual. It appears that the beliefs were diffused through extensive trading networks that criss-crossed the Midwest, transmitting both cult objects and the religious beliefs and rituals as well.

Migration involves the movement of a society and is based on a deliberate decision to enter new areas and leave the old. English settlers moved to North America, taking their own culture with them; the Spanish occupied Mexico. Such population movements result not only in the diffusion of ideas, but in mass shifts of people and in social and cultural changes over a wide front. Migration implies a complete, or at least an almost complete, transformation in culture. Perhaps the classic instance of migration in prehistory is that of the Polynesians; they settled the remote islands of the Pacific in consequence of deliberate explorations of the open ocean by their skilled navigators.[13] These superb seamen learnt the lore of the heavens and made long distance voyages of discovery when they found such remote islands as Hawaii and Easter Island. In most cases they returned safely to their homelands with detailed sailing directions to the new islands that could be repeated by later colonists. No one knows why the Polynesians set out on voyages to the unknown. Perhaps population pressure and political considerations played their part. But, undoubtedly, many long voyages of exploration were undertaken simply because the navigators were curious to learn what lay over the horizon.

The early study of invention, diffusion, and migration was based on data from dozens of excavations and anthropological fieldtrips led by experts. One such expert was Franz Boas (1858–1942), an anthropologist of German birth who immigrated to the United States and became a professor at Columbia University. Boas attacked those who sought general comparisons between non-Western societies; he helped to establish anthropology as a form of science, applying more precise methods to the collection and classification of minute details of human cultures, especially those of North America. He and his students sought explanations of the past based on meticulous studies of individual artifacts and customs. Boas instilled respect for the notion that data should not be subordinated to elaborate theoretical schemes. The myriad data provided by Boas and others gave a great impetus to the use of the comparative method and ethnographic analogy in anthropological archaeology.[14]

Boas on data

THE CONCEPT OF CULTURAL ECOLOGY

It was the American anthropologist Julian Steward who first developed the notion that human cultures were adaptations to the subsistence and ecological requirements of a locality. Steward saw this adaptation as constantly changing. "No culture," he wrote, "has ever achieved an adaptation to its environment which has remained unchanged over any length of time."[15] This viewpoint contrasted sharply with that of many archaeologists of the time, who felt that human cultures were built by accumulation of cultural traits through diffusion and not as responses to ecological factors.

Steward on environment

Another famous anthropologist, Leslie White, argued that human culture was made up of many structurally different parts that interacted; they reacted to one another within an overall cultural system.[16] He pointed out that cultures can change in response to changes in the environment, that one part of a cultural system could not change without triggering change in other segments. There was an equilibrium between a human cultural system and its natural environment, and the system was constantly adjusting to environmental changes. Steward and White assumed that successful adaptive patterns continued in use and acted as an important stabilizing influence over a long period of time. From their work has developed a new recognition of the importance of cultural evolution in prehistory — not the cultural evolution of Tylor and Morgan, which implied that some human races were superior to others, but evolution based on many and increasingly complex adaptations to the natural environment. The study of the total way in which human populations adapt to, and transform, their environments is called *cultural ecology*.

White on equilibrium

Archaeologists who study cultural ecology see human cultures as systems interacting with other systems: other human cultures, the biotic community (other living things around them), and the physical environment. They are concerned not only with cultural evolution, but with intellectually reconstructing ancient environments and ways in which past cultures made their living.[17]

The Evidence

The study of prehistoric lifeways depends on many types of archaeological evidence, including any or all of the three categories that follow.

Artifacts provide evidence for subsistence activities. For instance, the discovery of a plowshare implies much more elaborate agricultural practices than those used by hoe farmers.

Food remains, such as animal bones or seeds, provide direct evidence for types of food eaten and, by sophisticated analyses, can provide insights into overall dietary patterns as well. The remains of domestic animals or game can be identified by such parts as teeth, jaws, horns, and sometimes the articular ends of limb bones. Not only can one establish the proportion of the diet which each type of animal supplied, but also, in some cases, invaluable data on butchery practices, the ages at which animals were killed (determinable by study of the teeth), and even the seasons at which the site was occupied. For instance, when Grahame Clark excavated the 9,000 year old Stone Age campsite at Star Carr in northeast England, he found that hunters of red deer had used the settlement for a short time in the spring: most of the deer antlers came from animals killed at that time of year.[18]

Seeds are much harder to come by than animal bones, and are often recovered using a flotation method: the soil is passed through water so that the fine seeds float on the surface. Dry caves in the United States and Mexico have yielded tens of thousands of once-edible seeds. Those from caves in the Tehuacán Valley in Mexico have shown how the inhabitants scheduled their gathering of wild plants with great care. The seeds yield an excellent chronicle of their early experiments with maize and other crops.

Food remains can come in many other forms, too. Fish and bird bones are highly informative, and often provide evidence of specialist hunter-gatherer activities. Human feces can be subjected to detailed analysis and provide a fascinating insight into the diet of a site's inhabitants. The ultimate objective of studying food remains is to understand the minutest details of a prehistoric society's adaptation to its environment.

Environmental evidence comes from many sources — from geological and botanical studies, from soil analyses of occupation levels, and from the bones of animals eaten by a site's inhabitants. Archaeologists have even used mouse bones to establish the microenvironment around a settlement. The analysis of fossil pollen grains (palynology) has been used extensively to reconstruct the surroundings of sites in waterlogged areas. Star Carr, for instance, was shown to be situated in a reedy swamp surrounded by a dense birch forest. Pollen analysis has been used to show the dramatic changes in vegetational cover that resulted from the introduction of agriculture in northern Europe; it even documents the characteristic cultivation weeds that infested the newly cleared fields. Palynology and the study of food remains enable one to look at the constantly changing relationship between a human culture and its environment, at ways in which people made their living.

Cultural ecologists look closely at prehistoric lifeways in the context of their environments, at constantly changing cultural systems to which simplistic explanations of culture change simply do not stand up.

THE COMPARATIVE METHOD

The comparative method is the specialty of the ethnologist, a cultural anthropologist who compares patterns of thought, social institutions like marriage, and other culture traits in many different societies. Archaeologists, too, spend a great deal of time in comparative studies, examining minute details of artifacts, settlement patterns, and art styles in different archaeological cultures. The comparative method in archaeology is closely tied to the classification and analysis of artifacts like pottery and stone tools. Much of what we know of the prehistory of Bronze Age Europe is based on the study of swords, brooches, and pins, for example. Archaeologists of the American Southwest rely heavily on changing styles and distributions of painted pottery to construct the culture history of the region. Until the advent of radiocarbon dating in the 1950s, European archaeologists made great use of comparative studies of pottery and metal artifacts to refine their cross-datings of cultures far from the Mediterranean civilizations in which such artifacts had their origin.

Perhaps one of the best-known experts on the comparative method was an Australian-born archaeologist named Vere Gordon Childe (1892–1957).[19] Childe was a brilliant linguist, who made his life's work the study of prehistoric European civilization. He became familiar with even the most trivial sites and artifact assemblages, and with obscure Central European journals that few English-speaking archaeologists read. He used his encyclopedic knowledge to develop a thesis that Europe was a province of the Near East, an area that had received agriculture, metallurgy, and other major inventions by diffusion from the East. He traced these traits from one end of Europe to the other by comparing cultural sequences and artifact distributions from area to area. Childe combined cultural evolution and diffusionist ideas into unexpected notions of human prehistory. He held, for instance, that farming was introduced into Europe from the Near East; local cultures developed their own distinctive economies and social institutions in later millennia, he thought.

Childe's aim was to distill from archaeological remains "a pre-literate substitute for conventional history with cultures instead of statesmen as actors and migrations instead of battles."[20] He drew together approaches to the past from various schools, including the Marxists; he was convinced that humanity had made rational, intelligent progress from its earliest development. Gordon Childe was a brilliant and articulate popular writer whose syntheses of prehistoric times were widely read by generations of archaeologists. His meth-

Childe on cultures

ods influence archaeologists to this day, although his comparative studies are slowly being replaced by much more sophisticated studies based on far more data than was available to him. These new studies allow for one major variable which Childe downplayed — the natural environment.

American archaeologists adopted the comparative method as a result of Boas's work, and developed their own elaborate classification systems for New World prehistory that correlated local cultural sequences over thousands of miles.[21] Between 1930 and 1960, they constructed hundreds upon hundreds of local sequences of culture history based on pottery styles and other artifacts. Their concern was with classification and chronology rather than the explanation of culture change or reconstruction of past lifeways. Once again, the natural environment and any notion of cultural adaptation entered but little into archaeological research.

To say that Childe and his American contemporaries ignored the environment as a factor in human history in no way detracts from their valuable contribution to archaeology. They provided the raw data that has enabled archaeologists of the 1960s and 1970s to attempt much more ambitious researches into past lifeways and cultural process.

ETHNOGRAPHIC ANALOGY

Archaeologists have been comparing prehistoric societies with living peoples for over a century.[22] Originally, people believed that the Eskimo, for instance, were living examples of lifeways that had flourished in say, southwestern France, when it enjoyed an arctic climate in remote prehistoric times. Thus, they argued, one could make direct comparisons between Eskimo society and that of arctic hunter-gatherers in prehistory. But such direct comparisons are no longer made, for there are simply too many uncontrollable variables that can affect direct comparisons over thousands of years. Another problem is that suitable ethnographic evidence on living hunter-gatherers and subsistence farmers is rarely available. This is because ethnographers have tended to concentrate on social and ritual institutions rather than on more physical and every-day aspects of human culture such as are found in excavations. But in recent years a number of anthropologists have studied the ethnography and cultural ecology of living hunter-gatherers in an attempt to record details of their cultural adaptations before they vanish forever; these are studies in

Living archaeology

"living archaeology." The work of Richard Gould among the Australian aborigines and Richard Lee with the San hunter-gatherers of the Kalahari desert in Southern Africa is referred to constantly in these pages, for their work has combined archaeology and ethnography into a single integrated approach which tells us far more about population dynamics, cultural adaptations, and settlement patterns — to mention only a few topics — than either type of research on its own.[23]

Careful research design and controlled use of ethnographic data enable anthropologists to make analogies, under carefully controlled conditions, to aid in interpretation of prehistoric cultures. In particular, "living archaeology"

Prehistory

tells us much of the mechanics of different long-lived cultural adaptations, like hunting and gathering. It provides essential background to the complex explanations of world prehistory generated in recent years.

MULTILINEAR CULTURAL EVOLUTION

The work of Leslie White and Julian Steward resulted in the emergence of a new school of evolutionary thought — one with no pat formulas and more variables. Instead of seeing cultural evolution as a unilinear process, one that had people evolving from hunting and gathering through agriculture to civilization, anthropologists came to think of a multilinear evolutionary process. Elman Service, Morton Fried, and Marshall Sahlins argued that each human culture pursues its own individual evolutionary course, a course determined by the long-term success of its adaptation, via technology and social institutions, to its natural environment.[24]

Some societies achieve a broad measure of equilibrium with their environment, one that is relatively stable, where adaptive changes consist of little more than some refinements in technology and the fine tuning of organizational structures. The Australian aborigines appear to have achieved such an equilibrium over tens of thousands of years. Other societies become involved in cycles of growth that are triggered by environmental change or from within society. If these changes involve either greater food supplies or population growth, there can be accelerated growth resulting from the need to feed more people or the deployment of an enlarged food surplus. Continued growth can place additional strains on society, triggering technological changes, adjustments to social organization, or alterations in the belief system that provides the integrative force for society.

Growth cycles

Every society has its growth limits imposed by the environment and available technology, and some environments have more potential for growth than others. Certain types of sociopolitical organization, like, for instance, centralized control of specialized labor, are more efficient than others. The emergence of food production in Mesoamerica (Central America), the beginnings of urban civilization — both are instances where societies have entered on a major growth cycle after centuries of relatively slow cultural evolution in the same regions. Adaptive changes have triggered technological innovation that led to increased food supplies and higher population densities. Our own society is embarked on such a growth cycle today — with open ended and dangerous consequences.

This sophisticated concept of multilinear cultural evolution led Service, Fried, and others to develop four broad stages of societal complexity that were of great importance in prehistory, stages that are implicit throughout this book.[25]

Stages of society

Bands: associations of families that may not exceed twenty-five to sixty people. These bands are knit together by close social ties; they were the dominant form of social organization for most hunter-gatherers from the earliest times up to the origins of food production.

Approaches to World Prehistory

Tribes: clusters of bands that are linked by clans into tribes. A clan is a group of people linked by common ancestral ties, ties that cut across the narrow frontiers of bands and serve as unifying links between widely scattered communities. Clans are important because they are a form of social linkage that give people a sense of common identity with a wider world than their own immediate family and relatives. They are much more of a kin than political unit, and, as such, are not used as one of the major stages of social evolution in themselves.

Chiefdoms develop among some tribes, societies where clan groups assume a ranking within society. One clan may achieve dominance, because its members have extraordinary religious or organizational powers. The leaders of this clan may become chieftains who act as social instruments for the control and redistribution of goods and services within the tribe as a whole. Chiefdoms, such as those found among the Hopewell people of the Midwest some 1500 years ago, are a transitional stage between the tribe and the state societies of the earliest civilizations.

State-organized societies develop from chiefdoms and are governed by a full-fledged ruling class and a hierarchy of social classes below them that include such diverse groups as specialist craftspeople, merchants, peasants, even slaves. State-organized societies of the past were first ruled by priest-bureaucrats, then gradually came under the rule of secular kings who sometimes became despotic monarchs, often with alleged divine powers. This type of social organization was typical of the early literate civilizations, and was the forerunner of the Classical civilizations of Greece and Rome.

Multilinear cultural evolution assumes that similar developments can occur in different cultures in broadly similar environments separated by thousands of miles. The startling differences in human cultures can be explained by studying them as highly complex, ever changing systems that interact constantly with their environments. Modern archaeology uses this notion of societal stages to study both the dynamics of growth within a culture and the complex mechanisms that led to cultural evolution.

CULTURAL PROCESS AND OPEN SYSTEMS

The 1960s and 1970s have seen not only a mass of new information becoming available to archaeologists, but the development of new and much more complex methods and techniques for studying cultural process. At the heart of the new methodologies, which assume that human cultures are interactive systems, is an insistence that archaeological research be based on deductive research. This type of research, first advocated by Lewis Binford, involves the development of formal research designs and testable hypotheses which are then tested against data collected in the field. We lack the space to discuss the complex methodology involved here: the reader is referred to basic texts that discuss the subject. But the models which this complex type of research generates are designed to identify the factors responsible for changes within a cultural system.[26]

Both multilinear cultural evolution and cultural ecology are models of cultural change which assume that technology was a primary factor in change, something that determined the nature and speed of cultural modification. But both also take account of the sociopolitical and belief factors that may have influenced change as well. And both approaches pay close attention to the linkages between these factors and the natural environment. At the heart of modern studies are the principles of general systems theory, a body of theoretical constructs developed in the 1950s for looking at general relationships in the empirical world.

A system can be defined as "a whole which functions as a whole by virtue of the interdependence of its parts."[27] General systems theory argues that any organization, from a city to a human culture, must be studied as a system, so that one can understand the relationships between its various components and how change in any part of a system affects the remainder. Systems experts identify two basic types of system. *Closed systems* are those that receive no external input from their surrounding environment. A good example is the household thermostat, which is a self-regulating system that maintains a constant temperature in a room and a state of equilibrium. Changes in air temperature trigger a heating or cooling mechanism, which operates until control temperature is again reached. The closed system operates to maintain a stable state.

Open systems are those which exchange matter, information, and energy with their environment. An open system can change as a result of either external or internal factors. Cultural systems are obviously open systems, for they are adaptations to an external environment that is constantly changing. The feedback between the thermometer and the heating or cooling process in our closed system thermostat was negative, that is to say, it resulted in no change; the system functioned to maintain a state of stable equilibrium. But the feedback within an open system can accelerate change, simply because it can stimulate change which stimulates further change, through what is called *positive feedback*. Positive feedback can result in gradual, or accelerating change — simply by growth and decline in various subsystems within the total cultural system.

An excellent example of an open systems model in modern archaeology comes from the work of Kent Flannery on early agriculture in Mexico.[28] Flannery was trying to understand how the population of the southern highlands gave up food gathering and took up agriculture. He began by assuming that the southern highlands and their inhabitants were part of a single complex open system consisting of many subsystems — economic, botanical, social, and so on — which interacted with one another. Between 8000 and 2000 B.C. the highland peoples used no less than five different collecting systems, each with its own distinctive technology of artifacts, storage facilities, and carrying utensils. These five systems were carefully scheduled to take maximum advantage of the seasonal abundance of the different resources in each season. By being able to predict which plants would come into season, the society could schedule the harvesting of particular species at periods of abundance, and before animals beat them to it. At these times of abundance the people would congre-

General systems theory

Early Mexican agriculture

gate in larger groups; they scattered over the countryside in tiny bands during periods of scarcity. By a combination of scheduling and judicious use of seasonal foods, the highlanders were able to interact with their environment without overexploiting any of their available food sources. The balance of system was maintained by scheduling and relying on five basic food sources: deer, rabbits, maguey, tree legumes, and prickly pears. There was enough food to support the population and no one food source was overexploited.

Flannery pointed out that something must have happened to jolt the food procurement system towards the deliberate growing of wild grasses. So he looked more closely at these species, which included both foxtail grass and wild maize. The excavations in a series of dry sites yielded thousands of seeds dating to between 5000 and 2000 B.C., some of which underwent genetic change. For instance, wild maize increased its cob size and was crossed with related wild corn to produce a hybrid species that was the ancestor of modern domesticated maize. Some species of beans became more permeable in water and developed softer pods which did not shatter when collected. Thus the potential bean crop became more edible and easier to collect. The best seeds were saved for the next year's planting. Flannery suggested that the people began to experiment with the deliberate planting of maize and other grasses, intentionally expanding the areas where they would grow. After a long period of time these deviations in the food procurement system caused the importance of wild grass collecting to increase at the expense of other collecting activities until it became the dominant one. Eventually the Indians created a self-perpetuating food procurement system with its own vital scheduling demands — planting and harvest; these competed with other scheduled collecting systems and proved more durable. By 2000 B.C. the highly nutritious bean and corn staple diet of the highland peoples was well established.

We have dwelt on the highlands example at some length because it dramatizes the importance of looking at cultural change in the context of the interrelationships between many different variables. There is no one prime agent of cultural evolution, but a whole series of important variables, all with complex interrelationships. When we seek to explain the major and minor events of prehistory, we consider the ways in which change took place, the processes and mechanisms (cultural evolution, experimentation), and the socioeconomic stresses (population pressure, game scarcity, and so on) that select for these mechanisms.[29]

Our narrative of prehistory is a story first of human progress told within a framework of biological and cultural evolution, and second of increasingly complex interaction with the physical environment, leading to the alarming ecological imbalances of today. Complex models that use cultural ecology, systems theory, and multilinear evolution bring us better understanding of human progress.

Chapter Three

THE PLEISTOCENE EPOCH

PREVIEW

❧ The evolution of human culture has taken place against a backdrop of complicated geological events that are only imperfectly understood.

❧ The Pleistocene (the Age of Humanity) is the last of the major geological epochs, and is thought to have begun about 2 or 3 million years ago.

❧ Four major glacial and interglacial periods are known from studies made of the northern latitudes of the New and Old Worlds. These brought major changes in distribution of ice sheets, sea level heights, and faunal and floral populations throughout the world.

❧ There were major fluctuations during each glacial period which are still imperfectly understood, but those of the last (Weichsel) glaciation coincided with the emergence of modern humans.

❧ The end of the Pleistocene coincides with the final retreat of Weichsel ice sheets in northern Europe and the Americas and is conventionally dated to about 10,000 years ago. Major changes in world sea levels and vegetational zones have taken place since then.

❧ Scientists in many disciplines are working to reconstruct Pleistocene climate — among them geologists, pollen analysis experts, geomorphologists, and paleontologists.

Humankind and its environment are so tightly entwined that understanding human culture or cultural evolution requires us to know the natural environment as well. Major changes in climate during the past two million years have helped determine where people lived, what they ate, and how their population would be distributed.

For most of geological time, the world's climate was warmer and more

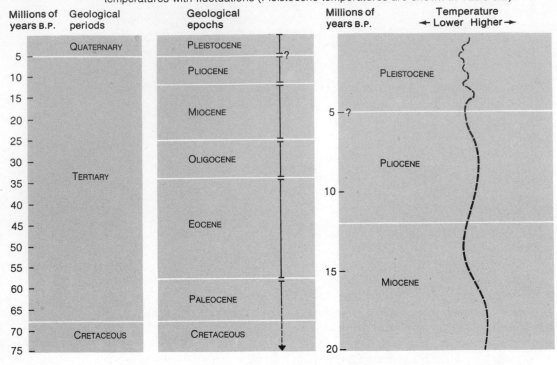

Table 3.1 Geological epochs, from more than 60 million years ago. The curve demonstrates lasting temperature changes on earth since the late Miocene; the dotted line indicates lack of data. Notice that the general trend is toward cooler temperatures with fluctuations (Pleistocene temperatures are shown in Table 3.2).

Millions of years B.P.	Geological periods	Geological epochs	Millions of years B.P.	Temperature ← Lower Higher →
5	QUATERNARY	PLEISTOCENE ?		PLEISTOCENE
10		PLIOCENE		
15				
20		MIOCENE	5 –?	
25				
30		OLIGOCENE		PLIOCENE
35	TERTIARY		10	
40				
45		EOCENE		
50				
55			15	MIOCENE
60		PALEOCENE		
65				
70	CRETACEOUS	CRETACEOUS		
75			20	

homogeneous than it is today. As early as the Miocene (Table 3.1), land began to uplift in many places and mountains began to form, continuing through the Pliocene into later time.[1]* Temperatures were lowered on the new highlands, and in the highest latitudes glaciers formed on the high ground. For a long time glaciers and their ice sheets were confined mainly to highlands and high latitudes, but in more recent times huge ice sheets have spread repeatedly over middle latitudes in the northern hemisphere, alternating with shrinking ice cover. The periods of extensive ice sheets are called *glacial* stages, which were interrupted by *interglacials* when warmer climates returned. The duration of each glacial or interglacial varied, and the details of many earlier glacials still are uncertain. Much of human history has unfolded against a backdrop of glacial advances and retreats during the Pleistocene epoch (see Table 3.2).[2]

The Pleistocene perhaps covers some 3 million of the 4 billion or more years of the earth's past. Plant life and animal life have existed for about half a billion years, but humanity first appeared between 2.5 and 5 million years ago. Although our origins may extend back into the Pliocene, the Age of Human-

Glacials and interglacials

* See pages 371–372 for notes to Chapter 3.

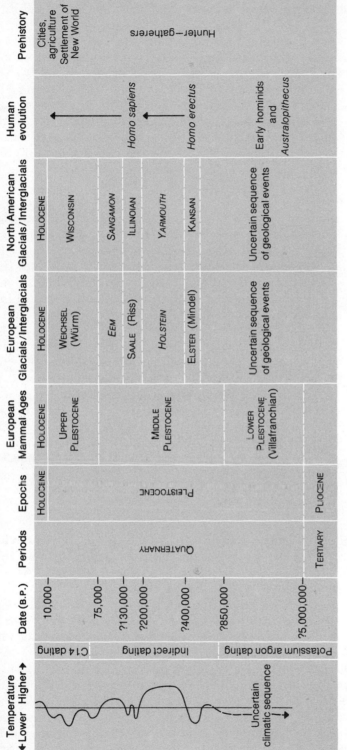

Temperature (Lower ← → Higher)	Date (B.P.)	Dating method	Periods	Epochs	European Mammal Ages	European Glacials/Interglacials	North American Glacials/Interglacials	Human evolution	Prehistory
(uncertain climatic sequence; temperature curve)	10,000	C14 dating	Quaternary	Holocene	Holocene	Holocene	Holocene	Homo sapiens	Cities, agriculture, Settlement of New World
	75,000	Indirect dating		Pleistocene	Upper Pleistocene	Weichsel (Würm)	Wisconsin		Hunter-gatherers
	?130,000					Eem	Sangamon		
	?200,000				Middle Pleistocene	Saale (Riss)	Illinoian	Homo erectus	
	?400,000					Holstein	Yarmouth		
	?850,000				Lower Pleistocene (Villafranchian)	Elster (Mindel)	Kansan	Early hominids and Australopithecus	
						Uncertain sequence of geological events	Uncertain sequence of geological events		
	?5,000,000	Potassium argon dating	Tertiary	Pliocene					

Note for the advanced reader and the instructor: Throughout this book I have used the glacial terminology applied to northern Europe in discussing the successive glaciations and interglacial periods in the Old World. This system follows Karl Butzer's definitive synthesis, *Environment and Archaeology,* 2nd ed. (Chicago: Aldina, 1973). Many still use the Alpine names preferred in earlier literature, but I have chosen to reduce confusion and recognize that not everyone will agree. For the newcomers, here are the equivalent names:

			Uncertain sequence
Alpine terms:	Würm	Riss	Mindel
Northern European terms:	Weischel	Saale	Elster	of geological events

[a] Data are from Flint, 1971 — the chronology of earlier glacial periods is controversial. Terms are greatly simplified and there are many local labels.

ity, is truly the Pleistocene, one of the most remarkable periods in the earth's history.

During Pleistocene times, climatic change repeatedly displaced plants and animals from their original habitats.[3] When a glacial period began, plants and animals usually fared better in lower altitudes and warmer latitudes. Populations of animals spread slowly toward more hospitable areas, mixing with populations that already lived in the new areas and creating new communities with new combinations of organisms. This repeated mixing surely affected the directions of evolution in many forms. No one knows exactly how many species of mammals emerged during the Pleistocene, althouth Björn Kurtén has estimated that no fewer than 113 of the mammal species now living in Europe and adjacent Asia appeared during the last 3 million years.

The Pleistocene is important for it is the only geological epoch contemporary with human activity. People lived and hunted over much of the terrain covered by its ice sheets and dwelt in arctic steppe zones during the more temperate interglacials. Stone Age humans killed many types of animals for food, animals whose butchered bones are often found in river gravels and other Pleistocene deposits in the Old World. Early hunters preyed on animals now extinct, whose carcasses sometimes sank into lake mud or washed into river backwaters, burying the skeletons for archaeologists to find thousands of years later.

With these fossils and careful study of geological deposits a complex chronological record of the Pleistocene has been assembled. Some Pleistocene sites, for example, can be dated very roughly by examining the fossilized teeth of elephants, for elephants changed radically during each glacial and interglacial period; each species of this animal has a tooth pattern that distinguishes it from earlier and later forms.[4] Numerous branches of science — botany, zoology, geomorphology (the study of landforms) and nuclear physics — have helped build up the story of the Pleistocene epoch we shall outline here.

THE GREAT ICE AGE

In the late nineteenth century, two Austrian geologists, A. Penck and E. Brückner, studied the glacial deposits in four northern Alpine valleys.[5] They identified four major Pleistocene glacial periods: Gunz, Mindel, Riss, and Würm, named after Alpine valleys; these designate times when the ice sheets of the mountains extended into much lower altitudes than today. At the same time vast ice sheets flowed southward from Scandinavia and arctic Canada, covering much of northern Europe and much of the midwestern United States.

These four glacial periods were separated from each other by prolonged interglacials, when sea levels rose and the world enjoyed warmer and often drier climates (Table 3.2). When the longest interglacial was at its height, such animals as the hippopotamus were living in the Somme, Thames, and other European rivers. The glaciations themselves were not all unrelenting cold, for temperatures fluctuated as the ice sheets advanced and retreated. During the height of the Weichsel (last) glaciation, the mean annual European temperature may have been 10° to 15° C lower than today's, and 2° to 3° C higher during interglacials. These figures are gross generalizations from inadequate evidence.

The glacial ages of the Pleistocene affected the higher latitudes most. Ice sheets covered up to three times as much land area as they do today. In latitudes that are now more tropical, less conspicuous and very complex climatic shifts took place. Climatic zones shifted, depending on the extent of arctic zones. The dry Sahara supported some grassland vegetation during colder spells; the Mediterranean became a temperate sea. Snow lines were sometimes lowered on tropical mountain ranges; rain forests expanded and contracted, depending on the abundance of rainfall. The world's sea levels fluctuated between periods of colder and warmer climate. The vast ice sheets locked up enormous amounts of the earth's water, lowering sea levels far under their present depths. Land bridges were formed as the continental shelf rose from the ocean that now covers it. Britain was joined to France. Many of Southeast Asia's islands (but not Australia) were part of the mainland. Siberia and Alaska had a vast land connection. When the ice sheets melted, sea levels rose and flooded many habitats of hunters and gatherers and vast herds of game.

The Pleistocene brought great diversity in world climates, forming or altering regional climatic zones with bewildering rapidity. Perhaps the effect of glaciations and ice sheets in prehistory has been exaggerated (even if they did periodically close off large areas of the world to human settlement). But the minor shifts in local climate in more southern latitudes, in annual rainfall or vegetative cover, were potentially significant to hunters and gatherers who depended on the environment for food, water, and shelter.

But do not be misled by the simple sequence of glaciations and interglacials derived from Penck and Brückner in this chapter. The European image of the Pleistocene has turned into a sort of idealized criterion that has been used world-wide. The drastic climatic changes are in fact a great oversimplification, for pollen analysis and other modern geological techniques have now produced details of at least eight interglacials during the last 700,000 years.[6] The major events are shown in Table 3.2, and it is advisable for you to study the table carefully as you read on.

Beginnings of the Pleistocene

The Pleistocene epoch is now calculated to be 2 to 3 million years long, although the beginning date remains uncertain.[7] For some 85 million years, until about 10 million years ago, the world had enjoyed a prolonged period of warm climate. In the Oligocene and Miocene epochs great mountain chains were formed, such as the Alps and the Himalayas. Land masses were uplifted; there was less connection between northern and southern areas, lessening the heat exchange between those latitudes and causing greater differences in temperature between them. Marine temperatures cooled gradually during the Pliocene. By about 3 million years ago, northern latitudes, still warmer than today, were much cooler than they had been 70 million years before. A cooling of the northern seas 3 million years ago can be detected from finds of marine deposits in northern Europe and North America that show temperate, northern mollusks replacing warmer species.

Lower Pleistocene

Attempting to summarize Pleistocene stratigraphy in a few pages is an act of temerity, but a summary is essential. Table 3.2 gives an approximate correlation of the stratigraphic data for Europe during the Pleistocene. We have added North America at the right of the table as glacial background for the first human settlement. The terminology is that advocated by Pleistocene geologist Richard F. Flint,[8] based on geological stratigraphy in northern Europe.

The terms Lower, Middle, and Upper Pleistocene break the epoch into large subdivisions according to their fossils. The Lower Pleistocene normally includes surviving Pliocene mammals and plants; the Middle Pleistocene does not. The Upper Pleistocene contains more northern mammals than the Middle Pleistocene.

Villafranchian
?5,000,000 B.P.

The earliest portion of the Pleistocene is named the *Villafranchian*, after a series of early fossil-bearing beds from southern Europe (Table 3.2). The French deposits hold many Pliocene animal fossils as well as wild horses, cattle, elephants, and camels, all of which appear for the first time in the Pleistocene. Fossil pollen grains from Villafranchian lake beds in southern France belong to both cool- and warm-loving species, as if spells of cooler climate had separated long periods of warmer weather.[9] Other Lower Pleistocene fossil beds are known from Africa, where early hominids hunted both large mammals and smaller animals. But the Lower Pleistocene is still almost a blank climatically, a time when early humans began toolmaking and the lakeside camps at Olduvai Gorge were in use (Chapter 4). It seems unlikely that the climatic changes of the early Lower Pleistocene were as drastic as those of later times.

Middle Pleistocene

The three most recent glaciations of northern Europe were named after three German rivers, the Elster, the Saale, and the Weichsel. Many details remain uncertain.[10] Elster glacial deposits covered much of central Britain, the

Elster
?500,000 B.P.

Low Countries, and central Europe as far east as the Ural Mountains. The Alpine ice extended northward and local glaciers sat on the Pyrenees and the Caucasus, so that much of Europe between latitudes 40° and 50° N was arctic plains country, with severe winters on the shores of the Mediterranean. The Kansan glaciation in North America was equivalent to the Elster and extended southward from three ice caps near the 60th parallel in Canada. Its southern limits were Seattle, St. Louis, and New York. At the height of the Elster, 32 percent of the world's land masses were covered with ice, and sea levels sank about 197 meters (650 ft) below their present heights.

Holstein
?400,000 to
200,000 B.P.

The succeeding interglacial, sometimes called the Holstein, or Great Interglacial, lasted from about 400,000 years to some 200,000 years ago. The climate was temperate, at times milder than today's in northern latitudes (Figure 3.1). It was during the Great Interglacial that human settlement of temperate latitudes really took hold, as small bands of hunters exploited the rich game populations of European river valleys.[11]

The Saale glacial began about 200,000 years ago, a glacial period that coincided with the Illinoian in North America. In places the Saale was fully as intense as the Elster, with an arctic climate persisting over much of the neighboring parts of Europe, marked by extensive deposits of windblown dust. The Saale did not last as long as the Elster, giving way to the Last Interglacial, or Eem, about 130,000 years ago; the Eem was a period of more temperate climate much shorter than the Holstein, lasting only about 60,000 years. The bones of large mammals like the elephant have been found in many Eem deposits in central Europe. Temperatures at the height of the interglacial may have been comparable to those of recent times.

Saale
?200,000 to 130,000 B.P.

Eem
?130,000 to 75,000 B.P.

Figure 3.1 Generalized distribution of vegetation in Europe during the height of the Holstein interglacial. (After Butzer.)

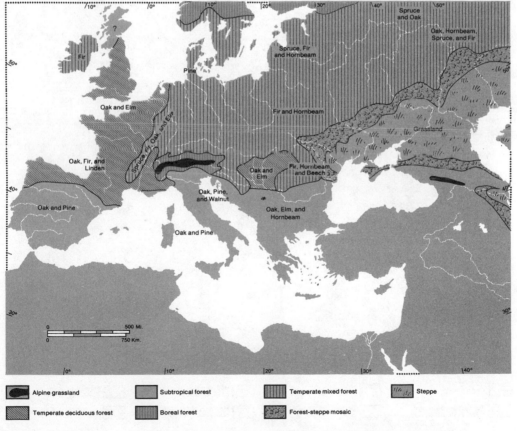

Upper Pleistocene

Weichsel
**75,000 to
10,000 B.P.**

The Weichsel glaciation (or Wisconsin, in North America) formed the last great Pleistocene ice sheet in Europe. About 70,000 years ago the climate cooled rapidly as tundra vegetation replaced forests in central Europe (Figure 3.2). By about 50,000 years ago the sea was more than 106 meters (350 ft) below its present height.

Geologists divide the Weichsel glaciation into three phases (Table 3.3).[12] An initial cold period, lasting 30,000 years from 70,000 B.P., was followed by a slightly warmer interval that ended in 30,000 B.P. The late Weichsel was an intensely cold phase dating from within the last 30,000 years, but by 10,000 to 11,000 B.P. the ice sheets had begun to retreat for the last time. Arctic cold continued to hinder human settlement in extreme eastern Europe and Siberia until the end of the Weichsel (Chapter 6). People first crossed the Bering Strait at a time of low sea level during the last glaciation and settled in North America (Chapter 7) by 25,000 years ago.

Figure 3.2 Generalized distribution of vegetation in Europe at the height of the Weichsel glaciation. Land areas were larger than today's. Notice, too, the extent of the ice sheet. (After Büdel.)

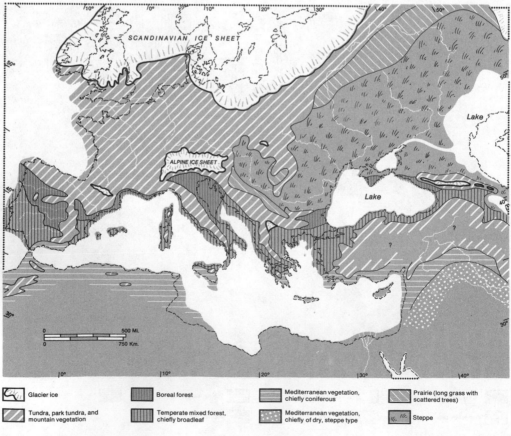

Glacier ice	Boreal forest
Tundra, park tundra, and mountain vegetation	Temperate mixed forest, chiefly broadleaf
	Mediterranean vegetation, chiefly coniferous
	Mediterranean vegetation, chiefly of dry, steppe type
	Prairie (long grass with scattered trees)
	Steppe

Table 3.3 The Weichsel glaciation. (After Butzer.)

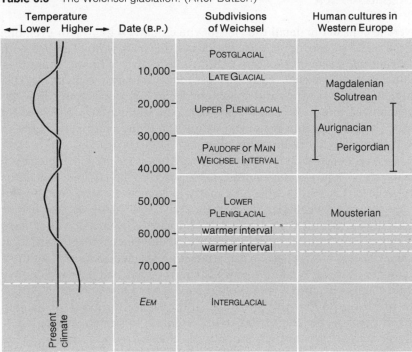

Temperature ← Lower Higher →	Date (B.P.)	Subdivisions of Weichsel	Human cultures in Western Europe
		POSTGLACIAL	
	10,000–	LATE GLACIAL	Magdalenian Solutrean
	20,000–	UPPER PLENIGLACIAL	
	30,000–		Aurignacian
		PAUDORF or MAIN WEICHSEL INTERVAL	Perigordian
	40,000–		
	50,000–	LOWER PLENIGLACIAL	Mousterian
	60,000–	warmer interval	
		warmer interval	
	70,000–		
Present climate		EEM	INTERGLACIAL

[a] After Butzer.

THE LAST TEN THOUSAND YEARS

The end of the Pleistocene is normally thought to have coincided with the final retreat of the ice sheets into the Scandinavian and Alpine mountains and arctic North America. We are said to live in Holocene or Recent Times. Another often-used label is Neothermal. But many scientists prefer to think of us as still living in the Pleistocene, for they have great difficulty defining the boundary between Pleistocene and Holocene.

> Holocene
> **10,000 B.P.**

The shrinking of the Weichsel ice sheets was accompanied by a rapid rise in world sea levels to modern heights. The North Sea was flooded, and Britain was separated from the Continent about 8,000 B.P.[13] The Bering land bridge was covered. Many climatic and environmental changes have taken place since the forests spread into temperate Europe at the end of the Weichsel glaciation some 10,000 years B.P. The climate was warmest during the Atlantic period (Hypsithermal in North America), about 6,000 years ago, when summers were warmer and winters milder. Warmer, cloudier, and moister climates have persisted since a little before the Christian era.

> Atlantic period
> **8,000 B.P.**

Most of the major new human adaptations have taken place since the beginning of the Weichsel glaciation, and the majority of them within comparatively temperate postglacial times.

If we were to consider in detail the Pleistocene climatic schemes for even one area of the world with any precision, the rest of this book would be filled with just that. But one major controversy is not to be missed: climatic changes in Africa during the Pleistocene. Early workers found evidence of major fluctuations in rainfall in East Africa and elsewhere. They compared events in northern latitudes in periods of glacial cold with periods in Africa of increased rainfall or *pluvials*. The four major glaciations (and four major pluvials) were separated by prolonged dry interpluvials.[14]

In fact the sequence of climatic changes in Africa is far more complex than anyone imagined. It now seems impossible to correlate pluvials and glaciations directly; indeed it is questionable how many pluvials there were. Analysis of pollen has shown how complex the picture really was. Many of the pluvials and interpluvials identified in deposits in the East African Rift Valley have been shown to have been caused by sudden earth movements that caused local floods and erosion, creating geological strata that seemed to be the result of major climate changes. We know now that Europe has had extreme, almost zone-wide changes in climate, with colder zones to the north. Here in Africa, though, life had a buffer, the mosaic of interpenetrating types of habitat. Habitats did change, but the various types — forest, savannah, and desert — were always present, even if their proportions changed. Africa's faunas therefore remained more stable and less subject to the drastic extinctions of northern latitudes. Current researchers are studying specific ancient environments, not the global correlations so favored in the earlier literature.[15] It is unlikely that such comprehensive efforts will ever be rewarded with success. At the moment, it is better to look at early human populations strictly in their own environment, as reconstructed by pollen analysis and by carefully observing modern processes forming geological deposits. After all, it is more useful to know a great deal about the habitat of an ancient campsite than it is to be able to assign it to a specific pluvial. All cultural systems are in constant interaction with their local environment; to understand these interactions is the first stage on the way to wider climatic reconstructions.

PART TWO

THE EARLY HUMANS

(c. 4 million to 40,000 B.P.)

"The art of fabricating arms, of preparing aliments, of procuring the utensils requisite for this preparation, of preserving these aliments as provision against the seasons in which it was impossible to procure a fresh supply of them — these arts, confined to the most simple wants, were the first fruits of a continued union, and the first features that distinguished human society from the society observable in many species of beasts."
— Marquis de Condorcet

We describe the origins of humankind, and the early evolution of human culture from the first toolmakers up to the emergence of modern humanity.

Chronological Table A

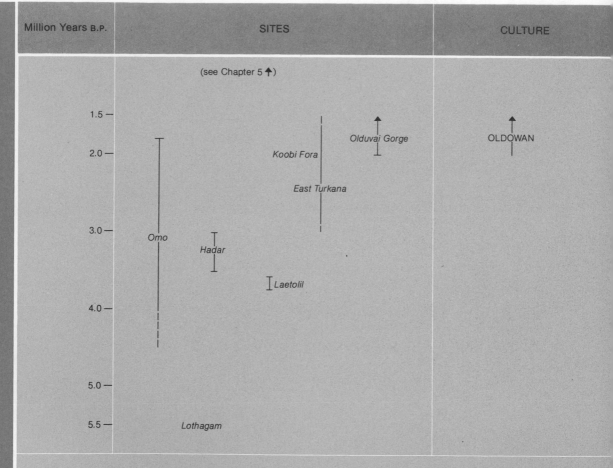

Million Years B.P.	SITES	CULTURE
	(see Chapter 5 ↑)	
1.5 —		
	Olduvai Gorge ↑	OLDOWAN ↑
2.0 —	Koobi Fora	
	East Turkana	
3.0 —	Omo Hadar	
	Laetolil	
4.0 —		
5.0 —		
5.5 —	Lothagam	

Note: In chronological tables in this book, cultures are indicated by all capital letters, sites by italic.

Chapter Four

HUMAN ORIGINS
(4 million to 1.5 million B.P.)

PREVIEW

🌿 There seems to be wide agreement that humanity separated from the apes about 20 to 30 million years ago.

🌿 The first toolmaking humans can be distinguished in the archaeological record about 2 million years ago, perhaps earlier.

🌿 At least three hominid forms were living in East Africa 2 million years ago.

🌿 Critical developments in the emergence of humanity were a change to an erect, bipedal posture, enlargement of brain size, and toolmaking. Major behavioral changes, and the development of some form of a more sophisticated communication system, were part of the process of constant interaction and feedback between different evolutionary forces.

🌿 The earliest stone tools are currently dated to about 2 million years ago. They were made by simple flaking techniques that lasted unchanged for at least a million years. This tool tradition is called the Oldowan, after the much-studied Oldowan culture which used it.

🌿 The earliest humans used home bases that were less transitory than those of apes. Their living sites, scatters of artifacts, animal bones, and other debris have been excavated at Koobi Fora and Olduvai Gorge in East Africa. Our earliest ancestors seem to have lived on small and medium-sized game they hunted, along with vegetable foods, fish, and rodents, they collected; in addition, they scavenged the carcasses of large game killed by carnivores.

Nineteenth-century scientists pointed out that our closest living relatives were apes such as the chimpanzee and the gorilla; all of us are members of the order of primates which are placental mammals, most of them tree-living, with two suborders — anthropoids (apes, humans, and monkeys) and prosimians

Chronological
Table A

Primates

47

Table 4.1 Human development: 10 million to 10,000 years ago.

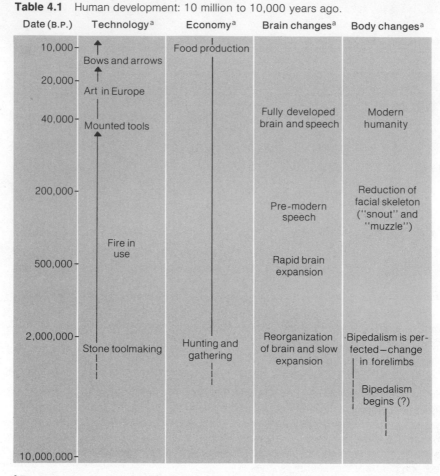

Date (B.P.)	Technology[a]	Economy[a]	Brain changes[a]	Body changes[a]
10,000	Bows and arrows	Food production		
20,000	Art in Europe			
40,000	Mounted tools		Fully developed brain and speech	Modern humanity
200,000			Pre-modern speech	Reduction of facial skeleton ("snout" and "muzzle")
500,000	Fire in use		Rapid brain expansion	
2,000,000	Stone toolmaking	Hunting and gathering	Reorganization of brain and slow expansion	Bipedalism is perfected—change in forelimbs
				Bipedalism begins (?)
10,000,000				

[a] The developments on this table appeared at the period indicated by their placement. They are assumed to continue until being either replaced or refined.

(lemurs, tarsiers, and other "pre-monkeys").[1]* The research of over a century has shown that the many similarities in behavior and physical characteristics

Hominids

between the hominids (primates of the family *Hominidae*, which includes modern humans, earlier human subspecies, and their direct ancestors) and these closest living primate relatives can be explained by identical characteristics that each group inherited millions of years ago from a common ancestor. Differences between us and the apes must have evolved since we separated because each group began its own separate development. (For an overview of human development covered in Part II, see Table 4.1.)

* See pages 372–374 for notes to Chapter 4.

Thomas Huxley, a Victorian zoologist, spelled out his own opinion about the divergences between humans and apes in his classic *Man's Place in Nature*: "the structural differences which separate man from the gorilla and chimpanzee are not so great as those which separate the gorilla from the lower apes." But Huxley realized that the gap which separates humans from the higher apes is a gap between parallel lines, not a gap between locations along a single line. The gap measures divergent evolution from a common ancestor. The question is, when did humankind separate from the nonhuman primates? Experts disagree violently when asked this question. There are at least three theories on the origins of the human line, which are summarized in Figure 4.1.[2]

Scheme A: Our Tarsier Forbears

The first school hypothesizes that humans separated into a distinct family before the monkeys and apes originated, about 40 million years ago. Proponents argue that a small, nocturnal insect-eater named the tarsier is more closely related to us than to any other living primate.[3] It is unlikely, however, that human ancestry passed through a stage that would be identified as a tarsier, although the fossil evidence is still very limited.

40 million B.P.

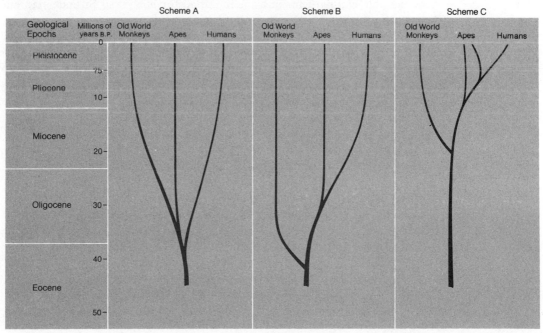

Figure 4.1 Three much-simplified versions of how Old World monkeys, apes, and humans evolved. For later human evolution, see Figure 4.10.

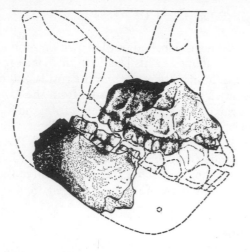

Figure 4.2 Composite reconstruction of the face of *Ramapithecus* from the Siwalik Hills, India, partly based on teeth from Kenya; it is highly tentative.

Scheme B: Was *Ramapithecus* One of Us?

A second group of paleontologists consider that apes and humans separated from a common stock in the Oligocene or the early Miocene era, 20 or 30 million years ago (Figure 4.1).[4] Widely accepted, this theory allows for an apelike ancestry for humans only to the extent that an early unspecialized ape may have been ancestral to both humanity and apes. Unfortunately, the fossil record before the early Pleistocene is very incomplete.

One possible claimant for our apelike ancestor is a fossil primate named *Ramapithecus* (*Rama*, a Hindu god; *pithecus*, from the Greek for ape), a dozen specimens of which have been found in Africa and India. *Ramapithecus* first came to light in 1932 in the Siwalik Hills, 200 miles (322 km) north of New Delhi in India. The fragmentary jaws and teeth were found in late Miocene deposits estimated to date to some 12 to 15 million years ago, but the chronology is very uncertain.[5] Further specimens have been found by Yale University paleontologists in the Siwalik Hills, and a highly tentative identification of another Ramapithecine comes from China. In 1961 Louis B. Leakey found several jaws that belonged to the same *Ramapithecus* genus at Fort Ternan in Keyna, potassium argon dated to about 14.5 million years ago. These Ramapithecines are all more recent than the date of 20 to 30 million years that, according to the supporters of the second theory, separated humans from apes.

Ramapithecus has also recently been found in Turkey, and possibly in Hungary as well.

Many physical anthropologists believe that *Ramapithecus* is not an apelike creature ancestral to both apes and humans, but an early hominid. They argue that the human family separated from the apes and left the forest before *Ramapithecus* lived in Africa and Asia during the late Miocene and early Pliocene. Paleontologist Elwyn Simons has claimed that *Ramapithecus* is the earliest known hominid. Its jaws and teeth bear some similarities to those of *Australopithecus* and later fossil humans (Figure 4.2). The jaws are smaller

20 to 30 million B.P.

Ramapithecus
12–15 million B.P.

than those of the Australopithecines of the Lower Pleistocene, but the muscle attachments for chewing appear better developed than those of apes. The snout is reduced and the teeth are smaller than those normally found in apes. The canines in particular are small, compared with those of the baboon, for example. Such teeth are used by modern apes to defend themselves and to find food. If Ramapithecines did not use their teeth for these purposes, they must have had other ways to protect themselves and survive in their intensely competitive environment, surrounded by many species of apes and predators. The small canines mean that *Ramapithecus* may have made greater use of hands both in feeding and in defense.

The Ramapithecines may have walked upright, but the bones we have are too incomplete to give an answer. Unfortunately, with little but jaws and teeth to go on, it is difficult to assess how close this early primate lies to the origin of our lineage among the apes.

Scheme C: Molecular Biologists Theorize

A third opinion of human origins has been proposed by some researchers in molecular biology, who argue that humanity separated from the apes as recently as 5 million years ago (Figure 4.1), a radically different approach to human evolution. Two biochemists, Vincent Sarich and Alan Wilson, believe that albumin protein substances found in primate blood have evolved at a constant rate.[6] Thus the difference between the albumins of any pair of primates can be used to calculate the time that has elapsed since they separated.

5 million B.P.

Sarich and Wilson have shown that the albumins of apes and humans are more similar than those of monkeys and humans. Thus, they argue, apes and humans have a more recent common ancestry. They estimate that apes and Old World monkeys diverged about 23 million years ago, the gibbon and humankind only about 12 million years ago, and that the chimpanzee, gorilla, and humans last shared a common ancestor 4 to 5 million years ago. The apparent separation of apes and humans is so recent that statistically reliable numbers of differences have not yet accumulated.

Sarich's work has been criticized because it deals with only one protein. Another biochemist, Morris Goodman, investigates similarities between different primates using antibodies and antigens and comparative analysis plates. He argues that evolution is slowing down in the higher primates, and is far less specific about the dates when apes and humans diverged.

The biochemists' short chronology conflicts with the longer timescale for the separation of humans and apes proposed by paleontologists. The objection to the longer timescale is simply lack of fossil evidence belonging to the time between *Ramapithecus* 14 million years ago and the Australopithecines, the earliest of whom flourished around 5 million years before the present; fossil-bearing deposits dating to this time are rare and are little studied. During this period between 14 million and 5 million years ago, the African savannah, with its islands of residual forests and extensive grassland plains, was densely populated by many mammal species as well as specialized tree dwellers and other primates. Both the chimpanzee and the gorilla evolved in the forests, surviving from earlier times. On savannah plains other primates were flourishing in small bands, probably walking upright, and, conceivably, making tools. No fossil remains of these creatures have been found, so that we do not know when primates first achieved the bipedal (two-footed) posture that is the outstanding human physical feature. If *Ramapithecus* is a hominid, then future discoveries of hip bones and limbs will show that it walked upright, a posture most suitable for open country. If it is not, then its hip bones will display anatomical features better suited to life in the trees. Whether human evolution has a long or short chronology will probably be resolved by future discoveries of both *Ramapithecus* and other Pliocene fossils. In the meantime, most scientists favor the theory that the primate line that led to toolmaking humans diverged from the apes 20 to 30 million years ago.

THE EVOLUTION OF HUMAN BEHAVIOR

The major gap in the fossil record comes toward the end of the Pliocene, a time when dramatic changes in primate behavior were occurring. The only way in which we can obtain insights into the evolution of human behavior is by studying living apes, the objective being to identify the kinds of behavior that distinguished early human populations from their ape relatives. We, like modern apes, are the end product (possibly) of the successful behaviors our ancestors evolved over millions of years of cumulative achievement.

Adaptations in Posture

The American anthropologist Sherwood L. Washburn has long argued that the close relationship between humans and the African apes makes it likely that our ancestors walked on four feet, with both hands and feet adapted to grasping.[7] This quadrupedal posture remained in use for a long time. Washburn goes on to suggest that the early apes evolved an arboreal (tree-living) adaptation, climbing in trees to feed on fruit as well as on ground-growing foods. Adaptations in their anatomy followed, modifying chests, shoulders, elbows, and wrists to allow swinging from branch to branch, climbing, hanging, and reaching for food, as well as other new behaviors. We lack the fossil bones that would tell us when these changes took place.[8]

An upright posture and two-footed gait are the most characteristic human physical features, probably gained from modified behavior patterns among the early apes. We can picture the modified behaviors from analogous actions by the modern African ape. The chimpanzees, ably studied by Jane Goodall, use objects for play and display, carry them in their hands, and use sticks to fish for termites (Figure 4.3). They take leaves for cleaning the body and sipping water, and actually improve their sticks slightly with their teeth, if need be, when searching for termites. Monkeys do none of these things. Chimpanzees have in fact inherited behavior patterns far closer to our own than to those of any monkey.

Figure 4.3 Chimpanzee using a stick as a tool to fish for insects.

Both the chimpanzee and the gorilla get around by knuckle-walking, a specialized way of moving in which the backs of the fingers are placed on the ground and act as main weight-bearing surfaces (Figure 4.4). Jane Goodall finds that chimpanzees knuckle-walk for long distances; but this posture is only occasionally used by humans, by football linemen or runners at the starting block.[9] With longer arms, like those that ancestral hominids might have had, that posture would have been easier to assume. Knuckle-walking may be an intermediate stage between the ape's arboreal adaptation and the human bipedal posture.[10]

Chimpanzees — as knuckle-walking, object-using apes — have been seen to prey on other primates and small antelopes. The change from knuckle-walking to bipedalism *may* have resulted from more frequent object use and more hunting; both these behaviors could have led to greater use of bipedalism and of the anatomy making it possible. The success of the whole behavior pattern led to the evolution of primates with the human attribute of upright posture, as well as the characteristic hunting and gathering and toolmaking patterns that went with it.

Bipedal posture

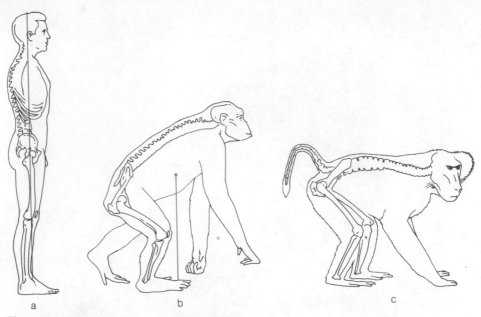

Figure 4.4 Bipedalism and quadrupedalism.

    a. Human bipedal posture. The center of gravity of the body lies just behind the midpoint of the hip joint and in front of the knee joint, so that both hip and knee are extended when standing, conserving energy.

    b. A knuckle-walking chimpanzee. The body's center of gravity lies in the middle of the area bounded by legs and arms. When the ape walks bipedally, its center of gravity moves from side to side and up and down. The human center of gravity is displaced much less, making walking much more efficient. (After Zihlman.)

    c. A baboon. Baboons are quadrupedal and adapted to living on the ground.

Cooperation, Hunting, and Gathering

    Animal behavior specialist George Schaller says it might be more productive to compare hominids with carnivores such as lions or wild dogs living on the African savannah than with primates.[11] Lions, hyenas, and wild dogs hunt in groups and share their food, engaging in a form of cooperative hunting that has several advantages. Animals that cooperate are more successful at killing, can prey on larger animals, and, by eating most of the kill at one time, waste less food. A solitary hunter is obliged either to protect the food he does not consume immediately after the kill or to hunt again when he is hungry. Group hunting allows some members of the pride or pack to guard the young while others hunt and bring back food. When they return, they regurgitate some of their kill for the rest of the group.

Cooperation   Social life for nonhuman primates is structured by hierarchies of dominance, a pattern that has been radically altered among humans, who, when they began systematic hunting, had to cooperate far more closely than their nonhuman, predominantly vegetarian relatives did.

    This account of human cooperative behavior is challenged by several anthropologists.[12] Some argue that hypotheses on the origins of culture wrongly make males the architects of all evolutionary change. Theories on the origins of human behavior advanced by Washburn and others have also been attacked because they do not adequately explain the trend toward smaller hominid teeth, which one would not expect if the major element of early humans' diets were in fact large animals. Clifford Jolly in particular talks of a lengthy period when "basal" hominids — immediate ancestors of humans — were predominantly, if not exclusively, seed eaters.[13] Through much of the Lower Pleistocene, he says, the earliest hominids subsisted on grass seeds and other vegetable foods that must be gathered by agile hands and accurately coordinated eye and hand. These are, states Jolly, an essential preadaptation for even a medium-sized animal to be able to gather enough seeds to support itself. With these preadaptations, the early hominids would have faced little competition in the exploitation of a concentrated, high-energy food. Jolly believes there were no major advances needed in social organization, intelligence, culture, or communication for such hominids over those attributable to some living nonhuman primates.

Gathering

It was not until much later that evolving hominids became more involved in hunting, when projectiles and fire began to be important in human culture.

Hunting

The Jolly model of human behavior has significant implications for male and female roles in human evolution. Kay Martin and Barbara Voorhies, writing on the position of women at the species level, follow anthropologist Ralph Linton in replacing the familiar model (a community organization based on a single male) with a social arrangement putting adult females at the head of their own matricentric units.[14] These individuals are mainly involved with "reproduction, infant care, and socialization, and the gathering of sufficient seeds or vegetable products for themselves and their dependent young." The adult males have no special attachment to the units of mother and child, adhering merely to the unit of their birth. In other words, all adults foraged for themselves in a community structure that may have survived almost unchanged for thousands of years.

But what happened when hunting became more important? Jolly argues that the increased importance of hunting led to the beginnings of food sharing, specialized tools, and new ideas on economic cooperation — and from these to kinship systems. Martin and Voorhies disagree and feel that these developments were foreshadowed in the matricentric family. Food sharing was part of the bond between mother and child. When males started hunting, they logically shared the meat with those who shared other food with them. Sexual divison of labor may have begun in the extended, matricentric family instead of with the rise of hunting. And marriage and kinship ties may have developed because of strengthened cooperation by exchange of mating partners and the ultimate development of kinship and marriage.

Language Development

Only humans have a spoken, symbolic language; scientists have long thought that nonhuman primates had much less sophisticated communication systems. True, but chimpanzees use gestures and many voice sounds in the wild, while other apes use sounds to communicate territorial information. Chimpanzees seem to have a natural talent for learning symbolic language under controlled conditions. A famous chimpanzee named Washoe was trained to communicate with humans, using no less than 175 sign language gestures similar to those of the American Sign Language.[15] After more than a year Washoe could associate particular signs with specific activities, such as eating and drinking. Another chimpanzee named Sarah was taught to read and write with plastic symbols and acquired a vocabulary of 130 different words, to the extent that she obeyed sequences of written instructions given with the symbols.[16] But such experiments in communication with primates are a far cry from the versatility and grace of human speech.

We cannot tell from fossil bones exactly when human speech first appeared, for detailed relationships between skeletal structure and soft tissue are lost forever. But Charles F. Hockett, a linguist at Cornell University, speculates that early in human evolution the development of bipedal movement, which freed the hands for toolmaking, may have also opened up the call system of vocal sounds, body movements, and facial expressions.[17] Over thousands of years, the three call systems were blended, new signals being developed from combinations of old ones. As this system took hold the vocal cords gradually became innervated, as did the tongue and the larynx. The portions of the brain cortex used in vocal expression also evolved until a transition to speech was possible. Although no one knows when it all took place, Hockett believes that speech evolved from a blended signal system, at the very beginning of the Pleistocene.

Many scholars disagree, arguing that the slow evolution of human technology and the small brain size of the earliest hominids are signs of only the most rudimentary communication systems. They feel that language did not develop until the Middle Pleistocene. Vocal communication came about with enhanced mental ability, which increased the probability that an anatomical mutation enhancing the phonetic repertoire and the rate of communication would be retained by natural selection. Increased anatomical phonetic ability would in turn mean that mutations enhancing the neural abilities involved in speech encoding, decoding, syntax, and so on would be retained.

The real value of language, apart from the stimulation it gives brain development, is that with it we can convey subtle feelings and nuances far beyond the power of grunts or gestures to communicate. We may assume that the early hominids had more to communicate than nonhuman primates, but we simply do not know, and may never know, when language began.

THE FOSSIL EVIDENCE FOR HUMAN EVOLUTION

For working purposes, we can correlate the emergence of the first human beings with the appearance in the archaeological record of:

people with erect posture and enlarged brain size
living sites that represent more lasting home bases than the sleeping places of apes

systematically manufactured artifacts
evidence for a cultural system which acts as an adaptive device.

With these attributes in mind, we will now examine the archaeological and fossil evidence for human evolution.

Australopithecus

Of all the fossil candidates as a direct ancestor for humankind, none is better known than *Australopithecus africanus* (Latin for Southern Ape of Africa), a primate first identified in 1924 by Raymond Dart, an anatomist at the University of Witwatersrand, South Africa.[18] Subsequently, a more robust form was also discovered, and named *Australopithecus robustus* to distinguish it from the lighter, gracile *A. africanus* form (see Figures 4.5, 4.6; see also Table 4.3 later in this chapter).[19]

Australopithecus africanus

A. robustus

Figure 4.5 *Australopithecus africanus* from Sterkfontein, South Africa. *A. africanus* was probably 107 to 127 centimeters (42 to 50 in.) tall; the females, weighing 18 to 27 kg (40 to 60 lbs) were somewhat lighter than the males. The posture was fully upright, with the spinal curvature that places the trunk over the pelvis for balanced walking. (Apes do not have this curvature, nor are their legs proportionately as long as those of *Australopithecus*.) The foot was small, with a well-developed big toe. *Australopithecus* looked remarkably human, but with an apelike snout that was, however, less prominent than the ape's. The canines were small, and the incisors were vertical in the jaw, where the ape's slope outward. A flat nose was combined with a well-developed forehead, and the brow ridges were much less prominent than those of his modern tree-living relatives. The brain had an average size of about 450 cubic centimeters, much less than that of a modern human male (1,450 cc) and slightly larger than that of the chimpanzee (400 cc).

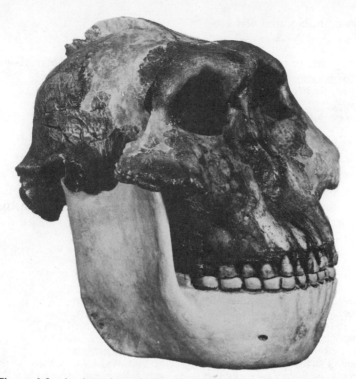

Figure 4.6 A robust Australopithecine from Olduvai Gorge, Tanzania. The robust Australopithecine was both larger and heavier than the *africanus* forms, with a more barrel-like trunk. The biggest contrasts were in the facial appearance and in the teeth. *Australopithecus robustus* had a low forehead and a prominent bony ridge on the crest of the skull, which supported massive chewing muscles. Its brain was slightly larger than the *A. africanus* form, and *A. robustus* had relatively well-developed cheek teeth as well as larger molars.

Although dozens of Australopithecine fragments have been recovered in South Africa, the sites are all undated. Only the animal bones from the sites provide a rough framework for dating most South African Australopithecines to between 3 million and 800,000 years ago; the robust forms may be somewhat later.

Early Humans of East Africa

Dozens of *Australopithecus* specimens have come from East Africa in recent years (Figure 4.7).

Lothagam
5.5 million B.P.

Lothagam The earliest Australopithecine fossil yet discovered is a solitary jaw found on the western shores of Lake Turkana, which has been potassium argon dated to 5.5 million years.

Omo
3.7 million B.P.

Omo In the late 1960s an American-French-Kenyan expedition found the

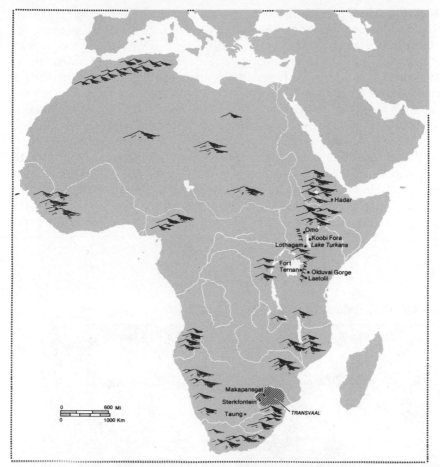

Figure 4.7 Archaeological sites in Africa mentioned in Chapter 4.

teeth and lower jawbones of both gracile and robust Australopithecines as well as possible traces of a more advanced hominid in late Pliocene and Lower Pleistocene fossil-bearing beds in the Omo Valley near the Kenya-Ethiopia border. These finds were dated to between 3.7 and 1.8 million years ago.[20]

Hadar When Maurice Taieb and Don Johanson found a remarkably complete skeleton of a small primate at Hadar on the Awash river in northern Ethiopia, they named it "Lucy."[21] She has been dated to about 3 million years ago. Nearby some further jaws and limb bone fragments came to light in lake deposits dated to earlier than 3.5 million years. Lucy was only about 3.5 to 4 feet tall, and 19 to 21 years old. Her primitive teeth and pelvis seem too small to be human, and she is probably an Australopithecine. Johanson has named this find *A. afarensis* (after the area where the fossil came from) a form of gracile Australopithecine.

Hadar
3.5 million B.P.

Laetolil   The fossil-bearing beds at Laetolil in northern Tanzania have been potassium argon dated to 3.59 to 3.75 years and have yielded not only the bones of long extinct animals but the incomplete jaws and teeth of at least twenty hominids.[22] The Laetolil specimens are said to have some similarities to Lucy from Hadar. But the most remarkable finds came from the buried bed of a seasonal river where thin layers of fine volcanic ash once formed a pathway for animals traveling to waterholes. The hardened surface of the ash, dated to older than 3.59 million years ago, bore the footprints of elephants, rhinoceroses, giraffes, a sabre-toothed tiger, and many species of antelope. Mary Leakey also identified a trail of six prints of a fairly large bipedal primate, which, she estimated, stood about 4 feet tall (Figure 4.8). "The tracks," she wrote," indicate a rolling and probably slow-moving gait, with the hips swivelling at each step, as opposed to the free-striding gait of modern man." Unfortunately, no traces of the bones of this primate have come from the excavations so far.

Figure 4.8   Pliocene footprint from Laetolil, Tanzania.

Figure 4.9 A tentative reconstruction of Skull 1470 from East Turkana. Provisionally identified as *Homo*, this cranium is remarkable for its large brain capacity and rounded back part of the skull.

East Turkana Lake Turkana lies in remote and hot northern Kenya, which today supports little more than desert scrub. In recent years Richard Leakey and Glynn Isaac have been working on the eastern side of the lake, searching for early hominids.[23] They have located a thousand square miles of Pliocene and Lower Pleistocene fossil-bearing sediments. The hominids include both Australopithecines and specimens of individuals with unmistakably enlarged brains, including the famous Skull 1470 (Figure 4.9), which has a brain capacity of 775 cc, far larger than that of *Australopithecus*. This specimen, with jutting face like an *Australopithecus* but the brain size of a human, is thought to date to about 2.9 million years ago. The East Turkana finds include another skull, almost complete, of a hominid that is clearly from the genus *Homo*, dated to about 1.5 million years, and contemporary with Australopithecines.

Olduvai Gorge Olduvai Gorge is one of the world's most famous archaeological sites and is closely associated with Louis and Mary Leakey.[24] The gorge is a spectacular rift in the great Serengeti Plains of northern Tanzania. Earth movements have exposed hundreds of meters of lake beds belonging to a long dried-up Pleistocene lake. In 1959 Mary Leakey found the almost complete skull of a robust Australopithecine, *Australopithecus boisei*, on a living floor in Bed I, the lowest of the four lakebed series in the gorge (Figure 4.6). Later, a more gracile hominid came from a level slightly lower than that of the original robust skull. Fortunately, fragments of lava were in the Olduvai floors, usable for potassium argon dating. The living floor upon which the Leakeys' first skull was found has been dated to approximately 1.75 million years ago. The earliest occupation levels at Olduvai date to about 2 million years ago (Table 4.2).

The more gracile hominid remains from the levels slightly below those of the original robust find consist of parts of the skull of a juvenile, together with a collarbone and hand bones from at least two individuals. The skull fragments are said to belong to a larger-brained hominid than *Australopithecus africanus*, with a dental pattern similar to that of the gracile Australopithecine. A reconstruction of the hand bones revealed an opposable thumb, which allows both powerful gripping and precise manipulating of fine objects. With the latter the individual could have made complex tools. Intermediate between the modern human hand and that of apes, the Olduvai hands were characterized by great flexure and muscularity in the fingers, perhaps attributable to their ancestry among knuckle-walkers.

Other fragments of the gracile hominid have come from the floor where *Australopithecus boisei* was found and from the lower part of Bed II. Louis Leakey and his colleagues named this gracile hominid *Homo habilis*, or "handy person," a new species of the genus *Homo*, more advanced anatomically and more skillful in toolmaking than *Australopithecus africanus*.

FROM HOMINIDS TO *HOMO SAPIENS*

A considerable number of fossil bones from various parts of Africa date to the period between 5.5 and 1.5 million years ago, most of them from the sites listed in the preceding section. But the question of how the first humans evolved generates arguments so fiery that no two specialists can agree on the answer, and no unified scheme of human evolution satisfies every school of thought.[25] What exactly is the archaeological evidence, and what major hypotheses have been formulated as frameworks for early human evolution?

Table 4.3 summarizes the fossil evidence. It shows that there are three groupings of East and Southern African hominids, two of them Australopithecines, the third *Homo*, with a larger brain capacity and more modern limb bones. Figure 4.10 gives a tentative timescale for the various major fossil finds. Much of the fossil evidence has been gathered in recent years and has generated three major hypotheses for early human evolution.

Diverse species
hypothesis

Scheme A in Figure 4.10 sees the Australopithecines as a highly diverse species, which suggests that all early hominids belonged to the same variable species. Their morphological differences could be accounted for by their separation in time and space and by normal variability within any species. This simple viewpoint has both *Australopithecus* and *Homo habilis* as a relatively

Table 4.2 Highly schematic chronology of Olduvai Gorge, Tanzania, with positions of fossils and tools.

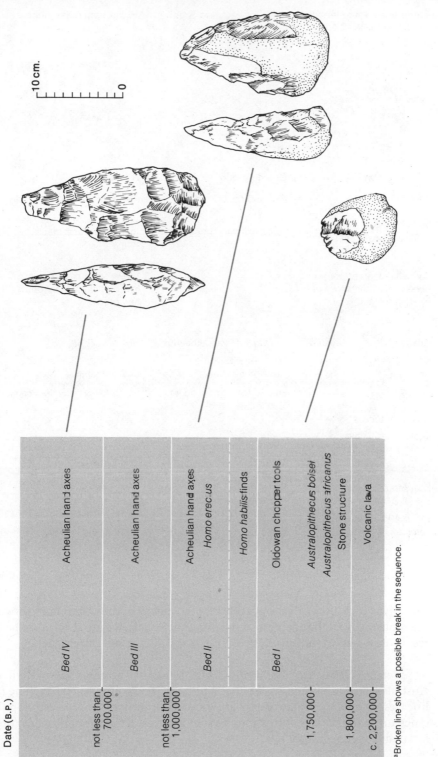

Date (B.P.)		
	Bed IV	Acheulian hand axes
not less than 700,000	*Bed III*	Acheulian hand axes
not less than 1,000,000	*Bed II*	Acheulian hand axes *Homo erectus*
		Homo habilis finds
1,750,000	*Bed I*	Oldowan chopper tools *Australopithecus boisei* *Australopithecus africanus*
1,800,000		Stone structure
c. 2,200,000		Volcanic lava

10 cm.
0

^aBroken line shows a possible break in the sequence.

Human Origins   63

Table 4.3   Three tentative groups of East and Southern African hominids, much simplified for this book.

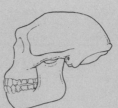

	Robust group	Gracile group	Homo group
Brain size	500-550 cc.	450-550 cc.	650-775 cc.
Teeth	Very large back teeth; relatively small front teeth	Large front and back teeth	Variable; generally smaller than robust and gracile forms
Limbs	Some elements of limb bones differ from those of modern humans		Lower limbs more modern in morphology than robust and gracile forms
Species and sites	*Australopithecus robustus* South Africa: Swartkrans, Kromdraai *Australopithecus boisei* East Africa: Olduvai, East Turkana, Omo	*Australopithecus africanus* South Africa: Taung, Sterkfontein, Makapansgat East Africa: Omo?, Hadar, East Turkana	*Homo* East Africa: Olduvai and East Turkana South Africa: Sterkfontein
	East Africa: 2,000,000 to c. 1,000,000 B.P. South Africa: no reliable dates	East Africa: 3,000,000 to c. 1,500,000 B.P. South Africa: no reliable dates	East Africa: c. 2,000,000 to c. 1,500,000 B.P.

short-lived stage between the apes and *Homo erectus*. The differences between the robust Australopithecine and its more gracile relative are thought to be the result of sexual dimorphism (size differences due to sex differences).

3-species
hypothesis

   Scheme B has three hominid species living at the same time, then the Australopithecines becoming extinct while the *Homo* group survives. The two lineages represent adaptations to different environments; the Australopithecines in their different forms represented a series of local populations, often isolated from one another.

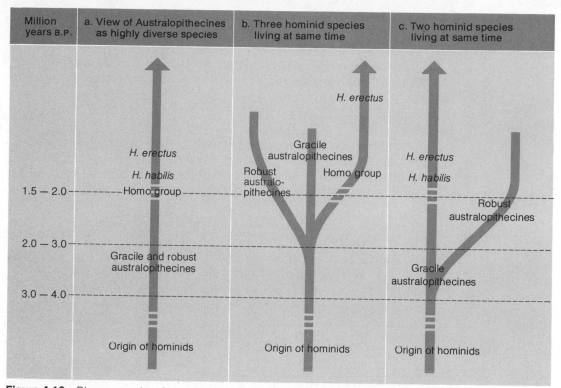

Million years B.P.	a. View of Australopithecines as highly diverse species	b. Three hominid species living at same time	c. Two hominid species living at same time

Figure 4.10 Diverse species, 3-species, and 2-species hypotheses of early hominid evolution.

Scheme C envisages two hominid species living at the same time, with only the robust Australopithecines becoming extinct and humanity evolving out of the gracile, *Australopithecus africanus*, populations. 2-species hypothesis

Scheme A is probably too simple, given the great variety of fossils found at East Turkana. The three-species proponents differ from their two-species colleagues of scheme C in believing that the Laetolil finds made by Mary Leakey are in fact *Homo* and that humans separated from the Australopithecines as early as 3.5 million years ago. Scheme C supporters believe that the Laetolil jaws and teeth are too fragmentary for firm identification and that *Homo* evolved from the gracile Australopithecines about 2 million years ago, while the robust *Australopithecus* had speciated from the gracile form somewhat earlier.

Despite the different interpretations of data, several points seem well established:

1. The Australopithecines were a long-lived and highly successful adaptation to the African tropical savannah, and perhaps elsewhere. (Nearly all the Australopithecine fossils so far have been discovered in Africa, but that is not to say they may not be found in other regions.) Then, about a million years

ago, they suddenly disappear from the archaeological record. The early dates for *Australopithecus* in the Omo show that these creatures flourished for at least 3.5 million years.

2. Robust Australopithecines are not found earlier than 2.5 million years ago. Although this gap may reflect a lack of discoveries, it may in fact be because the robust species were an evolutionary development from the much older gracile *Australopithecus* form, one that did not occur until about 3 to 2.5 million years ago.

3. There is a good evidence for at least two Australopithecine groups living alongside each other in East Africa for a considerable period of time. The robust lineage seems to have developed such a distinctive ecological and behavioral specialization that it survived alongside *Homo* for at least 2 million years.

4. The ancestral hominid population was probably a gracile primate closely resembling *Australopithecus africanus*.

5. At issue is the date at which *Homo* and *Australopithecus africanus* diverged, the former with larger brains and more complex societies that depended increasingly heavily on a new element — their own culture.

6. Human culture, in the form of stone implements, can be traced back to approximately 2 million years, maybe more, in East Turkana.

HOME BASES

The archaeological evidence for the earliest human culture comes from East Turkana and Olduvai Gorge where hominid living sites have been located and excavated with meticulous care. To date, no living sites or stone artifacts have been found with the South African Australopithecines, with the Omo or Laetolil hominids, or with the Lothagam find.

Koobi Fora

The earliest humanly manufactured tools in the world come from the Koobi Fora area of East Turkana.[26] Two localities have been excavated — one a dry streambed hollow where a group of hominids found the carcass of a hippopotamus. They gathered round and butchered the carcass with small stone knives, crudely flaked choppers and pebble hammers. The deposits in which these stones and the flaked debris from them are found are so fine grained that they contain no stones larger than a pea. Thus, every lump of rock there was carried in by the hominids to make tools. The lumps of stone they brought to the site were chipped into small knives at the carcass. The hominids visited the locality at least 1.8 million years ago. We do not know whether they killed the hippopotamus. In all likelihood, they simply cut up the carcass of a dead animal and scavenged the meat.

Only a mile away from this site, the archaeologists found another scatter of stone tool fragments and broken animal bones — these from several antelope and larger mammals. The scatter lay on the surface of a dry streambed where water could still be easily obtained by digging in the sand. The banks of the watercourse were probably shaded by dense stands of trees that provided both shelter and plant foods. Perhaps, too, the people who left the tools and bones climbed into these same trees at night. The site was so sheltered that even miniscule stone chips were still in place, unaffected by the strong winds that sweep over the area; the leaves, too, left impressions in the deposits there. The nearest source of toolmaking stone is two miles from the site, so the inhabitants must have carried in their tools, and, in all probability, portions of the several animals whose bones accumulated at the site. This type of behavior — the carrying in of food to a home base — is fundamentally different from that of the nonhuman primates.

Olduvai Gorge

Our present knowledge about the way of life of the earliest humans comes almost entirely from Olduvai Gorge where Mary Leakey plotted and recorded several living sites in Bed I at the base of the gorge.[27] The *Zinjanthropus* campsite at Olduvai was found to be 1,239 feet square, consisting of over four thousand artifacts and bones. Many artifacts and bones were concentrated in a working area some fifteen feet across. A pile of shattered bones and rocks lay a short distance away, the bones perhaps piled in heaps as the marrow was extracted from them. A barer, arc-shaped area between these bone heaps and the pile of more complete fragments may have been the site of a crude windbreak of branches, for the area lies in the path of today's prevailing winds.

Olduvai Gorge
2 million B.P.

One campsite at the very bottom of the gorge yielded not only stone artifacts but also a crude semicircle of stones in front of a slightly depressed area in the floor. Mary Leakey interprets this as the foundation of a two-million-year-old windbreak, perhaps the oldest living structure yet discovered.

The Olduvai living sites were well-established, temporary home bases to which the hominids returned to live, eat, and sleep. Bed I floors contain the remains of some medium-sized antelope and wild pigs, but smaller animals predominate; it seems that meat was scavenged from the carcasses of larger species that had been carnivore kills or had died of natural causes. The gathering of fruit and wild vegetable foods was probably of great importance, as it is to hunter-gatherers in Africa today.

OLDOWAN CULTURE

For many years the Leakeys had found crudely chipped stones in the long-buried lake beds at Olduvai. Similar artifacts came from the *Zinjanthropus* floor and from floors associated with more gracile fossils. *Oldowan* tools, named by Leakey after Olduvai Gorge, are nothing much to look at (Figure 4.11). They are broken pebbles and flakes, mostly the latter. Some Oldowan tools are so crude that only an expert can tell them from a naturally fractured rock — and the experts often disagree. All the Oldowan choppers and flakes strike one as extremely practical implements; many are so individual in design

Oldowan
2 million to 1 million B.P. or later

Figure 4.11 Early stone technology. The principles of fracturing stone were fully understood by early stoneworkers, who used them to make simple but very effective artifacts. Certain types of flinty rock fracture in a distinctive way, as illustrated below. Early stoneworkers used a heavy hammerstone to remove edge flakes or struck lumps of rock against anvils to produce the same effect. Oldowan choppers were frequently made by removing a few flakes from lava lumps to form jagged working edges. Such artifacts have been shown by modern experiments to be remarkably effective for dismembering and butchering game. Perhaps it is small wonder that this simple stone technology was so long lasting.

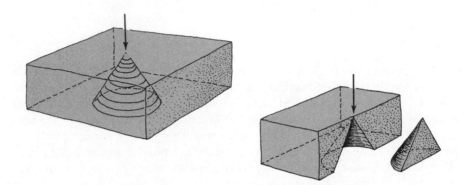

When a blow is struck on flinty rock, a cone of percussion is formed by shock waves rippling through the stone. A flake is formed (right) when the block (or core) is hit at the edge, and the stone fractures along the edge of the ripple.

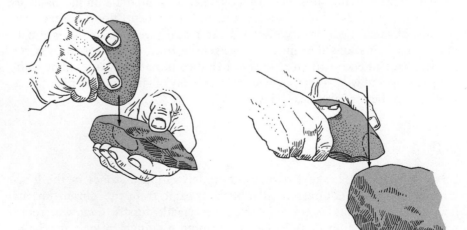

Using a hammerstone (left) and anvil (right).

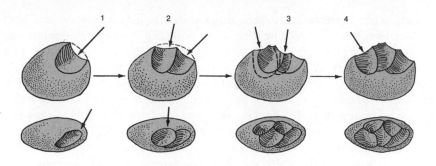

Making a chopping tool. First, sharp blows are struck near the natural edge of a pebble to remove flakes. The pebble is then turned over, and more blows are struck on the ridges formed by the scars of the earlier flakes. A chopping tool with a strong, jagged working edge results.

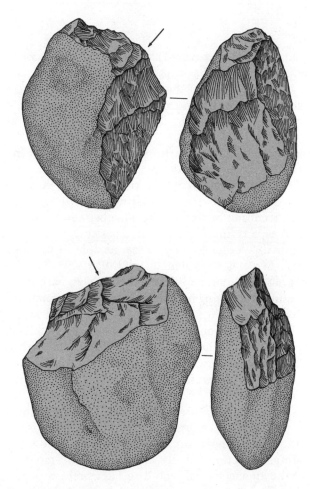

Two Oldowan chopping tools from Olduvai Gorge. Arrows show working edges. Front and side views (three-fifths actual size).

that they seem haphazard artifacts, not standardized in the way that later Stone Age tools were. Classifying them is very difficult, for they do not fall into distinct types. The tools cannot be described as primitive, for many display a sophisticated understanding of stone's potential uses in toolmaking. Although Oldowan stone tools are easily confused with naturally fractured stones when found in river gravels or away from sealed occupation sites, we now know that the Olduvai hominids were adept stone toolmakers, using angular flakes and lumps of lava to make weapons, scrapers, and cutting tools. The tools themselves were probably used for cutting skin too tough for teeth to cut. In all probability, the hominids made extensive use of simple and untrimmed flakes for widely differing activities. The earliest human toolkit could probably perform all the basic tasks of tropical, nonagricultural hunter-gatherers, whatever their primary means of subsistence.

THE EARLY ADAPTIVE PATTERN

The few early living sites that have been excavated show that the first phase of human evolution involved shifts in the basic patterns of subsistence and locomotion, as well as new ingredients — food sharing and toolmaking. These led to enhanced communication, information exchange, and economic and social insight, as well as cunning and restraint. And human anatomy was augmented with tools.

Opportunism

Archaeologist Glynn Isaac believes that opportunism is a hallmark of humankind — a restless process, like mutation and natural selection.[28] The normal pressures of ecological competition were able to transform the versatile behavior of the ancestral primates into the new and distinctive early hominid pattern. The change required feedback between cultural subsystems, such as hunting and sharing food. Weapons and tools made it possible to kill and butcher larger and larger animals. Vegetable foods were a staple in the diet, protection against food shortages. Foraging provided stability, and it may also have led to division of labor between men and women. Skin bags, bark trays, and perhaps baskets were useful in collecting food; sharing and manufacturing them encouraged the division of labor. The savannah was an ideal and vacant ecological niche for hominids who lived on hunting and foraging combined.

There was no single "prime mover" in the evolution of humankind, such as the upright posture or toolmaking. Rather, many different factors, of which bipedalism, toolmaking, and food sharing were only a few, interacted to influence the course of human evolution.

Were the first toolmakers human in the sense that we are? The most striking feature of early prehistory up to 400,000 years ago is the simple nature of human technology, with its basically opportunistic tools like simple stone choppers that performed simple functions highly effectively. The rapid increase in the complexity of the archaeological record in later prehistory can, one suspects, be connected to the great expansion of language and communication abilities, and the cognitive and cultural capabilities that are integrally related to speech and language.

Chronological Table B

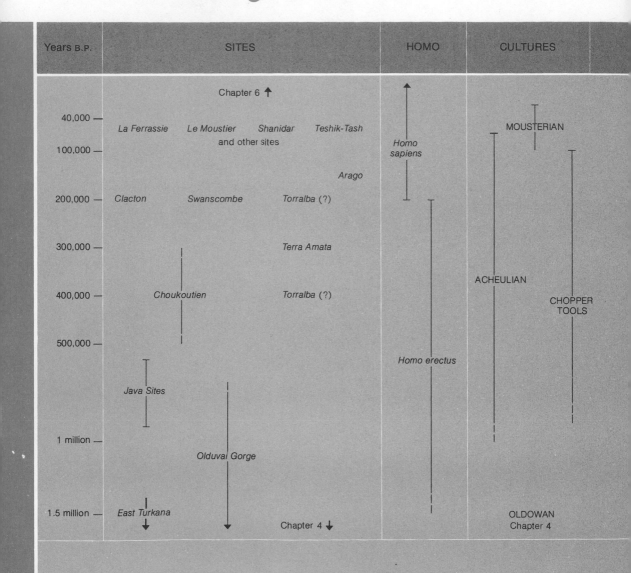

Years B.P.	SITES				HOMO	CULTURES
		Chapter 6 ↑			↑	
40,000 —						MOUSTERIAN
	La Ferrassie	*Le Moustier*	*Shanidar*	*Teshik-Tash*	*Homo*	
100,000 —		and other sites			*sapiens*	
				Arago		
200,000 —	*Clacton*	*Swanscombe*	*Torralba* (?)			
300,000 —			*Terra Amata*			
400,000 —	*Choukoutien*		*Torralba* (?)			ACHEULIAN
						CHOPPER TOOLS
500,000 —						
	Java Sites				*Homo erectus*	
1 million —						
		Olduvai Gorge				
1.5 million —	*East Turkana*		Chapter 4 ↓			OLDOWAN Chapter 4

Chapter Five

TOWARD MODERN HUMANITY

(1.5 million to 40,000 B.P.)

PREVIEW

- About 1.5 million years ago, the first indisputable human came into existence; he can be recognized in the archaeological record and has been classified by paleontologists as *Homo erectus.*

- *Homo erectus* was apparently the first hominid to adapt to environments as diverse as tropical forest, temperate, and near-arctic climates. These hominids had enlarged brains, improved communication skills, more elaborate culture, and larger home bases.

- The technology of *Homo erectus* was based on relatively simple stoneworking techniques that produced two major traditions: the hand ax and the chopper. Hand ax sites are mostly confined to southern and temperate latitudes, while chopper tools were favored in Asia and perhaps in northern Europe as well.

- *Homo erectus* relied heavily on big game hunting and cooperative game drives. The Terra Amata and Torralba sites show how people butchered big game and returned to the same localities year after year when favored foods were in season. These hominids practiced basic patterns of hunting and gathering that persisted for hundreds of thousands of years.

- The earliest *Homo sapiens* finds date to about 200,000 B.P.; these were the predecessors of modern human beings, *Homo sapiens sapiens,* who did not appear until about 40,000 years ago.

- The early sapiens populations, including the Neanderthalers, used a distinctive Middle Paleolithic technology, called Mousterian, that spread far over temperate and tropical latitudes of the world. Its regional variations were based on a wider variety of specialized tools than ever made before, including spearheads and scrapers. The more elaborate Mousterian tool kit may signify that Neanderthal populations made more diverse adaptations than those of earlier times.

- The Neanderthalers of 50,000 years ago were already burying their dead and practicing some simple hunting rituals that reflected a rudimentary belief in an afterlife. Religious beliefs reached a much fuller expression after 40,000 B.P.

↓ From 40,000 years ago, cultural evolution accelerated rapidly, after the emergence of *Homo sapiens sapiens.*

East Turkana
1.5 million B.P.

Whether or not the gracile Australopithecines evolved into *Homo*, we can be sure of one fact: from about 1.5 million years ago we are dealing with the biological and cultural history of our own genus, a genus that began to appear in various parts of the Old World. The earliest humans who are indisputably *Homo* are grouped under the taxonomic label *Homo erectus* ("person who stands upright").

HOMO ERECTUS

Homo erectus
**1.5 million to
?100,000 B.P.**

Chronological
Table B

The earliest unquestionable human discovered so far comes from East Turkana in Kenya, a skull known as "KNM-ER 3733," which is dated to between 1.5 and 1.6 million years ago.[1]* This fossil, with its massive brow ridges, enlarged brain size, and high forehead, is morphologically very close to much later examples of *Homo erectus* dating to a million years ago and later.

Java
**900,000 to
600,000 B.P.**

Homo erectus had first come to light in 1891 when a Dutch doctor named Eugene Dubois found the skullcap of an apelike human in the gravels of the Solo river near Trinil in central Java.[2] When, a year later at the same site, he found an upper limb bone that displayed many human features, he named his discovery *Pithecanthropus erectus* ("ape-man who walks upright"). A vicious outcry greeted his announcement; Dubois was accused of heresy and his findings dismissed with contempt. Then, in 1928, a Canadian anatomist named Davidson Black announced the discovery of human teeth at Choukoutien cave near Peking.[3] A year later Chinese archaeologist W. C. P'ei recovered a complete skullcap from the same cave; it closely resembled the Dubois's Java finds. The Choukoutien human remains were associated with stone tools, crude bone artifacts, and the bones of hundreds of animals. A Dutch physical anthropologist, G. H. R. von Koenigswald, examined the Chinese and Javanese remains and described a new human form: *Homo erectus* (Figure 5.1).

Choukoutien
**500,000 to
300,000 B.P.**

Olduvai Gorge
1,000,000 B.P.

Homo erectus is known to have lived over a wide area of the Old World. Louis Leakey found a skullcap of *Homo erectus* in the upper levels of Bed II at Olduvai Gorge.[4] This specimen came from levels dating to about a million years ago. In contrast, the Chinese finds are now estimated to date to between 500,000 and 350,000 years ago, while new *Homo erectus* finds from the Trinil area of Java have been potassium argon dated to between 900,000 and 600,000 years.[5] *Homo erectus* fossils have come to light in Morocco and Algeria and in Hungary and western Germany. None of the European finds can be dated, but probably belong to about 500,000 years ago. Further, although fossil remains of *Homo erectus* are rarely encountered, their distinctive toolkit of stone axes

* See pages 374–375 for notes to Chapter 5.

The Early Humans

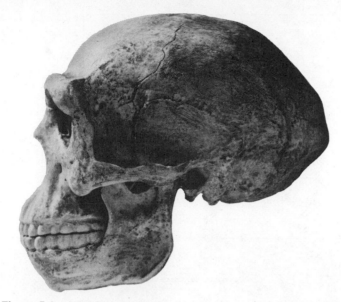

Figure 5.1 A plaster cast of *Homo erectus* from Choukoutien, China. The skull bones of *Homo erectus* show that these hominids had a brain capacity between 775 and 1,300 cc, showing much variation. It is probable that their vision was excellent and that they were capable of extensive thought. The *H. erectus* skull is more rounded than that of earlier hominids; it also has conspicuous brow ridges and a sloping forehead. With a massive jaw, much thicker skull bones, and teeth with cusp patterns somewhat similar to those of *Australopithecus atricanus* and modern humans, *H. erectus* had limbs and hips fully adapted to an upright posture. It stood about 5 feet high (153 cm) with hands fully capable of precision gripping and many kinds of toolmaking.

and choppers is relatively commonplace and tells us much about their distribution and adaptations.

Where and How *Homo erectus* Lived

Homo erectus' culture was complex enough to allow for adaptation to a wide range of environments — from the tropical savannah in East Africa to forested Javanese valleys, temperate climates in North Africa and Europe, and the harsh winters of China and northern Europe. By half a million years ago *Homo erectus* hunted big game and gathered on a scale that their predecessors would never have contemplated. The basic patterns of hunting and gathering that were to persist through millennia into modern times were already well developed by 500,000 B.P.

THE HAND AX TRADITION

The greater sophistication in hunting and gathering is reflected in the toolkits associated with *Homo erectus.* Olduvai Gorge tells us of the cultural changes

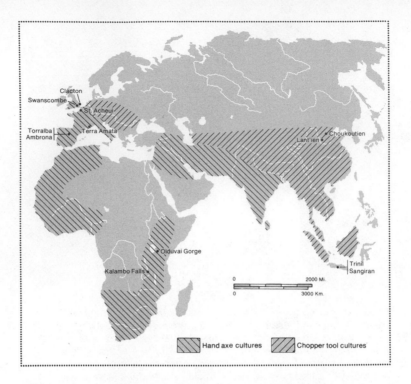

Clacton
Swanscombe
St. Acheul
Torralba
Ambrona
Terra Amata
Lant'ien
Choukoutien
Olduvai Gorge
Kalambo Falls
Trinil
Sangiran

0   2000 Mi.
0   3000 Km.

Hand axe cultures   Chopper tool cultures

Figure 5.2 (a) Distribution of hand ax and chopper traditions, also showing location of sites mentioned in first half of Chapter 5. (b) Distribution of Neanderthal cultures, with locations of sites mentioned in text.

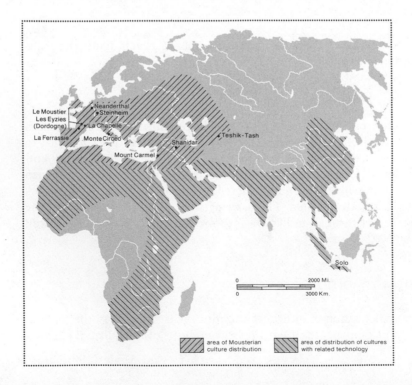

Le Moustier
Les Eyzies
(Dordogne)
La Ferrassie
Neanderthal
Steinheim
La Chapelle
Monte Circeo
Shanidar
Teshik-Tash
Mount Carmel
Solo

0   2000 Mi.
0   3000 Km.

area of Mousterian culture distribution   area of distribution of cultures with related technology that took place as the new hominids appeared. The long-lived Oldowan tool tradition survived throughout Bed I at Olduvai and into overlying Bed II, where the first traces of *Homo erectus* are found. In the upper levels of Bed II the first hand axes appear — tools with sharp cutting edges and rounded bases probably used for a multitude of purposes, from skinning animals to digging wild roots (Figures 5.2, 5.3).

Oldowan culture
**2 million to later
than 1 million B.P.**

Hand axes appear suddenly at Olduvai; they are made of larger rocks than those used for Oldowan choppers.[6] But their origins in the Oldowan technology are unquestionable, for the earliest hand axes are crudely shaped, jagged edged artifacts that are obvious developments of the chopper. The serpentine edges of the early hand axes in Bed II at Olduvai give way to more advanced artifacts in later levels of the gorge. The hand ax edges become straighter, often flaked with a bone hammer that gave a flatter profile to the ax. The bases are carefully rounded and finished.

In contrast to the earlier Oldowan, the Lower Paleolitic technology of *Homo erectus* varied greatly throughout its duration, reaching astonishing heights of delicate artistry (pages 78–79; Table 5.1). In addition to hand axes the new technology resulted in scrapers and other artifacts for woodworking, skinning, and other purposes. But hand axes remain the most characteristic artifact of many *Homo erectus* populations.

The hand ax technology associated with *Homo erectus* is known as the *Acheulian*, after the French town of St. Acheul. *Acheulian* is a term that covers many different cultural adaptations, for hand axes have been found over an enormous area of the Old World (Figure 5.2). Fine specimens are scattered in the gravels of the Somme and the Thames rivers in northern Europe, in North African quarries and ancient Sahara lakebeds, and in sub-Saharan Africa from the Nile Valley to the Cape of Good Hope. Acheulian tools are common in some parts of India, as well as in Arabia and the Near East as far as the southern shores of the Caspian Sea. They are rare east of the Rhine and in the Far East, where chopping tools were commonly used until comparatively recent times.[7] No one has been able to explain why hand axes have this restricted distribution. Were such multipurpose tools used only in big-game hunting camps? Was their use restricted by the availability of flint and other suitable raw materials? Did environmental conditions affect the hunters' choice of toolkits? We do not know.

Acheulian culture
**1,000,000 to
60,000 B.P.**

THE CHOPPER TOOL TRADITION

By no means all *Homo erectus* populations relied on hand axes as general purpose tools. The Chinese bands who lived at Choukoutien made their tools from quartzite and relied heavily on choppers with jagged edges.[8] They had no hand axes; most of their artifacts were little more than crudely shaped flakes, combined with a few simple bone points and clubs (Figure 5.4). This simple technology did not prevent the inhabitants of Choukoutien from hunting at least sixty species of animals including elephants, bears, deer, and many small

Choukoutien
**500,000 to
300,000 B.P.**

Figure 5.3 Lower Paleolithic (hand ax) technology. Acheulian tool technology first appeared over a million years ago. Although the Acheulians used wooden tools such as the spear and the club, few examples have been found. Their stone tools are much better known, and include the ubiquitous hand ax and numerous flake tools. The earliest Acheulian hand axes were crudely flaked with jagged edges but functional points. It is thought that their development was the logical extension of the chopping tool, as they had two cutting edges instead of one. Simple hammerstone techniques were used to make early hand axes. Later examples were much more finely made, with delicate, straight edges and flatter cross-sections. A bone hammer was used to strike off the shallow flakes that adorn the margins of these tools (bottom left). Hand axes are thought to have been multipurpose tools, equally at home skinning and butchering a carcass or digging for roots. A widely found variant is the cleaver, a butchering tool with a single, unfinished edge that has proved effective for skinning and dismembering game under experimental conditions. Later hand axes and cleavers are found in a wide variety of forms and lasted in some areas until as late as some 60,000 years ago.

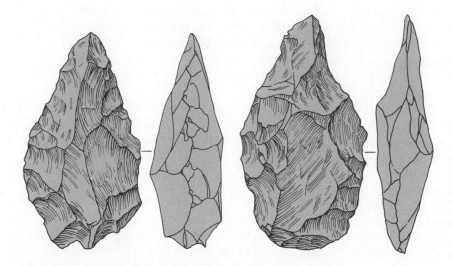

Two early hand axes from Bed II. Olduvai Gorge, Tanzania. Front and side views (three-quarters actual size).

Using an animal bone to make a hand ax.

The Early Humans

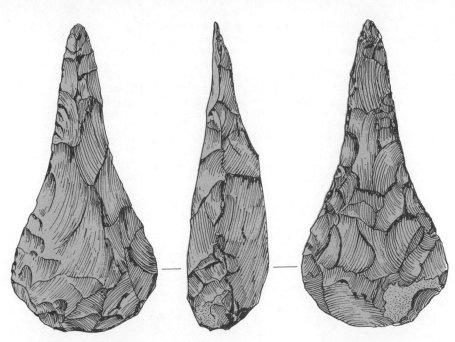

Acheulian hand ax from Swanscombe, England (one-third actual size).

Two Acheulian cleavers, from Baia Farta. Angola (left) and Kalambo Falls, Zambia (both one-half actual size).

Table 5.1 Classic technological stages of the Old Stone Age.

Approximate dates B.P.	Stage	Technology
After 10,000	No formal term	Trend to smaller tools (Figure 6.7), associated with wide use of bow and arrow.
?40,000 to 10,000	UPPER PALEOLITHIC	Pressure flaking first used. Blade technology and many specialized artifacts (Figure 6.3). More reliance on bone tools.
?100,000 to 40,000	MIDDLE PALEOLITHIC	"Disc" and "Levallois" prepared core technologies. Flakes used to make composite artifacts and some specialized tools (Figure 5.11).
Earliest times to ?100,000	LOWER PALEOLITHIC	Simple technology based on use of stone against stone, or bone or wood against stone. Choppers and hand axes are commonplace (Figure 5.3).

The terms *Paleolithic* or *Old Stone Age* are purely convenient labels, without specific time frames. We use them in this book just for convenience in describing a general level of technological achievement. It is inevitable that stone technologies dominate the definitions of the stages because technologies centered on tools of other materials cannot have been as well preserved. The table is cross referenced to pages describing each technology.

rodents. The Choukoutien people built large fires, presumably for both warmth and protection; theirs was the first recorded use of fire in prehistory.

Choppers were favored over hand axes in southeast Asia and, apparently, in parts of central Europe and Britain as well. Sites containing hundreds of choppers, flakes, and cores but no hand axes have been found in eastern England. The Clacton site near London, dating to about 200,000 B.P., yielded the point of a wooden spear as well (Figure 5.5).[9]

Many of the simple tools used by the Asians and Europeans resemble the Oldowan artifacts of the first Africans. Such similarities can be explained as merely the logical result of flaking a pebble to produce a jagged edge and sharp flakes. But did toolmaking originate in Africa, and in Europe and Asia as well, before the evolution of *Homo erectus*? Or were chopping tools carried into cooler latitudes by early, more adaptable *Homo erectus* populations before the hand ax was developed? No hominid fossils earlier than *Homo erectus* have yet been found in Europe or Asia, and, if such people did settle in temperate latitudes, there are few signs of their artifacts. One can perhaps best describe the chopper sites of Britain and Europe as specialized adaptations which are still imperfectly understood. There is a sameness about the tools of *Homo erectus* that is both depressing and remarkable. Acheulian hand axes from as

200,000 B.P.

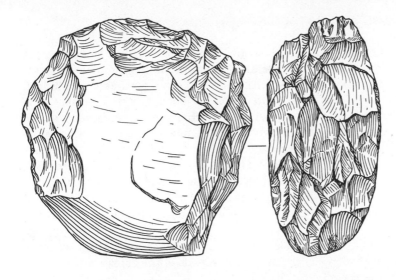

Figure 5.4 A crude chopping tool from Choukoutien, China, front and side views (one-half actual size).

far apart as Olduvai Gorge, the Thames Valley, and the Indian peninsula are similar in shape — the same is true of many other large and small artifacts possessed by *Homo erectus*. Most surviving Acheulian tools are made of stone and give us an extremely limited view of subsistence activities, ecological adaptations, or diet. It is quite possible that different Acheulian bands had ecological adaptations and social and cultural specializations that varied far more than their surviving artifacts suggest.[10] In the Acheulian culture, the long millennia of apparent equilibrium must be thought of in the context of the more rudimentary brain and economic adaptations of *Homo erectus*.

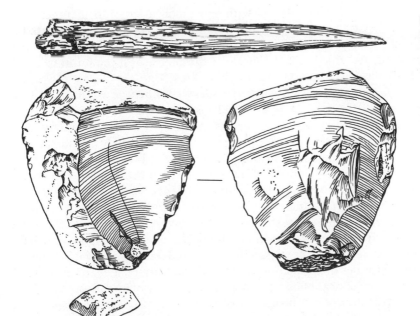

Figure 5.5 At top, a wooden spearhead from Clacton, England, from the Lower Paleolithic (about one-eighth actual size). Below, views of a flake from Clacton-on-Sea. The upper surface is shown at left, the flake (lower) surface on the right. The striking platform is at the base (one-third actual size).

Toward Modern Humanity

Big-game hunting was of more than passing importance to many *Homo erectus* bands. Dramatic evidence for cooperative big-game hunting comes from two Acheulian butchery sites at Torralba and Ambrona northeast of Madrid, Spain. The two sites were once located in a deep valley with abundant bubbling springs and muddy swamps, where big game were accustomed to feed. The experts disagree about the date of Torralba and Ambrona, but they probably belong in a period of temperate climate either 400,000 or 200,000 years ago.[11] American archaeologist F. Clark Howell exposed 278 square meters (333 sq. yd.) of the Torralba site, no less than 28 square meters (33 sq. yd.) of which were covered by the remains of the left side of a large elephant. The hindquarters were gone, but the tusks, jaw, and part of the backbone lay on the ground. Southeast of the carcass were broken remains of some of the rib cage and the right limbs of the same elephant, as well as traces of fire and skinning tools. The hunters had evidently cut up small parts of the carcass after removing them from the body.

Ambrona yielded two levels of occupation, the lower of which was a kill site where thirty to thirty-five elephants had been dismembered. The bones of wild horses were about half as common as the elephants'. Concentrations of broken food bones were found all over the site, but the center of the butchery area held very large bones, most of them from a nearly complete old bull elephant. The individual bones had been removed by the hunters, and the skull had been smashed, presumably to get at the brain. Most of the limb bones were missing. In one place elephant bones had been laid in a line, perhaps to form stepping stones in the swamp in which the elephants were dispatched (Figure 5.6).

The Spanish kill sites were littered with stone tools used for dismembering the hunters' prey. Crude Acheulian hand axes and cleavers were outnumbered by a range of scraping and cutting tools. The stone lumps from which the flakes were made are conspicuously absent at these sites, as if the hunters had brought their tools with them to the butchery areas.

The Torralba elephants were buried in clays, which must have been treacherous marsh for the heavy Middle Pleistocene beasts. Hunters could watch the valley floors where the elephants roamed. At a strategic moment, they would drive the unsuspecting herd into the swamps by lighting grass fires and shouting. The elephants could then be killed and butchered at leisure. Perhaps it is no coincidence that F. Clark Howell found scatters of charcoal over wide areas of the Torralba site, possible evidence of fiery game drives.

Gathering wild vegetable foods such as nuts, berries, and seeds was undoubtedly important although next to nothing survives in archaeological sites. Within their territory the hunters knew the habits of every animal and the characteristics of many edible vegetable foods and medicinal plants; they were familiar with the inconspicuous landmarks and strategic features. From sites like Terra Amata near Nice in France, we know that they returned to the same locality year after year at favored seasons of the year in search of specific foods.

The Early Humans

Figure 5.6 From Torralba, Spain, a remarkable linear arrangement of elephant tusks and leg bones that was probably laid out by those who butchered the animals in Ctono Ago times.

Terra Amata was excavated by Henry de Lumley and consisted of a series of oval huts that once stood on the shores of the Mediterranean at a time of cool and arid climate, some 300,000 years ago.[12] He found that the huts consisted of shallow hollows 8 to 15 meters (26 to 50 ft.) long and 4 to 6 meters (13 to 20 ft.) wide, with an entrance at one end (Figure 5.7). When he cleared the hollows he uncovered a series of posts about 7 centimeters (3 in.) in diameter that had once formed the walls. The bases of the posts were reinforced with lines of stones. The roof was supported by center posts, and some huts had a hearth in the center. The excavators recovered the bones of wild oxen, stags, and elephants, as well as those of small rodents. There were even imprints of skins once laid on the floors. De Lumley records that the inhabitants never cleaned out their huts. They lived among butchered bones, discarded stone tools, even their own feces. The feces yielded numerous fragments of nuts and seeds that had flourished in the late spring and early summer. De Lumley concluded that

Figure 5.7 Reconstruction of a hut at Terra Amata, France.

Terra Amata was a seasonal camp, occupied by the same band of hunter-gatherers who returned to the same locale year after year in search of vegetable foods and shellfish, another common find in the settlement.

Terra Amata and Torralba show that fire had become an important tool, already in use at Choukoutien 500,000 years ago. The very earliest humans must have been familiar with the hungry flames of brush fires caused by lightning or volcanic eruptions.[13] Grass fires destroy old vegetation, and game grazes happily on the green shoots that spring up through the blackened soil a few weeks later. This easy familiarity with natural fires may have led *Homo erectus* to keep fires alive, kindling wood from a brushfire or flames from a seepage of natural gas. As people moved into less hospitable environments, they needed fire constantly — to keep them warm at night, to protect them from nocturnal predators, to give them light, and to help them with game drives.

Improvements in language and modes of communication are thought to have been a distinctive feature of *Homo erectus*'s style of life. With improved language skills and more advanced technology, it became possible for people to achieve better cooperation in gathering activities, in storage of food supplies, and in the chase. Unlike the nonhuman primates, who strongly emphasize individual economic success, Middle Pleistocene hunter-gatherers depended on cooperative activity by every individual in the band. The economic unit was the group; the secret of individual success was group success. Individual ownership of property was unimportant, for no one had tangible possessions of significance. Nor did groups as a whole. People got along well with one another — as individuals, as families, and as entire groups. The hunter-gatherers who followed *Homo erectus* did not necessarily inherit this advantage.

Most people now believe that *Homo erectus* evolved into *Homo sapiens*, but there are few fossil remains available to document this vital transition. Those that have been excavated are tantalizingly incomplete. *Arago cave* in the French Pyrenees has yielded a skull and several jaws that seem anatomically intermediate between *H. erectus* and *H. sapiens*. Henry de Lumley, who found the site, dates these specimens to the Saale glaciation, between 200,000 and 130,000 B.P.[14] *Swanscombe*, a quarry in the Thames river gravels east of London, has yielded the back and sides of a skull associated with hundreds of beautifully made Acheulian hand axes. Unfortunately the face of the Swanscombe skull is missing, but the brain size is considerably larger than that of *Homo erectus*. The Swanscombe site dates to the Holstein interglacial (earlier than 200,000 B.P.).[15] A crushed skull from Steinheim, Germany, and some small cranial fragments from Fontechevade cave in southwestern France complete the inventory of early *Homo sapiens* finds in the West (Figure 5.8).

The Pleistocene deposits of the Solo river in Java have yielded several skull-caps and shin bones which appear to show features in common with earlier *Homo erectus* finds in the same area. The exact evolutionary status of the Solo material is uncertain, but they show that the same evolutionary transition that

Arago
**200,000 to
130,000 B.P.**

Swanscombe
c. 200,000 B.P.

Figure 5.8   The Steinheim (top) and Swanscombe (bottom) skulls (one-fourth actual size). The Swanscombe skull is shown with a tentative reconstruction of the missing parts.

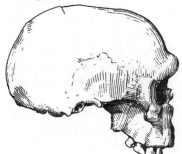
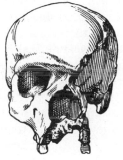
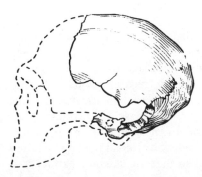

was occurring in the West was taking place in other parts of the Old World as well.

The status of all these finds is much debated. Bernard Campbell and other anthropologists argue that they are classifiable as early *Homo sapiens*, being far more like ourselves than like *H. erectus* — but they were quite distinct from modern humans.[16] Their brain capacity was larger than that of *Homo erectus*, yet they retain fairly massive chewing muscles and more pronounced brow ridges than the modern structures.

The Neanderthals

These so-called "early *Homo sapiens*" finds are modern looking compared with a primitive skull found at Neanderthal in West Germany in 1856, a discovery that caused a sensation at the time and still generates academic debate today.[17] Despite Neanderthal's primitive appearance, the remains post-date *Homo erectus* by over 150,000 years. In the century since the first Neanderthal skull was found, substantial numbers of Neanderthal individuals have been unearthed, most of them in western Europe, as well as contemporary human fossils from the Near East, Africa, and Asia. The Neanderthal people are now recognized as *Homo sapiens neanderthalensis*, a subspecies of *Homo sapiens* (Figure 5.9).

Neanderthalers
?100,000 to 35,000 B.P.

Le Moustier
?70,000 B.P.

Neanderthalers first appeared during the Eem interglacial, but they were not widespread. Large Neanderthal sites have been found in the Dordogne area, where deep river valleys and vast limestone cliffs offered abundant shelter during the Weichsel glaciation. One site is the cave of Le Moustier near Les Eyzies.[18] The Neanderthal skeletons found in French caves look like anatomical anachronisms, with massive brow ridges and squat bodies (Figure 5.9). This "classic" variety of Neanderthal is confined to western Europe and is more noticeably different from *Homo sapiens* than its contemporary populations found elsewhere, especially around the shores of the Mediterranean and in Asia (Figure 5.2). We find much variability among Neanderthals, who most often display less extreme features than the "classic" variety of western France. This variability shows in less extreme brow ridges and other cranial features. It is well demonstrated at the Mount Carmel sites of et-Tabūn and es-Skhūl in Israel as well as at Krapina in central Europe.[19]

Theories About *Homo sapiens*

These *Homo sapiens neanderthalensis* fossils from the Eem interglacial are the earliest fossils of *Homo sapiens* that are in no way transitional from *Homo erectus*. The first completely modern humans, with high foreheads, no brow ridges, and entirely contemporary features appear in the archaeological record about 35,000 years ago and are classified as *Homo sapiens sapiens*. On the face of it, the morphological differences between many "classic" Neanderthalers and modern *Homo sapiens* are startling. How do these heavily built, beetle-browed people fit into the picture of human evolution? The great French physical anthropologist Marcellin Boule believed that the classic Neanderthals

Boule's theory

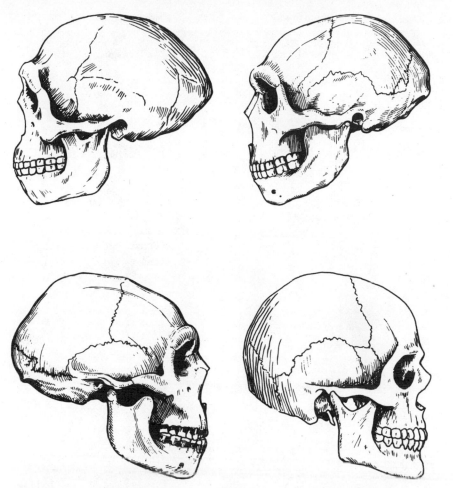

Figure 5.0 A reconstructed *Homo erectus* skull (top left) compared with a classic Neanderthal skull found in Monte Circeo, Italy (top right) and a less extreme example from Shanidar, Iraq (bottom left). A skull of a modern *Homo sapiens sapiens* is included for comparison (bottom right).

In general, Neanderthal skulls are lower and flatter than those of modern humans. But the Neanderthal brains were within the range of modern ones. Prominent brow ridges extend over the eye sockets; there is no chin. Neanderthal people stood just over 153 centimeters (5 ft.) high, and their forearms were relatively short compared to modern humans. The Neanderthalers walked fully upright and as nimbly as modern humans.

were so specialized that they became extinct while other populations provided the evolutionary basis for modern humans (Figure 5.10).[20]

F. Clark Howell has developed an alternative hypothesis based on far more discoveries and more sophisticated analytical techniques.[21] He points out that unspecialized, "progressive" Neanderthals are found in sites dating to the Eem interglacial and the early part of the last (Weichsel) glaciation. These progressive Neanderthals, who possessed few of the extreme features of the classic

Howell's theory

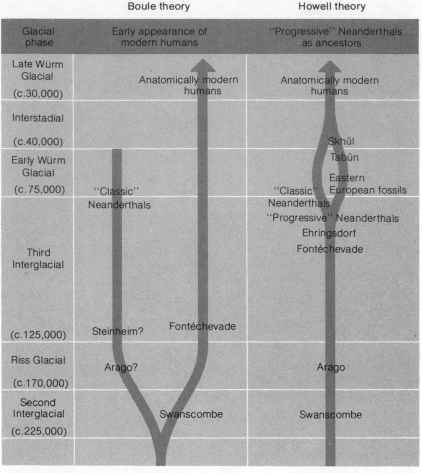

Glacial phase	Boule theory — Early appearance of modern humans	Howell theory — "Progressive" Neanderthals as ancestors
Late Würm Glacial (c.30,000)	Anatomically modern humans	Anatomically modern humans
Interstadial (c.40,000)		Skhūl
Early Würm Glacial (c.75,000)	"Classic" Neanderthals	Tabūn
		Eastern European fossils
		"Classic" Neanderthals
Third Interglacial		"Progressive" Neanderthals
		Ehringsdorf
		Fontéchevade
(c.125,000)	Steinheim? Fontéchevade	
Riss Glacial (c.170,000)	Arago?	Arago
Second Interglacial (c.225,000)	Swanscombe	Swanscombe
	Homo erectus	*Homo erectus*

Figure 5.10 Alternative hypotheses of the evolution of *Homo sapiens*: on the left, the Boule hypothesis; on the right, the Howell theory. A third theory, which sees the "classic" Neanderthalers as direct ancestors of modern humanity, is omitted here, as few people now subscribe to it.

form, are found all over Europe and the Near East. When the ice sheets of the Weichsel glaciation advanced southward over northern latitudes, the western Neanderthal populations became isolated from the people living in more temperate latitudes to the south and east. The Neanderthal skeletons found in the Mount Carmel caves of Israel and elsewhere in the Near East show great anatomical variation, so much so that some of them are almost identical to modern *Homo sapiens*. It was among these less specialized populations that modern humanity evolved, Howell argues, not at one particular location but in many places. Meanwhile, the western Neanderthalers, isolated by the Scandinavian and Alpine ice sheets and the inhospitable arctic plains of central Europe, became a separate breeding population subject to strong selective pressures to develop physical traits better suited to a harsh, glacial environment. Then, once the glaciers retreated for a while, about 35,000 years ago (Table 3.3), the classic Neanderthalers interbred with newcomers from less specialized populations and were soon submerged in the gene pool.

The Howell hypothesis is a popular one, although it does not answer one immediate objection: why didn't the later *Homo sapiens* populations of the west develop similar specialized characteristics? Perhaps the answer lies in the short duration of later (but more intense) Weichsel cold periods. It should also be pointed out that we do not know whether the extreme features of the classic Neanderthals were in fact the result of adaptation to a cold climate.

HOMO SAPIENS ADAPTS

Although many details of the biological evolution of early *Homo sapiens* remain unresolved, we know a great deal about the many and diverse adaptations of these people. Their distinctive hunter-gatherer culture, which continued in the basic hominid tradition, is known from hundreds of sites in Africa, Asia, and Europe. The Neanderthalers' *Mousterian* technology (named after the Le Moustier rockshelter in southwest France) was far more complex and sophisticated than its Acheulian predecessor, with many regional variations. Many of the Neanderthalers' artifacts were made for specific purposes (pages 90–91). Like their *erectus* predecessors, the early *Homo sapiens* bands occupied large territories which they probably exploited on a seasonal round, returning to the same locations year after year when game migrated or vegetables came into season. The Neanderthalers were skilled hunters who were not afraid to pursue large game animals like the mammoth as well as reindeer and wild horses. They also caught birds and fish. It appears that many western European bands lived in caves and rockshelters during much of the year as a protection against arctic cold. During the summer months they may have fanned out over the tundra plains, living in temporary, tented encampments. African hunter-gatherers developed woodworking toolkits for use in dense rain forests as well as on open savannah.

Mousterian culture
?100,000 to 35,000
B.P. (Chapter 6)

Mousterian Technology

Mousterian technology differs radically from earlier toolmaking traditions, both in its techniques and complexity. The Neanderthalers were the first to use:

Prepared core techniques, noticeably the Levallois and disc core methods of shaping flakes (Figure 5.11).

Composite tools, artifacts made of more than one component — for example, a spearpoint, the spear shaft, and the binding that secured the head to the shaft, making a spear.

For the most part Mousterian artifacts were made of flakes, the most characteristic artifacts being points and scraping tools. The edges of both

Figure 5.11 Middle Paleolithic tools. Middle Paleolithic stone technology was based on more sophisticated concepts than those of earlier times. Now artifacts of many types were *composite* form — they were made from several different parts. A wooden spear might have a stone tip; a flint scraper, a bone handle. Unfortunately we know almost nothing about bone and wood tools used.

The points, scrapers, and other stone tools were often manufactured by careful preparation of the core from which they were struck. Prepared cores were carefully flaked to enable the toolmaker to strike off large flakes of predetermined size. One form used was a Levallois core. The stoneworker would shape a lump of flint into an inverted bun-shaped core (often compared to an inverted tortoise shell). The flat upper surface would be struck at one end, the resulting flake forming the only product from the core. Another form was the disc core, a prepared core from which several flakes of predetermined size and shape were removed. The core gradually became smaller, until it resembled a flat disc. Disc cores were often used to produce points and scrapers.

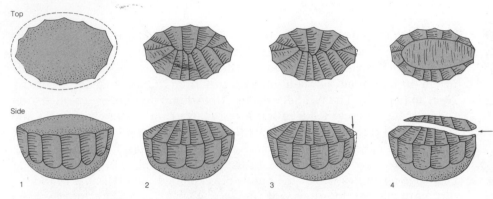

a. Making a Levallois core: (1) the edges of a suitable stone are trimmed, (2) then the top surface is trimmed, (3) a striking platform is made, the point where the flake will originate, by trimming to form a straight edge on the side, (4) a flake is struck from the core, and the flake removed.

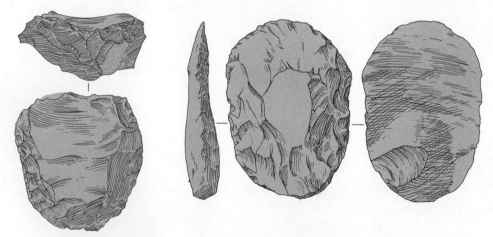

b. A Levallois core from the Thames valley, England (left) with the top of the core (bottom), shown from above and the end view shown above it. A typical Levallois flake is shown at the right: upper surface (center), lower (flake) surface (right), cross section (left). Both artifacts are one-third actual size.

The Early Humans

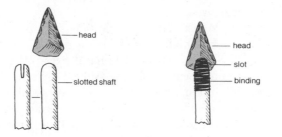

c. Stone-tipped Mousterian spear (a hypothetical example). The spear was made by attaching a pointed stone head to a wooden handle to form the projectile. The head probably fitted into a slot in the wooden shaft and was fixed to it with resin or beeswax: a binding was added to the end of the shaft.

Western European point

French Mousterian side-scraper

Mount Carmel point

Rhodesian Middle Stone Age point (Stillbay type)

cutting edge

French denticulated flake

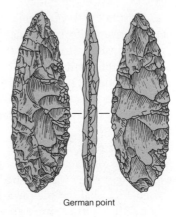

German point

d. Typical artifacts, all approximately one-half actual size.

points and scrapers were sharpened by fine trimming — the removal of small, steplike chips from the edge of the implement. These artifacts, almost universally distributed in Middle Paleolithic sites, were used in the chase, in woodworking, and in preparing skins.

The complexity of Mousterian technology is striking. This is well illustrated by the French sites, which have yielded a great diversity of Mousterian artifacts and toolkits. Some levels include hand axes; others, notched flakes perhaps used for strippng meat for drying. Subdivisions of Mousterian technology have been identified by the prevalence of specific tool types. The French archaeologist Francois Bordes identifies five traditions which he says represent the work of five distinct bands who were living in one territory at the same time.[22]

Not everyone agrees with Bordes. Many scholars believe that Mousterian technology evolved slowly, with different tools (like the side scraper or hand ax) in fashion at different times. In contrast, Sally and Lewis Binford argue that Bordes's traditions reflect different activities carried out within the same cultural system at different times of the year.[23] In all probability, there is some truth in all these hypotheses. People were developing tools for different activities far more quickly than ever before, perhaps at a time of increasing social complexity. For the first time, diversity in lifeway was possible.

The map on page 77 shows the distribution of Mousterian and related cultures in the Old World. Although Middle Paleolithic technology goes under many regional labels, the basic technological devices differed little from one area to another.

THE ORIGINS OF BURIAL AND RELIGIOUS BELIEF

Although the Neanderthals were still hunter-gatherers and the world's population still small, life was gradually becoming more complex. We find the first signs of religious ideology, of a preoccupation with the life hereafter. Many Neanderthalers were buried by their companions. Neanderthal burials have been recovered from the deposits of rockshelters and caves as well as from open campsites. Single burials are the most common, normally accompanied by flint implements, food offerings, or even cooked game meat (evidenced by charred bones). One band of Siberian mountain goat hunters lived at Teshik-Tash in the western foothills of the Himalayas. They buried one of their children in a shallow pit, surrounding the child's body with six pairs of wild goat horns.[24]

Another remarkable single burial came from Shanidar cave in the Zagros Mountains of Iraq.[25] There a thirty-year-old man (born, incidentally, with a useless right arm) was crushed by a rockfall from the roof of the cave. He was buried in a shallow pit on a bed of flowers and covered with more blooms (Figure 5.12). Other single graves from France and central Europe were covered with red ochre powder.

One rockshelter, La Ferrassie near Les Eyzies in France, yielded the remains of two adult Neanderthals and four children buried close together in a camp-

Burials at Teshik-Tash

Shanidar

La Ferrassie

The Early Humans

Figure 5.12 A Neanderthal skeleton buried at Shanidar with bunches of wild flowers including hyacinths, daisies, and hollyhocks.

site.[26] Group sepulchres occur at other sites, too, more signs that the Neanderthals, like most living hunter-gatherers, believed in life after death. They may also have had beliefs that went with deliberate burial, but details will always remain hypothetical.

Some glimmers of insight into Neanderthal beliefs may come from their remarkable bear cults. The Neanderthalers were skillful hunters who were not afraid to go after cave bears, which were about the size of Alaskan brown bears and weighed perhaps up to three quarters of a ton. Like some modern northern

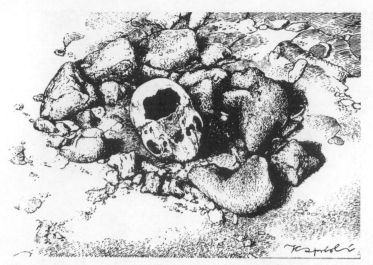

Figure 5.13 In the Guattari Cave of Monte Circeo, a human skull was found lying base upwards in the center of a ring of stones. The condition of the skull, as well as other artifacts in the cave, gives evidence of a sacrificial murder.

Rituals at
Regourdou

hunters, the Neanderthalers had a bear cult, known to us from bear skulls that were deliberately buried with ceremony. The most remarkable find was at Regourdou in southern France, where a rectangular pit lined with stones held the skulls of at least twenty cave bears.[27] The burial pit was covered with a huge stone slab. Nearby lay the entire skeleton of one of the bears. It seems likely that the cave bear became an integral part of these hunters' mythology, an object of reverence and an animal with a special place in the world.

Monte Circeo

Evidence of an even more remarkable ritual appeared in the depths of the Guattari Cave at Monte Circeo, sixty miles south of Rome. A Neanderthal skull was found in an isolated inner chamber surrounded by a circle of stones.[28] The base of the skull lay upward, mutilated in such a way that the brain could be reached. The right side of the skull was smashed in by violent blows. Near the circle of stones lay three piles of bones, from red deer, cattle, and pigs (Figure 5.13). Although ingenious explanations for this curious ritual have been proposed, we shall never know why this sacrificial victim was killed and beheaded outside the cave, his head then laid out as the centerpiece of an important ritual. But, like the bear cult, cannibalism and other hunting rituals appear to have been part of human life and subsistence. We find in Neanderthalers and their culture the first roots of our own complicated beliefs, societies, and religious sense.

PART THREE

HUNTER-GATHERERS

(40,000 B.P. to modern times)

"There is a passion for hunting something deeply
implanted in the human breast."
— Charles Dickens, *Pickwick Papers,* 1836–37,
Chapter 10

In this section we describe numerous cultural adaptations by hunter-gatherers
and the first settlement of Australia and the New World.

Chronological Table C

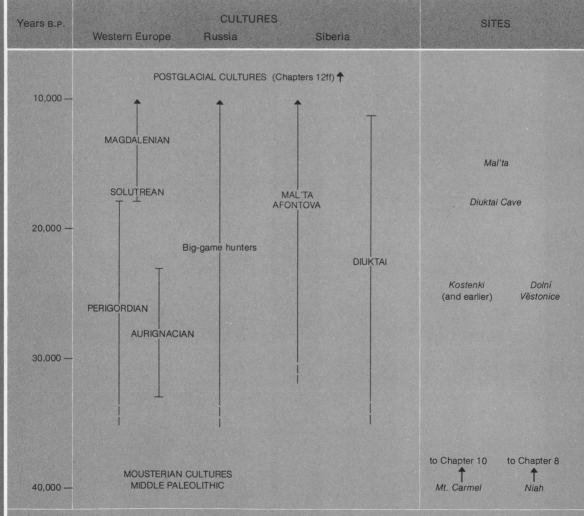

Years B.P.	CULTURES			SITES
	Western Europe	Russia	Siberia	

POSTGLACIAL CULTURES (Chapters 12ff) ↑

10,000 —

MAGDALENIAN

SOLUTREAN   MAL'TA
                   AFONTOVA

Mal'ta

Diuktai Cave

20,000 —

Big-game hunters

DIUKTAI

PERIGORDIAN

AURIGNACIAN

Kostenki   *Dolní*
(and earlier)   *Věstonice*

30,000 —

to Chapter 10   to Chapter 8
      ↑   ↑

MOUSTERIAN CULTURES
MIDDLE PALEOLITHIC

40,000 —

Mt. Carmel   *Niah*

Chapter 5 ↑

Chapter Six

EUROPEANS AND NORTHERN ASIANS

(40,000 to 10,000 B.P.)

PREVIEW

⬇ The emergence of *Homo sapiens sapiens* saw the development of many and diverse hunter-gatherer adaptations to the world's environments. The more specialized hunter-gatherer societies that flourished after 40,000 B.P. developed more elaborate toolkits; these toolkits contained regularly shaped, parallel-sided stone blades as well as bone and antler implements. This technology is named "Upper Paleolithic."

⬇ Western Europe was the home of some of the richest Upper Paleolithic cultures, of peoples adapted to an arctic environment in which hunting reindeer and other migratory game was important. These people lived in rockshelters and caves for much of the year and developed a magnificent art tradition of bone artifacts and decorated cave walls. They flourished from about 35,000 B.P. until the end of the Weichsel glaciation about 10,000 years ago. When the ice sheets retreated, these Europeans turned to more specialized hunting and gathering in which fishing and fowling played an important part.

⬇ Upper Paleolithic peoples of the Russian plains developed a distinctive mammoth and big-game hunting tradition adapted to the harsh climate. After 25,000 B.P. they lived in large dwellings of skins and mammoth bones.

⬇ The earliest settlement of Siberia and northeast Asia is still undated, but people are thought to have settled there by 30,000 years ago. Most archaeologists agree that the first Americans came from this cultural background, but the evidence is incomplete.

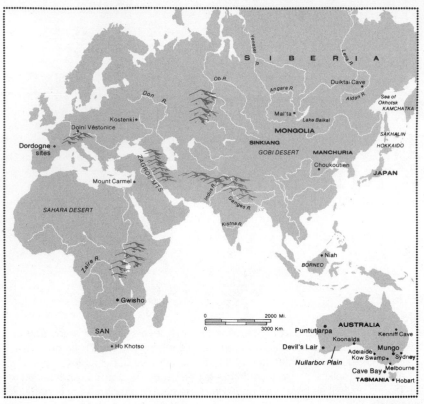

Figure 6.1 Map showing archaeological site, mentioned in Chapters 6 and 8.

For some 50,000 years the Mousterian culture flourished over a great part of the Old World. Then, immediately before or during the warm Paudorf inter-stadial of the Weichsel glaciation (Table 3.3), a sharp biological and techno-logical break appeared throughout western and central Europe. As radical a change is not found anywhere else in the world at that time. Biological change did not necessarily coincide with technological innovation. The biological break is the first appearance of *Homo sapiens sapiens;* the technological break is the appearance of numerous specialized tools for the chase, for bone- and woodworking, and for many other activities. For the first time hunter-gatherers were beginning to influence their environment. (See Figure 6.1 for sites mentioned in this chapter and Chapter 8.)

Homo sapiens
sapiens
40,000 B.P. to
modern times

GATHERING BECOMES SPECIALIZED

Specialized hunting and gathering can mean that a population needs large territories to support itself, for resources are not always fully exploited. Most of the available vegetable foods may be underutilized, leaving a significant reservoir of edible species to fall back on in times of scarcity. Hunter-gatherers rarely starve with this cushion behind them, yet more specialized hunting and gathering may lead groups into competition and even warfare as people compete for the same limited resources.

As we learn more about modern hunter-gatherers, we realize the tremendous importance of gathering in such societies. Although little normally survives in the archaeological record, it seems certain that foraging was always significant, indeed often the dominant activity. Kay Martin and Barbara Voorhies, studying ninety hunting and gathering societies, show that for 58 percent of them gathering is primary in subsistence, but hunting is the major activity for only 25 percent.[1]* Roughly averaged, hunting gives any hunter-gatherer people only 30 to 40 percent of its diet. Most of these societies take vegetable foods as their staple. The importance of gathering has been dramatized by Richard Lee's researches among the present-day !Kung San of the Kalahari Desert in Southern Africa.[2] He found that the !Kung live in an inhospitable, dry woodland environment, where game is now rare. They gather the nutritious mangetti nut as a primary food all year round. The remaining vegetable foods are selected from at least eighty-five edible species known to the !Kung, of which only eight are major foods (Figure 6.2). All of them are seasonal favorites; one is a root that provides water at times of the year when people have to venture far afield in search of food, away from water supplies. So plentiful are edible vegetable foods that the !Kung San have two choices when favorite species become exhausted: eat less desirable foods near home, or walk farther, perhaps shifting their camp. Long before the least desirable foods are eaten, the people have moved to a new site.

Few hunters and gatherers are left, and it is difficult to know whether the !Kung life of relative security and leisure was typical of most prehistoric hunter-gatherers. We can be sure that some groups — like the reindeer-hunting peoples of southwestern France 15,000 years ago or the Coast Indians of the Pacific Northwest — were far better off as far as potential food sources were concerned. What is revealing, however, is the way in which the !Kung relate to their environment, for this is surely typical of many hunter-gatherers throughout prehistory. The !Kung know their environment intimately, and they know what to expect from it. They can gather their food when they need it and do not have to store it for days. This subsistence strategy is a conservative adaptation, based on plants and animals that come back naturally year after year. Hunter-gatherers tend to put in a constant amount of work, unlike the agriculturalists' sharply seasonal activity of planting and harvest. One of Flexibility the most striking features of the hunter-gatherer lifeway wherever it can still be observed is its flexibility, both in food gathering and in a social organization normally based on the small band and the nuclear family. Perhaps it was this flexibility and resulting built-in insurance against lean years that made hunting and gathering the most lasting of all human lifeways.

* See pages 375–376 for notes to Chapter 6.

Figure 6.2 !Kung women gathering food.

Hunter-Gatherers

As we saw in Chapter 5, *Homo sapiens sapiens* may have evolved from early *Homo sapiens*, and ultimately from *Homo erectus*, by phyletic change and by hybridization from earlier populations that displayed considerable variation. Many of the predecessors of *Homo sapiens* displayed only moderately developed brow ridges and well-rounded skullcaps, so that they are virtually indistinguishable from their modern descendants. This variation is well documented in the caves of Mount Carmel, Israel, and also by an isolated specimen of *Homo sapiens sapiens* from the Niah Cave in Borneo which was carbon dated to at least 40,000 years ago.[3]

Mt. Carmel and Niah
c. 40,000 B.P.

The final chapter of this biological evolution was accompanied by major technological changes that, in their way, were as radical as the emergence of the humans who made them. These cultural changes are still imperfectly documented, except in the great caves and rockshelters of the Near East such as et-Tabūn and Mugharet el-Wad at Mount Carmel, Israel, and at Shanidar in Iraq. These sites were visited almost continuously by hunter-gatherer bands from Mousterian times more than 70,000 years ago right up to modern times. The Mousterian levels at these sites contain tens of thousands of carefully retouched points and side-scrapers, as well as the bones of large deer and wild cattle. These layers are covered by further occupation levels containing different toolkits that gradually replace earlier artifact forms and technologies. In these, the long, parallel-sided blades that were the first stage in making stone tools were removed from cylindrical flint cores with a punch and a hammerstone (Figure 6.3). Some blades were up to 15.2 centimeters (6 in.) long; the tools made from them varied greatly, many of them designed for specific tasks and, in later millennia, mounted in handles.

Upper Paleolithic technology, summarized in Figure 6.3, flourished during the later millennia of the Weichsel glaciation, from about 35,000 years ago (Table 5.1). Among its major innovations were:

The use of punchstruck blades.

Much greater reliance on composite tools, such as stone-tipped spears, harpoons, and spearthrowers (Table 6.1). The bow and arrow was the culminating innovation, one that appeared late in the Weichsel.

The use of a much wider range of toolmaking materials, including antler and bone.

Skins, horn, hair, and other byproducts from game went into housing, clothes, lighting, and coloring. Skins were sewn together with threads; weaving and plaiting were probably done for the first time. Flexible sewn materials make a tent a far more effective shelter than the crude and chilly windbreak of grass or branches. Skin boats for pursuing large sea mammals and deep-sea fish are another innovation made by sewing.

The result of these innovations was a dramatic explosion in diversity of cultures and toolkits, most of them fine tuned to local needs. We cannot possibly describe the full richness of hunter-gatherer peoples who flourished in

Figure 6.3 Upper Paleolithic tools. The stoneworking technology required for Upper Paleolithic tools was based on punchstruck blades. Various methods were used to strike off the blades, using a handheld or chest-impelled punch to produce parallel-sided blades to make tools. The punch allows intense pressure to be applied to a single point on the top of the core and channels the direction of the shock waves. Parallel-sided blades were made into a variety of tools, among them burins and scrapers, which were typical of all stages of the Upper Paleolithic. Burins were used for grooving wood, bone, and particularly antlers, which were made into spears and harpoon points. The chisel ends of burins were formed by taking an oblique or longitudinal flake off the end of a blade. Burins were also used to engrave figures. End scrapers were used on wood and bone as well as skins.

Upper Paleolithic technology was based to a great extent on composite tools, of which the stone elements were only a part. Some blade tools were used by themselves, however, for the blade offered a convenient and standarized way of making many fairly specialized artifacts. See also Table 6.1.

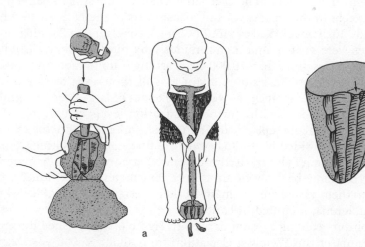

a   b

Two punch techniques (a) and a typical product (b) — a core and a blade struck from it. The dotted line and arrow show the point where the next blade will be struck off from the core.

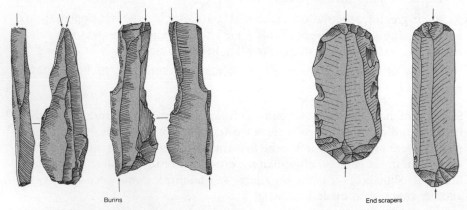

Burins   End scrapers

Burins and end scrapers. Arrows indicate the chisel ends of burins and the scraping edges of the end scrapers.

all parts of the globe after 35,000 B.P., so our narrative concentrates on these major developments:

The hunter-gatherer cultures that flourished in southwest France during the period 35,000 to 10,000 B.P. These cultures are of particular importance on account of their arctic adaptation to the last cold snap of the Weichsel glaciation and because of their remarkable artistic traditions.

The big game hunting cultures that developed on the West Russian plains and Siberia.

The early settlement of the arctic latitudes of north-east Asia from which the first settlement of the New World may have developed.

The first human settlement of the Americas and the cultural traditions that stemmed from it.

The early history of surviving hunter-gatherers in tropical latitudes, especially the Australians and the San peoples of Southern Africa.

EUROPEAN HUNTER-GATHERERS: 35,000 to 10,000 B.P.

The emergence of the new Upper Paleolithic technologies is partially documented in the great caves of Mount Carmel in the relatively benign climate of the Near East.[4] For thousands of years after 40,000 B.P. the inhabitants of this area hunted gazelle and other mammals and practiced a way of life that changed little for over 25,000 years. As their hunting and gathering became more and more specialized, their toolkits became smaller and more locally adaptive to the gathering of cereal grasses or to the intensive hunting of a single animal. We will examine the later prehistory of the Near East in much more detail in Parts IV and V; here in Part III, we are concerned with the flowering of the hunter-gatherer culture, which took place most dramatically in northern latitudes. The dramatic fluctuations in northern areas of Weichsel climate, from arctic cold to periods of more temperate weather and then back to bitter cold, caused human societies to make constant changes in their adaptations to what was a rich and diverse natural environment for hunter-gatherers.

Later levels of Mt. Carmel **40,000 to 10,000 B.P.**

Between 35,000 and 10,000 B.P., the caves and rockshelters of southwestern France and northern Spain housed some of the most elaborate hunter-gatherer cultures the world has ever seen.[5] These caves contain the remains of the "Cro-Magnon" people, who were modern in appearance, robust, tall, with small faces, high-domed foreheads, and few of the primitive features of the Neanderthalers. The earliest Upper Paleolithic horizons in French caves immediately overlie Mousterian levels in which Neanderthal fossils have been discovered. With Cro-Magnon new toolkits based on blade technology come into fashion, with a proliferation of tool types that is highly confusing to the nonspecialist (Table 6.1).[5] Table 5.1 shows where this phase of technology fits into the overall development. Inevitably, the subject is controversial, for the same arguments surround the various technological changes as those that applied to Mousterian artifacts: are the different tool traditions, changing

French Upper Paleolithic **35,00 to 10,000 B.P.**

Table 6.1 Much simplified table showing the Upper Paleolithic cultural traditions of western Europe from 40,000 to 10,000 B.P.

The most commonly accepted scheme, that of French archaeologists, has two parallel cultural traditions, the Perigordian and Aurignacian, flourishing in western Europe between about 32,000 and 25,000. The Perigordian possessed a technology that produced dozens of backed knife blades, while the Aurignacians favored scrapers and sharpened blades. The Perigordian was submerged by the Aurignacian for a considerable period before the former returned to prominence after 25,000.

The Solutrean is characterized by beautifully made lanceheads that were executed by pressure flaking flint blades. No one knows why these artifacts came into fashion, but they must have fulfilled some specific need, and, like so many innovations, have enjoyed a brief period of popularity before the Magdalenians began to rely more heavily on bone and antler tools.

It should be noted that all Upper Paleolithic cultures in this area relied heavily on blade technology and on scrapers, burins, and other simple blade artifacts that were common to all cultures.

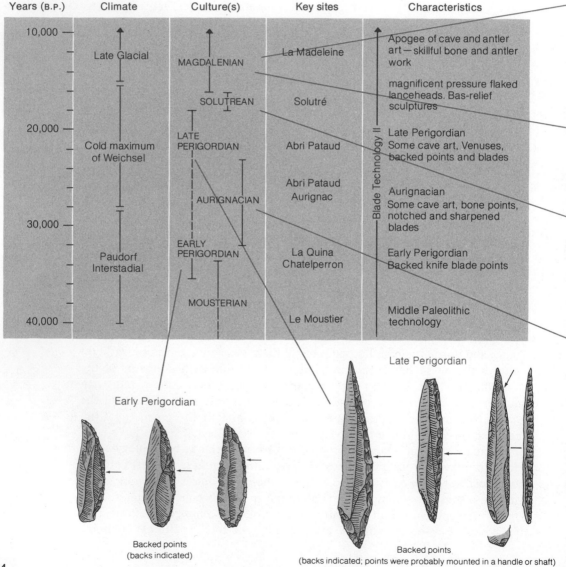

Years (B.P.)	Climate	Culture(s)	Key sites	Characteristics
10,000	Late Glacial	MAGDALENIAN	La Madeleine	Apogee of cave and antler art — skillful bone and antler work
		SOLUTREAN	Solutré	magnificent pressure flaked lanceheads. Bas-relief sculptures
20,000	Cold maximum of Weichsel	LATE PERIGORDIAN	Abri Pataud	Late Perigordian Some cave art, Venuses, backed points and blades
		AURIGNACIAN	Abri Pataud Aurignac	Aurignacian Some cave art, bone points, notched and sharpened blades
30,000	Paudorf Interstadial	EARLY PERIGORDIAN	La Quina Chatelperron	Early Perigordian Backed knife blade points
40,000		MOUSTERIAN	Le Moustier	Middle Paleolithic technology

(Blade Technology II)

Early Perigordian

Backed points
(backs indicated)

Late Perigordian

Backed points
(backs indicated; points were probably mounted in a handle or shaft)

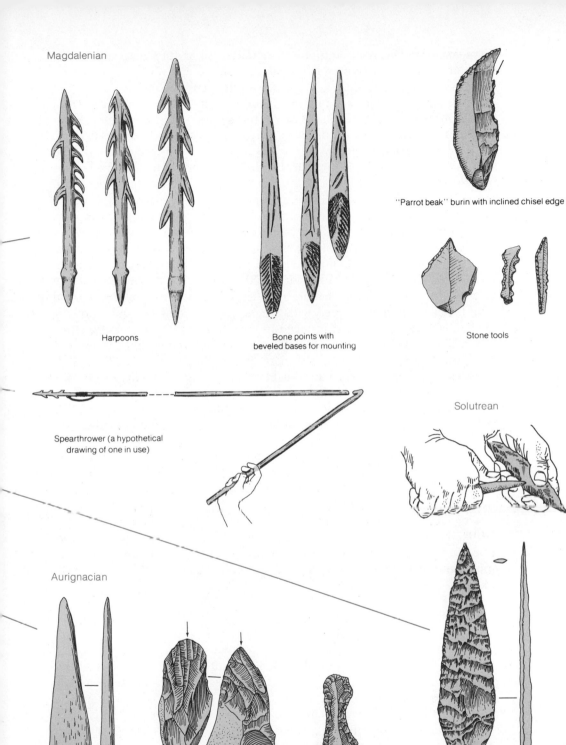

Magdalenian

Harpoons

Bone points with
beveled bases for mounting

"Parrot beak" burin with inclined chisel edge

Stone tools

Spearthrower (a hypothetical
drawing of one in use)

Solutrean

Aurignacian

Split-base bone point
(split used for mounting)

Steep scraper
(scraping edge indicated)

Blade with sharpened
notches

technologies, and evolving cultures truly a reflection of different peoples, or of different specialized activities? No one knows for sure.

The first Upper Paleolithic cave occupations were fleeting, but above the evidence for these brief stays are dense layers of living debris which show that later people lived in the caves and rockshelters more or less continuously for thousands of years. Many of the French caves are located in the sides of deep, sheltered river valleys that provided welcome haven from the bitter winds of the tundra to the north and east. The Dordogne, Vezère, and other rivers were rich in fish which could be caught with lines fitted with bone hooks and gorges. Bottom fish could be trapped in shallow pools and speared with barbed weapons. The hunters engraved salmon from the Dordogne on their weapons. Even more important than fish and seasonal vegetable foods were herds of migrating reindeer who passed through the river valleys during their annual migrations. Many of the hunters followed the migrating reindeer, and probably moved out into open country during the summer with the herds; there they lived in tented camps that are represented rarely in the archaeological record. Reindeer were pursued with spears, harpoons, clubs, and throwing sticks. They were probably dispatched in large numbers in cooperative game drives.[6] The spearthrower was a useful invention, for it allowed the hunters to stalk game less closely and to hurl a spear a much longer distance (Table 6.1). They used it to pursue such formidable beasts as the wild ox, the woolly rhinoceros, and the mammoth. Sometimes, especially in periods of slightly milder climate, the wild horse was a primary source of meat. Not that the hunters concentrated on big game alone. They trapped arctic foxes, beavers, birds and other small animals.

Magdalenian
17,000 to 10,000
B.P.

The zenith of these cultures was reached after 17,000 years ago with the evolution of the Magdalenian culture (Table 6.1). The Magdalenians achieved a higher population density in parts of western Europe than any of their predecessors. They occupied groups of rockshelters that extended along the base of cliffs along the larger rivers, often moving to open camps on the riverbanks at favored seasons of the year.[7] These remarkable Stone Age artisans developed an astonishing artistry with bone and antler that played a far more important role in their culture than mere personal adornment or art for art's sake.

UPPER PALEOLITHIC ART

These hunter-gatherers of the Magdalenian culture, and their immediate predecessors, developed one of the first of the world's artistic traditions, a tradition painted and engraved on the walls of caves and rockshelters and repeated on hundreds of small artifacts and bone and antler fragments.

The earliest art objects are a series of female figurines with pendulous breasts and grossly exaggerated sexual characterstics (Figure 6.4a).[8] Some people think such figures are fertility symbols, although other explanations have been advanced. These female figurines are found from Russia in the east to the Dordogne in the west, most of them in cave deposits dating to about 25,000 years ago. Sometimes called "Venus" figurines, few have facial features, although the hair is often depicted. They seem to be associated with a relatively short-lived religious cult that spread over a wide area of what is now temperate Europe. Venus figurines

No one knows when the first cave paintings were made, but the earliest engravings and paintings are distinctive. The same cave walls were covered again and again with depictions of wild horses, bulls, reindeer, and many other animals. Many of the animals are painted with long, distorted necks and thick bodies, as if the artists were unaware of perspective (Figure 6.4b). By studying the superimpositions of painting after painting in the same locations, experts have been able to show a gradual evolution of Upper Paleolithic art to more naturalistic animals. Lascaux, the most famous rock art site in France, dates to the earlier period.[9] A Great Hall of the Bulls features four immense wild bulls, drawn in thick, black lines, with some of the body details filled in. Horses, deer, a small bear, and a strange, unicorn-like beast prance with the great bulls in a fantastic display of blacks, browns, reds, and yellows that truly brings the animals to life in a flickering light. It is hard to believe that these paintings are at least 15,000 years old. Lascaux

The earliest tradition reaches its height with an explosion of antler and bonework after 15,000 B.P. The hunters engraved their harpoons, spearpoints, spearthrowers, and other artifacts with naturalistic engravings, fine carvings of

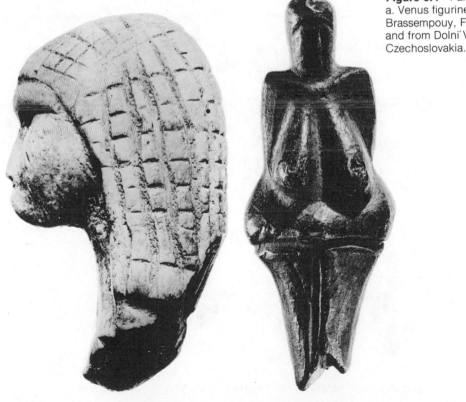

Figure 6.4 Paleolithic art. a. Venus figurines from Brassempouy, France (left) and from Dolní Věstonica, Czechoslovakia.

Figure 6.4   b. A giant stag from Lascaux, France. An example of the Perigordian style.

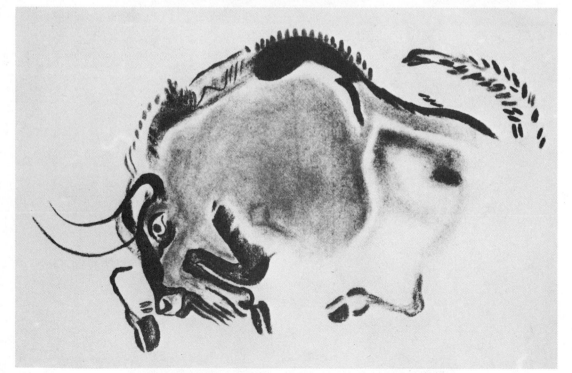

Figure 6.4   c. A bison in a polychrome cave painting at Altamira, Spain.

wild animals, and elaborate schematic patterns. Even fine eye details and hair texture were shown by delicate graving strokes. But the Magdalenians are most famous for their beautiful rock art, paintings and engravings deep in the caves of northern Spain and southwestern France. At Altamira, in northern Spain, Altamira you walk deep into the hillside to enter a low-ceilinged chamber, where the painters left fine renderings of bison in red and black (Figure 6.4c).[10] By painting and engraving the animals around natural bulges in the rock the artists managed to convey a sense of relief and life to the animals. At cave after cave, the hunters left jumbled friezes of large and small game animals, hand impressions, dots, and signs, many of which must have had religious significance. An enormous and highly speculative literature concerns itself with the motives behind this remarkable art, which is thought to be tied, at least partially, to the continued prosperity of the hunt. Some of the paintings are so lively and naturalistic that one cannot help wondering whether they were painted simply for the pleasure of it.

The motifs on the antler and bone artifacts have led Alexander Marshack to study the patterns of symbols on the tools.[11] He has perfected a system of microphotography that enables him to study the engraved pieces in minute detail. Instead of concentrating on the naturalistic pictures of animals, he studied the hundreds of nonnaturalistic pieces, with their patterns of lines, notches, dots, and groupings of marks (Figure 6.5). On some pieces the marks were made with different tools at different times. These pieces, which Marshack named "time-factoral" objects, were used, he believes, as sequential

Figure 6.5 Engraved bone (21 cm long) from La Marche, France, which was intensively studied by Marshack. The close-up shot shows tiny marks separated in two groups, each engraved by a different point, with a different type of stroke. © Alexander Marshack 1972.

notations of events and phenomena, predecessors of calendars. Marshack has examined hundreds of specimens stretching back as far as the early millennia of the Upper Paleolithic. He found duplicated designs, systematic groups of dots and notches that were either counting tallies or the beginnings, he felt, of a writing system. But, he suggests, they differed from later, more formal writing systems that could be read by everyone: the Magdalenian and earlier notations were for the engraver alone to read, even if he explained them to others on occasion. To formulate such a notation system required thought and theoretical abstractions far more advanced than those hitherto attributed to hunter-gatherers of this age. Of course Marshack's ideas are controversial, but they are the type of ground-breaking research that produces exciting new interpretations and insights into Stone Age life.

The glorious artistic traditions of the Upper Paleolithic lasted until the Weichsel ice sheets began to retreat about 12,000 years ago. As the climate warmed up, the great herds of reindeer, horses, and bison retreated north or vanished forever, to be replaced by smaller forest game. The successors of the Magdalenians turned more and more to lakeside dwelling and to a life among forests and along seashores. The artistic traditions cherished by their arctic predecessors withered with the passing of big-game hunting in favor of more specialized hunting and gathering.[12]

SETTLEMENTS IN RUSSIA AND SIBERIA

The vast, undulating plains of western Russia and central Europe were a much less hospitable environment for hunter-gatherers than the deep, well-watered valleys of the West. There were no convenient caves or rockshelters. For warmth and shelter, the inhabitants of the plains had to create artificial dwellings with their own tools and raw materials.

By 35,000 B.P. a scattered population of Upper Paleolithic people had begun to adapt to life on the plains. The hunter-gatherers lived in large, irregular dwellings partially scooped out of the earth, probably roofed with bone and huge mammoth skins (Figure 6.6).[13] Movable bone "poles" probably supported the hides; the edges of the tents were weighted with huge bones and tusks, which were found lining the house hollows at Kostenki and other famous sites. The house plans are so irregular that it is difficult to be sure what the floor plan was. In some cases several circular structures, up to 4.6 meters (15 ft.) in diameter, were built together in a huge depression with a row of hearths down the middle. There is every reason to believe that bands of considerable size congregated in these tented areas.

We have no means of telling how long the hunter-gatherers dwelt in their camps, nor whether they moved seasonally. The plains dwellers' lives were partly determined by the mammoth, whose migrations and habits must have influenced both the movements of the hunters and the size of their bands. At times during the year the beasts undoubtedly moved to new pastures, feeding on young grass in the spring. Cooperative hunting and game drives could have yielded rich hauls of meat and skins.

12,000 B.P.

Nonnaturalistic pieces

West Russia 35,000 B.P.

Kostenki 25,000 B.P.

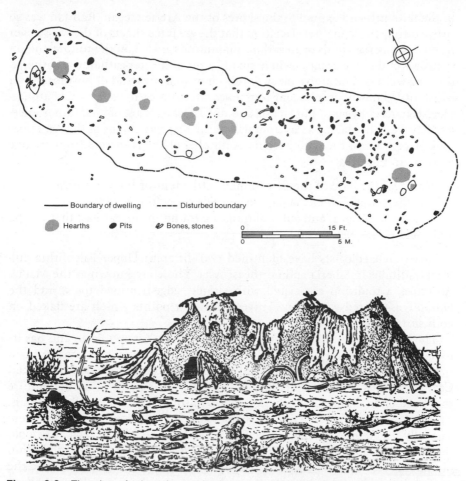

Figure 6.6 The plan of a long house (top) from Kostenki IV, USSR, and a reconstruction based on finds at Push Karl. The latter was nearly 12 meters long by 3.7 meters wide (40 ft. by 12 ft.) and stood in a shallow depression.

Mammoth skins, bones, sinews, and marrow were valuable for many purposes. Bone was especially important for fuel; burned mammoth bones have come from Kostenki and other sites. House frames, digging tools, pins, needles, and many small tools were made from the bones of the hunters' prey. Wood was naturally less important in the treeless environment of the steppe. In this difficult environment we would expect an economy based at least in part on lumbering beasts whose carcasses could support many hungry mouths and fuel fires. The technology of the plains made much use of fire for warmth and for hardening the tips of spears, as well as in preparing flint for pressure-flaking. Indeed, fire was vital in the human armory as people moved outward to the arctic frontiers of the Paleolithic world.

Remote from Atlantic and Pacific weather patterns, Siberia is dry country with harsh, dry winters and short, hot summers. Treeless plains predominate

Siberia

in the far north and extend to the shores of the Arctic Ocean. Rainfall was so sparse during the Weichsel glaciation that the great ice sheets of the west never formed in Siberia. Herds of gregarious mammoths grazed on the tundra and on the edges of the river valleys where small bands of hunter-gatherers weathered the long winters. The archaeology of this enormous area and of northeast Asia is still little known, despite long-term excavation campaigns by Soviet archaeologists in recent years.[14] But Siberia and northeast Asia are of vital importance, for they were the staging areas from which the first settlement of the Americas took place — across the Bering Straits. A number of key issues confront anyone working in this area:

What was the date of the first human settlement of the far northeast?
Was there a pre-*sapiens* population in Siberia before 35,000 B.P.?
What technological and cultural traits are found in the Far East that can be identified in the New World?

Soviet archaeologists have identified two different Upper Paleolithic cultural traditions in Siberia and northeast Asia. These are known as the Mal'ta-Afontova, a tradition associated with simple, edge-trimmed tools; and the Diuktai, associated with stone knives and spear points which are flaked on both surfaces.

Diuktai tradition
?35,000 to 11,000 B.P.

The Diuktai tradition is mostly found east of the Yenesei Basin and has its roots in Middle Paleolithic technology. The earliest Diuktai sites are found on the Aldan river and have been[15] dated to around 35,000 to 33,000 B.P. Diuktai Cave itself adds to the picture of a long-lived hunting and gathering culture that lived on mammoth, woolly rhinoceros, bison, and some smaller animals. By at least 18,000 B.P. the Diuktai people were making spearpoints that were carefully flaked on both sides, as well as using large pebbles known as *skreblo* that may have served as butchery tools (Figure 6.7). The effective exploitation of this area depended on a successful adaptation to the open tundra and on the special skills of big-game hunting. As in the west, the plains people would have had to range widely over a huge territory in search of their prey, camping near the kills for a few days and returning to favored spots year after year when the prey were plentiful.

Most Soviet experts believe that the Diuktai cultural tradition evolved from earlier hunter-gatherer cultures of *Homo erectus* and early *Homo sapiens*. There is no reason to doubt that the same evolutionary pressures existed among isolated Asian human populations as occurred in the western parts of the Old World. Few sites yet document this evolutionary model, but it seems likely that the first human settlement of the tundra took place when *Homo sapiens* managed to adapt successfully to the arctic plains and the specialized lifeway that went with big-game hunting there.

Mal'ta-Afontova tradition
earlier than 21,000 B.P. to 10,000 B.P. and later

The Mal'ta-Afontova tradition is best known from the Yenesei Valley and the Lake Baikal region. The Mal'ta site itself was occupied by people who lived in long houses and hunted both arctic and plains game.[16] Their tools include Upper Paleolithic scrapers and burins, as well as edge-trimmed points and scraping tools that are obvious survivals from earlier, Middle Paleolithic traditions. The Mal'ta people were expert boneworkers, who carved female and bird

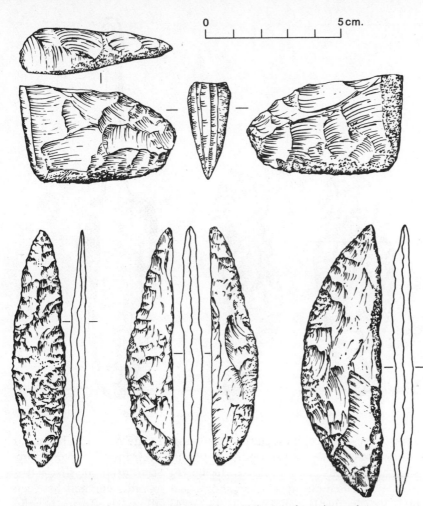

Figure 6.7 Artifacts of the Diuktai tradition. At the top, four views of a wedge-shaped core, used to make tiny blades. At the bottom, three bifacially flaked projective heads. The wedge-shaped core is a characteristic artifact that is found on both sides of the Bering Strait in contexts about 10,000 B.P. It is, of course, a byproduct of the production of fine microblades.

figurines (Figure 6.8). The Mal'ta-Afontova tradition has been radiocarbon dated to as early as 20,900 ± 300 B.P. in the Yenesei Valley, and Mal'ta itself has been carbon dated to around 14,500 B.P.

About 11,000 years ago, at the end of the Weichsel glaciation, the mammoth hunters of the Aldan were replaced by Mal'ta-Afontova peoples from the south, who had already adapted successfully to a more broadly based hunter-gatherer economy that flourished in the relatively warmer climate of postglacial times. By that time Stone Age hunter-gatherers had long since settled in the New World, carrying with them the basics of cultural traditions that had been evolving for millennia in northeast Asia.

Figure 6.8 Figurines from Mal'ta, Siberia: a bone figurine (actual size), two views, and an ivory bird (two-thirds actual size).

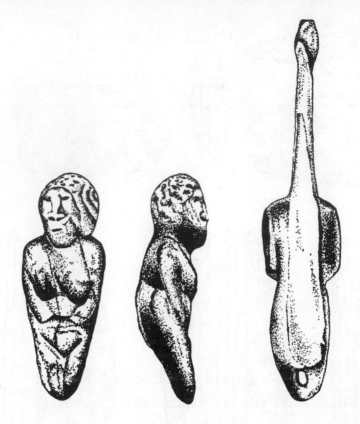

To identify these very earliest cultural traditions in the Americas has so far proved almost impossible. There are many possibilities, for there were probably almost continuous contacts across the Bering Strait after the first settlements were established on the Alaskan shore, and sporadic contacts between the Kamchatka Peninsula and Japan and the Aleutian islands are beyond doubt. Japan, for example, was not isolated from the Asian mainland for most of the Pleistocene and there is evidence of continuous human settlement of the archipelago from at least 30,000 years ago.[17] The sophisticated Japanese blade tools and projectile heads flaked on both surfaces have been compared to somewhat similar artifacts in the Americas, so far with few definite conclusions being drawn.

The technology of the Asian hunter-gatherers evolved over a long period of time; in the far northeast, this technology depended on crudely flaked stone pebbles and some small blade artifacts, a toolkit well adapted to the forest environment of the region. In the coastal zones of the Arctic Ocean and the Bering Strait, people were developing adaptations 10,000 years ago that were eventually to be perpetuated by the rich Eskimo, Aleut, Chukchi, and Koryak hunter-gatherer cultures that survived into modern times; these extended finally over the northern latitudes of the New World as far east as Greenland and the Atlantic coast.

Japan
30,000 to 10,000 B.P.

Bering Strait
10,000 B.P.
(Chapter 7)

Chronological Table D

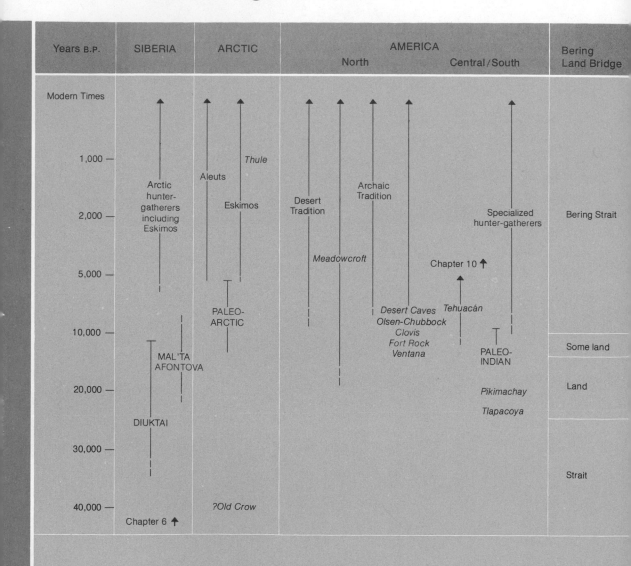

Years B.P.	SIBERIA	ARCTIC	AMERICA North	Central/South	Bering Land Bridge
Modern Times					
1,000	Arctic hunter-gatherers including Eskimos	Aleuts / Thule	Desert Tradition		Bering Strait
2,000		Eskimos	Archaic Tradition	Specialized hunter-gatherers	
5,000		PALEO-ARCTIC	Meadowcroft	Chapter 10 ↑	
10,000	MAL'TA AFONTOVA		Desert Caves Olsen-Chubbock Clovis Fort Rock Ventana	Tehuacán PALEO-INDIAN	Some land
20,000	DIUKTAI			Pikimachay Tlapacoya	Land
30,000					
40,000	Chapter 6 ↑	?Old Crow			Strait

Chapter Seven

THE FIRST
AMERICANS

PREVIEW

- The earliest human settlement of the New World is now generally agreed to have taken place across the Bering Strait during the Weichsel glaciation. During the coldest phases of that glaciation a land bridge known as Beringia connected Alaska and Asia. It is known to have existed from 25,000 to 14,000 B.P. and to have vanished altogether about 10,000 years ago.
- Few traces of very early human settlement have come to light in the Americas; the earliest in Alaska is the Old Crow site, perhaps dating to as early as 41,000 B.P.
- People were hunting big game in Mexico by 22,000 B.P. and were living at Meadowcroft rockshelter in the Ohio Valley by 19,000 B.P. Pikimachay Cave in the Andes was occupied about the same time.
- These little-known cultural traditions developed into specialized Paleo-Indian hunter-gatherer cultures that are best known from their 10,000 year old kill sites on the North American plains. After 9,000 years, other specialized hunter-gatherer cultures developed in many parts of the Americas. Prominent among these cultures are the Desert and Archaic traditions of North America. Many varieties of hunter-gatherer adaptation, often involving precise scheduling of gathering activities, developed in Central and South America during the same period. It was among some of these specialized groups that early American agriculture began.
- The hunter-gatherer cultures of the Aleutian Islands and the Arctic developed from earlier cultural traditions based on sea mammal hunting and fishing. Eskimo and Aleut culture can be recognized in the archaeological record at least three, perhaps four, thousand years ago.

Figure 7.1 Prehistoric hunter-gatherers in the New World. Sites mentioned in the text are indicated, as well as the limits of ice sheets during the last glaciation. (For the Bering Land Bridge, see Figure 7.2.) The diagonally hatched areas show the distribution of specialized hunter-gatherers after 7,000 B.P.

Ever since the Americas were first colonized, people have speculated about where the pre-Columbian populations of the Western Hemisphere came from.[1]* The claimants have been many: Canaanites, Celts, Chinese, Egyptians, Phoenicians, and even the ten Lost Tribes of Israel have been proposed as ancestors of the native Americans.[2] By the early nineteenth century, field research and museum work had begun to replace the wild speculations of earlier scholars. People began to dig in Indian mounds. Spanish and American explorers rescued the temples of Mesoamerica from the rain forest.

A wise and sober scholar named Samuel Haven summarized myths and legends about pre-Columbian Indian beginnings in 1856.[3] He concluded that the New World was initially settled from across the Bering Strait, designating the earliest Americans as northeastern Asiatics who migrated into North America at an unknown date. (See Figure 7.1 for sites mentioned in this chapter.) Most archaeologists now agree with Haven that the first Americans set foot in the New World by way of the Bering Strait. The Bering route is accepted because at times the strait formed a land bridge between Asia and Alaska during the Wisconsin (equivalent to Weichsel) glaciation (Table 3.2).

ICE SHEETS AND LAND BRIDGES

Human settlement in Siberia and northeastern Asia intensified during the Weichsel glaciation (see Chapter 6). Few traces of earlier hunters exist in Siberia; indeed, it has been argued that not until the technology of shelter and clothing was sufficiently advanced to cope with the climatic extremes of Siberia were people able to settle the arctic tundra.

Small bands of hunter-gatherers were living in Siberia and northeastern Asia during the last Weichsel cold snap, when sea levels were as much as 100 meters (330 ft) lower than today — so low that a land bridge stood where the Bering Strait now separates Asia and Alaska. (Sea level drops when quantities of ocean water are frozen into ice sheets.) The low-lying plain was a highway for such Asian mammals as the caribou and the mammoth, as well as for people, who presumably ventured eastward toward Alaska in pursuit of game. The Pacific coastal plain was much expanded by lower sea levels, enabling movement farther south as well (Figure 7.2).

The Bering Strait was dry land between about 50,000 and 40,000 years ago and again from 25,000 to 14,000 B.P. Great ice sheets covered much of North America during the later phases of the Wisconsin glaciation, extending in a formidable barrier from the Atlantic to the Pacific, and making any southward movement by man or beast almost impossible. Southerly corridors through the ice were clear for only a few thousand years before and after the glacial

* See pages 376–377 for notes to Chapter 7.

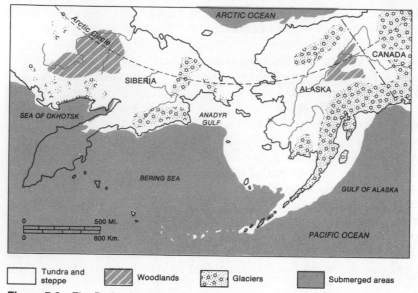

Tundra and steppe | Woodlands | Glaciers | Submerged areas

Figure 7.2 The Bering Land Bridge as reconstructed by the latest research.

Bering Land Bridge

maximum. Just how large the ice sheets were during various periods of the Wisconsin is a burning controversy, however. Since the Bering Land Bridge was submerged about 10,000 years ago, the only way people could reach the Western Hemisphere has been by water; aboriginal societies developed in almost complete isolation until ships filled with European colonists and missionaries arrived.[4]

Beringia
50,000 to 40,000 B.P. and 25,000 to 14,000 B.P.

The dry shelf between Asia and the New World formed by the low sea levels of the last glaciation is often called Beringia. It was a continuation of the Siberian tundra, which probably abounded in herds of large grazing animals. The tundra extended like a peninsula from Asia eastwards to the vast ice sheets that covered North America (see Figure 7.2). Beringia was a dry plain, with brief, warm summers, long winters, and continual winds. It is thought that Beringia was last exposed from about 25,000 to 14,000 B.P. As the ice sheets began to retreat, the shelf gradually became submerged under water until Asia and the New World were separated about 10,000 years ago.

With such a harsh environment and extensive glaciation, it is hardly surprising that much of Canada was not occupied until about 7,000 years ago, and that traces of the earliest peoples to cross into the New World are sparse. Intense controversy surrounds the origins of human settlement in the Americas:[5]

How long ago did humans settle in the Americas?
What toolkit did they bring with them?
Are there cultural connections between American and Asian sites of the time of first settlement?

ALASKA

The obvious place to look for traces of early settlement is Alaska, where field work is, unfortunately, very difficult on account of the remote terrain and severe climate.[6] Few traces of early occupation have been found in Alaska, and those that have are controversial. The eroding deposits of the Old Crow Flats near the border between Alaska and Canada have yielded a large number of fossil mammal bones, of which about a hundred are claimed to have been made into artifacts and hundreds more altered for casual use.[7] Several of these bones have been radiocarbon dated to between 25,000 and 29,000 years ago. Unfortunately, none of the artifacts or altered bones have been found in their original contexts. All of them are from redeposited levels — geological horizons consisting of materials that have been shifted by water action, erosion, or some other natural force from their original position. By careful geological observation, Richard Morlan and his colleagues have tried to establish the date of the bones through relative chronology and suspect that they may be as old as 41,000 B.P. However, these scientists are quick to admit that their dating is insecure and must await the discovery of artifacts in precise association with geological levels, and, if possible, charcoal for radiocarbon dating.

Old Crow
?41,000 B.P.
(date uncertain)

The bone artifacts themselves consist of a caribou limb bone that may have been used as a device for removing flesh from hides and some wedge-shaped tools perhaps used for woodworking or dressing skins. There are bone flakes, too, apparently removed from bone cores. No stone tools have been found in association with the Old Crow bones. So far, all efforts to find an undisturbed archaeological site in the area have failed. As Richard Morlan says, it is rather "like looking for a needle in a haystack (and a frozen one at that)."

It is difficult to know what to make of the Old Crow artifacts. Most people accept at least the flesher as a tool. Some scholars go as far as to claim that the artifacts are the only surviving traces of a highly distinctive bone and wood technology used by the hunter-gatherers who first adapted to this harsh arctic steppe environment.

The earliest relatively well-attested occupation of Alaska is estimated to date to between 15,000 and 13,000 B.P., although there are few dated sites to support this estimate. This *Paleoarctic tradition* covers a scatter of sites that have yielded microblades, wedge-shaped cores (Figure 6.4), and some leaf-shaped bifacially flaked artifacts. The tradition was practiced at the Dry Creek site near Fairbanks, which has been radiocarbon dated to about 10,700 B.P.[8] The most famous locality, however, is the 10,000 year old Akmak site at Onion Portage, which lies in a river valley that has been a migration route for caribou ever since the earliest human settlement in the region. This site consists of little more than a scatter of characteristic tools that once lay by a house long since eroded away.

Paleoarctic tradition
15,000 to
?6,000 B.P.
Dry Creek
11,000 B.P.

Akmak
10,000 B.P.

Some archaeologists believe that there are some connections between the Diuktai artifacts of northeast Asia (Chapter 6) and those of the Paleoarctic tradition, but it would be unwise to pursue these analogies too far until many more sites have been dug on both sides of the Bering Strait. Some of the stoneworking techniques practiced by the Paleoarctic people are similar to those used in Japan between about 14,000 and 10,000 B.P. Again, it would be easy to read a great deal into these parallels; but in fact their very existence has hardly been established, and that from only a mere scatter of sites.[9]

We still lack precise answers to the questions posed at the beginning of this section, but we can say that:

People *may have settled* in Alaska by 40,000 B.P., but the evidence is still highly uncertain.

The first well-attested human settlement is about 11,000 B.P. or a few millennia earlier.

There are some technological parallels between Paleoarctic artifacts of about 10,000 B.P. and those of contemporary Asia.

Beringia provided an environment suitable for regular contact between Asia and the New World until as late as 10,000 B.P.

THE EARLIEST SETTLEMENT OF MORE SOUTHERLY LATITUDES

Exactly the same archaeological problem — lack of sites — arises when we turn our attention to the earliest settlement of the vast continents south of the great ice sheets.[10] Until fairly recently most archaeologists believed that the first settlement took place about 13,000 years ago, after the retreat of the ice sheets when access from Alaska became possible. Now that more is known of the distribution of Pleistocene ice sheets and about American cultures of the period, there is agreement that the first settlement must have taken place earlier. The American hunter-gatherer cultures of 13,000 B.P. are simply too distinctive for them to have any links with contemporary Asian peoples. The distinctive features of early American toolkits probably resulted from isolation, which occurred after a much earlier initial settlement from the Arctic that took place at a time when access from north to south was possible, and there were no intervening groups to hinder progress southward. There are so few sites documenting this settlement that almost nothing is known of the settlers.

North America:
Meadowcroft
**?19,000 to 10,000
B.P. and later**

Meadowcroft rockshelter southwest of Pittsburgh was used as a home base for hunting, gathering, and food processing from at least 16,000 years ago, and perhaps as early as 19,000 B.P.[11] The earliest levels of the site contain a relatively sophisticated blade technology which produced delicately flaked knives, small bifaces, most of them made of small river pebbles. Later levels of Meadowcroft contain typical Paleo-Indian and Archaic artifacts (see pages 124–130), but excavators are convinced that the lowest horizons are the prototype technology for the fine projectile heads and other artifacts made after 12,000 B.P. To date, Meadowcroft is one of the very few North American sites which contain absolutely indisputable evidence for human occupation before 13,000 B.P. (By indisputable, we mean stratified and dated artifacts, in a precise context of time and space.[12])

A lancelike point found in a level dating to about 12,000 B.F. at Meadow-

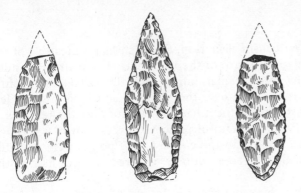

Figure 7.3 Points found with mammoths in Mexico. The length of the middle point is 8.1 cm (about 3 in.) long.

croft is similar to other such points found in the base levels of Fort Rock Cave in Oregon, Ventana Cave in Arizona, and some locations in Texas. But virtually nothing is known of the lifeway or technology of these people, discovered as they invariably are at the base of deep cave sites. There are numerous reports of humanly struck tools in caves, river gravels, and lakebeds. But almost invariably there are doubts about the stratigraphy and dating of the finds. There have been claims of human occupation of Santa Rosa Island, off the southern California coast, dating to earlier than 40,000 years ago, and claims for amino acid racemization dates of 40,000 to 50,000 years B.P. for skeletal material from San Diego.[13] These findings have not yet been published in detail and can only be described as highly controversial.

Fort Rock
12,000 B.P.

Ventana

Central and South America

Somewhat better evidence for early settlement comes from the Tlapacoya site near Mexico City, where some crudely flaked stones associated with the bones of extinct animals have been dated to between about 24,000 and 22,000 B.P. (Figure 7.3).[14] A scattering of early sites has been found in South America, among them Pikimachay Cave, where Richard MacNeish found simple cores and retouched flakes in a level dated to 20,200 ± 1,050 B.P.[15] People using a stone technology that produced simple flake tools were widespread in South America by 12,000 B.P. Their artifacts have come from rockshelters in Patagonia (southernmost South America), Columbia, and Brazil; but these tools do not include the fine projectile heads that are so characteristic of later South American hunter-gatherers.

Tlapacoya
**24,000 to
22,000 B.P.**

Pikimachay
20,200 B.P.

12,000 B.P.

A scatter of artifacts, dated levels, and a handful of fossil bones represent the total evidence for the earliest human settlement of North and South America. This is all we can conclude:

Any evidence for human occupation south of Alaska prior to 25,000 years is still unproven.

People were living in Mexico, and probably farther south, by 22,000 B.P.

The earliest stone technologies appear to have been a series of generalized core and flake traditions that did not involve the use of projectile heads (characteristic of later times).

These generalized technologies were the base from which the more specialized cultural traditions and technologies after 11,000 B.P. evolved in both North and South America.

The First Americans   123

THE PALEO-INDIANS

Clovis
10,500 B.P.

Toward the end of the Wisconsin glaciation, the High Plains area east of the Rockies lay immediately to the south of the ice sheets. The plains abounded with herds of mammoths, bison, camels, and horses. By 12,000 B.P. we find small mammoth kill sites scattered over the plains. The Clovis site in New Mexico is one of the most famous, for it has yielded not only the remains of mammoths but also a distinctive form of projectile head known as a Clovis point, which was used by hunters in the chase. Clovis points were carefully flaked on both sides and then given a "fluted," grooved base for hafting the point on a shaft (Figure 7.4).

In the plains areas where big-game hunters flourished, numerous varieties of hunting cultures began to appear. They can be distinguished by the styles of their projectile heads, which include Clovis, Eden, Folsom, Plainview, and Scottsbluff.[16] Projectile heads are found over an enormous area of North America, from Nova Scotia to northern Mexico, as well as in South America, from Venezuela to Chile. All of them are grouped together under the label *Paleo-Indian tradition*. Most Paleo-Indian sites occur in more temperate latitudes. But as the Pleistocene ice sheets retreated northward, bands of people moved with the big game into more northern latitudes, also toward the Atlantic and Pacific coasts.

Paleo-Indian
tradition
**12,000 to
9,000 B.P.**

For much of their livelihood many plains bands relied on big-game drives and communal hunting. Both the bison and the mammoth were formidable prey for hunters equipped only with spears. We have remarkably complete

Figure 7.4 Points from plains cultures (all actual size). Arrows show fluted bases.

Clovis   Folsom   Scottsbluff   Eden

knowledge of their hunting methods thanks to discoveries of kill sites where herds of bison were driven down narrow gullies to be dispatched by waiting hunters. When Joe Ben Wheat dug the Olsen-Chubbock kill site in Colorado, he examined the orientation of the dead bison, and found that all of them faced north.[17] Since the hunters would have approached the herd from downwind, he concluded that the wind on the day of the hunt was blowing from the south. At Olsen-Chubbock the hunters' artifacts were scattered around the carcasses of their quarry: scraping tools, stone knives, and flakes used for dismembering the bison (Figure 7.5).

Olsen-Chubbock
10,000 B.P.

In many areas gathering must have been vital, especially in marginal regions where desert encroached on the plains, as in parts of southern Arizona. These people are thought to have lived by seasonal exploitation of game herds and vegetable foods.[18] That seems likely from the many milling stones and other artifacts used in processing vegetable foods found on sites in this area.

Paleo-Indian hunting and gathering economies must have varied a great deal from region to region — some bands specializing in big game, others in fishing or gathering — depending on the resources available in each territory. This variation is reflected in the sites, which range from kill sites to shell middens (refuse heaps). Perhaps best known are kill sites, where hunters sometimes butchered entire herds. Campsites were maintained as much more permanent bases, normally close to regular water supplies; they yield many kinds of tools that were used for hunting and gathering and for domestic tasks. The celebrated Lindenmeier site in Colorado has long been recognized as such a more lasting settlement; it is very different from the many temporary locations where vegetable foods were collected and processed.

Lindenmeier

BIG-GAME EXTINCTIONS

In the northern latitudes of both Old World and New at the end of the Pleistocene, many big-game species became extinct. But nowhere were the extinctions so drastic as in the Americas; three quarters of the large mammalian genera there abruptly disappeared at the end of the Pleistocene.[19] Extinguished were the mammoth and the mastodon and the Pleistocene camel and horse, to say nothing of several bison species and numerous smaller mammals. Why did the American fauna die off just like that? Speculations have been long and lively. One theory that has long held on is that the large mammals were killed off by the Paleo-Indian bands' intensive hunting as they preyed on large herds of animals that had formerly had relatively few predators to control their populations. This overkill hypothesis has flaws that have become apparent as more is discovered about how extinction comes about. Many of the animals disappeared before the heyday of the Paleo-Indians. Besides, the Indians existed in very small numbers; also, they had other subsistence activities than the chase. Surely the animals would have adapted to changed conditions and new dangers. Instead, the extinctions accelerated after the hunters had been around for a while.

Overkill

The First Americans   125

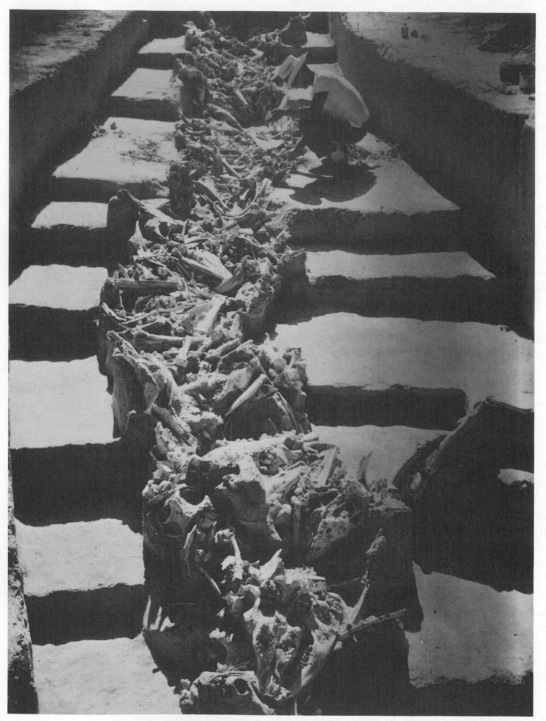

Figure 7.5 A layer of excavated bison bones from the Olsen-Chubbock site in Colorado, where a band of hunters stampeded a herd of bison into a narrow arroyo.

Hunter-Gatherers

Change in climate gives a second hypothesis for the cause of extinction. Climate change Changing environments, spreading aridity, and shrinking habitats for big game may have reduced the mammalian population drastically. Strong objections face this hypothesis too. The very animals that became extinct had already survived enormous fluctuations in Pleistocene climate without harm. If they had once migrated into more hospitable habitats, they could have done so again. Furthermore, the animals that became extinct were not just the browsers; they were selected from all types of habitat. Extinctions spared none. This too-simple hypothesis about climate change stands on the notion that desiccation leads to mass starvation in game populations, an idea refuted by ecological research on African game populations. All that happens is that the smaller species and those with lower growth rates adapt to the less favorable conditions, leaving the population changed but not defunct.

A third hypothesis cites the great variation in mean temperatures at the end of the Pleistocene as a primary cause. In both New and Old Worlds, the more pronounced seasonal contrasts in temperate climates would have been harder on the young of species that are born in small litters, after long gestation periods, at fixed times of the year. These traits are characteristic of larger Seasonal contrasts mammals, precisely those which became extinct. The less equable climate at the end of the Pleistocene, then, would have been a major cause of late Pleistocene extinctions in North America.

All three hypotheses have truth in them. Complex variables must have affected the steps that led to extinction, with intricate feedback among the effects of intensive big-game hunting, changing ecology, and the intolerance of some mammalian species to seasonal contrasts in weather conditions. It may be that the hunters, being there as persistent predators, were the final variable that caused more drastic extinctions among the mammalian fauna than might otherwise have occurred.

LATER HUNTERS AND GATHERERS

As the world climate warmed up at the end of the last glaciation, New World environments changed greatly. The western and southwestern United States became drier, but the East Coast and much of the Midwest grew densely forested. The large Pleistocene mammals of earlier times became extinct, but the bison remained a major source of food. In the warmer Southeast, the more favorable climate brought drier conditions that meant less standing water, markedly seasonal rainfalls, and specialization among humans for fishing or intensive gathering instead of big-game hunting. Many areas had much economic diversity, as we see among the desert gatherer peoples of the Tehuacán Tehuacán **12,000 to 9,000 B.P.** Valley in Mexico. They flourished between 12,000 and 9,000 B.P., at the same time other hunter-gatherers were still hunting an occasional mammoth. Hunter-gatherers in the Pacific Northwest were probably taking advantage of seasonal salmon runs in the fast-moving rivers.

Desert Tradition

Economic emphasis shifted in the arid West and Southwest. In the great basin west of the Rockies, hunting became less important. Smaller animals such as rabbits, squirrels, and antelopes were more common game. At the same time gathering vegetable foods grew dominant in economic life, combined with some fishing and, in maritime areas, exploitation of shellfish. We are fortunate that arid climates in Utah, Nevada, and elsewhere have preserved many plant and vegetable foods eaten by these early desert hunter-gatherers. By 9,000 B.P. a distinctive desert form of culture had been developed over much of the western United States by small bands camping in caves, rock-shelters, and temporary sites.

The excavations at Danger Cave in Utah and at the Gypsum and Lovelock sites in Nevada reveal that the hunters were making nets, mats, and baskets, as well as rope (Figure 7.6).[20] The Hogup Cave in Utah has yielded one of the world's most complete, longest, and best-analyzed archaeological culture sequences.[21] The site displays gradual adaptations at one settlement, changing it from a base camp to a short-stay camp that was associated with other base camps or with horticultural villages after people learned how to produce food. At all these sites the inhabitants used digging sticks to uproot edible tubers, and much of their toolkit consisted of grinding stones used in preparing vegetable foods. Those who lived in this way were obliged to be constantly on the move, searching for different vegetable foods as they came into season and camping near scanty water supplies.

Desert life in the United States survived almost without change into the eighteenth and nineteenth centuries A.D., when many hunter-gatherer groups were just about exterminated by expanding European settlement.

Archaic Tradition

A distinctive hunter-gatherer tradition appeared in the wooded areas of the eastern United States between 9,000 and 7,000 B.P. and lasted until 4,000 years ago. The term *Archaic tradition* is used to group many regional variations of hunter-gatherer culture under a single archaeological umbrella.[22] The Archaic people exploited more fish and vegetables and less game for food. Where it was possible, fish and shellfish were the largest part of their diet. Ground stone axes were in wide use, and the more northern hunters relied on gouges for woodwork. Between 8,000 and 7,000 B.P., the Archaic people began to develop extensive trading networks, handling seashells from the Florida coast and many exotic raw materials. One of the most widespread trade items was copper, first traded before 5,000 B.P. and collected from rich outcrops near Lake Superior; it was traded in the form of crude weapons and tools, such as spearheads, knives, and pins, in New England and New York and, in ingot form, in the southeastern United States (Figure 7.7).[23] The copper trade was associated with the appearance of quite elaborate burial cults, which may reflect the earliest development of chiefdoms, where high status was acquired at least partly by trading activity (Chapter 2).

Desert tradition
9,000 B.P. to modern times

Danger Cave
Gypsum Cave
Lovelock Cave
Hogup Cave

Archaic tradition
9,000 to 4,000 B.P. and modern times

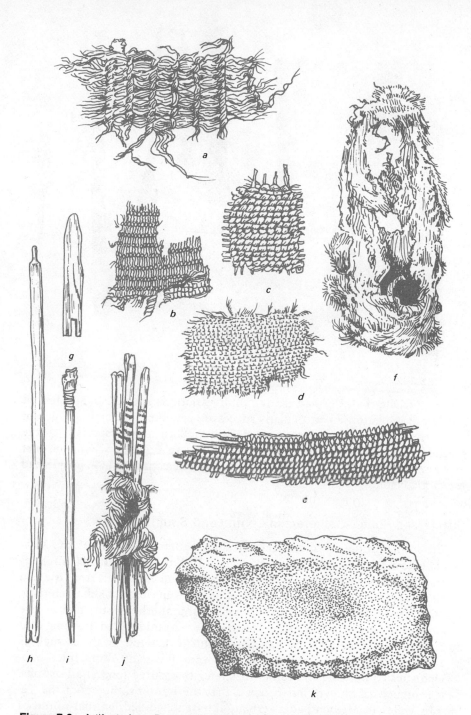

Figure 7.6 Artifacts from Danger Cave, Utah, preserved by the dry climate: (a–b) twined matting; (c) twined basketry; (d) coarse cloth; (e) coiled basketry; (f) hide moccasin; (g) wooden knife handle, 7.4 cm (4.5 in.) long; (h) dart shaft, 41 cm (16 in.) long; (i) arrow shaft with broken projectile point in place, 84 cm (33 in.) long; (j) bundle of gaming sticks, 29 cm (11.5 in.) long; (k) milling stone.

Figure 7.7 Archaic copper artifacts, about half actual size.

The Archaic tradition had many minor variations because of specialized ecological adaptations or particularly successful economic strategies. Much of the Archaic hunting tradition survived until modern times, especially in the northern parts of the eastern United States and in Canada, where the first explorers found hunters and gatherers living much as the Archaic people had millennia before.[24]

Specialized Hunter-Gatherers in Central and South America

The hunter-gatherers of the central and southern portions of the New World enjoyed a wide variety of specialized adaptations after 10,000 B.P. Sites of these specialized hunter-gatherer groups have been excavated from Mexico to Tierra del Fuego, at the southern tip of South America. One characteristic adaptation has been identified in the Andes, and another flourished on the uplands of eastern Brazil.[25] As in North America, intensified hunting and gathering concentrated the human population in favored localities such as lake shores and sea coasts, where resources were unusually abundant.

Sophisticated hunting and gathering strategies ensured food at all seasons. Kent Flannery has shown, for instance, that the hunter-gatherers of the Tehuacán Valley in Mexico had a regular, almost scheduled, annual round of hunting and gathering activities that caused the population to gather in large camps during the plentiful season and scatter into small groups during the lean months.[26] The people obtained a balanced diet by using different food procurement systems that varied in importance with the time of year.

Tehuacán
12,000 B.P.

Some of these specialized hunter-gatherers remained at the simple hunting and collecting level because of limitations in their environment and plentiful natural resources, making economic change unnecessary. But in some areas of Mesoamerica and on the coasts and highlands of Peru, hunter-gatherer bands began to experiment with the deliberate planting of vegetable foods, perhaps in attempts to expand the areas in which certain favored vegetable foods were found. These experiments became one of the vehicles of dynamic cultural change that resulted from the first development of agriculture in the New World (Chapter 13).

The southernmost extremities of Latin America were inhabited until recent times by scattered bands of hunters and fishermen. The Ona, Yaghan, and Alacaluf peoples are vividly described by early missionaries who settled among them. They lived in small bands, using only the crudest shelters of skins or grass and driftwood, with nothing but skin for body covering during the height of the antarctic winter. Shellfish, some game, fruits, berries, and fish provided a simple diet, and for tools they had none of the more sophisticated weapons made by more northern hunters. Tierra del Fuego, however, was occupied remarkably early, and it is thought that the Fuegian tradition began as early as 6,000 B.P., if not earlier. Many roots of these most southerly prehistoric humans lie back in early hunting cultures that elsewhere were replaced thousands of years before by more advanced farming cultures.

Fuegian Indians
**6,000 B.P. to
modern times**

ALEUTS AND ESKIMOS

We started the story of the first Americans with Alaska, and now end with a brief return to Arctic latitudes to trace the origins of the Aleuts and Eskimos, whose remarkable hunter-gatherer cultures survived long beyond European contact into recent times. The origins of both the Aleut and the Eskimo go back many thousands of years into prehistory, and their ultimate ancestry may lie both in Asian roots and in local cultural evolution. The differences between them are more cultural than physical, and reflect different adaptations to arctic maritime environments. It is logical for us to end this chapter with the Arctic, for the Eskimos were the first native Americans to come in touch with Europeans, in Greenland and in the extreme continental northeast.[27]

As we have seen, there is good reason to suspect that people have been living in Alaska and parts of northern Canada for at least 20,000 years, and perhaps for double that time. But the earliest cultural tradition which makes any archaeological sense at the moment is the Paleoarctic tradition, which was flourishing by 15,000 B.P. and had some connections with contemporary cultures in Siberia. The Paleoarctic people were tundra-dwelling hunter-gatherers, whose culture and language *may* be the ancestor of both Eskimo and Aleut culture and language. It should be noted that both peoples are the most Asian of all indigenous Americans. By 9,000 B.P. these two peoples had moved south as far as the Alaskan peninsula. Only a millennium later they had settled in the Aleutian Islands.

Paleoarctic tradition
**15,000 to
?6,000 B.P.**

9,000 B.P.

By 6,000 B.P. there was more cultural diversity in the Arctic, as specialized adaptations developed on the coast and in the interior, and some American Indian groups moved northwards into formerly glaciated regions in the interior. On the Pacific Coast and in the eastern Aleutians, the Aleutian tradition was among those which emerged. Centered on the Aleutian Islands and the tip of the Alaskan peninsula, this distinctive cultural tradition lasted from about 4,500 B.P. until recent times, when Russian fur traders shot and enslaved the islanders.

The Aleutian tradition is typified by the archaeological sites on Anangula Island, which was occupied by maritime hunter-gatherers for at least 4,000 years, and probably as early as 8,500 to 7,700 B.P.[28] Economic specialization on Anangula was built on fishing, sea mammals, and birds — a strategy developed in an isolated and stable environment (Figure 7.8). The Anangula archaeological site lies on a cliff 20 meters (65.5 ft) above sea level and was probably occupied for at least 500 years, with a population estimated to be at least a hundred souls. Chaluka, a later site nearby, carried the story of Aleutian occupation up to recent times.

The origins of the Eskimo cultural tradition of modern times lie in the Arctic Small-Tool tradition, a distinctive small-artifact technology that appears in Alaska about 4,200 B.P. The Arctic Small-Tool people may have had strong connections with Siberia, and are thought to have been nomadic land mammal hunters who preyed on caribou and musk ox. Some settled in Alaska;

Figure 7.8   Aleuts returning from a sea otter hunt, probably in the 1890s. They are wearing eye visors made of wood. Photograph by an unknown Government Surveyor.

Figure 7.9 Ornamented ivory object, perhaps a comb from the Seward Peninsula in Alaska (Northern tradition, Ipiutak stage). Length 26 cm.

others of them wandered as far east as Greenland by 4,000 B.P., the first people to settle in the eastern Arctic. The eastern Small-Tool tradition eventually evolved into the long-lived Thule tradition, whose people were the first native Americans to come in touch with Europeans.[29]

The Arctic Small-Tool tradition began to disappear in Alaska around 3,500 B.P., to be replaced by cultures based on the intensive hunting of both sea mammals and land animals. This hunting tradition, called the Norton tradition (Figure 7.9), in turn gave rise to a magnificent Eskimo sea mammal hunting culture, the Thule tradition, that is thought to have originated among whale hunters in the Bering Strait. The Thule tradition first emerged in the first millennium A.D. and developed into a highly distinctive sea mammal hunting culture with all the characteristic Eskimo artifacts so well known from popular publications — among them, the kayak, the umiak (open skin boat), and toggled harpoons, as well as fine ivory work (Figure 7.9). Many of the Eskimo lived by then in larger settlements, especially those who hunted whales. About A.D. 900 the Thule people started to expand to the south, and then to the east. Thule whale hunters appeared in the Arctic islands of the east about A.D. 1000, where their open-water hunting techniques could be used with great effect. By the time the Thule reached northwest Greenland, the Norsemen had been living in the southern parts of the island for some time.

Eskimo cultural traditions, like those of the Fuegians and other hunter-gatherer groups, continued to flourish after European contact. But within a few centuries, traditional lifeways were modified beyond recognition and exotic diseases decimated hunter-gatherer populations. Today, few of America's hunter-gatherers still practice their millennia-old life styles: there are no longer the resources nor the territorial space for them to do so.

Norton tradition (west)
3,500 to 1,500 B.P.

Thule tradition
A.D. 500 to modern times

A.D. 1,200

Chronological Table E

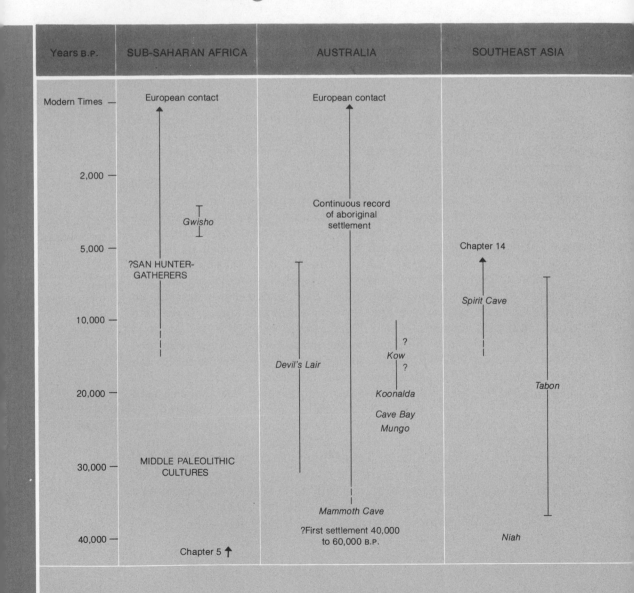

Years B.P.	SUB-SAHARAN AFRICA	AUSTRALIA	SOUTHEAST ASIA
Modern Times —	European contact	European contact	
2,000 —		Continuous record of aboriginal settlement	
	Gwisho		Chapter 14
5,000 —	?SAN HUNTER-GATHERERS		Spirit Cave
10,000 —		Kow ?	
	Devil's Lair	?	
20,000 —		Koonalda	Tabon
		Cave Bay	
		Mungo	
30,000 —	MIDDLE PALEOLITHIC CULTURES		
		Mammoth Cave	
40,000 —		?First settlement 40,000 to 60,000 B.P.	Niah
	Chapter 5 ↑		

Chapter Eight

AFRICANS AND AUSTRALIANS

PREVIEW

🌿 Like hunter-gatherers in northern latitudes, the post-Pleistocene peoples of tropical regions adopted increasingly specialized economies after 10,000 B.P. They
also made much use of the bow and arrow, and toolkits became smaller and
more lightweight as a result.

🌿 This chapter concentrates on the San hunter-gatherers and Australian aborigines, whose traditional lifeways originated many thousands of years ago in prehistoric times.

🌿 The San of southern Africa flourished in savannah woodland country that was
rich in game and vegetable foods. Their lively rock art depicts their hunting and
gathering activities. These paintings, and the waterlogged Gwisho sites in central Zambia, have shown that their portable toolkits changed little over the centuries. The San's highly flexible band organization of today doubtless ensured
the continued viability of prehistoric hunter-gatherers as well. They also lived at
small campsites which were often reoccupied at certain seasons of the year for
many generations.

🌿 Human occupation of Australia goes back over 35,000 years, probably to a time
when large marsupials were still flourishing. The archaeological record shows
that the Australian lifeway changed little during its long history; there were,
however, steady, slow changes in tool technology. The Tasmanians were isolated in their homeland as sea levels rose at the end of the Pleistocene and,
as a result, did not acquire some of the later mainland tool types, such as the
boomerang.

🌿 Living archaeology and ethnographic analogy play an important part in our
modern interpretation of the prehistory of tropical hunter-gatherers.

The end of the Weichsel glaciation had less profound effects on tropical latitudes than it had on northern latitudes. However, it did result in minor shifts in rainfall patterns, which may have had a significant effect on the distribution of critically important game populations and cereal grasses. The archaeological record for the many hunter-gatherer populations of southern latitudes consists for the most part of thousands of stone implements from dozens of isolated sites.[1]* Instead of attempting a detailed chronicle of isolated local cultures, we concentrate on two adaptations of particular interest — those of the San peoples of southern Africa, and those of the Australian aborigines. Both these peoples continue to display a wide range of relatively specialized adaptations that include not only hunting and gathering, but fishing and exploitation of shellfish as well.

The modern hunter-gatherer populations of Africa and Asia are among the very few survivors of the longest-lived and perhaps most viable of all human lifeways. Only 15,000 years ago, probably everyone lived by hunting and gathering. Ethnographer George Peter Murdock has estimated that perhaps 15 percent of the world's population were still hunting and gathering at the time Columbus landed in the New World.[2] We are fortunate that modern anthropological studies of the San and Australians have given us at least a few insights into the traditional lifeways of southern hunter-gatherers.

AFRICAN HUNTER-GATHERERS: PAST AND PRESENT

15,000 B.P.

Until about 10,000 years ago many hunter-gatherers in Africa were still making prepared cores and flake tools characteristic of the Middle Paleolithic. These were replaced in part by tools made with blade technology after 15,000 B.P.[3] By the end of the Pleistocene, savannah woodland groups were beginning to rely heavily on the bow and arrow. Stone technology was modified to produce enormous numbers of tiny, stone arrow barbs that are known to archaeologists as "microliths." These were fitted onto arrow shafts (Figure 8.1). Later stone toolkits were much smaller than earlier ones. The bow has the important advantage that it can be used to dispatch game from a distance, especially if the arrow is smeared with vegetable poison. Thousands of microlithic arrow barbs are found in the caves and rockshelters and open living sites of the woodland cultures. In more densely forested regions the people relied on heavy stone-headed picks and a variety of woodworking tools to exploit the closed-in environment of dense woodland and rain forest.

In Africa, as elsewhere, we find increasing economic specialization. The peoples of the open savannah lived off the abundant game populations and supplemented their diet with seasonal gathering of the rich vegetable resources of the woodland. Other bands settled on the shores of lakes and on riverbanks and lived by fishing. This valuable and reliable source of protein encouraged more lasting settlement and increased specialization. The rain forest peoples of the Zaire river basin in central Africa were unable to hunt such a wide range

* See page 378 for notes to Chapter 8.

of game as their savannah counterparts, so they relied heavily on vegetable foods and wild roots for much of their livelihood.

The lifeway of the savannah hunter-gatherers of eastern and southern Africa has been immortalized by the people themselves. They lived in open living sites, under convenient rocky overhangs, and in the mouths of deep caves. It was on the walls of these caves and rockshelters that the people

Figure 8.1 Microliths. Stages in manufacturing a microlith, a small arrow barb or similar implement made by notching a blade and snapping off its base after the implement is formed.

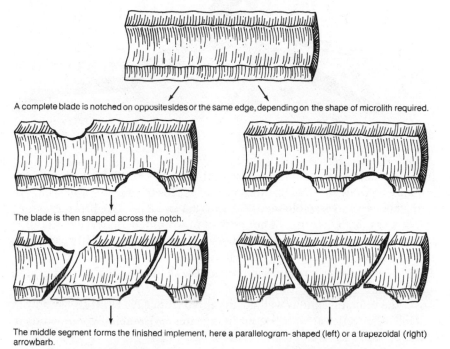

A complete blade is notched on opposite sides or the same edge, depending on the shape of microlith required.

The blade is then snapped across the notch.

The middle segment forms the finished implement, here a parallelogram-shaped (left) or a trapezoidal (right) arrowbarb.

Microliths (Actual size)

Mounted barbs
(hypothetical)
(Actual size)

Figure 8.2 A running San hunter from Ho Khotso, Lesotho, southern Africa, from a late Stone Age painting colored purple-red. The figure is 21 centimeters (about 8 in) high.

painted vivid depictions of the game they hunted, of the chase, and of life in camp.[4] The San drew running hunters, people fishing from boats, and scenes of gathering honey and vegetable foods (Figures 8.2 and 8.3). The hunters can be seen stalking game in disguise, in hot pursuit of wounded quarry, even raiding cattle herds of their agricultural neighbors of later centuries. This extraordinary artistic tradition is found on the walls of caves that were occupied as early as 8,000 B.P., perhaps earlier. The San returned to the same sites year after year, occupying some of them until very recent times. Their lifeway changed but little over the millennia and is well documented from cave paintings and from remarkable discoveries at waterlogged living sites in Zambia, where bands of San camped regularly over 4,000 years ago.

Gwisho
4,500 B.P.

The Gwisho hot springs in central Zambia were a favored location for San bands for thousands of years.[5] Because the lower levels of the campsites there are waterlogged, some artifacts were preserved by the water and give us unique insights into the peoples who used them. The economy and material culture of these peoples show a striking resemblance to those of modern San peoples in the Kalahari, although, of course, there are environmental differences.[6] The Gwisho people hunted many species of antelope and caught fish in shallow pools of the nearby Kafue river. The waterlogged levels contained over ten thousand plant remains, which came from only eight species, all of which were apparently collected to the exclusion of many other edible species. Nearby lay some fine arrowheads and some of the wooden artifacts made by the inhabitants, including some simple digging sticks used for uprooting tubers. These tools were identical to those used by Kalahari San today. There were traces of a grass and stick shelter, of hearths, and of layers of grass that may have served as bedding. Thirty-five burials were deposited in the soil of

the campsites. The deposits were littered with hundreds of stone arrow barbs and tiny scraping tools that lay alongside pestles and grinding stones used to process the vegetable foods that were an important part of the Gwisho diet. So little have gathering habits changed in the past three thousand years that a San from the Kalahari was able to identify seeds from the excavations and tell archaeologists what they were used for.

The Gwisho hot springs are informative, for they confirm ethnographic observations made about the present-day San of the Kalahari. Like that of their modern successors, the toolkit of the Gwisho people was highly portable and much of it was disposable. Except for bows and arrows, the Kalahari San improvise many of their tools from the bush as they need them, making snares from vegetable fibers and clubs from convenient branches. The women use digging sticks like the Gwisho artifacts for digging tubers and a softened antelope hide, or kaross, as a garment and carrying bag. Their only other artifacts are a pair of pounding stones for breaking up nuts. The Gwisho site contains both the digging sticks and pounders. We know from cave paintings that the San used karosses for thousands of years, and we can assume they were used at Gwisho and elsewhere.

Like those of the San, the Gwisho home bases were little more than small clusters of brush shelters. The average present-day !Kung San camp holds about ten to thirty people. The small population of !Kung territory leads to a constant turnover of the composition of camp populations. This constantly changing composition is a reality reflected in the !Kung's highly flexible kinship system. Every member of a band has not only close family ties, but kin connections with a much wider number of people living all over !Kung territory. The !Kung kinship system is based on an elaborate network of commonly

Africans and Australians   139

possessed personal names which are transmitted from grandparent to grandchild. People with similar names share kin ties even if they live at some distance from one another. This network of personal names and kin ties is such that individuals can move to a new camp and find a family with which they have kin ties to accept them. The resulting flexibility of movement prevents total social chaos. Presumably, the prehistoric San had a similar pragmatic and flexible social organization to aid survival.

2,000 B.P.

Prehistoric hunter-gatherers enjoyed the savannah woodlands of eastern and southern Africa undisturbed until about 2,000 years ago, when the first farming peoples (other African natives) settled by the banks of the Zambezi and Limpopo rivers.[7] The San came off second best in the resulting competition for land: the farmers wanted grazing grass and prime land for cultivating, so they drove off the bands of San hunter-gatherers who had to retreat into less favored areas. Some took up the new economies and married into farming communities. White settlement in South Africa increased the isolation of the San still further. As the pressure on their hunting grounds increased, the San

A.D. 1800

moved into mountainous areas and into desert regions. Even there they were harassed and hunted. Some of the white settlers even went shooting them on Sunday afternoons. The doomed San of South Africa calmly continued to paint scenes of cattle raids and of European ships and wagons. They even depicted red-coated English soldiers on their expeditions into the mountains. By the end of the nineteenth century, there were no artists still painting in South Africa and the art of stone toolmaking had all but died out. The last

A.D. 1890

stoneworkers made use of glass fragments to make their sharp arrowheads. They found this unusually pure "stone" vastly preferable to their usual quartz pebbles.[8]

PREHISTORY OF THE AUSTRALIANS

The Australian aborigines encountered by Captain Cook and other early explorers were still living in the Stone Age; they were all hunter-gatherers and used a technology that could have stepped right out of prehistory (Figure 8.4). Their ancestry has excited the interest of anthropological archaeologists ever since:[9] Where did the Australians come from, and how long ago did people first settle on this remote continent?

The natural area to look in for Australian origins is, of course, southeastern Asia. When sea levels were at their lowest during the height of the Weichsel glaciation, perhaps 50,000 years ago, only a relatively short open water passage separated Australia from the islands which lie off Asia and the mainland.[10] Unfortunately archaeological research in southeastern Asia has been too sparse to demonstrate close connections between the toolkits of the earliest Australians and those of their Asian contemporaries. No one, however, challenges the accepted hypothesis that Australian origins lie in the north.

We do know that the stone technologies of southeastern Asia were startlingly conservative for long periods of time. And at both Niah Cave in Borneo and at Tabon Cave on the island of Palawan the same crude flake and chopper

Figure 8.4 An Australian aborigine with his lightweight hunting kit. This somewhat romanticized portrait was drawn by François Peron, a naturalist attached to the Baudin Expedition of 1802.

stone technology remained in use almost unchanged from 40,000 to 7,000 years ago.[11] The same long-term conservatism is found in Australia, where the simplest of stone technologies proved effective for tens of thousands of years.

The earliest traces of human settlement in Australia date to far earlier than 30,000 years ago, indeed are older than the outer limits of radiocarbon dating (over 60,000 B.P.). Many scholars have pointed out that if humans entered Australia at a time of low sea level (which would have resulted during a

Niah
40,000 B.P.

First settlement
?60,000 B.P.

Africans and Australians   141

glaciation) they must have done so before the last cold snap of Weichsel (30,000 to 10,000 B.P.) — because by that time people were already living there. From 40,000 to 30,000 B.P., was an interstadial, so the first crossing must have been before 40,000 B.P., which marked the end of an earlier ice age — conceivably much earlier.

During the late Pleistocene, Australia was inhabited by large marsupials (pouched animals) who became extinct at the threshold of modern times. How did these animals die out? Some people believe that overhunting caused their ultimate demise, but a more likely hypothesis sees drought at the end of the Pleistocene as a major cause. As the drought took hold, the big-game populations were concentrated in smaller areas where their food supplies were still plentiful and water abundant. Many larger animals would die out fairly rapidly, as food supplies near the water they needed every day became very scarce. There are almost no firm associations of human artifacts with big-game bones, so we cannot say whether overhunting accelerated the extinction of larger animals. Some cut and charred bones of large extinct animals have come from Mammoth Cave near Devil's Lair in southwest Australia and are dated to "more than 37,000 years."[12] Similar cut and charred bones occur with hearths and steep-ended scraping tools in now arid parts of southeast Australia. Even earlier associations of human artifacts and extinct fauna were found in geological deposits in the Murchison river basin and on the margins of the Nullarbor plain. Some collections of large artifacts from South Australia are also considered to be of high antiquity, but they are still undated.[13]

While the earliest date of human settlement in Australia is still a mystery, there is abundant evidence for later occupation, from 30,000 years ago until recent times. One of the problems with identifying the earliest occupation is that the tools used by the early Australians were very unspecialized artifacts, of a form that almost defy classification into specific tool types.

There are two groups of Pleistocene human fossils in Australia. One includes the famous Mungo skeleton from New South Wales, which dates to 35,000 B.P. This group consists of entirely modern people, *Homo sapiens sapiens*, who may have reached Australia during a period of low sea level, perhaps as early as 50,000 years ago.[14] The second is a more robust, "archaic" group, represented by such finds as the burials of some forty individuals discovered in the dunes around Kow Swamp, about 120 miles (193 km) north of Melbourne. These skeletons, with thick skulls, large jaws, and other archaic features, are dated to between 10,000 and 20,000 years. Some anatomists see this group, despite the late date of the Kow specimens, as a relic of an earlier population, which could have entered Australia as early as the beginning of the Weichsel glaciation, perhaps around 100,000 B.P. But the relationships between these Australian finds and the few fossil discoveries from southeast Asia remain to be established.

Just how conservative the early Australians were is shown by a long cultural sequence recovered from Devil's Lair, a cave in the southwestern part of Western Australia.[15] There Charles Dortch and Duncan Merrilees excavated a limestone cave which contained occupation levels dated from earlier than 31,000 B.P. up to 6,000 years ago. The same traditions of stoneworking and bone technology survived almost unchanged for thousands of years. For instance, flakes showing wear patterns characteristic of adze blades made by modern aborigines are found back as far as 25,000 B.P. The same bone points used to fasten skin clothes in historic times are found deep in the prehistoric levels of Devil's Lair as well.

The Australian aborigines are celebrated for their artistic traditions and elaborate ceremonial life. Abundant traces of ritual beliefs are found in Australian sites. The Devil's Lair site yielded engraved stone plaques, a deep pit, and human incisors that had been knocked out with a sharp blow: the evulsion of teeth was a long-lived Australian tradition. At Koonalda Cave, close to the south coast of Australia, engravings have been found in a completely dark chamber dating back at least 20,000 years, if not further, into prehistory.[16] These engravings are as old as much Upper Paleolithic art in Europe. Koonalda was a quarry where the people obtained flint from 61 meters (200 ft.) below ground.

Koonalda
c. 20,000 B.P.

Despite the essential conservatism of Australian stoneworking practices, some regional variations in stone technology did appear over the millennia. Steep-edged scrapers which were probably used as woodworking tools were made over a wide area of Australia during much of the Late Pleistocene. These, and crude flake tools, remained in use until recent times; they were joined after 6,000 B.P., in some areas, by stone points set on shafts and other microliths. There is good reason to believe that Australian aboriginal technology developed within Australia over a very long period of time in response to local needs, and without the benefit of cultural innovation from outside (Figure 8.5).

Some idea of the simple level of early Australian life can be obtained from the saga of the Tasmanians.[17] When the first European voyagers visited Tasmania in 1642, they found bands of hunter-gatherers living on the island, separated from the mainland by the stormy Bass Straits. The Tasmanians lasted precisely eighty years after European settlement. They had no hafted tools (that is, tools composed of stoneheads or points with wooden shafts or handles) and relied instead on scrapers and choppers somewhat like those used by early hunter-gatherers on the mainland; they lacked the boomerangs, spearthrowers, shields, axes, adzes, and lightweight stone tools the Australians of the mainland had when they first entered written history. Tasmania was settled when it was attached to the mainland during the Weichsel glaciation, but many of the earliest sites are probably buried under the sea. The earliest archaeological record of occupation is from a cave at Cave Bay on Hunter Island, now isolated from Tasmania by the higher sea level that cut Tasmania away from Australia as well. The cave was used by occasional visitors who left sparse occupation levels behind them dating from 23,000 B.P.[18] The result of Tasmania's isolation was that its populations, although forming part of the Australian cultural group, never received the later cultural innovations that spread through Australia after the sea levels rose.

Cave Bay
23,000 B.P.

Fortunately for archaeology, at least some investigations of aboriginal culture have been made that have important bearing on the interpretation of the archaeological record. Richard Gould spent many months among the Ngatat-

Africans and Australians   143

jara people of the Western Desert carrying out ethnographic investigations that had objectives somewhat similar to those of Richard Lee among the San in Africa:[19] he was interested in their cultural ecology and in the ways in which ethnographic observations could be used to interpret the archaeological record. His aboriginal informants took him to Puntutjarpa rockshelter, a site that they still visited regularly. Gould excavated the occupation levels in the shelter and found that people had lived there for more than 6,800 years. The later stone implements at the site were almost indistinguishable from modern Ngatatjara tools, to the extent that Gould was able to compare the wear patterns on both ancient and modern artifacts and decide which 5,000-year-old tools had been mounted on shafts and which had not. He also compared modern living surfaces with equivalent features found in the rockshelter (Figure 8.6).

The study of living aborigine bands shows just how conservative Australian lifeways have been. There were few major technological innovations during Australian prehistory. Indeed, it was possible for the prehistoric Australians to maintain a thoroughly viable lifeway with minimal technology and but the simplest of artifacts. The Tasmanians, for instance, used only about two dozen

Figure 8.5 Australian aborigines making stone tools.

Hunter-Gatherers

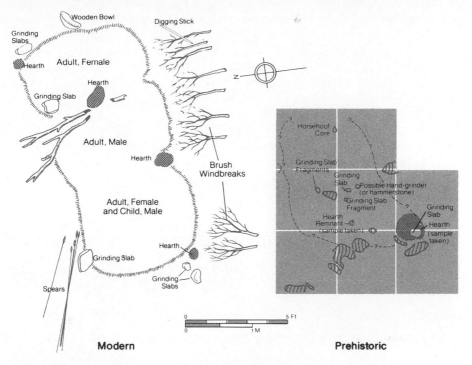

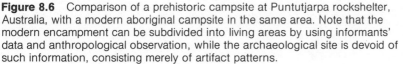

Modern   **Prehistoric**

Figure 8.6 Comparison of a prehistoric campsite at Puntutjarpa rockshelter, Australia, with a modern aboriginal campsite in the same area. Note that the modern encampment can be subdivided into living areas by using informants' data and anthropological observation, while the archaeological site is devoid of such information, consisting merely of artifact patterns.

tools to hunt and forage. The great elaboration of Australian and Tasmanian culture was in social and ritual life, neither of which can readily be recovered by archaeological investigation. That much of this activity was designed to maintain the delicate balance between the aborigines and their available resources in their environment was no coincidence.[20] A belief in such balance lay at the very core of Australian life.

PART FOUR

FARMERS

(c. 12,000 B.P. to Modern Times)

"Agriculture is not to be looked on as a difficult or
out-of-the-way invention, for the rudest savage, skilled as
he is in the habits of the food-plants he gathers, must
know well enough that if seeds or roots are put in a
proper place in the ground they will grow."
— Sir Edward Tylor, 1883

The beginning of food production — of agriculture and animal domestication —
was one of the catalytic events of human prehistory. Part 4 not only describes the
sequence of farming cultures in all parts of the world but also analyzes some of the
recent theories about the origins of farming. We will start with the theoretical background first and then study farming in geographical areas. With the beginnings of
food production we find the first signs of rapidly accelerating cultural evolution, of
processes that are still operating at a record pace today. But our understanding of
the early millennia of farming is incomplete. The archaeological evidence outlined
here is extremely sketchy and often stretched to the limit to produce a coherent
narrative. Future research is certain to modify drastically the story set forth in the
chapters of Part 4.

Chapter Nine

PLENTEOUS HARVEST— THE ORIGINS

PREVIEW

⚜ The domestication of plants and animals was one of the momentous developments in world prehistory because the new economic strategies resulted in increased and stabilized food supplies — but generally at a higher energy cost.

⚜ Food production proved dramatically successful. Ten thousand years ago almost everyone in the world was hunting and gathering. By 2,000 B.P. hunter-gatherers were in a minority.

⚜ The advent of food production brought more sedentary settlements, improved storage facilities, and new toolkits designed for agriculture and food storage. Population increases appear to have preceded, and followed, the beginnings of food production.

⚜ The first theories for the origins of food production were formulated in terms of a single genius who invented agriculture. Others hypothesized that increased desiccation at the end of the Pleistocene concentrated plants, humans, and animals in a close symbiosis, which resulted in domestication. V. Gordon Childe refined this theory and postulated a Neolithic Revolution.

⚜ Modern theories have moved away from a Neolithic Revolution toward ecological explanations, which suggest that a variety of factors interacted to cause humankind to experiment with the deliberate cultivation of cereal and root crops. According to this ecology-based account, food production was developed in several areas of the world more or less at the same time.

⚜ Braidwood with his nuclear zones, Binford with theories of demographic stress, and Flannery with a systems approach to agricultural origins all argued that the development of food production was a gradual process, one in which hunter-gatherers moved from scheduled gathering activities to experimentation with food crops at the edge of areas where potential domesticates were abundant.

⚜ Recently, Mark Cohen has suggested that population pressure was a major factor in the development of food production. He argues that the only significant puzzle is why people turned from hunting and gathering, a relatively low-risk activity, to agriculture, which, at any rate initially, was a high-risk and much more arduous venture. It could be that the changeover occurred when environmental imbalance caused people to fall back on less desirable foods and to trying to grow food for themselves. This would be, after all, a logical step for people familiar with the germination of plants.

↓ We end by looking at some of the genetic changes in plants and animals that resulted from domestication, and at the technological changes that followed in the train of domestication.

It is difficult for us, buying our food from supermarkets, to appreciate how awesome were the consequences to human history of agriculture and the domestication of animals. For over 99 percent of our existence as humans, we were hunter-gatherers, tied to the seasons of vegetable foods or movements of game. But with economies based on the production of food, people could now influence their environment and sometimes control its ecological balance — with drastic consequences for their descendants.[1]*

CONSEQUENCES OF FOOD PRODUCTION

The new food-producing economies proved dramatically successful. Ten thousand years ago virtually everybody in the world lived by hunting and gathering. By 2,000 B.P. most people were farmers or herders and only a minority were still hunter-gatherers. The spread of food production throughout the world took only about 8,000 years. The problem for anthropologists is not only to account for why people took up agriculture, but also to explain why so many populations adopted this new, and initially risky, economic transition in such a short time. Food production spread to all corners of the world except where an environment with extreme aridity or heat rendered agriculture or herding impossible, or where people chose to remain hunters and gatherers. In some places, food production was the economic base for urbanization and literate civilization. But most human societies did not go further than subsistence-level food production until the industrial power of nineteenth- and twentieth-century Europe led them into the Machine Age.

Food production resulted, ultimately, in much higher population densities in many locations, for the domestication of plants and animals can result in an economic strategy that increases and stabilizes available food supplies, although at the expense of more energy used to produce it. Farmers use concentrated tracts of territory for agriculture and for grazing cattle and small stock, if they practice mixed farming. Their territory is much smaller than that of hunter-gatherers (although pastoralists need huge areas of grazing land for seasonal pasture). Within a smaller area of farming land, property lines are

---

* See pages 379–380 for notes to Chapter 9.

carefully delineated, as individual ownership of land and problems of inheritance of property arise. Shortages of land can lead to disputes and to the founding of new village settlements on previously uncultivated soil.[2]

More enduring settlements brought other changes. The portable and lightweight material possessions of many hunter-gatherers were replaced by heavier toolkits and more lasting houses (Figure 9.1). Grindstones and ground-edged axes were even more essential to farming culture than they were to gathering societies. Hoes and other implements of tillage were vital for the planting and harvesting of crops. New social units came into being as more lasting home bases were developed; these social links reflected ownership and inheritance of land and led to much larger settlements that brought hitherto scattered populations into closer and more regular contact.

Food production led to changed attitudes toward the environment. Cereal crops were such that people could store their food for use in winter (Figure 9.1). The hunter-gatherers exploited game, fish, and vegetable foods, but the farmer did more; he *altered* the environment by the very nature of the exploitation. Expansion of agriculture meant felling trees and burning vegetation to clear the ground for planting. The same fields were then abandoned after a few years to lie fallow, and more woodland was cleared. The original vegetation began to regenerate, but it might be cleared again before reaching its original state. This shifting pattern of farming is called slash-and-burn agriculture. Voracious domesticated animals stripped pastures of their grass cover, then heavy rainfalls denuded the hills of valuable soil, and the pastures were

Figure 9.1 A pole-and-mud hut typical of the Middle Zambezi Valley, Africa (left). Such dwellings, often occupied fifteen years or longer, are more lasting than the windbreak or tent of the hunter-gatherer. At right is a grain bin from an African village, used for cereal crops. Storing food is a critical part of a food-producing economy.

never the same again. However elementary the agricultural technology, the farmer changed the environment, if only with fires lit to clear scrub from gardens and to fertilize the soil with wood ashes. Hunter-gatherers had deliberately set fires to encourage the growth of new grass for their grazing prey. In a sense, shifting, slash-and-burn agriculture is merely an extension of the age-old use of fire to encourage regeneration of vegetation.

Food production resulted in high population densities; but growth was controlled by disease, available food supplies, water supplies, and particularly famine. Many peoples controlled their populations by deliberately spacing births. Early agricultural methods depended heavily on careful selection of the soil. The technology of the first farmers was hardly potent enough for extensive clearance of the dense woodland under which many good soils lay, so the potentially cultivable land could only be that which was accessible in the first place. Gardens probably were scattered over a much wider territory than is necessary today with modern plowing and other advanced techniques. One authority on African agriculture estimates that, even with advanced shifting agriculture, only 40 percent of moderately fertile soil in Africa is available for such cultivation.[3] This figure must have been lower in the early days of agriculture, with its simpler stone tools and fewer crops.

In regions of seasonal rainfall like the Near East, sub-Saharan Africa, and parts of Asia, periods of prolonged drought are common. Famine was probably a real possibility as population densities rose. Many early agriculturalists must have worriedly watched the sky and must have had frequent crop failures in times of drought. Their small stores of grain from the previous season would not have carried them through another year, especially if they had been careless with their surplus. Farmers were forced to shift their economic strategy in times of famine. We can assume that the earliest farmers made heavy use of game and vegetable foods to supplement their agriculture, just as even today some farmers are obliged to rely heavily on wild vegetable foods and hunting to survive in bad years.[4] Many hunter-gatherer bands collect intensively just a few species of edible plants in their large territories. Aware of many other edible vegetables, they fall back on those only in times of stress; these less favored foods can carry a comparatively small population through to the next rains. A larger agricultural population is not so flexible and quickly exhausts wild vegetables and game in the much smaller territory used for farming and grazing. If the drought lasts for years, famine, death, and reduced population can follow.

THEORIES ABOUT THE ORIGINS OF DOMESTICATION

Why did people choose to grow their own crops? What caused food production to be adopted in thousands of human societies and with such rapidity?

Speculations about the origins of agriculture go back over a century. The first theories envisaged a solitary genius who had suddenly had the brilliant idea of planting seed.[5] Others argued for a severe drought at the end of the Pleistocene which concentrated animals, plants, and humans in oases with permanent water supplies where people tamed the flora and fauna for their own purposes. No one still looks for a single genius, or for the earliest maize cob. Rather, modern theory concentrates on the complex processes that caused gradual changes in human subsistence patterns.[6]

Childe: Neolithic
Revolution

One of the first scholars to work with excavated data was V. Gordon Childe, who proposed a major economic revolution in prehistory — the Neolithic Revolution.[7] His Neolithic Revolution took place during a period of severe drought, a climatic crisis that caused a symbiotic relationship to be forged between the humans and animals in fertile oases. The new economies ensured a richer and more reliable food source for people on the edge of starvation.

Childe's Revolution hypothesis was a refinement of the oasis theory and was widely accepted. But no one has yet found convincing traces of drier climate at the end of the Pleistocene. Other early scholars began to examine the hilly regions above the lowlands of Mesopotamia to see if they might have been the cradle of early food production, for it was there that fossils of potentially domesticable animals and wild cereals were found.[8]

Braidwood: nuclear
zones

Systematic fieldwork into the origins of food production began only in the late 1940s. Robert J. Braidwood of the University of Chicago mounted an expedition to the Kurdish foothills of Iran to test Childe's theories. Geologists and zoologists on the expedition produced field evidence causing Braidwood to reject the notion of catastrophic climatic change at the end of the Pleistocene, despite minor shifts in rainfall distribution. Nothing in the environment, Braidwood argued, could have necessitated the radical shift in human adaptation proposed by Childe.[9] Braidwood felt the economic change came from the "ever increasing cultural differentiation and specialization of human communities." Thus, he argued, the people were culturally receptive to innovation and experimentation with cultivation of wild grasses. People had begun to understand and manipulate the plants and animals around them in "nuclear zones," that is to say, areas where potentially domesticable cereals and animals flourished in the wild. One of these zones was the hilly flanks of the Zagros Mountains in Iraq and the upland areas overlooking the Mesopotamian lowlands. Braidwood was convinced that the human capacity and enthusiasm for experimentation made it possible for people to domesticate animals and grow crops — but his hypothesis does not explain why food production was adopted.

Sauer: ecology

In 1952, Carl O. Sauer published a remarkable essay on agricultural origins, in which he analyzed the ecology of food production.[10] He saw the origins of food production as a change in the way in which culture and environment interacted. Sauer proposed Southeast Asia as a major center of domestication, where root crops were grown by semisedentary fishing folk. Few scholars were prepared to accept Sauer's theory that the idea of domestication diffused from Southeast Asia to the Near East. But Sauer has proved remarkably prophetic on the importance of root crops and the antiquity of food production in southeast Asia. He insisted on the importance of continuous adaptation to the origin of food production. Sauer's was a pioneer interpretation of how food production began.

Binford:
demographic stress

Lewis Binford rejected Braidwood's contention that human nature brought about agriculture and argued that demographic stress favored food production.[11] At the end of the Pleistocene, he hypothesized, population flowed from some of the world's sea coasts into less populated areas because of rising sea levels as the world's glaciers retreated. These movements led to demographic stress where potentially domesticable plants and animals were to be found; so the development of agriculture was adaptively advantageous for the inhabitants of these regions. Like Braidwood's, Binford's theory has several weaknesses, not least among them being the repeated fluctuations of sea levels in earlier interglacials. Why did they not lead to similar demographic stress and culture change?

Kent Flannery has argued that the transition from hunting and gathering to food production was a gradual process.[12] In a classic paper that examined the mechanisms by which Mesoamericans took up agriculture (Chapter 2), he maintained that the preagricultural peoples of Mesoamerica who later became agriculturalists adapted not to a given environment but to a few plant and animal genera whose range cut across several environments. Using pollen and animal bone analyses from preagricultural sites, Flannery listed the animals and plants upon which these people depended — including century plant leaves, cactus fruits, deer, rabbits, wild waterfowl, and wild grasses, including corn. Foods like the century plant were available all year. Others, like mesquite pods and deer, were exploited during the dry season, but cacti were eaten only during the rains.

Flannery: mechanisms

To obtain these foods the people had to be in the right place at the right season, and the time depended on the plants, not the people: foragers had to plan around the seasons. In other words, their system for procuring food was scheduled. A minor change in any part of the system was reflected in the group's scheduling and might preclude their exploiting foods whose season conflicted with the new schedule.

Genetic changes in two food plants, corn and beans, eventually made these plants increasingly important to the people who used them. Both plants became slightly more productive; so they tended to become more important in the diet. Gradually more and more time was spent on beans and corn, and the groups had to reschedule their activities to accommodate this change. Because a group could not be in two places at once, foods that were procured at times when corn and beans had to be planted or harvested would necessarily be neglected.

In another paper Flannery considered the problems of Near Eastern food production.[13] He stressed that it was not the planting of seeds or the herding of animals that was important but the fact that people moved out to niches to which they were not adapted and removed pressures of natural selection, which now allowed more deviants to survive and eventually selected for characteristics not beneficial under natural conditions. According to Flannery and his colleague Frank Hole,[14] about 20,000 years ago people began to shift from a hunting and gathering way of life to a more specialized economy, including the use of both storage pits and ground stone tools used to crush pigments and tough grass seeds. Seasonal utilization of the environment was typical of many parts of the Near East and Mesoamerica, with different wild foods scheduled for separate seasons. But what upset this equilibrium between culture and environment?

Flannery took Binford's demographic model, in which population growth in some areas of southwestern Asia was greatest in the optimum habitats of the seasonal hunters and gatherers of the hilly flanks and the Palestine woodlands. The population increases caused new groups to split off into more marginal areas where the inhabitants tried to produce artificially, around the *margins* of the optimum zone, stands of cereals as dense as those in the heart of the zone.

Here are the implications of this hypothesis. First, the hunter-gatherer populations in the optimum areas increased before food producing began. This can be tested in the archaeological record by searching for evidence of dense settlement in the optimum areas and large kill sites and other signs of a culture that hunted and collected food intensively to support its large numbers. Second, the earliest evidence of food production will appear on the margins of the hilly flanks and the woodland areas of Palestine in sites where the material culture is strikingly similar to that of the hunter-gatherers in the best areas. Finally, there will be more than one center of domestication for both plants and animals. The advantage of Flannery's hypothesis is that it can be tested in the field, although the testing is likely to be arduous and time consuming. Measuring population increases before food production started will be particularly difficult, if indeed such increases took place.

Now that we can look at world prehistory on a far wider canvas than the pioneers could, we know that agriculture appeared in widely distributed parts of the world at about the same time — in the Near East, China, southeastern Asia, and the Americas. An increasing preoccupation with population has caused those following up on Flannery's work to look more closely at prehistoric demography. Mark Cohen has recently argued that population pressure on a global scale caused many widely separated hunter-gatherer cultures to abandon gathering because their traditional economy could not sustain their growing populations, which had reached the limit that their food resources could support.[15] This point, argues Cohen, was reached at about the same time on all the major landmasses except Australia. Cohen assumes that early agriculture was a logical development of existing gathering and plant conservation techniques, and that agriculture was neither easier nor a more secure subsistence base than hunting and gathering. All that can be said for it is that it does yield more calories per acre of land. He went on to assume that hunter-gatherer populations had mechanisms for controlling excessive local population growth, but that population densities rose steadily throughout early prehistory, so that the same pressures arose all over the world at about the same time. Thus, he concludes, a single explanation for the appearance of agriculture can be invoked for the entire world — population pressure.

Cohen's tantalizing hypothesis is difficult to support from archaeological evidence because some variables such as population size, age-sex structures in society, and many demographic factors are very difficult to recover from archaeological research. The crux of his hypothesis is the point that early agriculture offered only one major advantage — increased food yield. In the short term, the per capita workload and quality of the diet probably declined. An

Cohen: population growth

Farmers

agriculturalist's life is far more arduous than that of a hunter-gatherer. The only circumstances under which people would experiment with a new food procurement system would be if there were a serious ecological imbalance; such an imbalance can be accounted for only by population growth that upset the efficiency of hunting and gathering for small populations. Once less palatable wild foods were being consumed, then the only possible recourse for a growing population is to start producing its own food. And this, after all, is a logical step for people familiar with the germination of plants and used to manipulating vegetable foods for their use.

The Cohen hypothesis is an attractive one as a general explanation, one that is bound to cause discussion and controversy. But how does one account for local variations in the time it took for people to adopt the new economies? David Harris has gone beyond Flannery's work in Mesoamerica. He argues that the more complex the distribution of plant species in an area, the more likely it is that people will settle down in permanent home bases and experiment with cultivation.[16] Conversely, when hunter-gatherers concentrate on one or two plant species to the exclusion of others, in an environment where there are relatively few food resources, they are obliged to move frequently as they exhaust available vegetable staples. This type of rather mobile situation, Harris believes, is not conducive to the emergence of agriculture. Furthermore, he argues, the most likely places for experimentation with food crops are on the edges of major ecosystems. In such areas, maximum local and seasonal variation in vegetable foods is possible.

Harris: local models

Harris's essay points out that there are many variables which have to be understood before we can reconstruct the conditions under which agriculture was first regarded as a profitable activity. We are searching for a set of conditions in which population pressure, distribution of plants, the rate at which the environment is changing, even techniques of harvesting wild grasses, all played their part in making agriculture work. Then there are variations among the potentially domesticable plants and animals, some of which resist domestication because of their long life span, or because parts of their lives take place outside human control. The seasonal distribution of wild vegetable foods or game could also have prevented experiments in domestication, when the seasons during which these wild foods were exploited coincided with the times of year when it was important that the experimenting farmers stay near their growing crops. Under these circumstances, people would tend to pursue their traditional food-getting strategies, rather than risk their lives for an uncertain outcome.

As is obvious, research into the origins of food production has shifted its emphasis from a hunt for origins into a study of conditions under which agriculture and domestication became profitable. Unfortunately, many of the studies which throw light on these conditions involve intangibles such as productivity, caloric intake, and other variables that can only be recovered by scientific use of data from living populations. Unfortunately, too, we have no means of knowing if our projections from living populations into the past are reliable. Kent Flannery, for example, has calculated some productivity figures for maize in Mexico that can be applied to early farming sites in the Tehuacán

Valley.[17] Perhaps similar figures can be generated for other plants, but even if they are, there are numerous intangible factors that could affect the reliability of both historic and prehistoric figures. The new hypotheses on early food production are beginning to change our thinking about culture change. Previously, people had thought that cultural systems remained in equilibrium unless jogged into changing by environmental or other changes. In fact, human culture may have been changing all the time — with our developing technology acting as a means by which humanity has tried to retain the status quo as we occupy more and more diverse environments and are forced to eat more and more unpalatable foods. As Cohen points out, people in prehistory concentrated on big game, then increasingly specialized in vegetable foods, fish, shellfish, and other foods which were not eaten in earlier times. Agriculture was another way of adjusting to changed circumstances; the technology developed to practice it was one of many continual adjustments to the growing population and the increasingly higher costs for food in humanpower terms. Today, humanity is facing the prospect of synthetic foods, another adjustment to growing numbers and the need to feed more and more people. Like other cultural adaptations in human history, this one will probably take place without major disruptions, for people tend to choose the easiest way to preserve the status quo they have enjoyed in their own and earlier generations.

In the final analysis, people probably turned to food production only when other alternatives were no longer practicable. The classic example is the aborigines of extreme northern Australia, who were well aware that the neighbors in New Guinea were engaged in intensive agriculture. They knew, too, how to plant the top of the wild yam so it regerminated. But they never adopted food production, simply because they had no need to become dependent on a lifeway that would reduce their leisure time and produce more food than they needed.

HERDS: DOMESTICATION OF ANIMALS

Potentially tamable species like the wild ox, goat, sheep, and dog were widely distributed in the Old World during the late Pleistocene. New World farmers domesticated only such animals as the llama, the guinea pig, and the turkey, and then only under special conditions and within narrow geographic limits. It is possible that the dog was domesticated in the American Northwest as well, but the evidence is uncertain.

Having one's own herds of domesticated mammals ensured a regular meat supply. The advantages to having a major source of meat under one's own control are obvious. Later, domesticated animals provided byproducts, such as milk, cheese, and butter, as well as skins for clothes and tent coverings, and materials for leather shields and armor. In later millennia, people learned how to breed animals for specialized tasks like plowing, transportation, and traction.

Domestication implies a genetic selection emphasizing special features of continuing use to the domesticator.[18] Wild sheep have no wool, wild cows produce milk only for their offspring, and undomesticated chickens do not produce surplus eggs. Changes in wool-bearing, lactation, or egg production could be achieved by isolating wild populations for selective breeding under human care. Isolating species from a larger gene pool produced domestic sheep with thick, woolly coats and domestic goats providing regular supplies of milk, which formed a staple in the diet of many human populations.

No one knows exactly how domestication of animals began. During the Upper Pleistocene, people were already beginning to concentrate heavily on some species of large mammals for their diet. The Magdalenians of southwestern France arranged much of their life toward pursuing reindeer. At the end of the Pleistocene, hunters in the Near East were concentrating on gazelles and other steppe animals. Wild sheep and goats were intensively hunted on the southern shores of the Caspian Sea. Gregarious animals are those most easily domesticated — they follow the lead of a dominant herd member or all move together.

Hunters often fed off the same herd for a long time, sometimes deliberately sparing young females and immature beasts to keep the source of food alive. Young animals captured alive in the chase might be taken back to camp, becoming dependent on those who caged them, and partially tamed. A hunter could grasp the possibility of gaining control of the movements of a few key members of a herd, who would be followed by the others. Once the experience of pets or of restricting game movements had suggested a new way of life, people might experiment with different species.[19] As part of domestication, animals and humans increased their mutual interdependence.

The archaeological evidence for early domestication is so fragile that nothing survives except the bones of the animals kept by the early farmers. But differences between wild and domestic animal bones are initially often so small that it is difficult to distinguish them unless very large collections are found. In the earliest centuries of domestication, corralled animals were nearly indistinguishable from wild species.

One way of distinguishing between domestic and wild beasts is to age a fossil find by its dentition — the number, kind, and arrangement of its teeth. Hunters normally kill animals of all ages but strongly prefer adolescent beasts, which have the best meat. For breeding, however, herd owners slaughter younger sheep and goats for meat, especially surplus males, but keep females until no longer productive as breeding animals. In some early farming sites such as Zawi Chemi in the Zagros Mountains of the Near East (page 166), the only way domestic sheep could be identified was by the early age at which they were slaughtered.[20]

The process of animal domestication was undoubtedly prolonged, developing in several areas of the Near East at approximately the same time. Although animal bones are scarce and often unsatisfactory as evidence of early domestication, most authorities now agree that the first species to be domesticated in the Near East was the sheep — about 10,500 years ago. Sheep are small animals living in herds, whose carcasses yield much meat for their size. They can readily be penned and isolated to develop a symbiotic relationship with people.

Figure 9.2 *Bos primigenius*, the aurochs or wild ox, as depicted by S. von Heberstain in 1549. It became extinct in Europe in 1627, although recent breeding experiments have reconstructed this formidable beast.

Cattle are much more formidable to domesticate, for their prototype was *Bos primigenius*, the wild ox much hunted by Stone Age people (Figure 9.2). Perhaps cattle were first domesticated from wild animals who were penned for food, ritual, and sacrifice. They may have been captured from wild herds grazing in the gardens.

It should be noted that some animals, like sea mammals, resist domestication because much of their lives are spent out of range of human influence. As mentioned, most early successes with domestication took place with gregarious animals. Kent Flannery has pointed out that penned, gregarious animals can, in a sense, be regarded as a "bank" of food protected and maintained against hard times.[21]

CROPS: DOMESTICATION OF PLANTS

An astonishing range of wild vegetable foods have been domesticated over the millennia.[22] In the Old World wheat, barley, and other cereals that occur wild over much of Asia and Europe became cultivated. In the New World, a different set of crops was tamed. These included Indian corn *(zea mays)*, the only important wild grass to be domesticated. Root crops such as manioc and sweet potatoes, chili peppers, tobacco, and several types of beans were all grown. Common to both Old and New Worlds are gourds, cotton, and two or three other minor crops.

Carl Sauer pointed out that seed crops such as maize were first grown in Mesoamerica, and root crops such as manioc and potatoes were grown more commonly in South America.[23] This fundamental distinction between root and seed crops also applies in the Old World, where tropical regions had many potential domesticates such as the yam and gourds. In southeastern Asia and tropical Africa a long period of intensive gathering and experimenting with the deliberate planting of wild root crops probably preceded the beginnings of formal agriculture. Perhaps, however, the transition from gathering to cultivation of root crops was almost unconscious, for many tubers are easy to grow deliberately. The African yam, for example, can be germinated simply by cutting off its top and burying it in the ground. The hunter-gatherer bands who were familiar with this easy means of conserving their food supplies may simply have intensified their planting efforts to supplement shortages caused by changed circumstances. As with animals, however, certain heavily ex-ploited species tended to resist domestication, among them the long-lived trees and plants, whose life spans were so long that they inhibited human selection. They also tended to cross-pollinate, a process that undoubtedly discouraged human efforts to trigger or control genetic variation.

In the Old World, the qualities of wild wheat, barley, and similar crops are quite different from those of their domestic equivalents. In the wild, they occur in dense stands.[24] The grasses can be harvested easily by simply tapping the stem and gathering the seeds in a basket as they fall off. This technique is effective because the wild grain is attached to the stem by a brittle joint, or *rachis.* When the grass is tapped, the weak rachis breaks and the grass falls into the basket.

The conversion of wild grass to domestic strains must have involved some selection of desirable properties in the wild grasses (Figure 9.3). To cultivate cereal crops extensively, the yield of an acre of grass has to be increased significantly before the work is worth it. If the yield remains low, it is easier to gather wild seeds and save the labor of cultivation. A tougher rachis must be

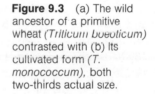

Figure 9.3 (a) The wild ancestor of a primitive wheat *(Triticum boeoticum)* contrasted with (b) its cultivated form *(T. monococcum),* both two-thirds actual size.

developed to prevent the seed from falling on the ground and regerminating. By toughening the rachis, people could control propagation of the grass, sowing it when and where they liked and harvesting it with a knife blade or sickle.[25] Certain patterns of grass harvesting, like the hand and sickle methods used in the Near East even today, tended to select for useful mutants like the tough rachis, thereby reinforcing the trend toward control of the grasses by humans. The mutations that did take place helped already adaptable wild grasses to grow outside their normal wild habitats.[26] Early farmers seem to have grown cereals with remarkable success, but probably only succeeded after long experimenting in different places.

TECHNOLOGY AND DOMESTICATION

The technological consequences of food production were, in their way, as important as the new economies. A more settled way of life and some decline in hunting and gathering slowly led to long-term residences, lasting agricultural styles, and more substantial housing. As they had done for millennia, people built their permanent homes with the raw materials most abundant in their environment. The early farmers of the Near East worked dried mud into small houses with flat roofs; these were cool in summer and warm in winter. At night, they slept on the flat roofs during the hot season. Some less substantial houses had reed roofs. In the more temperate zones of Europe, with wetter climates, timber was used to build thatched-roof houses of various shapes and sizes. Early African farmers often built huts of grass, sticks, and anthill clay. Nomadic pastoralists of the northern steppes had no concern with a permanent and durable home, yet they, too, took advantage of the side benefits of having a domestic food supply: they made clothing from the skins as well as tents to shelter them during the icy winters.

Agriculture is a seasonal activity, with long periods of the year when the fields are lying fallow or are supporting growing crops. Any farmer is confronted with the problem of storing food in ways the hunter-gatherer never has to ponder. A new technology of storage came into being. Grain storage bins, jars, or clay-lined pits became an essential part of the agricultural economy for stockpiling food for the lean months and against periods of famine. The bins (Figure 9.1) might be made of wattle and daub, clay, or timber. Basket-lined silos protected valuable grain against rodents.

The hunter-gatherer uses skins, wood containers, gut pouches, and sometimes baskets for carrying vegetable foods back from the bush. But the farmer faces far more formidable transport problems: he must carry his harvest back to the village, keep ready-for-use supplies of foods in the house as opposed to storage bins, and store water. So early farmers began to use gourds as water carriers, and to make clay vessels that were both waterproof and capable of being used to carry and cook food (Figure 9.4). They made pots by coiling rolls of clay or building up the walls of vessels from a lump and firing them in simple hearths. Clay vessels were much more durable than skin or leather receptacles. Some pots were used for several decades before being broken and

Figure 9.4 Pottery manufacture. A common method of potmaking was to build up the walls from coils of clay (a). The pot was then smoothed and decorated (b), and fired, either in an open hearth (c) or a kiln. These pictures illustrate Pueblo Indian pottery manufacturing techniques from the Southwestern U.S., and are, of course, not necessarily typical of all potters.

Figure 9.5 Using a stone adze to fell a tree. A Tefalmin farmer at work in 1966, in New Guinea.

abandoned. Pottery did not appear simultaneously with the appearance of agriculture. The Jomon hunter-gatherers of Japan were making simple clay pots at least 14,000 years ago. They lived a more-or-less sedentary life by their shell middens, using clay vessels long before agriculture became part of their way of life. However, pottery was first used by farmers in the Near East about 8,000 B.P.[27]

The technology of gathering consisted in most places of a simple digging stick, sometimes with a stone weight. The first farmers continued to use the digging stick, but placed considerable emphasis on the wooden and clay bladed hoe. The hoe blade was made of metal in later millennia, the handle either long or short, depending on cultural preference. The plow, with its wooden or iron blade, was a relatively late development (Chapter 15), which enabled people to turn over the soil to a much greater depth than ever before. Every farmer has to clear wild vegetation and weeds from the fields, and it is hardly surprising to find a new emphasis on the ax and the adze. The simple axes of pioneer farmers were soon replaced by more elaborate forms in metal. Present-day experiments in Denmark and New Guinea have shown that the ground and polished edges of stone axes are remarkably effective in clearing woodland and felling trees (Figure 9.5).[28] In later millennia the alloying of copper and bronze, and later, the development of iron cutting edges, made forest clearance even easier.

New tools meant new technologies to produce tougher working edges. At first the farmers used ground and polished stone, placing a high premium on suitable rocks, which were traded from quarry sites over enormous distances. Perhaps the most famous ax quarries are in western Europe, where ax blanks were traded the length of the British Isles, and Grand Pressigny flint from France was prized over thousands of square miles. In the Near East and Mexico, one prized toolmaking material was obsidian, a volcanic rock prized for its easy working properties, and for its ornamental appearance. Early obsidian trade routes carried tools and ornaments hundreds of miles from their places of origin. By using spectrographic techniques, scientists have been able to trace obsidian over long distances to such places of origin as Lipari Island off Italy and Lake Van in Turkey.[29]

All these developments in technology made people more and more dependent on exotic raw materials, many of which were unobtainable in their own territory. We see the beginnings of widespread long-distance trading networks that were to burgeon even more rapidly with the emergence of the first urban civilizations.

Chronological Table F

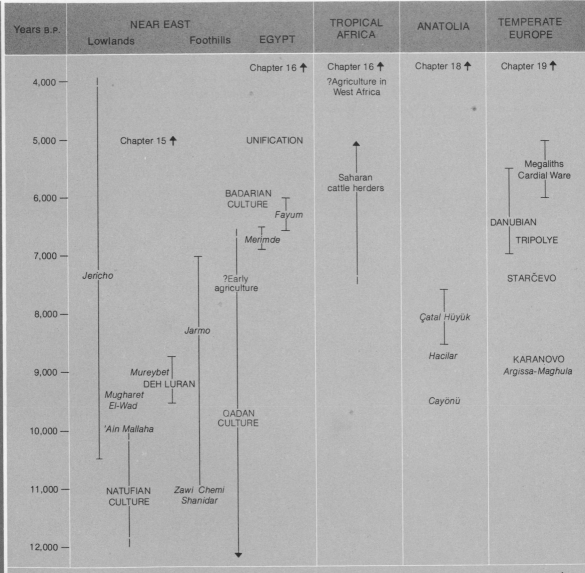

Years B.P.	NEAR EAST			TROPICAL AFRICA	ANATOLIA	TEMPERATE EUROPE
	Lowlands	Foothills	EGYPT			
			Chapter 16 ↑	Chapter 16 ↑	Chapter 18 ↑	Chapter 19 ↑
4,000 —				?Agriculture in West Africa		
5,000 —		Chapter 15 ↑	UNIFICATION			Megaliths Cardial Ware
6,000 —			BADARIAN CULTURE	Saharan cattle herders		
			Fayum			DANUBIAN
7,000 —			*Merimde*			TRIPOLYE
	Jericho		?Early agriculture			STARČEVO
8,000 —					Çatal Hüyük	
		Jarmo				
9,000 —		*Mureybet* DEH LURAN			Hacilar	KARANOVO *Argissa-Maghula*
	Mugharet El-Wad		QADAN CULTURE		*Çayönü*	
10,000 —	*'Ain Mallaha*					
11,000 —	NATUFIAN CULTURE	*Zawi Chemi Shanidar*				
12,000 —						

Chapter 8 ↑   Chapter 6 ↑

Chapter Ten

ORIGINS OF FOOD PRODUCTION: EUROPE AND THE NEAR EAST

PREVIEW

- Both the Kurdish foothills and the Jordan Valley have yielded traces of a gradual technological shift from hunting and gathering to food production.

- The Natufian culture of the Jordan Valley flourished as early as 12,000 B.P. and lasted to at least 10,000 years ago. The Natufians were intensive gatherers and their settlement at Jericho formed the nucleus of a more lasting settlement with massive defense walls. These Jericho people engaged in extensive trading in obsidian and other commodities.

- The hilly flanks of the Near East were occupied by seasonal hunter-gatherers about 11,000 years ago. By 8,000 B.P. the people were living in more permanent settlements and were on their way to food production. By 7,500 B.P. a village farming economy was widespread in the Near East, fostered by extensive inter-village trading networks. One well-known site is Jarmo in the Zagros foothills, a cluster of mud houses that yielded abundant evidences of cereal agriculture.

- The agricultural towns of Hacilar and Çatal Hüyük in Turkey provide evidence both of agriculture and of extensive trading in Anatolia by 9,000 B.P. Çatal Hüyük was a substantial trading settlement with shrines and a distinctive artistic tradition.

- European agriculture is thought to have developed from Balkan roots at least as early as 7,500 B.P. The Starčevo culture flourished for a considerable period, while the Danubian people settled the fertile soils of Central Europe and the Low Countries, probably by 7,000 B.P. Western Europe was settled by farming peoples by 6,500 B.P.

- Megalithic tombs are found over a wide area of western Europe and the Mediterranean around 6,000 B.P. The origins and inspiration of these monumental sculptures and the rituals associated with them are a mystery.

- Scandinavia was settled by farming peoples by 5500 B.P.; Britain a few centuries earlier. Hunter-gatherers continued to flourish in arctic latitudes where agriculture was impracticable.

Much of the theorizing about early food production has stemmed from ar-chaeological research in the Near East, where many early farming settlements are found.[1]* (See Figure 10.1.)

JERICHO AND THE LOWLANDS

At the end of the Pleistocene both highlands and coastal plains in the Near East were inhabited by hunter-gatherers who hunted wild sheep, goats, gazelles, and other mammals, as well as relying heavily on wild vegetable foods.[2] Their microlithic toolkits included many grindstones used for processing cereal

* See pages 380–381 for notes to Chapter 10.

Figure 10.1 Early farming sites in the Near East, Europe, and the Nile Valley.

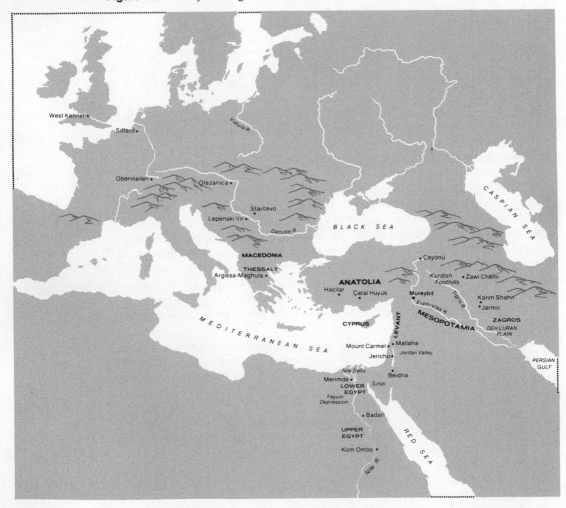

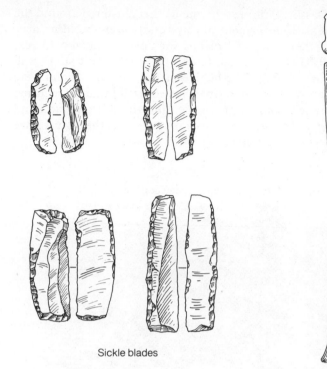

Figure 10.2 Natufian sickle blades and a bone handle for such blades. This handle (about one-half actual size) bears a deer's head.

Sickle blades

Sickle handle

grasses. One such culture was the so-called Natufian, named after a cave in Israel, which flourished over much of the coastal strip from southern Turkey to the fringes of the Nile Valley.

15,000 to 11,000 B.P.

The Natufians hunted gazelle but obtained much of their food from stands of wild cereal grasses.[3] Their toolkits included flint sickle blades, of which the cutting edges bear a characteristic gloss that was achieved by friction against grass stalks; the kits also contained bone handles in which the blades were mounted (Figure 10.2).

Natufian 12,000 to 10,000 B.P.

Natufians began to live in fairly permanent settlements. 'Ain Mallaha in northern Israel, for example, covers at least half an acre, with circular houses on stone foundations. Storage chambers were an integral part of the houses, a clear sign of increasing sedentariness. Stone bowls, mortars, and paved floors are also common, and many burials reflect greater social differentiation by their varying amounts of adornment. This increasing social complexity logically precedes the more elaborate class structure of later, urban life. But other Natufians were still living in rockshelters and caves. A relative abundance of trade objects, such as seashells, seems to indicate expanded bartering in both house communities and rockshelter communities. Trading was an activity destined to spread greatly in future millennia.

'Ain Mallaha 10,000 B.P.

Mughared el-Wad

By 10,500 B.P. a temporary Natufian settlement at the bubbling Jericho spring had formed the locus of later farming villages.[4] But the Natufians were

Jericho 10,500 to 9,500 B.P.

soon succeeded by more lasting farming settlements that clustered around the spring. Soon these people, without benefit of clay vessels, were building massive defense walls around their town. A rock-cut ditch over 2.7 meters (3 yds) deep and 3.2 meters (10 ft) wide was bordered by a finely built stone wall complete with towers (Figure 10.3). The behive-shaped huts of Jericho were clustered within the defenses. The communal labor of wall building required both political and economic resources on a scale unheard of a few thousand years earlier. Why walls were needed remains a mystery, but they must have been for defense, resulting from group competition for scarce resources.

Figure 10.3 Excavated remains of the great tower in early Jericho.

Farmers

The Jericho people engaged in extensive trading activities, which brought to their town bitumen, salt, obsidian, and shells from the Mediterranean and Dead Sea. They also kept large flocks of goats and sheep. Another site, Beidha, has produced many specimens of wild barley, which must have been either gathered in enormous quantities from natural stands or sown deliberately. The emmer wheat (goat grass) seeds from Beidha show a wide range in size, as if domestication had only recently begun. Several other minor crops were either grown or gathered. Large numbers of young goats were also found; their ages imply selective slaughtering, strongly suggesting domestication rather than hunting.[5]

HILLY FLANKS IN THE NEAR EAST

The hilly flanks of the Near East, which are inland from the Mediterranean Sea and at a higher elevation, witnessed a long and complex transition from hunting and gathering to food production. Around 11,000 B.P., wild goats were a primary quarry for the hunters and gatherers exploiting the resources of the foothills. An adaptive trend like that of the Natufian is found in this region. Open seasonal sites such as Zawi Chemi Shanidar were occupied by people living in round, semisubterranean houses. The people killed many immature wild sheep, as if they had either fenced in the grazing grounds, penned herds, or even so tamed the sheep that they could control the age at which they would be killed.[6]

Zawi Chemi
Shanidar
11,000 B.P.

About 9,000 B.P., the inhabitants of Mureybet in northern Syria were gathering wild wheat as well as barley.[7] Conceivably they were cultivating these wild grasses, but there is no certain evidence for farming at the village, which covered about a hectare (2.5 acres). Mureybet lies outside the wild distribution of einkorn today, for its habitat is cooler and wetter than the Euphrates Valley. Either the climate was different when the village was occupied, or the people were experimenting with cultivation of einkorn outside its natural habitat.

Mureybet
9,000 B.P.

Experimentation was certainly complete by 8,000 B.P., when village life became more widespread. A fairly intensive agricultural economy was widely distributed over southwest Asia by 7,500 B.P., fostered by extensive trade networks distributing obsidian, much prized for ornaments and sickle blades. Farming villages dating to this time flourished at Jericho and along the Syrian and Palestinian coasts.

One of the best-known early villages is Jarmo, in the Zagros foothills southeast of Zawi Chemi Shanidar, mainly dated to about 7,000 B.P.[8] Jarmo was little more than a cluster of twenty-five houses built of baked mud, forming an irregular huddle separated by small alleyways and courtyards. Storage bins and clay ovens were an integral part of the structures. The Jarmo deposits yielded abundant traces of agriculture: seeds of barley, emmer wheat, and minor crops were found with the bones of sheep and goats. Hunting had declined in importance; only a few wild animal bones testify to such activity. But the

Jarmo
**11,000 to
7,000 B.P.**

toolkit still included Stone Age-type tools together with sickle blades, grinding stones, and other implements of tillage.

The lowlands to the southwest of the Kurdish foothills are a vast alluvial delta watered by the Tigris and the Euphrates rivers. As early as 9,500 to 8,750 B.P., goat herdsmen were wandering over the Deh Luran plain east of the Tigris River.[9] In the late winter and spring they harvested wheat, but nine-tenths of their vegetable diet came from wild plants.

Deh Luran
7,500 to 8,750 B.P.

ANATOLIA

By 9,500 B.P., scattered farming villages began to appear in the headwaters of the Tigris River and to the west in Anatolia. At Çayönü in southern Turkey, a small community of food producers roughly contemporary with Jarmo used tools resembling those from the Levant and Zagros regions. Obsidian was plentiful and native copper was hammered into simple ornaments. Domestic pigs and sheep were in use, flax domesticated.[10]

Çayönü
9,500 B.P.

The first evidence of food production on the Anatolian plateau to the west extends back to about 7,000 B.P. But farming could have flourished even earlier in the rolling highlands of Turkey. British archaeologist James Mellaart excavated a remarkable early farming village at Hacilar in southwestern Anatolia, which was founded about 8,700 B.P.[11] Seven phases of village occupation took place at Hacilar before its inhabitants moved. They lived in small rectangular houses with courtyards, hearths, ovens, and plastered walls.

Hacilar
8,750 B.P.

Figure 10.4 Schematic reconstruction of houses and shrines from Level VI at Çatal Hüyük, Anatolia, showing their flat-roof architecture and roof entrances.

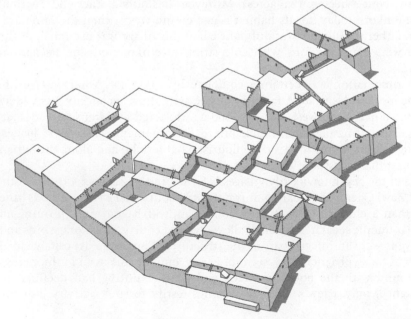

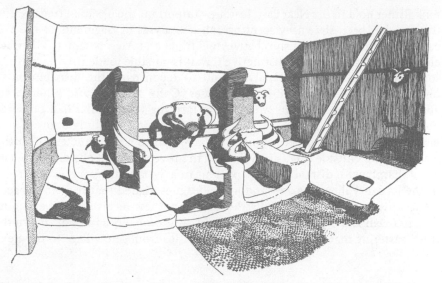

Figure 10.5 Reconstruction of the east and south walls of Shrine VI.14 at Çatal Hüyük, Anatolia, with sculptured ox heads, horns, benches, and relief models of bulls and rams. The shrine was entered by the ladder at right.

No pottery was used at Hacilar, but basketry and leather containers probably were. Barley and emmer wheat were cultivated, and some wild grass seeds were also eaten. The bones of sheep or goats and cattle and deer are present, but there was no evidence for the domestication of any animal except the dog. Hacilar was a simple and unsophisticated settlement, probably typical of many communities in the Near East in the early millennia of farming.

The simplicity of Hacilar contrasts dramatically with the Çatal Hüyük mound, 200 miles (322 km) to the east.[12] Çatal Hüyük covers 13 hectares (32 acres); it was a town of numerous small houses built of sun-dried brick, which were designed to back onto one another, occasionally separated by small courtyards. Roofs were flat, and the outside walls of the houses provided a convenient defense wall (Figure 10.4). The town was rebuilt at least twelve times after about 8,000 B.P., presumably when the houses began to crumble or the population swelled.

Çatal Hüyük
8,000 to 7,600 B.P.

A most remarkable feature of Çatal Hüyük was its artistic tradition, preserved in paintings on carefully plastered walls and in sculptures, some of them parts of shrines (Figure 10.5). Most depicted women or bulls. Some paintings show women giving birth to bulls. Many art themes were about fertility and the regeneration of life, and figurines of women in childbirth have been found.

Much of Çatal Hüyük's prosperity resulted from its monopoly of the obsidian trade from quarries in nearby montains. Seashells came to Çatal Hüyük from the Mediterranean for conversion into ornaments. In later millennia trade in raw materials and ornaments between Anatolia and southwestern Asia continued to flourish, as metallurgy and other attributes of urban life took firmer hold in the Near East. Just how important the obsidian trade was in the area has been shown by spectrographic analyses of fragments of the volcanic glass in hundreds of sites between Turkey and Mesopotamia. The trace elements in obsidian are so distinctive that it is possible to identify the natural source of the glass by this analysis, and to reconstruct the distribution of obsidian from dozens of different localities. Colin Renfrew and others were able to identify no less than twelve early farming villages that had obtained obsidian from the Ciftlik area of central Turkey.[13] The study showed that eighty percent of the chipped stone in villages within 300 kilometers of Ciftlik was obsidian. Outside this "supply zone," the percentages of obsidian dropped away sharply with distance, to five percent in a Syrian village, and 0.1 percent in the Jordan Valley. Renfrew and his colleagues argued that regularly spaced villages were passing about half the obsidian they received to their more distant neighbors. Much early farming trade was probably a form of "down the line" bartering that passed various commodities from one village to the next.

AN EXPLANATION OF CHRONOLOGY

For years, European archaeologists like V. Gordon Childe believed that agriculture, metallurgy, and most significant technological developments had spread into temperate Europe from the Near East.[14] Today, people no longer think in terms of vast hordes of farmers and metallurgists flooding into temperate latitudes from the innovative East. Radiocarbon chronologies have radically altered our view of European prehistory.

Childe and other pioneers worked before radiocarbon dates were available. All chronologies of epochs before about 5,000 B.P., when civilization emerged in the Near East, were based on artifact typologies and inspired guesswork. The first radiocarbon dates showed that European agriculture and metallurgy had begun much later than in the Near East and there seemed nothing wrong with the traditional hypotheses.

When people started to calibrate radiocarbon dates against tree-ring chronologies, they found that European timescales between 3,500 and 7,000 B.P. had to be corrected several centuries backward.[15] But Egyptian historical (that is, from the written record) chronology from 5,000 B.P. now agrees more closely with calibrated C14 dates, rather than being several centuries too recent, as they were before (Table 10.1)

British archaeologist Colin Renfrew has now moved the dates for temperate Europe back far enough to rupture the traditional diffusionist links between the Near East and Europe (Figure 10.6). That is, it is now apparent that events in Europe were contemporary with those in the Near East and not a later result of the spread of Near East culture, as was once thought. Using historical dates for the Mediterranean has thrown what Renfrew aptly calls a "fault line" across the Mediterranean and southern Europe. This fault line marks a chronological boundary, to the west of which radiocarbon (C14) dates after 3,000 B.C. have been pushed back by calibration, making them older than the accurate, historically attested dates for the eastern Mediterranean and the Balkans,

Table 10.1 Calibration of C14 dates.

C14 / corrected date	Radiocarbon date (Half-life of 5,568 years)	Calibrated date: Corrected date in years[a]
Earlier Later	150 B.P.	265 B.P.
	450 B.P.	510 B.P.
	950 B.P.	920 B.P.
	1450 B.P.	1415 B.P.
	2250 B.P.	2320 B.P.
	2500 B.P.	2550 B.P.
	3000 B.P.	3250 B.P.
	3500 B.P.	3835 B.P.
	4000 B.P.	4520 B.P.
	4500 B.P.	3245 B.P.
	5000 B.P.	5785 B.P.
	5500 B.P.	6375 B.P.
	6000 B.P.	6845 B.P.
Corrected C14	6500 B.P.	7350 B.P.
date date		

Note: Except for those dates set in boldface, the C14 dates in this book are not calibrated to allow for errors caused by variations in the amount of C14 in the atmosphere. This correction is made by using tree-ring readings for calibrating C14 dates to correspond with actual dates in years. The dates were not calibrated because we were unable to locate a conversion table that had wide enough acceptance. The latest table to be published is an objectively derived conversion based on statistical treatment of the most generally used calibration tables now active. I have used this table in my conversion because it seems to be the best now available for my purposes. See R. M. Clark, "A Calibration Curve for Radiocarbon Dates," *Antiquity*, 49, 196 (1975), pp. 251–266, which includes suitable tables. I have added this simple conversion table so that you can make approximate calibrations. Treat this table as an approximate guide to the amount of variation in C14 dates from about 7,000 years ago to the present. *Readers who want greater accuracy are strongly advised to consult Clark's original paper.* Many statistical variables are involved.

[a] These dates give approximate variations at about 500-year intervals. In addition, there are numerous minor variations

which are east of the fault. Of course this fault line is a theoretical boundary. But it serves to show that, with the new calibrated chronologies, prehistoric Europeans were much less affected by cultural developments in the Near East than Childe had suggested. They adopted metallurgy and other innovations on their own, just as early as many such inventions were brought into use in the Near East.

EUROPEAN FARMERS

The temperate zones north and west of Greece and the Balkans provided environments contrasting to the seasonal rainfall areas in the Near East. Timber and thatch replace the mud brick used effectively for houses in Near Eastern villages. Agricultural techniques had to reflect the European climate. The initial development of agriculture in Europe coincided with a warm, moist phase. Midsummer temperatures were at least 2° C warmer than now.[16]

Origins of Food Production　　173

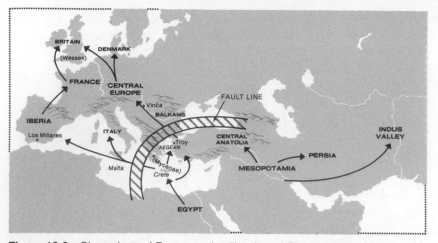

Figure 10.6 Chronology of Europe and calibration of C14 chronology. With the uncalibrated chronology, the traditional view of European prehistory had agriculture and other innovations spreading northwestward from the Near East and eastern Mediterranean into continental Europe. The calibrated chronology has hardly affected the dates after 3000 B.C. for the eastern Mediterranean and sites to the southeast of the fault line marked on the map. The calibrated dates after 3000 B.C. for sites to the west and northwest of the fault line have been pushed back several centuries by calibration, so that the old notion of innovation from the east is replaced by new theories postulating less eastern influence.

The forest cover was mainly mixed oak woodland, shadier tree cover that reduced the grazing resources of larger game animals like deer and wild cattle. As a result, hunter-gatherer populations may have shifted to coastal and lakeside settlements where fish, waterfowl, and sea mammals were readily available.[17]

Argissa-Maghula **9,000 B.P.**

The earliest evidence of food production in Europe comes from the Argissa-Maghula village mound in Greek Thessaly (Figure 10.7). Domestic cattle, sheep, and pig bones in the lower levels of the site have been C14 dated to c. 9,000 B.P.[18] These now are the earliest tame cattle in the world. The early dates for cattle and pig domestication argue strongly for independent domestication of animals in southeastern Europe. The Argissa-Maghula farmers were cultivating emmer wheat and barley and keeping sheep. Hunting was still important.

Karanovo culture

The earliest agricultural people of the Balkans settled in compact villages of one-room dwellings built of baked mud plastered on poles and wicker. These Karanovo culture settlements were occupied over long periods. Farming villages occur on brown forest soils and alluvial river plains. The economy was based on cultivated wheat and barley and domesticated sheep and goats. Ruth Tringham argues that cereal agriculture reached this area from the Near East, claiming a lack of continuity between earlier hunting artifacts and the new farming cultures.[19] A number of culture traits, including *Spondylus* shells (a characteristic Mediterranean mussel much valued because it could be used for

Farmers

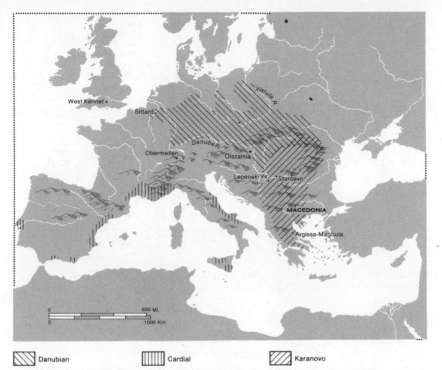

| 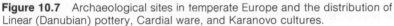 Danubian | Cardial | Karanovo |

Figure 10.7 Archaeological sites in temperate Europe and the distribution of Linear (Danubian) pottery, Cardial ware, and Karanovo cultures.

ornamentation), clay seals and figurines, and reaping knives, show continuing connections with the Mediterranean world. The Starčevo site near Belgrade gives a vivid picture of the economic life and pottery styles of this widespread farming culture. It was in this area that metallurgy developed around 5,000 B P (see Chapter 19).

Starčevo
7,500 B.P.

Danubian (Linear Pottery) Culture

Farther north, in the fertile plains and the valley of the Danube, we find the most distinctive early European farming tradition, on the middle Danube extending as far west as southern Holland and eastward toward the Vistula River and the upper Dniester. These people were the *Danubians* (Linear pottery culture group), known to generations of European archaeologists because of their characteristic pottery.[20] The Danubians made round-based vessels with lines (Figure 10.8), spirals, and meanders carefully incised on the clay. They cultivated barley, einkorn, emmer wheat, and minor crops including flax. These they planted on the fertile loess soils (rich, fine, wind-deposited soils) of central Europe using a simple form of shifting agriculture that involved careful soil selection and use of lighter soils. The Danubians rapidly settled the loess

Danubian
7,000 to 5,500 B.P.

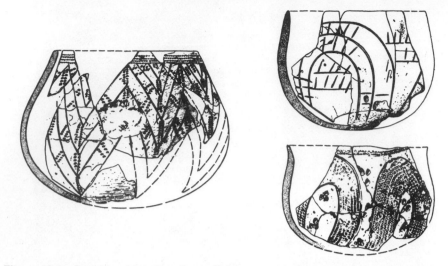

Figure 10.8 Danubian *Linearbandkeramik* (Linear pottery) from Sittard, Holland, with characteristic line decoration (one-fourth actual size).

zones from the Danube to the Low Countries. Cattle, goats, sheep, and dogs were domesticated, and domestic herds were important in the Danubian diet.

6,800 B.P.
7,370 B.P.

The Danubians were living in southern Holland by 6,800 B.P., and introduced food production to northwestern Europe much later than it appeared in areas to the southeast.* By 7,000 B.P. Danubian villages contained rectangular houses from 20 to 50 meters (18 to 46 yd) long, which were made of timber and thatch; presumably these houses sheltered stock as well as several families (Figure 10.9).

Originally, the Danubians practiced their wasteful agricultural techniques on the loess lands. Growing populations obliged some of them to move onto heavier and poorer soils. We find regional developments of Danubian culture in parts of central Europe. Some farmers had to rely more on hunting and gathering because the soils of their gardens did not yield enough food to support their families. Defensive earthworks appeared later, as if vigorous competition for land had caused intertribal stress.

Tripolye Culture
6,800 B.P.

While the Danubians were settling in central Europe, other peoples were moving onto the Russian plains in the east. People somewhat similar to the Danubians occupied farming settlements in the Ukraine and around the Dnieper River. Like the Danubians, they lived in rectangular houses. They reached the height of their prosperity during the period of the Tripolye culture, a period when many villages were laid out with houses in a circle (Figure 10.10).

* In this chapter I apply the new tree-ring calibrated radiocarbon dates instead of the conventional radiocarbon chronology used in many other chapters. For your convenience I have placed C14 dates in Roman type with the calibrated reading in bold type below. You can make comparisons with other areas using conventional C14 chronology. For calibrated dates used, see Table 10.1 on page 173 listing radiocarbon dates with their equivalent corrected dates.

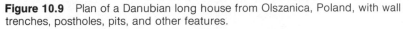

Figure 10.9 Plan of a Danubian long house from Olszanica, Poland, with wall trenches, postholes, pits, and other features.

Mediterranean and Swiss Lake Cultures

As the Danubians were cultivating the plains of western and central Europe, new farming economies were becoming established around the shores of the Mediterranean. Extensive bartering networks from one end of the Mediterranean to the other exchanged seashells, obsidian, exotic stones, and, later, copper ore. A characteristic type of pottery decorated with the distinctive imprint of the *Cardium* (scallop) shell is widely distributed on the northeastern shores of the Mediterranean, on Adriatic coasts, and as far west as Malta, Sardinia, southern France, North Africa, and eastern Spain (Figure 10.11).[21] Cardium-decorated wares spread widely because of trading. The new economies were flourishing in the western Mediterranean and in France and Switzerland by 6,000 B.P.

A series of farming villages were thriving on the shores of the Swiss lakes at about this time.[22] They were occupied by cattle-owning farmers, who cultivated barley and wheat as well as many minor crops, including cider apples and flax (used for textiles). The houses were built on the damp ground be-

Cardium-decorated wares
6,000 B.P.
6,845 B.P.

Figure 10.10 A Tripolye culture village.

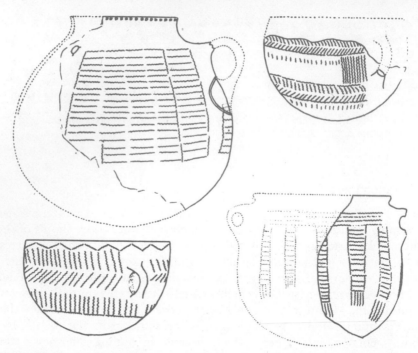

Figure 10.11 Cardium-shell-impressed pottery from southern France (one-fourth actual size).

tween the lake reed beds and the scrub brush of the valley behind. Small rectangular huts were replaced by larger two-room houses. Some villages grew to include between twenty-four and seventy-five houses clustered on the lake-shore, a density of population much the same as modern Swiss villages which have about thirty households. The Swiss farming cultures were contemporary with other scattered agricultural communities between the Mediterranean and the English Channel, far beyond the western frontiers of Danubian territory.

Northern and Western European Cultures

As early as 5,000 B.P., some French farmers were building large communal tombs of stone, known to archaeologists as *megaliths* ("large stone" in Greek). Megaliths are found as far north as Scandinavia, in Britain, Ireland, France, Spain, the western Mediterranean, Corsica, and Malta. For years, archaeologists thought that megaliths had originated in the eastern Mediterranean about 4,500 B.P. and spread westward into Spain with colonists from the Aegean, who had carried a custom of collective burial and their religion with them. Megalithic tombs were believed to have then been built in western Europe, witnesses to a lost faith perhaps spread by pilgrims, missionaries, or merchants. With their massive stones and large burial chambers, megaliths remained one of the mysteries of European prehistory (Figure 10.12).[23]

This popular and widely accepted hypothesis was badly weakened by C14 dates from France that turned out to be earlier than others from western Europe. Furthermore, new calibrated dates have dated Spanish megalithic sites and their associated culture to as early as c. 6,000 B.P., much earlier than their alleged prototypes in the Aegean. Thus, megaliths were being built in western Europe at least a millennium before massive funerary architecture became fashionable in the eastern Mediterranean. This remarkable freestanding architecture is a unique, local European creation.

Agriculture and domestic stock were in use in southern Scandinavia and on the north European plains by 5,500 B.P. A vigorous hunting and gathering **5,500 B.P.** cultural tradition had flourished on the shores of the Baltic for thousands of years.[24] Then it seems that some hunters adopted the new economy from the Danubian farmers on their southern boundaries; pollen diagrams from Scandinavian bogs show a striking disturbance in the natural forest cover at this time. The forest, especially elm trees, diminishes in the diagrams; cereal grasses and the pollen of typical cultivation weeds appear for the first time. Layers of charcoal fragments testify to forests being cleared by burning. The drop in elm cover is thought to mean that this tree was used for cattle fodder.

General features of this early farming activity are familiar — growing of cereal crops and grazing of stock, sizable settlements of rectangular houses, and forests cleared with polished stone axes. The farmers began building sizable family tombs. They developed a characteristic clay beaker with a flared neck, later widely distributed over central and northwestern Europe.

Figure 10.12 Interior of a megalithic chamber tomb at West Kennett, England, C14 dated to about 5,500 B.P. (After Piggott.)

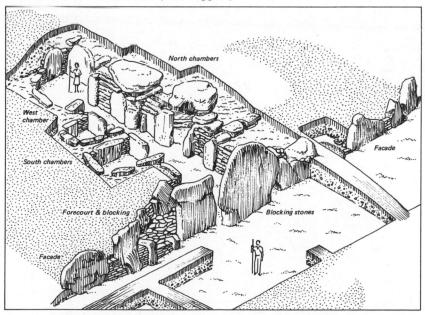

The British Isles stand at the extreme northwest corner of Europe, the receiving end of culture traits from many peoples. Before 6,000 B.P., farming communities were established in southern Britain. Communal burial chambers and large cattle camps with extensive earthworks came into use. British sites reflect cultural influences from both western France and Scandinavia. Flourishing barter networks carried stone blades, and the material to make them, throughout England. Similar exploitation of flint and other stone outcrops is persistent in early European farming.[25]

By 5,000 B.P. or thereabouts, stone-using peasant farmers were well established over most of temperate Europe. Many Stone Age hunters had adopted the new economies; still others lived by hunting and gathering alongside the farmers. Both subsistence patterns survived side by side for many centuries. In Scandinavia fishermen and fowlers of the Ertebølle culture absorbed some new economic practices without making major changes in their traditional way of life. They traded fish for grain products grown by their neighbors, and lived on the outskirts of cleared farmlands.

Chapter Eleven

EARLY FARMERS OF AFRICA

PREVIEW

☙ The Nile Valley was a rich environment for human settlement in late Pleistocene times. The Qadan culture flourished by the Nile from 14,500 years ago, until as late as 6,550 B.P. It was typical of hunter-gatherer traditions in Egypt at the end of the Pleistocene.

☙ There are no signs of extensive agricultural settlement in Egypt before 6,500 B.P., although evidence of earlier farming may someday be found. Opinion is divided over whether the Egyptians developed food production on their own, or with the aid of cereals or animals from the Near East or the west.

☙ The earliest Egyptian farmers probably had little need for irrigation agriculture, the appearance of which appears to coincide with the political unification of Egypt in about 5,000 B.P.

☙ The Sahara was sufficiently well watered to support cattle herding peoples from about 7,500 to 5,000 B.P. With the desiccation of the desert, Saharan peoples moved southward into sub-Saharan Africa, where they domesticated summer rainfall crops like sorghum and millet.

☙ Cattle herding people were living in East Africa by 3,000 B.P., but agriculture and domesticated animals did not spread to tropical Africa as a whole until the advent of ironworking about two thousand years ago.

The Nile Valley was a rich environment for human settlement in the late Pleistocene times.[1]* The Nile 14,000 years ago already flowed through desert, although intervals of higher rainfall did occur, the last between about 13,000 and 11,000 B.P. At that time the Nile Valley was occupied by hunting and

Chronological
Table F

* See pages 381–382 for notes to Chapter 11.

gathering populations, making much use of wild grains and seeds as well as large game animals, fish, and birds.[2]

HUNTER-GATHERERS ON THE NILE

Quadan culture
**14,500 to
6,550 B.P.**

One such culture of hunter-gatherers, named the *Qadan*, flourished between about 14,500 and 6,550 B.P. It is best known from microlithic tools found on riverside campsites near the Nile. In the earlier stages of the Qadan, fishing and big-game hunting were important. But large numbers of grindstones and grinding equipment came from a few localities, which seems to show that gathering wild grains was significant to at least part of the culture. Some Qadan settlements were probably large and occupied for long periods. The dead were buried in cemeteries in shallow pits covered with stone slabs. Some pits held two bodies. In six instances, small stone tools were embedded in the bones of these Qadan people, who must have met a violent end.[3]

Other distinct cultural traditions are known to have prospered in the Nile Valley at this time. Around Kom Ombo, upstream of Qadan country, Stone Age hunter-gatherers lived on the banks of lagoons and flood channels of the Nile, seeking game in the riverside woodlands and on the plains overlooking the valley. They fished for catfish and perch in the swamps. Here too, wild grasses were important in the hunter-gatherer economy from about 14,000 B.P.[4]

The valley is unusual in that its water supply depends on the seasonal floods from Ethiopia, not on rainfall. Its boundaries are severely constricted by the desert, confining humans to the Nile banks. This highly favorable environment was being exploited by hunters with a bow and arrow toolkit superior to that of earlier millennia, so that population densities inevitably rose, increasing competition for a habitat that was the only means of survival for the people of the valley. They could not move away from the river, for the arid deserts would not support them. The logical solution was more specialized exploitation of natural resources — or agriculture.

EARLY FARMING IN EGYPT: FAYUM AND MERIMDE

Although there are claims of finds of barley (possibly wild-growing) and grindstones in the Nile Valley dating to as early as 14,500 B.P., there is no sign of extensive agricultural settlement in Egypt before about 6,500 B.P.[5] Conventional scholarship has always held that cereal crops and domesticated animals were introduced into the valley from southwest Asia. But recent researches have suggested that the picture is more complex and that both wheat and a species of sheep were introduced into the Nile valley from North Africa. In all probability, agricultural techniques were introduced into Egypt from several different areas, and were adapted to local conditions of summer floods and winter growing season.[6]

The earliest undoubted farming settlements on Egyptian soil date to as early as 6,500 B.P. and were discovered by British archaeologist Gertrude Caton-Thompson on the shores of a former lake in the Fayum Depression to the west of the Nile Valley.[7] The sites belong to a time when the deserts were better watered and partly covered with stunted grasslands.

The Fayum settlements were transitory and lacked the substantial houses found in contemporary Near East settlements. The farmers may have used crude matting or reed shelters. They stored their grain in silos lined with baskets. The arid environment has preserved traces of their coiled baskets as well as grains of emmer wheat and flax. Sheep and goats roamed the shores of the lake, and cattle and pigs were probably domesticated. The Fayum people engaged in little trade and lived at a simple subsistence level by the shores of their lake. They fished and hunted both crocodiles and hippopotamuses.

**Fayum:
6,600 to 6,000 B.P.**

One floodplain settlement is the village of Merimde near the Nile Delta, where a cluster of oval houses and shelters were built half underground and roofed with mud and sticks.[8] An occupation mound 2 meters (7 ft) high accumulated over six hundred years from c. 6,130 B.P. Simple pottery, stone axes, flint arrowheads, and knives were in use. Agriculture and the cultivation of cereal crops is evidenced by grains stored in clay pots, baskets, and pits. Dogs, cattle, sheep or goats, and pigs were kept. Farming at a subsistence level may well have been characteristic of large areas of the Nile floodplain for thousands of years.

Merimde:
6,900 to 6,500 B.P.

Other farmers who flourished in the Upper Nile are known to us mainly from cemetery burials. Like their northern neighbors they used bows and arrows in the chase, many of them tipped with finely flaked arrowheads. Emmer wheat and barley were cultivated, and cattle and small stock provided much of their meat. Settlements here were typified by transient architecture. The dead, however, were buried with some ceremony — in linen shrouds, and the bodies were covered with skins. The women wore ivory combs and plaited their hair. This culture, named the *Badarian* after a village where the first settlements were found, is thought to be broadly contemporary with Merimde.[9]

Badarian:
6,000 B.P.

The early farming communities of the Nile continued to use the forested river banks for settlement.[10] Animals grazed in the flat grasslands of the plain for most of the year and crops were planted on wet basin soils as the waters receded. Game was still abundant in the Nile Valley six thousand years ago; even so, the people ventured to the edge of the deserts in search of gazelle and other small animals. They buried their dead in huge cemeteries overlooking the Nile, where the graves would not take up valuable agricultural land.

The unification of Egypt into a single state took place about 5,000 B.P. Agriculture was practiced for at least two thousand years before this event. The density of population was probably low enough that the people had no need of either government or government-regulated irrigation canals. They made use of natural floods and drainage basins to grow their crops. One authority has estimated that an average Nile flood would have allowed early Egyptian farmers to harvest grain over perhaps two-thirds of the flood plain of the Nile.[11] The first appearance of irrigation seems to coincide with the unification of Egypt and is described in Chapter 16.

Early Farmers of Africa

THE SAHARA BECOMES A DESERT

During the early millennia of Egyptian agriculture much of the Sahara was stunted grassland, and occasional vast, shallow lakes contained fish and crocodiles. Saharan grasslands supported sparse populations of Stone Age hunter-gatherers. Traces of their camps have been found by the shores of long-dried-up Pleistocene lakes deep in the desert.[12]

Saharan cattle
7,500 B.P.

The grasslands were a favorable environment for cattle-owning nomads as well. By 6,600 B.P., sheep and goats were being kept on the Libyan coast.[13] Domestic cattle bones have been found in Saharan caves dating to as early as 7,500 B.P. It is thought that farmers were living in the Sahara at least a thousand years earlier, but uncertainties still surround this early chronology. We can be sure that herds of cattle were roaming the Sahara by 7,000 B.P. Whether they were introduced into the desert or domesticated there from wild cattle remains to be seen.[14] The Saharan people have left a remarkable record of their lives on the walls of caves deep in the desert. Wild animals, cattle, goats, humans, and scenes of daily life are preserved in a complicated jumble of artistic endeavor extending back perhaps to 7,000 B.P.[15]

5,000 B.P.

The increasing aridity of the Sahara after 5,000 B.P. caused many of its inhabitants to move southward to the northern fringes of sub-Saharan Africa. The Saharan cattle people are thought to have used domestic crops, experimenting with such African summer rainfall cereals as sorghum and millet as they moved southward out of areas where they could grow wheat, barley, and other cereal crops used in the Mediterranean basin.[16]

SUB-SAHARAN AFRICA

Vegeculture

At the end of Pleistocene times the indigenous inhabitants of sub-Saharan Africa were already adapted to many kinds of specialized environment. Some lived by intensive fishing, others by gathering or hunting, depending on their environment. In a primitive way the techniques of food production may have already been used on the fringes of the rain forests of western and central Africa, where the common use of such root plants as the African yam led people to recognize the advantages of growing their own food.[17] Certainly the yam can easily be germinated by replanting the tops. This primitive form of "vegeculture" may have been the economic tradition onto which the cultivation of summer rainfall cereal crops was grafted as it came into use south of the grassland areas on the Sahara's southern borders.

East Africa
3,000 B.P.

By 3,000 B.P. when Europe and the Near East were beginning to enjoy the benefits of iron tools, Stone Age food producers were living on the East African highlands of Kenya, northern Tanzania, and parts of West Africa.[18] We don't know much about these early African farmers, nor do we know how deeply they penetrated into the vast rain forests of the Zaire basin.

About two thousand years ago, with the arrival of ironworking, the practices of food production and keeping domestic animals spread throughout the

African continent.[19] For thousands of years after the Near East had started to 1,900 B.P. enjoy literate civilization, San hunter-gatherers continued to flourish on the rich savannah woodlands of east and southern Africa. Their environment was so rich that they had no incentive to take up the new economies, even if they were aware of them. Agriculture finally came to the savannah when wide-spread forest clearance was made easier by iron tools and tougher working edges, from about 2,000 years ago.

Chronological Table G

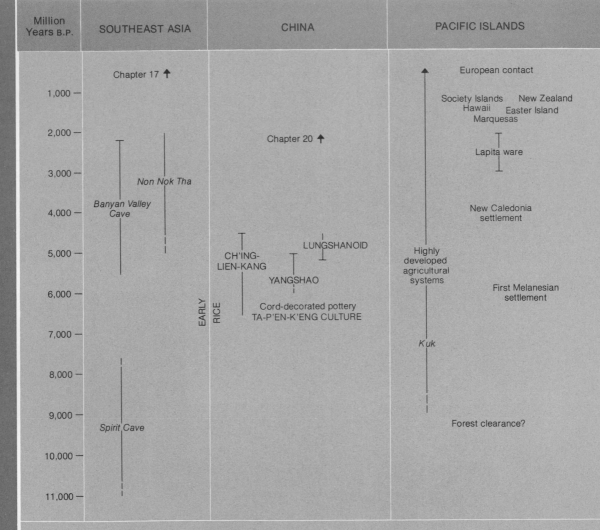

Million Years B.P.	SOUTHEAST ASIA	CHINA	PACIFIC ISLANDS
	Chapter 17 ↑		↑ European contact
1,000 —			Society Islands New Zealand
			Hawaii Easter Island
			Marquesas
2,000 —		Chapter 20 ↑	Lapita ware
3,000 —	Non Nok Tha		
	Banyan Valley Cave		New Caledonia settlement
4,000 —			
		LUNGSHANOID	Highly developed agricultural systems
5,000 —		CH'ING-LIEN-KANG	
		YANGSHAO	First Melanesian settlement
6,000 —	EARLY RICE	Cord-decorated pottery TA-P'EN-K'ENG CULTURE	
7,000 —			
			Kuk
8,000 —			
9,000 —	Spirit Cave		Forest clearance?
10,000 —			
11,000 —			

Chapter 8 ↑

Chapter Twelve

ASIA: RICE, ROOTS, AND OCEAN VOYAGERS

PREVIEW

🌿 Southeast Asia is widely believed to be an early center of root crop domestication. The archaeological evidence from Spirit Cave, Thailand, and other sites, is still insufficient to establish whether people were hunting and gathering a broad spectrum of animal and vegetable foods 11,000 years ago, or were deliberately planting some single species.

🌿 Another center of early crop domestication may be northern China, where distinctive farming cultures were flourishing in the Huagho Valley as early as 6,000 B.P. The first agriculturalists in this region had a wide range of potential domesticates to choose from.

🌿 Rice was, and still is, a key cereal crop in Asia. Its origins are still not certain. Rice cultivation appears at Non Nok Tha in Thailand about 5,000 B.P., but may be earlier in many areas. It is identified in Taiwan by 4,200 B.P. Rice cultivation spread into northern China early, but the date is unknown. The wide dispersal of rice cultivation in China is thought to be associated with the Lungshanoid cultures, which originated in the Yangshao culture of northern China.

🌿 The human settlement of the Pacific was dependent on Asian root crops and the development of deepwater canoes. The Kuk Basin in New Guinea has yielded traces of forest clearance and drainage as early as 9,000 B.P., with the cultivation of taro and yams probably beginning as early as 6,000 years ago.

🌿 The first settlement of Melanesia is believed to be associated with the development of trading networks, which later were elaborated into ceremonial trade routes. First settlement may have occurred as early as 6,000 B.P., with the widespread Lapita pottery tradition flourishing between 3,000 and 2,000 years ago and being used as far east as Samoa.

🌿 Polynesia was settled within the last 2,500 years: the Marquesas were colonized about 1,600 B.P., Hawaii some 1,350 years ago, and Easter Island about 1,450 B.P. The Polynesians were technologically in the Stone Age, but developed powerful chiefdoms that were at the height of their power when the first Europeans arrived in the eighteenth century.

⚓ New Zealand was first colonized by Polynesians around 1,000 B.P., but the introduction of the sweet potato led to rapid population buildup that coincides with
the emergence of Maori culture about 600 years ago. The Maori developed a
warlike society with constant competition for prime agricultural land and for
prestige that reached its peak about three hundred years ago.

Chronological
Table G

Fifteen thousand years ago much of Southeast Asia was inhabited by hunter-
gatherers whose stone toolkits reveal remarkable uniformity over large areas of
the mainland and islands.[1]* These stone assemblages do not necessarily reflect
a stagnation of cultural innovation, or a simple lifeway. Rather, it seems certain that these people were exploiting a broad range of game and vegetable
foods.[2]

15,000 B.P.

Very few scientific excavations have been made on sites that cover the
period 15,000 to 8,000 B.P., the period when food production may have begun
in this region.[3] The controversies about early food production in Southeast
Asia surround two questions:

When did people first start to cultivate root crops?

What are the origins of rice cultivation (rice being the vital staple cereal
crop in much of Asia throughout later prehistory)?

EARLY FOOD PRODUCTION IN THAILAND

The domestication of root crops is difficult to identify in the archaeological
record at the best of times. The only way that one can deduce cultivation is by
examination of vegetable remains found in excavations, comparing these finds
with the modern flora, and extrapolating modern uses of the flora into the
past — on the assumption that use patterns have not changed.

Spirit Cave
11,000 to
9,000 B.P.

Chester Gorman's excavations at Spirit Cave in northeastern Thailand took
him to a limestone cave overlooking a small stream (see Figure 12.1). He found
that the lowest levels of the site were formed more than 11,000 years ago. What
he called Hoabhinian tools, including small flakes and choppers, came from
these horizons and it was clear that such tools were used for a long time.
Gorman was able to identify quantities of seeds from the Hoabhinian levels.
When botanists examined these finds, they found that the people had eaten
almonds, betel nuts, broad beans, gourds, water chestnuts, peppers, and cu-
cumbers. D. E. Yen of the Bishop Museum in Honolulu visited the area and
collected modern floral specimens for comparative purposes.[4] He even ate
some of the wild foods himself. He noted that there were at least eight wild
species of yam in the area, and that the seeds found in the Spirit Cave were
from plants that can be collected in the wild and have a variety of dietary,
medicinal, and other uses. The botanists had great difficulty in establishing

* See pages 382–383 for notes to Chapter 12.

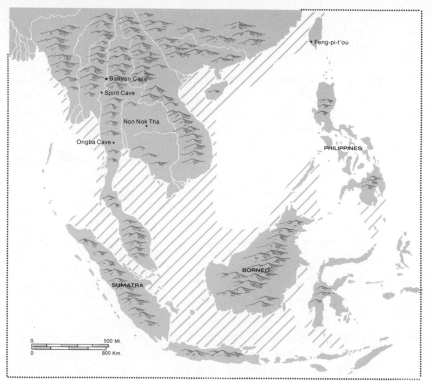

Figure 12.1 Southeast Asian sites mentioned in Chapter 12. Shaded areas are extent of low sea levels during the Weichsel glaciation.

whether the Spirit Cave seeds were domesticated or wild and in fact have produced no definite grounds for calling them deliberately planted.

The Spirit Cave finds provide no firm evidence for domestication of plants as early as 11,000 B.P., but, despite the uncertainty of the botanical evidence, Wilhelm Solheim and others have claimed that Southeast Asia was a major center of early plant and animal domestication.[5] There is certainly insufficient evidence from the few excavations in the area to make such a claim. However, there are indications of the following:

There was a wide variety of yams and other potential domesticates in Thailand and elsewhere; these were exploited by hunter-gatherers at the end of the Pleistocene.

In the case of the yams, there were enough species present for people under demographic or other stress to experiment with hybridization if they wished.

In view of these two factors, there is no reason to doubt that food production could have begun in this area quite independently from other regions.

As we have pointed out before, yam planting is very simple, and hunter-gatherers are well aware that deliberate cultivation is possible. The problem is to identify the factors that led people to deliberate experimentation with various plants. In the absence of firm archaeological evidence, we can speculate that primitive shifting agriculture, with a combination of diverse crops and some animal herding, may have had its roots in a broad spectrum of hunting and gathering, as it did in other regions of the world. In the final analysis, all that is needed for a culture to make the transition are some clearings at the edge of the forest and a simple digging stick, already used for gathering, to plant the crop.[6]

Charles Higham, who studied the animal bones from Spirit Cave and other localities in northern Thailand, argued that the large range of species found in the sites indicated a broadly based hunting economy that focused on deer, pigs, and arboreal creatures like monkeys.[7] Perhaps the caves reflected only the hunting aspect of an otherwise agricultural economy; in any case, there was no sign of domestic animals in the collections. Chester Gorman believes that this broadly based hunting was a preadaptation to early animal domestication.[8]

The case for indigenous development of agriculture and animal domestication in Southeast Asia is still unproven, although there is no reason to believe that it did not take place.

RICE CULTIVATION IN SOUTHEAST ASIA

Spirit Cave
9,000 to 7,000 B.P.

The material culture of the Spirit Cave people shows a distinct change after 9,000 B.P. From then until about 7,600 years ago the inhabitants began to use adzes, pottery, and slate knives. These last strongly resemble later artifacts used for rice cultivation in parts of Indonesia and may suggest that cereal was cultivated near the site.

8,500 B.P.

About 8,500 B.P. people were moving from the hills onto river plains and into lowland areas. River plains were the best place for the intensive cultivation and simple irrigation needed for rice agriculture. Crop yields, far superior to those from small highland root crop gardens, were ample and easily obtained. While everyone agrees that rice was domesticated in an Asian lowland area, there is little agreement about where or when it was cultivated, partly because there is no archaeological evidence bearing on the problem. In all probability, the wild ancestor of rice was a perennial grass that grew wild in lowland areas from India to southern China, and in the Pacific islands. Perhaps rice was first encountered as a weed in taro gardens; if so, it would have been transplanted, then harvested with a knife. In any case, it seems probable that rice was first cultivated by root crop farmers.

Banyan Valley Cave
5,500 to 1,200 B.P.

The earliest rice specimens from Southeast Asia come from relatively late sites, among them Banyan Valley Cave in northern Thailand and Non Nok Tha, a deep mound in the Mekong River floodplain in the same area.[9] Gorman found husks of rice in Banyan levels dating to between 5,500 and 1,200 B.P., none of which the botanical experts could positively identify as being fully domesticated. Experiments with milling stones were carried out which showed that the husks had been ground by a quite different method from that used by modern rice farmers in the area. Yen, whose studies of the rice can surely be described as comprehensive, speculates that the Banyan finds were the result of a form of gathering plus selective cultivation of wild rice — a stage in the gradual domestication of the cereal. There are many wild species in the region, several of which were possible candidates for cultivation.

Non Nok Tha was first occupied before 5,000 to 4,000 B.P., but it was abandoned at some time before 2,000 years ago. The excavators found traces of rice in the form of grain impressions on clay pots in the lowest levels. They pointed out that the site dates to the time when the lowlands were already settled and argued that this means that the rice was probably cultivated, not wild. The bones of domesticated cattle came from the same site. The inhabitants were sedentary farmers depending on rice and cattle for most of their diet. Hunting and gathering were less important than in earlier millennia when highland sites were occupied all year. Copper smelting may have been practiced by 5,000 B.P. at this site.

> Non Nok Tha
> **?5,000 to 2,000 B.P.**

Rice cultivation has become the major cereal crop agriculture of the world, but its origins are still uncertain. Southeast Asia did not suffer from the drastic climatic changes of northern latitudes. No prolonged droughts or major vegetational changes altered the pattern of human settlement. Only dramatic rises in low sea levels altered the geography and environment of Southeast Asia, creating islands from dry land, and reducing the amount of coastal floodplain available to hunters and gatherers. Conceivably these major changes in coastline and available land surface were among many factors that moved the inhabitants of Southeast Asia to experiment with plants and domestic animals.

EARLY FARMING IN CHINA

Southern China and Taiwan

"In the wealth of its species and in the extent of the genus and species potential of its cultivated plants, China is conspicuous among other centers of origin of plant forms." Thus wrote the great Russian botanist N. I. Vavilov over thirty years ago.[10] Like the archaeology of early agriculture in Southeast Asia, that of China is still in its infancy. But agriculture seems to have appeared separately in three major areas of China: the southern coastal, the north, and the eastern coastal area.

A widespread culture of possible farmers has been identified in the southern coastal regions of Fukien, Kwangtung, and Taiwan.[11] This Ta-p'en-k'eng culture is characterized by coarse cord-decorated pottery as well as beautifully polished axes, arrowheads, and grooved barkcloth beaters. The Ta-p'en-k'eng culture dates to earlier than 6,500 B.P. and is thought by Chinese-American archaeologist Kwang-Chih Chang to be that of root and tuber cultivators who were exploiting a wide range of food plants. They may have begun such exploitation as early as 12,000 years ago, although the date is a guess. It appears, however, that the same broad spectrum of exploiting wild vegetable foods may have been practiced in southern China as was commonplace in neighboring Southeast Asia.

> Ta-p'en-k'eng
> **6,500 B.P.**

Asia: Rice, Roots, and Ocean Voyagers

Northern China

If it is true that root crops were developed in Southeast Asia and southern China very early, that course of history would lead us to ask: What was the relationship between early agriculture in the south and the first farming in the north? Did agriculture spread from the south, or did food production develop quite independently in both regions?

North Chinese agriculture has one great contrast with the south: it is based heavily on cereals and seeded plants. The first northern agricultural communities were sited in the central regions of the Huangho Valley (Figure 12.2). The area is a small basin, forming a border between the wooded western highlands and the swampy lowlands to the east. Pollen analysis has provided evidence for a prolonged period of warmer climate from about 8,000 to 4,000 years ago, when favorable rainfall patterns and greater warmth made this nuclear area a fine place for agriculture.[12]

During the glaciations of the Pleistocene, loess soils were formed over a wide area of the north. The fine, soft-textured earth was both homogeneous and porous and could be tilled by simple digging sticks. Because of the concentrated summer rainfall, cereal crops, the key to agriculture in this region,

Figure 12.2 One approximate nuclear area (shaded) of early Chinese agriculture. Yangshao sites occur both within the nuclear area and outside it. Southern sites of corded pottery are found in Kwangtung, Fukien, and Taiwan areas.

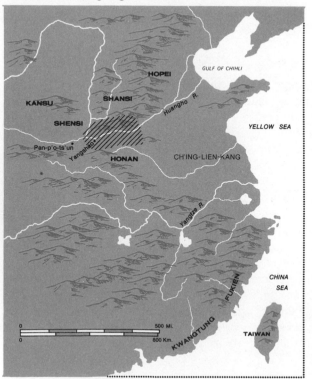

Farmers

Figure 12.3 Reconstructions of Yangshao huts from Pan-p'o-ts'un, China.

could be grown successfully. The indigenous plants available for domestication included the wild ancestors of foxtail millet, broomcorn millet, sorghum, hemp, and the mulberry. Ancient Chinese farmers developed their own cultivation techniques, which persisted for thousands of years before irrigation was developed. Although irrigation gradually became the basis of the agricultural economies of Egypt, the Indus Valley, and Mesopotamia, it was not important in northern China until much later.[13]

The earliest millennia of northern Chinese agriculture are still a blank on the archaeological map. Two hypotheses are possible. We can assume that the inhabitants of the Huangho region passed through a long phase of experimental cultivation and intensive exploitation of the indigenous flora before developing their own distinctive agricultural techniques. Or we can assume that food production was developed farther south in China and adopted later in the north. Neither hypothesis can be tested with the available evidence. Early farming villages are associated with coarse cord-marked pottery, found on the banks of the Huangho River in western Honan Province and on the lower Weishui River. Perhaps these cord-marked vessels are related to the cord-decorated pottery traditions of Southeast Asia and Taiwan.

Some of the earliest traces of agricultural settlement were first found in the 1920s on low-lying loess soils in the middle reaches of the Huangho River, especially at a site named Yangshao.[14] Similar villages have been found over much of the Huangho River basin, which is as large as early centers of agriculture in Egypt and Mesopotamia. Radiocarbon dates for Yangshao sites belong in the period 5,900 to 5,200 B.P.[15]

Many Yangshao villages were undefended settlements built on ridges overlooking the floodplains, sited to avoid flooding or to allow maximal use of floodplain soils. The villagers lived in fairly substantial round or oblong houses partly sunk into the ground. Yangshao houses had mud-plastered walls, timber frames, and steep roofs (Figure 12.3). Usually there were cemeteries outside

Cord-decorated wares

Yangshao culture
5,900 to 5,200 B.P.

the villages. Sometimes the villages had a special area for pottery kilns where the characteristic Yangshao painted funerary vessels favored by the house-holders were manufactured.

Some Yangshao people moved their settlements regularly, but returned to the same sites again and again. Using hoes and digging sticks, they cultivated foxtail millet as a staple crop. Simple dry-land slash-and-burn farming probably supplemented riverside gardens. Irrigation may have been practiced as early as the fifth millennium B.C., however. Dogs and pigs were fully domesticated. Cattle, sheep, and goats were less common. Hunting and gathering were still significant, as was fishing, for which hooks and spears were employed.

Each Yangshao village was a self-contained community, thousands of which flourished in the river valleys of northern China. The Yangshao farmers were distributed over a comparatively limited part of northern China from eastern Kansu in the west to Huangho and northwestern Honan in the east. Many regional variations of Yangshao culture remain to be distinguished, but the features of a characteristic, and thoroughly Chinese, culture are already clear. The earliest Chinese farmers had already developed a distinctive naturalistic art style (Figure 12.4). The unique Chinese style of cooking with steam is attested by the discovery of cooking pots identical to later specialized cooking vessels. Jade was worked; hemp was used for making fabrics; skilled basketry

Figure 12.4 Yangshao pottery from Kansu Province, China (about one-fourth actual size). In the photographs the fish motifs often used to decorate Yangshao pottery are clearly seen.

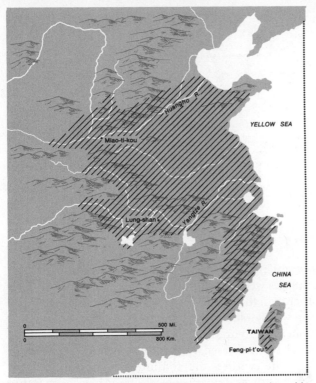

Figure 12.5 Approximate distribution of the Lungshanoid cultures in China (shaded area).

was practiced; even the Chinese language may have roots in Yangshao. Of the indigenous origins of Chinese cereal agriculture there can be little doubt, although, theoretically, long-established trade routes to the West could have brought new ideas to the Far East — including some crops, especially in later millennia.

The Yangshao culture itself had a relatively restricted distribution in northern China, centered on the Huangho Valley. The expansion of the Yangshao was largely confined to gradual taking up of land by villages that split off from larger settlements and needed new gardens. But the success of the agricultural adaptation led in part to population increases and greater elaboration of material culture, resulting in the evolution of the Lungshanoid cultures. Inevitably, too, farming settlements spread into hitherto unfarmed areas (Figure 12.5). Soon many regional variations of Lungshanoid culture were flourishing both in the north and in more southerly areas.[16] At least six regional variants of the Lungshanoid have been identified. Their village settlements follow a pattern of river valleys and sea coasts, each regional variant connected to others by a network of waterways. Their inhabitants may have spread into eastern and southeastern China from the nuclear area, perhaps pressured by population growth in the north.

Lungshanoid cultures **5,200 to c. 4,500 B.P.**

Asia: Rice, Roots, and Ocean Voyagers

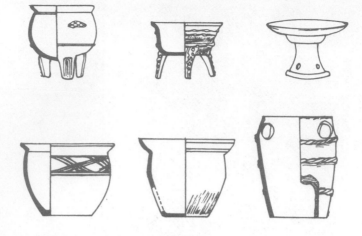

Figure 12.6 Some typical Lungshanoid vessels used for cooking and other purposes, from Miao-ti-kou, China (scale not recorded).

The typical Lungshanoid settlement was larger than those of the Yangshao. Their settled, permanent villages were often protected by earthen walls. Millet seems to have been a staple crop in the north, while domestic cattle, sheep, and goats, and perhaps the horse were added to the economy. Hunting and gathering as well as fishing were locally important. The economy changed but little from Yangshao times, except for increased productivity, some evidence for better organization of village life (witness the communally built walls), and the addition of rice to the crops grown. Remains of rice grains have been found in Lungshanoid villages, which gives reason to believe that rice cultivation spread into northern China from the south, where fertile floodplains with their lush water meadows provided an effective environment for rice growing. The introduction of rice to the north would have reduced dependence on dry agriculture, and, presumably, led to the use of irrigation and the modification of agricultural technology.

The Lungshanoid people are thought to have been one of the groups responsible for the rapid spread of rice cultivation not only through the mainland but on the offshore islands of Southeast Asia and far into the Pacific. Certainly, their more intensive agriculture, substantial settlements, and more elaborate material culture were among the roots of Chinese civilization (Figure 12.6).

AGRICULTURE IN THE PACIFIC ISLANDS

The origins of the peoples of the Pacific islands have fascinated scientists since the eighteenth century (Figure 12.7).[17] But most authorities now look to southeast Asia for the origins of the Melanesians and Polynesians. They point out that settlement of the offshore islands depended on the successful cultivation of root crops like taro and the yam, as well as breadfruit, coconuts, and sugar cane. Chickens, dogs, and pigs were also valued as food and were domesticated in Asia before being introduced to the Pacific. Why did these foods

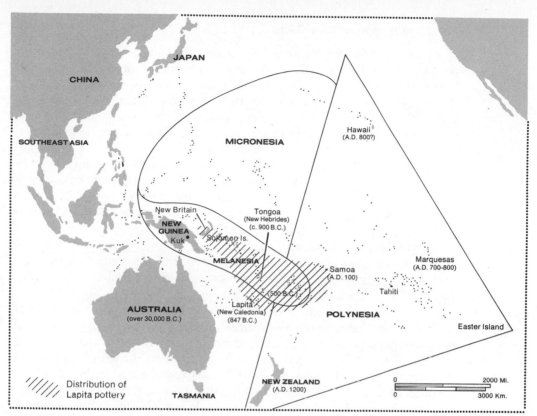

Figure 12.7 Map of Pacific sites and early farming settlements in the Americas. Shading shows distribution of Lapita pottery.

have to be established in the diets and farming repertoires of the island settlers? Small animals like pigs and chickens could readily have been carried from island to island in canoes, as could easily germinating root plants like the yam. Both food sources allowed a sizable population to spread to many hundreds of small islands separated by miles of open water.

The Pacific islanders show no features attributable to American Indian stock. Their physical attributes had probably stabilized before any cultivators left the Asian mainland. Their languages are similar to Thai and other Southeast Asian dialects and bear no resemblance to native American speech. Artifacts such as ground and polished axes and adzes, shell fishhooks, and canoes can be paralleled generally on the western shores of the Pacific.

The first settlement of the Pacific islands is closely connected with the early cultivation of yams, and especially of taro. As we pointed out earlier in this chapter, taro and yams were probably domesticated in Southeast Asia before the development of rice cultivation. But exactly when and where they were first grown is unknown. In all probability there were several centers of early domestication within Southeast Asia.

Asia: Rice, Roots, and Ocean Voyagers   **197**

Food Production in New Guinea

As far as the Pacific islands are concerned, a potential center of great importance is New Guinea, where both taro and yams are important crops. Taro is grown in naturally rich soils or as a first crop in newly cleared forest gardens. The older New Guinea crops, which include both taro and yams, flourish at higher elevations. Today, they are combined with the sweet potato, an American cultigen introduced only relatively recently which allows agriculture at lower altitudes and with far greater crop yields.

Jack Golson, Peter White, and others have studied early agriculture in the New Guinea highlands using both pollen analysis and the study of old irrigation channels to amplify the archaeological record.[18] There are traces, at about 9,000 B.P., of deliberate diversion of river water in the Kuk Basin, which have been interpreted to mean that the people were cultivating taro or yams at a very early date. The evidence is still uncertain, although signs of increased erosion in the area may be the result of forest clearance for taro or yam gardens, or, possibly, for the deliberate growing of indigenous New Guinea plants.

Kuk
9,000 B.P.

6,000 B.P.

By 6,000 to 5,500 B.P. much more organized agricultural works are found in the Kuk Basin. There is pollen evidence for quite extensive forest clearance in the general area. These more organized works may have been created for yam and taro crops, while indigenous plants were grown on the better drained soils between the channel banks. After 4,000 years ago, the first highly developed drainage systems occur in the area, a sign that a much more intensive agriculture is expanding. After 2,500 B.P. the people depended more and more heavily on dry and wet agriculture, for the forest resources they had relied on were replaced by an environment which had been altered permanently by human activity. A slow population growth would have resulted in the taking up of uncleared land. Then, after that was exhausted, the only option was to shorten the fallow periods on cleared gardens — something which, if taro was the crop, would result in lower crop yields.

4,000 B.P.

2,500 B.P.

The archaeological and pollen analysis investigations of Golson and others have produced firm evidence for sedentism, forest clearance, agricultural stone tools, and water control techniques in the New Guinea highlands by five to six thousand years ago. What is uncertain, however, is the means by which food production began in New Guinea. Was it developed locally with introduced plants after the local hunter-gatherers had manipulated local indigenous plants for centuries? Or did the people manipulate local plants as a result of adopting a few introduced crops first? Whatever the answer to these questions, it appears that the New Guinea highlands were an area where people created an artificial garden environment as a result of a long period of experimentation, in which they were raising plants *within* their natural environment. By exploiting a wide range of tropical animals and plants, the people may have become more sedentary, then later, might have started to plant small plots of root crops; ultimately, they would have intensified their food production until they modified their environment beyond recognition. This hypothetical model for early agriculture in New Guinea may serve as a possible model for other tropical areas in Asia as well.

Trading Systems Linked the Islands

Current archaeological research in lowland and island Melanesia sees maritime trade as a major factor in the settlement of the hundreds of islands of the western Pacific. The social and economic complexities of Melanesian trading systems have long excited anthropologists, starting with Bronislow Malinowski, whose immortal work on Trobriand island trading still forms part of the basic training of all anthropologists.[19] It is now known that related trading systems link all parts of coastal New Guinea and much of Melanesia. Although Malinowski concentrated on the ceremonial aspects of the trade, these networks carried an enormous diversity of different everyday and exotic goods and commodities ranging from foodstuffs to manufactured goods. The anthropologists have shown that these trade networks circulated commodities in huge rings that were reciprocal and self-perpetuating. Concerned as they are with material culture and technology, archaeologists have begun to look closely at this trade and the objects carried by it as a means for interpreting the archaeological record of early settlement on the islands.[20]

Most long distance trade was conducted by middlemen or specialist merchants who traveled in sea-going canoes. They made their living by trading food surpluses for manufactured goods. The navigational abilities of the Pacific islanders have long been the subject of vigorous academic controversy, much of which, however, has now been dispelled by some compelling studies of indigenous navigational techniques; these studies were done by anthropologists and practical small-boat seamen like David Lewis. One school of thought argued that long distance voyages by early islanders were one-way accidental trips, when canoes were blown out to sea.[21] Early navigators were helpless, this school argued, to counteract ocean currents. Their views have been sharply challenged by those who have studied the well-developed maritime technology of the Polynesians.[22] They point out that nearly all the long trips attributed to the Polynesians were from north to south, which involved simple dead-reckoning calculations and a simple way of measuring latitude from the stars. Anthropologist Ben Finney made detailed studies of Polynesian canoes and navigational techniques; his findings support a notion of deliberate one-way voyages, sparked as much by necessity — drought or warfare — as by restless adventure.[23] Evidence for the carrying of women, animals of both sexes, and plants for propagation, however, shows that colonization was the deliberate aim.

Amateur seaman David Lewis completed a remarkable study of Polynesian navigation, voyaging under prehistoric conditions and accumulating navigators' lore from surviving practitioners of the art.[24] He found that navigators were a respected and close-knit group. Young apprentices learned their skills over many years of making passages and from orally transmitted knowledge about the stars and the oceans accumulated by generations of navigators. The navigational techniques used the angles of rising and setting stars, the trend of ocean swells, and the myriad inconspicuous phenomena that indicated the general direction and distance of small islands. The navigators were perfectly capable of voyaging over long stretches of open water, and their geographic knowledge was astonishing. They had no need of the compass or other modern aids and their landfalls were accurate. Lewis's findings confirm those of Finney and others who believe that deliberate voyages colonized even remote islands.

Melanesia

6,000 B.P.
4,000 B.P.

By looking at oral traditions, archaeological excavations, and some linguistic data, A. Pawley and R. C. Green have dated the expansion of farming peoples into island Melanesia to about 6,000 B.P.[25] and as far as New Caledonia to at least 4,000 years ago.[26] These settlers are thought to have introduced agriculture, domesticated animals, and pottery to Melanesia. A later manifestation of this maritime expansion is associated with a characteristic pottery

Lapita ware
3,000 to 2,000 B.P.

style known as Lapita.[27] This is seen as a specialized invention that spread widely through the islands at a time when the double hulled canoe came into use. This canoe was part of the evolution, we are told, of efficient trading networks that were maintained by regular two-way voyages over distances up to 600 kilometers. Obsidian trade was conducted down these networks and has been identified by using trace elements in the raw material to trace rocks from the eastern Solomon islands to a source in New Britain.[28] Some people believe that the makers of Lapita pottery were traders and seafarers, but so little is

Figure 12.8   Lapita pottery from Melanesia.

Farmers

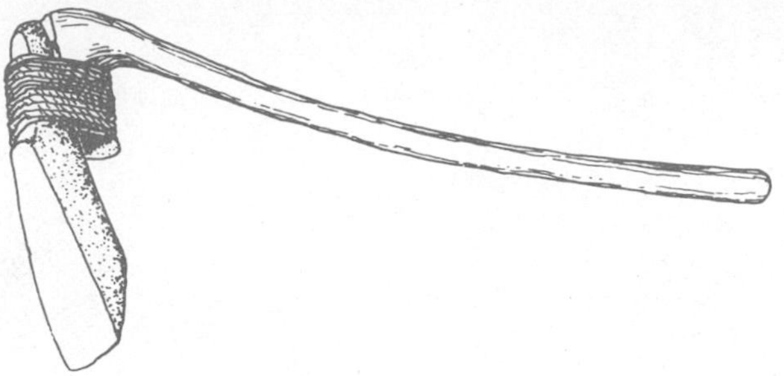

Figure 12.9 Stone ax from eastern Polynesia, mounted in a wooden handle (hypothetical reconstruction).

known about them that this is probably a premature hypothesis. Certainly, trade played an important role in the colonization of Melanesia.

Lapita pottery itself was decorated with impressed designs and made of clay tempered with shell (Figure 12.8). It is found from the Santa Cruz islands as far east as the New Hebrides, Fiji, Tonga, and Samoa. It is generally dated to the last thousand years before Christ, but seems to have gone out of fashion about 2,000 years ago.

From Melanesia canoes voyaged to Polynesia, taking the plants and domestic animals of their home islands with them. The antiquity of human settlement in Polynesia is about two thousand years.[29] It is thought that the Polynesians originated in the Fiji area before the great elaboration of Melanesian culture after 2,000 B.P. After a lengthy period of adaptation in western Polynesia, small groups began to settle the more remote islands. The Marquesas were settled by 1,600 B.P., the Society Islands and Tahiti by 1,200 years ago. The first canoes arrived at Hawaii some 1,350 years ago, and at Easter Island by 1,450 B.P.[30] The human settlement of Polynesia seems to have taken about 2,500 years from its very first beginnings, in the hands of people who were still technologically speaking in the Stone Age. They relied heavily on stone axes and adzes (Figure 12.9) and an elaborate array of bone and shell fish hooks. The crops the people planted varied from island to island, but breadfruit, taro, coconut, yams, and bananas were the staple crops. The food surpluses generated on the larger islands were used as a form of wealth.

Polynesia
2,500 to 1,200 B.P.

When the French and British visited Tahiti in the eighteenth century they chanced upon the center of a vigorous eastern Polynesian society.[31] The islands were ruled by a powerful hierarchy of chiefs and nobles, many of them descendants of original canoe crews who had settled the archipelago. The chiefs acquired prestige by controlling and redistributing wealth and food supplies. Their formidable religious and social powers led them to warfare and to the undertaking of elaborate agricultural projects and the erection of monumental shrines and temples of stone: the famous *maraes* of Tahiti are typical examples (Figure 12.10). On remote Easter Island the chiefs erected vast stone heads, as much as 19 meters (62 feet) high. No one knows what they signify.

The full diversity of Polynesian culture is still imperfectly understood, for archaeological research has hardly begun in the South Seas. But it is certain that the Polynesians were making ocean voyages on a large scale at a time when the Greeks and Romans were little more than coastal navigators.

Figure 12.10 A *marae* from Tahiti.

Settlement of New Zealand

New Zealand is the largest and among the most remote of all the Pacific islands; it is actually two large islands. It has a temperate climate, not the tropical warmth enjoyed by most Polynesians. Despite this ecological difference, New Zealand was first settled by Polynesians who voyaged southward in comparatively recent times and settled on the North Island. Maori legends speak of a migration from Polynesia in the mid-fourteenth century A.D. Settlers may have arrived 400 years before, including Toi Ete'huatai who came to New Zealand in search of two grandsons blown away from Tahiti during a canoe race. The earliest C14 dates for New Zealand archaeological sites are a matter of controversy, but are within the present millennium.[32]

First settlement
?1,000 B.P.

The temperate climate of the North Island formed a southern frontier for most of the basic food plants of Polynesia. The yam and gourd can be grown only there, but the sweet potato could be cultivated in the northern part of the South Island, if adequate winter storage pits were used. The Polynesian coconut never grew in New Zealand. The earliest settlers relied heavily on hunting, fishing, and gathering. Even later, though some peoples specialized in food production, others did not, especially in the South Island, where many settlements were on the coasts close to abundant ocean resources.

The first settlers found great flocks of flightless Moa birds, cumbersome and helpless in the face of systematic hunting. They hunted the Moa into extinction within a few centuries. Fish, fern roots, and shellfish were important throughout New Zealand's short prehistory. The introduction of the sweet potato made a dramatic difference to the New Zealanders, for the tubers, if carefully stored from winter cold, could be eaten in the cold months, and some could be kept for the next year's planting. Sweet potato has a large crop yield and is thought to have contributed to a rapid population build up, especially in the North Island. This, in turn, led to competition among different groups for suitable agricultural land to grow the new staple.

When the Moa became extinct the Maori had few meat supplies except birds, dogs, and rats. Their only other meat source was human flesh. The archaeological record of Maori culture from about 600 B.P. onwards shows not only population growth but an increasing emphasis on warfare, evidenced by the appearance of numerous fortified encampments or *pa*'s, protected with earthen banks. The distribution of *pa*'s coincides to a large extent with the best sweet potato lands. In the course of a few centuries warfare became a key element in Maori culture, to the extent that it was institutionalized, and an important factor in maintaining cohesion and leadership in Maori society. The booty of war was not only *kumara* (sweet potato), but the flesh of captives, which became part of Maori diet.

Maori warfare, mainly confined to North Island, where over five thousand *pa*'s have been found, was seasonal and closely connected with the planting and harvest of sweet potatoes, when everyone was busy in the gardens. Military campaigns were short and intense, very often launched from the sea in large war canoes up to 24 meters or more in length (Figure 12.11). These elaborately carved vessels could hold up to 150 men on a short expedition. So formidable was the reputation of the Maori that European ships avoided New Zealand ports for years before permanent white settlement was achieved. The last Maori war ended in 1872, by which time the indigenous population had been decimated by disease, warfare, and European contact.

Figure 12.11 Maori war canoe recorded by Captain Cook in the eighteenth century.

Chronological Table H

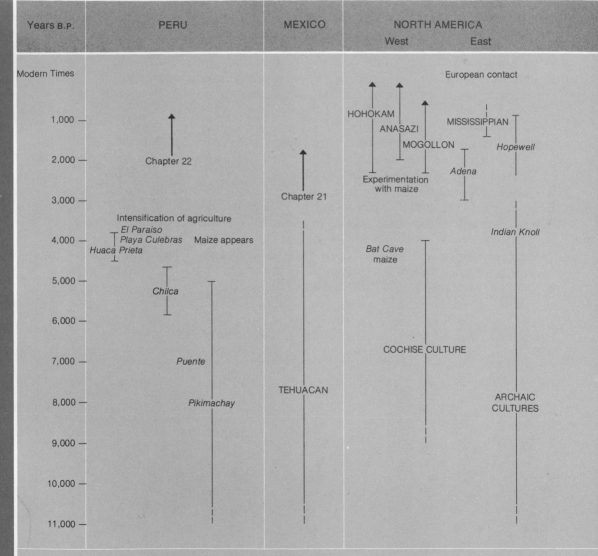

Years B.P.	PERU	MEXICO	NORTH AMERICA West East
Modern Times			European contact
1,000 —			HOHOKAM MISSISSIPPIAN
			ANASAZI
	Chapter 22		MOGOLLON Hopewell
2,000 —		Chapter 21	Adena
			Experimentation with maize
3,000 —	Intensification of agriculture		
	El Paraiso		Indian Knoll
4,000 —	Playa Culebras Maize appears		
	Huaca Prieta		Bat Cave maize
5,000 —	Chilca		
6,000 —			
7,000 —	Puente		COCHISE CULTURE
8,000 —	Pikimachay	TEHUACAN	ARCHAIC CULTURES
9,000 —			
10,000 —			
11,000 —			

Chapter 7 ↑

Chapter Thirteen

NEW WORLD AGRICULTURE

PREVIEW

🌾 New World agriculture was based on crops quite different from those grown in the Old World. The root crops included manioc and sweet potato, while maize was the most important staple cereal. Domesticated animals included the llama, turkey, and guinea pig.

🌾 The early history of food production and of maize agriculture is best chronicled from excavations in the Tehuacán Valley, Mexico, where food production was well established by 6,000 years ago. A long tradition of fishing and gathering in coastal Peru gave way to agriculture in some areas about 5,000 years ago. The Ayacucho area of the Andes provides evidence for food production in the highlands of Peru by 5,500 B.P. The origins of food production in the New World were a shift in ecological adaptation chosen by peoples living where economic strategies necessitated intensive exploitation of vegetable foods.

🌾 Maize agriculture reached the American Southwest by about 4,000 years ago. The Archaic Cochise hunter-gatherer peoples of the area gradually adopted the new economy, experimenting with the cultivation of various hybrid strains of maize. By 2,300 years ago sedentary villages and a much greater dependence on farming were characteristic of the Southwest, leading to the emergence of the Hohokam, Mogollon, and Anasazi cultural traditions. Hohokam and Anasazi are thought to be ancestral to modern American Indian groups still living in the Southwest.

🌾 The Archaic hunter-gatherer cultures of the eastern and midwestern parts of the United States gradually adopted food production after 3,000 years ago. A series of powerful chiefdoms emerged in the East and Midwest, peoples amongst whom elaborate burial customs and the building of burial mounds and earthworks were commonplace. The Adena tradition emerged about 3,000 B.P., and was replaced by the Hopewell about 1,750 years ago. Both traditions depended on long distance trade in essential commodities and cult objects for much of their prosperity. A preoccupation with death and status was at the center of Hopewell life, for their burials show extraordinary lavishness. Fourteen hundred years ago the center of economic, religious, and political power shifted to the Mississippi Valley with the emergence of the Mississippian tradition, which is thought to owe much to Mexican cosmology. The Mississippian was a state-organized society having powerful religious and secular leaders; it survived in a modified form until European contact in the eighteenth century.

The American Indians domesticated an impressive range of native New World plants, some of which — like maize, potatoes, and tobacco — were rapidly adopted by European farmers after contact.

Figure 13.1 Archaeological sites and culture areas mentioned in Chapter 13. (After Meggers.)

Nuclear areas for agriculture	Mogollon	Hohokam	Anasazi	Woodland (Adena and Hopewell)

Mississippian

Farmers

The most important staple crop was Indian corn, properly called maize — the only important wild grass in the New World to be fully domesticated. It remains the most important food crop in the Americas today, being used in more that 150 varieties as both food and cattle fodder. Root crops formed another important food source, especially in South America, and included manioc, sweet potatoes, and white potatoes. Chili peppers were grown as hot seasoning; amaranth, sunflowers, cacao, peanuts, and several types of bean were also significant crops. Some crops like cotton and gourds are common to both Old and New Worlds but were probably domesticated separately.

In contrast to Old World farmers, the Indians had few domesticated animals, including the llama of the Andes, and alpacas, which provided wool. Dogs appear in the Americas, and the raucous and unruly turkey, also muscovy duck, were domesticated.[1]*

Most archaeologists now agree that there were two major centers of plant domestication in the Americas: for maize in Mesoamerica, and for root crops in the highlands of the central Andes. There are also four major areas of later cultivation activity: tropical (northern) South America and Peru, Mesoamerica, and eastern North America.

MESOAMERICA: TEHUACÁN AND THE ORIGINS OF AGRICULTURE

Traces of early experimentation with the deliberate cultivation of crops like maize and squash have come from regions in Mexico, noticeably from Sierra Madre, Sierra de Tamaulipas, and the Tehuacán Valley (Figure 13.1).

The dry, highland Tehuacán Valley in Mexico has many caves and open sites and is sufficiently arid to preserve seeds and organic finds in archaeological deposits. This was the valley that archaeologist Richard MacNeish chose as a promising area in which to seek the origins of domesticated maize.[2] What he was looking for was a corn with a light husk that allowed the seeds to disperse at maturity — something that people seek to prevent by breeding the domestic strain with a tougher husk. While Paul Mangelsdorf and other botanists had hypothesized about the ancestor of maize, no one had actually found a specimen of ancestral maize (Figure 13.2).[3]

MacNeish soon found domestic maize cobs dating back to about 5,000 B.P. But not until he began digging in the small Coxcatlán rockshelter in the Tehuacán Valley did he find maize that met Mangelsdorf's specification. Coxcatlán contained twenty-eight occupation levels, the earliest of which dated to about 12,000 B.P. MacNeish eventually excavated twelve sites in Tehuacán, which gave a wealth of information on the inhabitants of the valley over nearly 12,000 years of prehistory.

MacNeish found that the earliest Tehuacán people lived by collecting wild vegetable foods, but mainly by hunting horses, deer, and other mammals.[4] These hunters used stone tipped lances in the chase. They also took large numbers of jackrabbits, probably in organized drives. MacNeish estimates that

* See pages 384–385 for notes to Chapter 13.

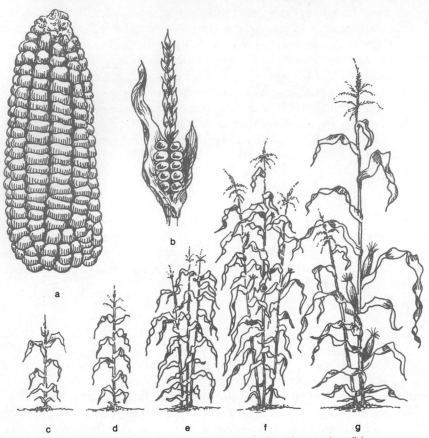

Figure 13.2 Development of maize: (a) a typical ear of modern maize; (b) probable appearance of extinct wild maize; (c–g) evolution of the domesticated maize plant.

12,000 to 9,000 B.P.

50 to 60 percent of the people's food came from game in 12,000 B.P., only 30 to 40 percent in 9,000 B.P. Hunting seems to have been the major activity all year round (Table 13.1).

After 10,000 B.P. the game population declined slowly, and the people turned more and more to wild vegetable foods. Instead of hunting all the year round, the Tehuacán bands scheduled their food gathering on a seasonal basis, and were able to exploit the vegetable and other foods in their environment very effectively without overtaxing the available resources. About 7,000 B.P.,

7,000 B.P.

the first deliberate planting took place, stemming from a desire to improve the location and prolificacy of favorite foods. This cultivation resulted in genetic changes, and soon the planted seeds were being laid out in special gardens.

Coxcatlán

The inhabitants of Coxcatlán Cave seem to have continued this trend after 7,000 years ago, planting potential domesticates, including some form of maize, in spring or summer. They grew foods that when stored would tide them over lean months: beans, chili peppers, amaranth, and gourds. The

208   Farmers

people lived in larger and more permanent settlements, grinding their maize with quite well-made grindstones (metates). The maize itself was smaller than modern strains and probably much like the hypothesized ancestor of present-day wild corn (Figure 13.2). Still, only a tiny proportion of Tehuacán's diet came from domestic sources, compared with the period after 5,400 B.P., when up to 30 percent of the diet came from agriculture; much of the produce was maize cobs that were larger than those of earlier centuries, clearly the descendants of earlier wild forms.

5,400 B.P.

By this time, the scheduled gathering and nomadic settlement patterns of

Table 13.1 MacNeish's sequence for Tehuacán summarized. Note: for full details, see Richard MacNeish, *The Science of Archaeology?*, Duxbury Press, North Scituate, Mass., 1978.

Years B.P.	Phase	Characteristics
1,250 to 431	VENTA SALADA	Spanish contact: A.D. 1531
2,100 to 1,250	PALO BLANCO	Village life
2,800 to 2,100	SANTA MARIA	Village life
3,450 to 2,800	AJALPAN	Establishment of village life. Single season economy with spring and summer agriculture.
4,250 to 3,450	PURRON	Hamlet villages and appearance of pottery. Agriculture important, but few details known.
5,350 to 4,250	AREJAS	Seasonal economy, with hunting important in the winter, collecting in spring, simple agriculture in summer and fall. Some year-round settlements, small food surpluses.
6,950 to 5,350	COXCATLÁN	Seasonal scheduling of hunting and gathering. Planting of domesticates in spring and summer. Very limited food surpluses. Maize cultivated.
8,950 to 6,950	EL RIEGO	Seasonally scheduled gathering and hunting. Seed planting appears late in phase during summers. Food storage more important.
11,950 to 8,950	AJUEREADO	Lance ambushing of game important. Rabbit drives and small game significant. Less gathering than in later phases? Seasonal camps, no food storage.
Before 12,000	Hunter-gatherers	

New World Agriculture

earlier times had been replaced by more sedentary villages; these were small hamlets that moved very rarely and depended on agricultural systems that planted crops in fields. The villages were sited near fertile flat lands, and consisted of pit houses with brush roofs. Their ample storage facilities helped the people live through the lean months.[5]

The sequence of events at Tehuacán is by no means unique, for other peoples were also experimenting with cultivation. Different hybrid forms of maize are found in Tehuacán sites; these were not developed locally and can only have been introduced from outside. Dry caves elsewhere in northern Mesoamerica show that other cultures paralleled the cultural events in Tehuacán.[6]

Plant domestication in Mesoamerica was not so much an invention in one small area as a shift in ecological adaptation deliberately chosen by peoples living where economic strategies necessitated intensive exploitation of vegetable foods. Kent Flannery has hypothesized as to how this shift in adaptation might have occurred in Mesoamerica. In a classic paper on the southern highlands of Mesoamerica he tried to understand how the human population of this area took up agriculture.[7] He assumed that the people and their homeland were part of a single, complex system composed of many subsystems — economic, botanical, social, and so on — that interacted with one another. Flannery pointed out that these people had no less than five carefully scheduled food-gathering systems that were in careful use at different seasons of the year. By being able to predict what vegetable foods came into season at different times of the year, the people were able to schedule their harvesting activities. Scheduling and use of seasonal food permitted these and many other Mesoamerican peoples to exploit their environment highly effectively without overtaxing any of the available food sources. Between 10,000 and 4,000 B.P. the people lived by using these basic procurement systems. But something caused the Mesoamericans to concentrate more heavily on wild grasses: both maize and foxtail millet. Between 7,000 and 4,000 B.P. wild maize increased its cob size and was crossed with related wild corn to produce a hybrid species that was the ancestor of modern maize. Some species of beans became more permeable in water and developed softer pods. Flannery argues that the highland people began experimenting with the planting of maize and other grasses, deliberately increasing the areas where they would grow. After a long time these deviations in the food procurement system caused the importance of grass collection to increase at the expense of gathering other seasonal foods until the new activity, with its vital planting and harvesting schedules, became the dominant activity, one that was self-perpetuating from one year to the next.

EARLY FOOD PRODUCTION IN PERU

Peruvian coast

The Peruvian coast forms a narrow shelf at the foot of the Andes, crossed by small river valleys descending from the mountains to the sea. These valleys are oases in the desert plain, with deep, rich soils and blooming vegetation where water is plentiful. For thousands of years Peruvians have cultivated these valley floors, building their settlements, pyramids, and palaces at the edges of their agricultural land. Because conditions for preservation in this arid country are exceptional, the archaeological record is often quite complete. The coast itself forms a series of related microenvironments, such as rocky bays where shellfish are abundant, places where seasonal vegetable foods nourished by damp fogs are common, and the floors or sides of river valleys flowing into the Pacific. A combination of these microenvironments provides a rich and uniform constellation of food resources that could be exploited with ease from relatively sedentary base camps.[8]

The archaeological evidence for the Peruvian coast is incomplete for the period immediately preceding early food production. During the dry winter months the inhabitants collected shellfish and other marine resources, and hunting and vegetable foods were more important in the summers. After 7,000 B.P., however, more efficient collecting strategies came into use, with greater attention to maximally exploiting natural food sources. Fishing, in particular, became more important. Between about 6,200 and 4,500 B.P., Peruvian coastal peoples depended on marine resources — fish, sea birds, and mollusks — for much of their diet. During the warmest and driest period after the Pleistocene, the coastal people moved closer to the shore, dwelling in larger and more stable settlements. Along with the shift to more lasting coastal dwelling came the development of sophisticated equipment for deep-sea fishing. Somewhere around 5,000 B.P., two species of cultivated squash were added to the coastal diet. At this point the population split into two groups: the large, coastal villages were established in areas where agriculture was impossible, but they flourished on rich maritime resources; the small, sedentary inland hamlets lived by farming. The prehistoric Peruvian coast is remarkable for its very large permanent settlements based on fishing and gathering rather than agriculture.

A typical coastal camp for this period flourished at Chilca, 45 miles (72 km) south of present-day Lima. Frederic Engel excavated refuse heaps there and C14 dated the earlier Chilca occupation between 5,800 and 4,650 B.P.[9] When the site was in use, it probably lay near a reedy marsh, which provided both matting and building materials as well as sites for small gardens. The Chilca people lived on sea mollusks, fish, and sea lions; they apparently hunted few land mammals. They cultivated jack and lima beans, gourds, and squashes, probably relying on river floods as well as rainfall for their simple agriculture.

One remarkable Chilca house was uncovered: a circular structure, it had a domelike frame of canes bound with rope and covered with bundles of grass (Figure 13.3); the interior was braced with bones from stranded whales. Seven burials had been deposited in the house before it was intentionally collapsed on top of them. The skeletons were wrapped in mats and all buried at the same time, perhaps because of an epidemic.

The new emphasis on fish, increased use of flour ground from wild grass seed, and availability of cultivated squashes provided new sources of nutrition for some coastal groups. This may ultimately have set off a sustained period of population growth. Certainly the succeeding millennia of coastal history saw many permanent settlements established near the ocean; the people combined

7,000 B.P.

6,200 to 4,500 B.P.

5,000 B.P.

Chilca
5,800 to 4,650 B.P.
6,750 to 5,300 B.P.

New World Agriculture

Figure 13.3
Reconstruction of a Chilca
house. (After Donan.)

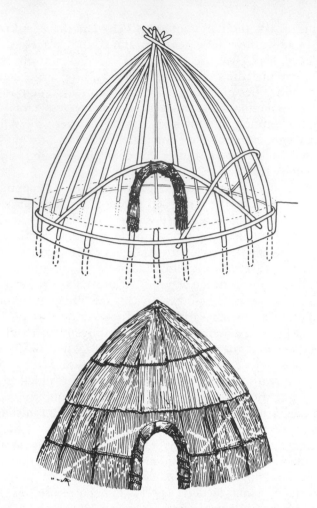

agriculture with fishing and mollusk gathering. Domesticated cotton first appeared somewhere around 4,500 B.P. Squashes, peppers, lima beans, and other crops remained as staple foods until recent times. Maize and other basic foods were still unknown. Agriculture remained a secondary activity much later than it did in Mesoamerica.

4,500 B.P.

One later site is Huaca Prieta, a sedentary village that housed several hundred people on the north coast of Peru between 4,500 and 3,800 B.P.[10] The vast refuse mound here contains small one- or two-room houses built partially into the ground and roofed with timber or whalebone beams. The inhabitants were remarkably skillful cotton weavers who devised a sophisticated art style with animal, human, and geometric designs.

Huaca Prieta
4,500 to 3,800 B.P.

Playa Culebras

Maize makes its first appearance on the coast at Playa Culebras, another important and contemporary settlement south of Huaca Prieta.[11] This and other settlements show greater emphasis on permanent architecture, not only in domestic buildings but also as large ceremonial structures. A complex of stone and mud mortar platforms lies at El Paraíso on the floodplain of the Chillón Valley, some distance from the sea. At least one mound had complexes of connected rooms built in successive stages. Settlements such as El Paraíso obviously depended more on agriculture than earlier sites had. By the time the temple complexes were built there, after 3,800 B.P., loom-woven textiles and pottery had come into widespread use (Figure 13.4). All the major food plants that formed the basis of later Peruvian civilization were employed.

3,800 B.P.
4,300 B.P.

Most of our knowledge about the early history of food production in the highlands is from discoveries by MacNeish and others in the Ayacucho region of central Peru.[12] Food resources in the highland valleys are separated in vertically spaced microenvironments, like layers of a cake. Rarely was it possible for the inhabitants of a valley to exploit all these microenvironments from one locality, nor are they uniformly distributed in all highland valleys. Economic variability between mountain valleys was great, and no one food provided a staple diet. The carrying capacity of the highland valleys depended on the ways in which their populations exploited the resources. On the coast, intensified exploitation of the marine and vegetal resources led to population growth, but the reverse ultimately occurred in the highland valleys. There,

Peruvian highlands

Figure 13.4 A double-headed snakelike figure with appended rock crabs revealed by plotting the warp movements in a preceramic twined cotton fabric from Huaca Prieta, Peru. The original length was about 41 centimeters (16 in). The shaded area indicates the surviving textile. Double-headed motifs have persisted through more than 3,000 years of Peruvian art. (Courtesy of Junius Bird.)

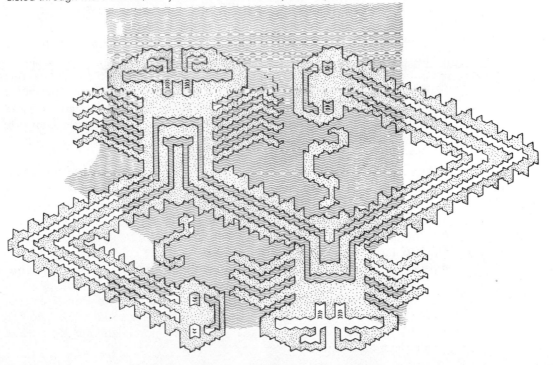

deforestation, soil erosion, and temporary desiccation partly generated by agriculture reduced carrying capacities after A.D. 500.

The hunter-gatherers of the highland valleys are thought to have exploited only a small portion of the potential resources. According to MacNeish, finds at Pikimachay Cave and elsewhere indicate several subsistence options — hunting various sizes of mammal including the great sloth and varied small creatures, and collecting many species of plant foods. These options were exercised by priority rather than by season, the notion being that one acquired food with the minimum effort. Around 11,000 B.P., however, the subsistence strategies changed. There is reason to believe that seasonal exploitation had replaced other options, with hunting, trapping, and plant collecting at high altitudes important in the dry season. During the wetter months, collecting and possibly penning small game, as well as seed collecting, were dominant activities.

After 7,000 to 6,500 B.P., the archaeological evidence becomes more abundant. In the Ayacucho-Huanta region twenty-five dry- and wet-season camps have been found that provide signs of continued exploitation of wild vegetables as well as game during the dry season. The Pikimachay Cave levels of this period yielded wet-season living floors. There, wild seeds are abundant along with remains of gourds and seeds of domesticated quinoa and squash. Game remains are very rare, as if a vegetable diet, whether wild or domesticated, was of prime importance during the wet months. Another wet-season locality, Puente Cave, yielded a few bones of tame guinea pigs as well as the remains of many small wild mammals. Grinding stones and other artifacts used for plant collecting, or perhaps incipient agriculture, are also common at Puente. Throughout this period, many wet-season camps became larger and more stable, their use extending over longer periods of the year.

After 6,000 B.P., the Ayacucho peoples relied more on food production. The potato was cultivated. Hoes appear, as well as domesticated corn, squashes, common beans, and other crops. Guinea pigs were certainly tamed, and llama were domesticated in central Peru by at least 5,500 B.P. By this time, too, there was more interaction between coast and interior, trade in raw materials, and some interchange of domesticates. MacNeish believes corn spread from the north, ultimately from Mesoamerica, into Ayacucho. Root crop agriculture may have diffused from highland Peru into the lowlands, too.

The Ayacucho sequence is illustrative of the complex adaptive shifts that took place in many parts of South America after 7,000 B.P. As in Mesoamerica, the beginnings of agriculture were a gradual process of adjustment, with food production eventually supplanting gathering as the major subsistence activity. As agriculture took hold, settlements became more sedentary. And, as agricultural production intensified after 5,500 B.P., so more substantial settlements appear, large villages often with small ceremonial buildings. These settlements were linked by complex barter networks that distributed a wide range of day-to-day and exotic commodities from highlands to lowlands and vice versa. It was the interaction between a whole series of complex social and economic, as well as environmental, factors that led to the more elaborate societies of Peru in later millennia.

11,000 B.P.

7,000 to 6,500 B.P.

Pikimachay

Puente

6,000 B.P.

5,500 B.P.

Eleven thousand years ago the southwestern United States was populated by hunter-gatherers whose culture was adapted to desert living.[13] A distinctive foraging culture, the Cochise, flourished in southeastern Arizona and southwestern New Mexico from about this time. The Cochise people gathered many plant foods including yucca seeds, cacti, and sunflower seeds. They used small milling stones, basketry, cordage, nets, and spearthrowers. Many features of their material culture survived into later times, when cultivated plants were introduced into the Southwest.

Cochise **11,000 to 3,000 B.P.**

We say introduced, because there is good reason to believe that a primitive form of maize and squashes were diffused into the Southwest from Mexico about 4,000 B.P. The earliest finds of maize in Southwestern sites, at Bat Cave and in northwest New Mexico, date to about this time.[14] As early as 5,200 B.P. the inhabitants of the area were living in larger and more numerous base camps, using many grindstones and other gathering artifacts. Conceivably, the population rose, partly because of more favorable climatic conditions and partly because of more efficient resource exploitation. The first appearance of primitive maize occurred around 3,800 B.P. and a gradual change in the settlement pattern resulted. A fall or winter base camp that brought several bands into one place came into fashion — a place where the people may have lived while they consumed the agricultural surplus and local abundances of wild vegetable foods. This lifeway continued until about 2,800 years ago, after which the gradual evolution of the culture into the later Anasazi tradition can be traced.

Bat Cave **4,000 B.P.**

2,800 B.P.

Cynthia Irwin-Williams and Vance Haynes have suggested that an elementary Southwestern culture emerged about 5,000 B.P., at a time when there was slightly higher rainfall and increased food resources for growing hunter-gatherer populations to feed on.[15] The various bands of the Southwest maintained widespread communication networks which enabled them to share information about new plant foods and other innovations. It seems likely not only that the Archaic peoples were familiar with the germination of seeds, but also that they occasionally manipulated wild plants by careful irrigation and weeding, as Great Basin peoples did in historic times. But there is a considerable difference between occasionally helping wild foods grow, while not disturbing your annual gathering round, and taking up deliberate cultivation as a priority which competes with your basic lifeway schedule.

How did the changeover occur? One scenario has agricultural peoples from Mexico moving northward into the Southwest. Archaic people may have been absorbed by the newcomers, or may have adopted the new economies on their own account after the initial colonization by newcomers. If one follows Flannery's arguments for Mesoamerica and applies them to the Cochise, then one would see the continued introduction of improved maize strains as new food energy sources that triggered cultural change of the kind Flannery described in Mesoamerica.[16] Another hypothesis sees population growth as a major factor. Under this argument, the Southwest received surplus population from hunter-gatherer territories in coastal California.[17] These newcomers tried to

New World Agriculture   215

adapt to the same favorable locations as the indigenous inhabitants but found themselves forced to settle in marginal areas where storage of food and greater dependence on agriculture were essential. Thus, cultural change was stimulated by mechanisms similar to those postulated by Flannery. Even without population growth, increased aridity in the Southwest could have produced a similar effect among people already living in the area.

2,300 B.P.

By 2,300 B.P. experimentation and new hybrid varieties of maize introduced from the south had led to sedentary villages and much greater dependence on farming. The cultural changes of the period culminated in the great Southwestern archaeological traditions: Hohokam, Mogollon, and Anasazi.

Hohokam
2,300 B.P. to recent times

The Hohokam tradition has long been thought to have originated in the Cochise. But Emil Haury, who dug the world famous Snaketown site in the Gila River Valley believes that the Hohokam people were immigrants from northern Mexico who brought their pottery and intensive irrigation agriculture with them.[18] The newcomers soon influenced the lifeway of the local people, and a desert adaptation of Hohokam resulted. Unfortunately, Haury's theory is based on very limited evidence and the origins of the Hohokam remain obscure.

Hohokam subsistence was based on maize, beans, cucurbits, cotton, and other crops, as well as gathering. They planted their crops to coincide with the biannual rainfall and flooding patterns. Where they could, they practiced irrigation from flowing streams; otherwise they cultivated floodplains and caught runoff from local storms with dams, terraces, and other devices. Hohokam people occupied much of what is now Arizona. Their cultural heirs are the Pima and Papago Indians of today.

Hohokam culture evolved slowly over two thousand years. There are at least five stages of Hohokam culture, culminating in a Classic period from about 850 to 500 years ago when large pueblos — communal villages — were built and canal irrigation was especially important. It was at this time and somewhat earlier that Mexican influences are detected in Hohokam culture. These include new varieties of maize, the appearance of platform mounds and ball or dance courts at Snaketown and elsewhere, and of imports such as copper bells. Does this mean that Mexican immigrants transformed Hohokam culture, or were there internal factors that caused greater elaboration of local society at the same time as some ideas arrived from Mexico? Archaeologists remain divided on this point.

Mogollon
2,300 to 500 B.P.

The Mogollon tradition emerged from Archaic roots between 2,300 and 1,700 B.P. and disappeared as a separate entity between 1,100 and 500 years ago, when it became part of Anasazi.[19] The Mogollon culture is well known from dry caves in New Mexico as an agricultural culture in which hunting and gathering in the highlands were always important. Mogollon agriculture depended on direct rainfall, with only very limited use of irrigation. The people lived in small villages of pit dwellings with timber frames and mat or brush roofs. Their material culture was utilitarian and included milling stones, digging sticks, bows and arrows, fine baskets, and characteristic brown and red pottery.

At least six regional variants of Mogollon are known, and there are five chronological stages, the fifth ending in about 500 B.P. Early Mogollon villages were often located on high promontories close to more fertile lands. The settlement pattern varied from area to area, but with a tendency toward larger sites and increased populations throughout the life of the tradition. By 600 B.P. pueblos of several hundred rooms had developed in some areas, but by this time Mogollon had become part of the western pueblo Anasazi tradition.

The Anasazi tradition is, in general terms, ancestral to the cultures of the modern Pueblo Indians — the Hopi, Zuni, and others.[20] Its emergence is conventionally dated to 2,000 B.P., but this is a purely arbitrary date, for Anasazi's roots lie in Archaic cultures that flourished for a long time before. The Anasazi people made heavy use of wild vegetable foods, even after they took up maize agriculture seriously, after 1,500 B.P. Most of their farming depended on dry agriculture and seasonal rainfall, although they, like the Hohokam, used irrigation techniques when practicable. They made use of flood areas, where the soil would remain damp for weeks after sudden storms. Moisture in the flooded soil could be used to germinate seed in the spring and to bring ripening crops to fruition after later rains. But this type of agriculture is very high risk, and the Anasazi relied on wild resources to carry them through lean years.

Anasazi
2,000 B.P. to recent times

Anasazi chronology is well established thanks to the use of dendrochronology on beams from abandoned pueblos. The tradition is centered in the "Four Corners" area where Utah, Arizona, Colorado, and New Mexico meet. There are at least six Basketmaker and Pueblo subdivisions of Anasazi; each marked a gradual increase in the importance of agriculture and the emergence of some larger sites with *kivas*, ceremonial sweathouses. Pueblos, which are complexes of adjoining rooms, occur more frequently after 1,000 B.P.; the population congregated in fewer, but larger, pueblos after 800 B.P. These were located in densely populated areas, some of them moved from the open to under cliff overhangs, the so-called "cliff-dwellings" (Figure 13.5). Some of the features of these sites such as turrets and loopholed walls appear to be defensive. At the same time as people concentrated in larger sites, there was depopulation of many areas of the northern Southwest. The reasons for these changes are imperfectly understood. In some areas, like Chaco Canyon, New Mexico, the concentrated populations may have enjoyed more elaborate social and political organizations as well as trading connections with widespread areas of the Southwest. But most pueblos seem to have been more egalitarian in their organization, and relatively self-sufficient in meeting their needs. It may be that the changes generated by the developments in Chaco and elsewhere caused people to congregate more closely. Alternatively, it has been argued that some climatic and environmental changes, as yet imperfectly understood, may have caused major shifts in the settlement pattern. More likely, a combination of environmental, societal, and adaptive changes set in motion a period of turbulence and culture change.

By about 1,400 B.P. the basic Anasazi settlement pattern had evolved and above-the-ground houses were being substituted for the pit dwellings of earlier centuries. The latter developed into kivas, subterranean ceremonial structures that existed in every large village. Large settlements of contiguous dwellings became the rule after 1,100 B.P., with clusters of "rooms" serving as homes for

New World Agriculture   217

Figure 13.5 Pueblo Bonito, New Mexico, the first site to be dated by tree-ring chronology, to A.D. 919–1130. The round structures are kivas.

separate families or lineages. Large settlements like Pueblo Bonito developed around 800 B.P.; this was a huge D-shaped complex of 800 rooms rising several stories high around the rim of the arc (Figure 13.5). The room complexes surrounded courts, with the highest stories at the back. They formed a blank wall; a line of one-story rooms cut off the fourth side. Within the court lay the kivas, always one great kiva and usually several smaller ones. The great kivas were up to sixty feet in diameter with wide masonry benches encircling the interior. The roof was supported by four large pillars near the center, where a raised hearth lay. Two subterranean, masonry-lined rooms were situated on either side of the fireplace. A staircase leading from the floor of the kiva to the large room above it gave access to the sacred precinct.

The period between 900 and 600 B.P. was one of consolidation of population into a few, more congested settlements where more elaborate social organizations may have developed. The pueblos were probably communities that were run for the collective good with at least some ranking of society under a chieftain. In modern Hopi society, clan superiority and kinship lineages played an important role in the election of chieftains. Thrust into close intimacy by the nature of pueblo architecture, the people developed well-integrated religious and ceremonial structures to counteract the tensions of close quarters living.

The Anasazi enjoyed a relatively elaborate material culture at the height of their prosperity; at this time they were making distinctive black and white pottery, well-formed baskets, and fine sandals. But their architecture was neither very sophisticated nor particularly innovative. Baked mud and rocks were formed into boxlike rooms; a roof of mud rested on horizontal timbers. Room after room was added as the need arose, using local materials and a simple architectural style entirely appropriate for its environment.

The southwestern farmer won success by skillfully using limited scarce water resources and by bringing together soil and water — by means of dams, floodwater irrigation, and other systems for distributing runoff. Planting techniques were carefully adapted to desert conditions and short water supplies, and myriad tiny gardens supplied food for each family or lineage. This successful adaptation is also reflected in their unique architecture which made full use of local materials.

AGRICULTURAL SOCIETIES IN EASTERN NORTH AMERICA

The Archaic hunter-gatherer traditions of eastern North America enjoyed many regional variations in material culture; these occurred because the people concentrated on different, locally abundant food sources.[21] In general, however, the lifeway was similar among them: a seasonal one, based on a very broad spectrum of game and vegetable foods. As long as the population density was low, every band could react relatively easily to changes in local conditions. Since many of their favorite vegetable foods were subject to cycles of lean and abundant years, a flexibility in choice and movement was essential. But as population grew slowly throughout the Archaic, this flexibility was increasingly restricted and the people tended to specialize on local resources that were available most of the year. They developed better storage techniques and fostered closer contacts with their neighbors through exchange networks that handled foodstuffs and other commodities. The development of these types of response may have required more complex social organization than the simple band structure of earlier times. And it is no coincidence that burial patterns during the late Archaic, about 3,700 B.P., reflect greater differentiation in social status.

3,700 B.P.

The eastern hunter-gatherer societies were so efficient that the people may have been aware of agriculture for centuries before adopting the new economies. The transition to food production seems to have taken place almost imperceptibly. Perhaps some crops like the sunflower were domesticated independently in the East before maize was cultivated. It seems clear, however, that the first eastern farmers relied heavily on hunting and foraging for much of their diet, in some areas to the virtual exclusion of agriculture. Conventionally, the beginnings of the Woodland tradition — a general name for farming sites with pottery and burial mounds — is placed at the moment when the

Figure 13.6 Reconstruction of an Adena house from the posthole pattern shown at left.

first "grit-tempered" clay vessels appear in the archaeological record, about 2,600 B.P.

It is thought that the use of local strains of corn, beans, and squash after 3,550 B.P. gave people the surplus of food and time to engage in some communal activities. About 3,000 B.P. the first signs of mound building appear in the Midwest. Some villages began to bury their dead under low earth mounds, a new custom that became widespread within a few centuries. The more elaborate early mounds are centered on the Ohio Valley; some of them were built in the middle of vast, earthwork enclosures. This first mound-building culture is called the Adena, and lasted from about 3,000 to 1,750 B.P. The Adena people lived in small, scattered villages and built round houses of wattle and thatch (Figure 13.6). To what extent they relied on agriculture is unknown.[22]

The Adena people were much preoccupied with death rituals and erected large communal burial mounds in which individuals, groups of people, perhaps clan leaders, or dozens of bodies, were deposited. The grave goods found with such burials suggest that Adena society was organized in lineages and clans, with chiefs whose power lay in their special economic and social status that resided in their clan and lineage associations. These chiefs organized the long distance trade networks that linked Adena villages over an enormous area of Ohio, Indiana, Kentucky, West Virginia, and Pennsylvania.

The Adena people flourished for a thousand years, but their distinctive religious and burial cults were eventually replaced by new rituals that made their first appearance in Illinois and then spread eastward into Ohio and a huge portion of the eastern United States from the Mississippi River to Florida.

This new culture, the Hopewell culture, emerged in about 2,400 B.P. and survived until around 900 years ago. The Hopewell people probably cultivated maize and other crops, but hunting and gathering were important as well. Hopewell settlements are still somewhat of a mystery, but most of the people seem to have lived in rectangular and oval-shaped houses with domed and thatched roofs. Most villages were permanent settlements, linked with one another by clan and lineage ties that extended for hundreds of miles. The Hopewell seems to have been a society without social classes in general, but clan or lineage leaders enjoyed a special prestige that is reflected in the wealth of their burials. A preoccupation with death and status seems to have been at the heart of Hopewell life, for their burials display extraordinary lavishness.

Hopewell burial mounds were on a larger scale than those of the Adena people. At Crooks' Mound in Louisiana the builders erected a vast earthen platform and buried 164 people in it. Then they deposited another 214 corpses on top of the platform before erecting a burial mound on top of it. Some mounds were over forty feet high. Important individuals were buried with lavish arrays of ceremonial vessels and other valuable objects of soapstone, mica, wood, and clay. Although the Hopewell culture heartland was relatively small, the cult objects buried with important people came from thousands of square miles of trade networks.

Crook's Mound

Hopewell miners exploited the copper outcrops of Lake Superior, which they heated and hammered into thin ornaments (Figure 13.7a). Sheets of mica were cut into striking lustrous silhouettes of bird talons, human hands, and other designs (Figure 13.7b). For some time people traded obsidian all the way from Wyoming, conch shells from the Gulf Coast, and soapstone from several areas to make fine pipe bowls carved in the forms of animals and humans (Figure 13.7c).

Figure 13.7 Hopewell artifacts: (a) raven or crow in beaten copper; (b) bird claw in mica; (c) soapstone frog.

This array of raw materials can only have been assembled by sophisticated and well-organized trading relationships. Many archaeologists believe that the various cult objects — pipe bowls and so on — were made by a few craftspeople at certain locations, then distributed far and wide through trade networks that moved not only cult materials but essential commodities as well. The result was the concentration of luxury goods in the hands of a few individuals, who enjoyed high prestige and special status in society.

The decline of the Hopewell is still imperfectly understood, but it is possible that a rapid and dramatic population explosion may have strained the limits of the economic system, causing competition between different trading networks and rupturing long-established economic and political relationships. By 1,400 B.P. the cultural primacy of the Hopewell area had passed to the fertile floodplain between St. Louis and New Orleans, which nurtured the greatest of North American Indian states, that of the Mississippian.[23] We use the term "state," because the Mississippian people were organized in a rigid hierarchy of social classes, headed by a religious elite of priests and nobles. The scale and flamboyance of Mississippian society dwarfed anything known before in North America. Its enormous ceremonial centers, brilliant artistic traditions, and elaborate cosmology seem to recall those developed by Mesoamerican civilizations. They appear at least partially alien to the simpler traditions of the earlier cultures of the East. The Mississippian lasted for at least eight hundred years, until the threshold of modern times and European settlement.

Mississippian
1,400 to 600 B.P.

Figure 13.8 A reconstruction of Cahokia during the period 700 to 450 B.P. by A. W. Hodge.

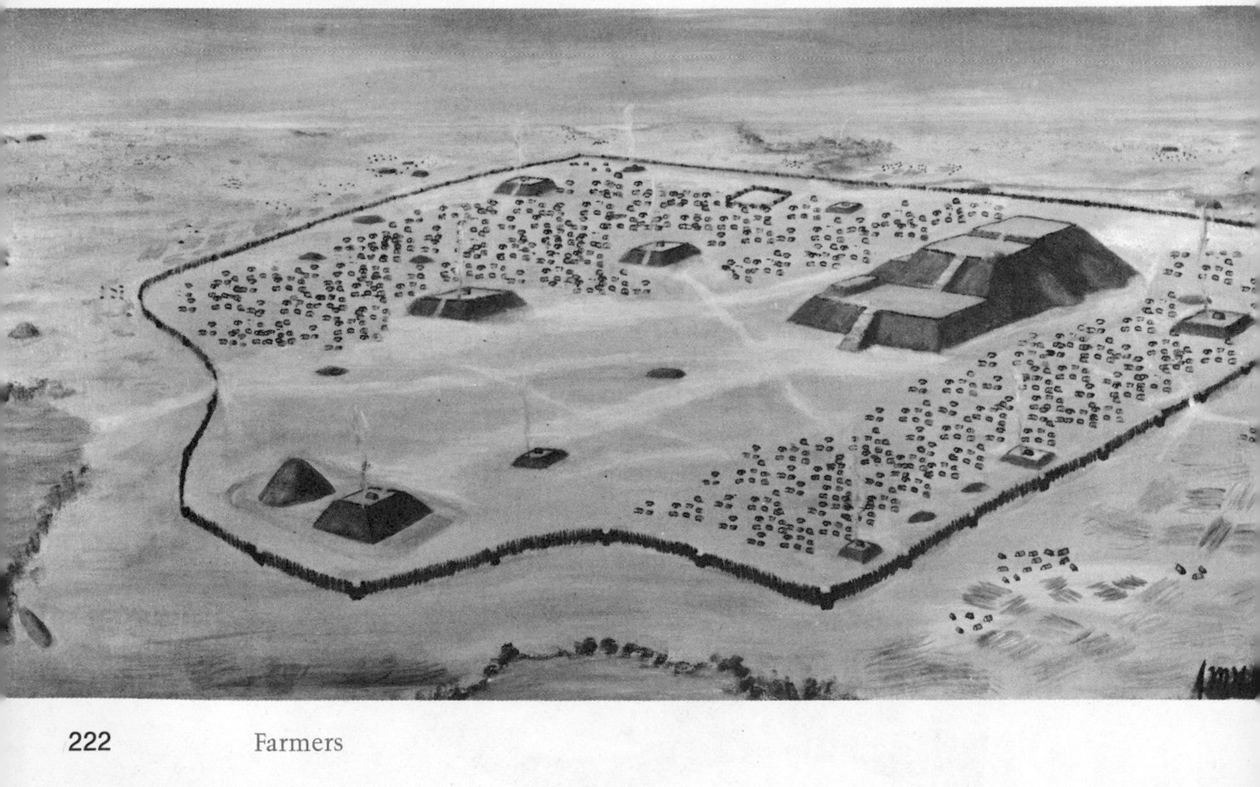

Figure 13.9 Monk's Mound, Cahokia, Illinois, from the southeast during excavation in 1966.

Many people believe that the Mississippian developed its remarkable elaboration as a result of the intensification of bean, maize, and squash agriculture in the floodplain areas. The new culture was centered on the Mississippi Valley, but extended into southeastern Missouri, southern Illinois, Georgia, Alabama, and Kentucky. The Mississippians had few technological advantages over their predecessors, but their leaders seem to have developed the political capacity to organize huge public works projects involving hundreds, if not thousands, of people. These leaders organized the development of larger towns centered around conspicuous rectangular temple mounds and large open spaces; these towns reflected a preoccupation with religious and ceremonial matters (Figure 13.8).

The greatest of these centers is the Cahokia site near St. Louis, a vast complex of mounds and plazas that may have housed, in its general area, some 30,000 souls in its heyday.[24] The largest mound at Cahokia covers 16 acres and the temple on its summit was over a hundred feet above the ground (Figure 13.9). A great plaza at its foot was surrounded with other mounds that formed the foundations for warehouses, administrative buildings, and the houses of

Cahokia

nobles. Stretching out into the countryside were the villages of the farmers who supported the nobles and craftspeople with their food surpluses. Dozens of smaller satellite communities linked by extensive trade routes and clan or lineage ties formed a multitiered settlement pattern in the floodplain, all of them controlled directly and indirectly by the religious leaders who presided over the affairs of state at Cahokia and elsewhere.

The Mississippian seems markedly different from the Adena and Hopewell, despite the same underpinning of subsistence agriculture and gathering. The vast ceremonial centers, pyramids, and plazas recall Mexican religious patterns and cosmology. This cosmology is reflected in cult objects — pots with human heads and copper ornaments bearing portraits that recall the abstract symbolism of Mexican cults, with their preoccupation with the sun, rain, and gods of fire. Many of the human figures are thought to represent shaman priests who played a dominant role in sacrifices and public ceremonies. The notion of Mexican influence on Mississippian culture is attractive, conceivably in the form of trading contacts by Mexican *pochteca*, or traders, who may have settled among the local inhabitants. However, it is only fair to point out that no Mesoamerican artifacts have yet been found in Mississippian sites.

The formal organization of the Mississippian state was akin to that of Mesoamerican civilizations. An elite of priests and nobles headed the pyramid of social classes, probably with absolute and despotic powers. The ranks of society were probably structured with some rigidity, under clan rules that regulated and perpetuated social organization at every level. As a result, everyone probably knew exactly where he or she stood in society, even slaves.[25]

When Spanish conquistadore Hernando de Soto came across the Mississippians in the sixteenth century, he found them living in large communities headed by powerful chiefs who were allied in loosely knit confederacies. Within a few centuries smallpox, measles, and other European diseases had depopulated much of the Southeast and South, and the economic and political structure of Mississippian life had collapsed forever.

400 B.P.

PART FIVE

OLD WORLD CIVILIZATIONS

(5,000 B.P. to Modern Times)

"The great tide of civilization has long since ebbed,
leaving these scattered wrecks on the solitary shore. Are
those waters to flow again, bringing back the seeds of
knowledge and of wealth that they have wafted to the
West? We wanderers were seeking what they had left
behind, as children gather up the coloured shells on the
deserted sands."
— Austen Henry Layard

As in Part 4 a discussion of the theoretical background and the major controversies precedes the narrative prehistory. Part 5 deals with the beginnings of complex states and urban civilization. These chapters present an unconventional
account of early civilization in that they deal with lesser known parts of the world
such as Africa and Southeast Asia, as well as the Near East. Research in Africa
and Asia has hardly begun; future excavations in these regions are likely to throw
significant new light on such much-debated issues as the importance of ceremonial
centers and long distance trade in the emergence of complex societies. Once
again, the reader is urged to start with the theoretical background before embark-
ing on the narrative culture history.

Chapter Fourteen

THE DEVELOPMENT OF CIVILIZATION

PREVIEW

✤ Most scholars consider civilization a stage in human development that has dimensions of time and space and is defined by its artifacts and other cultural attributes.

✤ V. Gordon Childe's pioneer definition of the Urban Revolution was widely accepted; it centered around the development of the city, metallurgy, food surpluses, writing, and a unifying religious force. Unfortunately, his criteria are not universal enough to be generally applicable.

✤ Evolutionary models of the development of sociopolitical units give us a framework for looking at the mechanisms that led to the emergence of urban societies.

✤ We summarize various commonly held theories about how complex societies began, describing the various major potential causes for civilization. These include ecological stress, population stress, technological change, irrigation agriculture, and the notion of the hydraulic civilization. Religion, ceremony, and exchange networks have all been espoused as potential factors in the development of civilization.

✤ Current research stresses a systems approach to the origins of civilization, regarding the emergence of complex societies as a gradual process caused by many interacting factors. Kent Flannery has argued that complex societies are not susceptible to simple analysis, and that there were many causes of cultural change. He urges us to look at the processes and mechanisms by which the necessary changes took place.

✤ The ultimate objective is to establish the set of rules by which a complex state could have come into being. Religious and informational factors seem to be key elements in the regulation of environmental and economic variables in early civilization.

Everyone who has studied the prehistory of human society agrees that the emergence of civilization in different parts of the world was a major event in human adaptation. The word *civilization* has a ready, everyday meaning. It implies "civility," a measure of decency in the behavior of the individual in a civilization. Such definitions inevitably reflect ethnocentrism or value judgements because what is "civilized" behavior in one civilization might be antisocial or baffling in another. These simplistic definitions are of no use to students of prehistoric civilizations seeking basic definitions and cultural processes.

Civilization

The generally agreed, special attributes that separate civilizations from other societies include monumental architecture, intensive agriculture, a state-organized society, metallurgy, writing, and, above all, cities. That not all these features are found in every early civilization has made the task of defining a civilization unusually difficult. Indeed, there are almost as many definitions of civilization as there are archaeologists. Most scholars consider it to be a stage in human cultural development, one that has dimensions of time and space and is defined by its artifacts and other cultural attributes, such as writing.

The well-known anthropologist Clyde Kluckhohn devised one widely used definition of civilization: towns with a population of more than 5000 persons, writing, and monumental architecture, including ceremonial centers. This very general definition is adequate for our purposes, for, in archaeological terms, the primary focus of research is the city, a new form of human settlement whose development is closely associated with the emergence of the world's first civilizations. This focus has developed simply because it is easy enough to excavate a city, whereas the nature of archaeological evidence makes it much harder to recover many of the intangible subtleties of a civilization.

CITIES

Archaeological research into early civilization concentrates on the origin and development of the city. Today the city is the primary human settlement type throughout the world, and has become so since the Industrial Revolution altered the economic face of the globe. The earliest cities assumed many forms, from the compact, walled settlement of Mesopotamia to the Mesoamerican ceremonial center with a core population in its precincts and a scattered rural population in villages arranged over the surrounding landscape. The cities of the Harappan civilization of the Indus were carefully planned communities with regular streets and assigned quarters for different living groups. The palaces of the Minoans and Mycenaeans functioned as secular economic and trading centers that served as focus for a scattered village populations nearby.

A *city* is best defined by its population, which is generally larger and denser than that of towns or villages. As we've said, a good and generally used rule of

City

thumb is a lower limit of 5000 people for a city. But numbers are not a sufficient determinant: many people can congregate in a limited area and still not possess the compact diversity of population which enables the economic and organizational complexity of a city to develop. It is this complexity that distinguishes the city from other settlement types. Most cities have a complexity in both organization and nonagricultural activities which is supported by large food surpluses. The city is not merely complex; it is a functioning part of a complex system of different settlements who rely on its many services and facilities.

AN URBAN REVOLUTION?

Since archaeological research into early civilization has concentrated on excavations into ancient cities and ceremonial centers, it was perhaps inevitable that the first attempts to explain the origins of civilization focused on the city and its implications.

Early scholars who debated the origins of civilization were concerned with the cultural evolution of humankind from a state of savagery toward the full realization of human potential. This, in their eyes, was Victorian civilization. They considered that their civilization had originated in Ancient Egypt and that bold mariners had spread the ideas of civilization all over the globe. These simplistic hypotheses collapsed in the face of new archaeological discoveries in Mesopotamia and the Nile Valley in the early decades of this century. With the discovery of the Sumerians and early Egyptian farming villages, scholars came to realize that early civilization had developed over a wide area and over a considerable period of time.

The first relatively sophisticated theories about the origins of urban civilization were formulated by V. Gordon Childe, of Neolithic Revolution fame (Chapter 2). Childe claimed that his Neolithic Revolution was followed by

Urban Revolution

an Urban Revolution, when the development of metallurgy created a new class of full-time specialists and changed the rules of human social organization.[1*] Childe argued that the new full-time specialists were fed by food surpluses raised by the peasant farmers. The products of the craftsworkers had to be distributed, and raw materials had to be obtained from outside sources. Both needs reduced the self-reliance of peasant societies. Agricultural techniques became more sophisticated as an increased yield of food per capita was needed to support the nonagricultural population. Irrigation increased productivity, leading to centralized control of food supplies, production, and distribution. Taxation and tribute led to the accumulation of capital. A new class-stratified society came into being. Writing was essential for keeping records and for developing exact and predictive sciences. Transportation by water and land was part of the new order. A unifying religious force dominated urban life as priest-kings and despots rose to power. Monumental architecture testified to their activities.

* See pages 385–386 for notes to Chapter 14.

The notion of an Urban Revolution dominated archaeological and historical literature for years. But the revolution hypothesis has flaws as an all-embracing definition of civilization and a description of its development. Childe's criteria are far from universal. Some highly effective and lasting civilizations like those of the Maya and the Mycenaeans never had cities.[2] The Maya built elaborate ceremonial and religious centers surrounded by a scattered rural population clustered for the most part in small villages. Writing is absent from the Inca civilization of Peru. The Mayan and Aztec scripts were used in part for administering an elaborate calendar. Some craft specialization and religious structure is typical of most civilizations, but it cannot be said that these form the basis for an overall definition of civilization.

American archaeologist Robert Adams stresses the development of social organization and craft specialization during the Urban Revolution. He raises objections to the Childe hypothesis, arguing that the name implies undue emphasis on the city at the expense of social change — the development of social classes and political institutions. Many of Childe's criteria, like the evolution of the exact sciences, have the disadvantage of not being readily preserved in the archaeological record. Furthermore, Childe's Urban Revolution was identified by lists of traits, although the name implies emphasis on the *processes* of cultural change as time passed. Childe believed technological innovations and subsistence patterns were at the core of the Urban Revolution. Adams directed his work toward changes in social organization; he described early Mesopotamia and central Mexico as following "a fundamental course of development in which corporate kin groups, originally preponderating in the control of land, were gradually supplemented by the growth of private estates in the hands of urban elites."[3] The eventual result was a stratified form of social organization rigidly divided along class lines.[4]

Adams:
Social organization

LATER THEORIES ABOUT
THE ORIGINS OF CIVILIZATION

By the time Adams was critiquing Childe's Urban Revolution, people were beginning to investigate the many interacting factors that led to the emergence of complex states. Everyone agreed that complex societies appeared during a period of major economic and social change, but different scholars gave emphasis to different possible factors that contributed to the rise of civilization. These factors included ecology, irrigation, population growth, trade, religious beliefs, and even warfare. In the pages that follow, we examine some of these factors, realizing that no one development led, on its own, to the emergence of cities and civilization.

Ecology

Many have said that the exceptional fertility of the Mesopotamian floodplain and the Nile Valley was a primary reason for the emergence of the cities and states in these regions. This fertility and benign climate led to the food surpluses that were capable of supporting the craftsworkers and the other specialists who formed the complex fabric of civilization.[5] This notion was the basic foundation of what was known in the 1920s and 1930s as the Fertile Crescent theory.

Reality, of course, is much more complicated. The true surplus is probably one of capacities, a *social surplus*, which is one that consciously reallocates goods or services. A social surplus is created by a society's deliberate action, through some form of governmental force achieving the reallocations. In a sense this is a taxation authority. This taxation authority is a person or organization that wrests surplus grain or other products from those who grow or produce them. Another problem with the Fertile Crescent theory is that the environments of all the major centers of early civilizations are far too diverse in altitude above sea level, for example, for any assemblage of environmental conditions to be defined and set forth as the requisite conditions which led to civilization's start.

Even on the Mesopotamian floodplain, which superficially appears to be a uniform environment, specialized zones of subsistence vary greatly. Wheat was grown on the Assyrian uplands; barley did better on the margins of swamps and near levees on the plain. Both these winter cereals were staples. Near the permanent watercourses low-lying orchards ripened in the summers, together with garden crops such as dates. The date crop was a beautiful supplement to the spring cereal harvests, ripening in the fall. Mesopotamian agriculture was combined with cattle herding on cereal stubble and fallow land in the permanently settled areas; many herds were grazed by nomads on the semiarid steppes beyond the limits of settled areas. Fish too provided vital protein, taken from the rivers and swamps that also had reeds for building material. Robert Adams argues that these ecological niches, effectively exploited, forged between adjacent segments of society an interdependence that was reflected in increased specialization in subsistence activities, as each segment of Mesopotamian society provided a part of the food supply and, ultimately, social surplus.[6]

Complex subsistence patterns like these were almost certainly active in Mesoamerica and Southeast Asia, to say nothing of Egypt, although the evidence is very incomplete. Even in the best-documented areas, evidence comes from later, well-documented periods, and we can only surmise that complexities were similar in earlier times. The integration of several ecological zones, each producing a different food as a main product, into one sociopolitical unit probably took place as the first ceremonial centers came into being. A localized center of power could control different ecological zones and the products from them, a more deliberate hedge against famine that was indispensable for planning food surpluses. This is not at all the same as saying that favorable ecological conditions were the cause of trade and redistributive mechanisms, and therefore some form of centralized authority, to develop. Rather, ecology was only one component in a close network of the many changes that led to civilization, a subsystem of interactive forces among a great many subsystems in equilibrium.

Population Growth

Thomas Henry Malthus argued as long ago as 1798 that people's reproductive capacity far exceeds the available food supply. Many people have argued that new and more intensive agricultural methods created food surpluses. These in turn led to population growth, more leisure time, and new social, political, and religious institutions, as well as the arts.

Malthus and Boserup

Ester Boserup, among others, has criticized this point of view. She feels that population growth provided the incentive for irrigation and intensive agriculture.[7] Her theories have convinced others that social evolution was caused by population growth. No one has explained, though, why the original population should have started to grow. By no means all farming populations, especially those using slash-and-burn cultivation, live at the maximum density that can be supported by the available agricultural land. And population is often artificially regulated. To claim that population growth explains how states were formed means finding out why such decisions would have been made.

Slash-and-burn, or swidden, agriculture with its shifting cultivation is very delicately balanced with the rest of its ecosystem. Populations are dispersed and have relatively little flexibility in movement or growth because the land has low carrying capacity and relatively few ecological niches to carry edible crops.[8] More lasting field agriculture is far more intensive, and exploits much more of the environment in an ordered and systematic way. The Mesopotamian example shows how effectively a sedentary population can manipulate its diverse food sources. The more specialized ecosystem created by these efforts supports more concentrated populations. It creates conditions in which more settlements per square mile can exist on foods whose annual yields are at least roughly predictable.

Most significant concentrations of settlement that might be called proto types for urban complexes developed in regions where permanent field agriculture flourished. But, unlike the period immediately after food production began, there is no evidence for a major jump in population immediately before civilization appeared. Nor does a dense population seem to have been a precondition for a complex society or redistribution centers for trade. We have no reason to believe that a critical population density was a prerequisite for urban life.

Technology

In Mesopotamia, again our best-documented area, agricultural technology did not advance until long after civilization began. The technological innovations that did appear were of more benefit to transportation (the wheel, for example) than to production. Copper and other exotic materials were at first used for small-scale production of cult objects. Not until several centuries after civilization started were copper and bronze more abundant, with demand for transportation and military needs burgeoning. Then we see an advance in technology or an increase in craftsworkers. Technology did evolve, but only in response to developing markets, new demands, and the expanded needs of the elite.

Irrigation

Most scholars now agree that three elements on Childe's list seem to have been of great importance in the growth of all the world's civilizations. The first was the creation of food surpluses, used to support new economic classes whose members were not directly engaged in food production. Agriculture as a way of life immediately necessitates storing crops to support the community during the lean times of the year. A surplus above this level of production was created by both increased agricultural efficiency and social and cultural changes. Specialist craftsworkers, priests, and traders were among the new classes of society that came into being as a result.

Second, agricultural economies may have tended to concentrate on fewer, more productive crops, but they remained diversified so that the ultimate subsistence base was still relatively wide. The ancient Egyptians relied on husbandry, especially in the Nile Delta. The diversity of food resources not only protected the people against the dangers of famine but also stimulated the development of trade and exchange mechanisms for food and other products and the growth of distributive organizations that encouraged centralized authority.

The third significant development was intensive land use, which probably increased agricultural output. Intensive agriculture usually implies irrigation, often hailed as one fundamental reason for a civilization's start. Archaeologists have long debated how significant irrigation was in getting urban life started. Julian Steward and Karl Wittfogel argue that irrigation was connected with the development of stratified societies.[9] The state bureaucracy had a monopoly over hydraulic facilities and created the Hydraulic State; in other words, the social requirements of irrigation led to the development of states and urban societies. Robert Adams takes a contrary view.[10] He feels that the introduction of great irrigation works was more a consequence than a cause of dynastic state organizations, however much the requirement of large-scale irrigation subsequently may have influenced the development of bureaucratic organizations.

Adams's view is based on studies of prehistoric irrigation in Mesopotamia, as well as observations of irrigation in smaller societies. Large-scale irrigation had its roots in simpler beginnings, perhaps in simple cooperation between neighboring communities to dam streams and divert water into fields where precious seeds were sown. The floodplain of the Tigris and the Euphrates rivers, with its long, harsh summers, could be cultivated only by irrigation with canals, which had to be dug deep enough to carry water even when the rivers were at their lowest. No means of lifting water was found until Assyrian times, so that the earliest inhabitants of the delta were obliged to dig their canals very deep and to keep them that way. Silting, blockage, and flooding were constant dangers, requiring endless manhours to keep the canals working. It paid the earliest delta farmers to live within a limited geographic area where canal digging was kept to a minimum. But even then organizing the digging would have required some centralized authority and certainly more restructuring of social life than the simple intercommunity cooperation typical of many smaller agricultural societies who used irrigation.

Building and maintaining small canals requires neither elaborate social organization nor population resources larger than those of one community, or several communities cooperating. Large-scale irrigation requires technical and social resources of a quite different order. Huge labor forces had to be mobilized, organized, and fed. Maintenance and supervision require constant attention, as do water distribution and resolving disputes over water rights. Because those living downstream are at the mercy of those upstream, large irrigation works are viable only so long as those who enjoy them remain within the same political unit. A formal state structure with an administrative elite is essential.

Early irrigation in Mesopotamia was conducted on a small scale.[11] Natural channels were periodically cleaned and straightened; only small artificial feeder canals were built. Maximum use was made of the natural hydrology of the rivers. Most settlement was confined to the immediate vicinity of major watercourses. Irrigation was organized by individual peoples. Large-scale artificial canalization did not take place until long after urban life appeared. The same is true of Ancient Egypt, where construction of large artificial canals seems to have been the culmination of long evolution of intensive agriculture.

Growth of Trade

The origins and evolution of complex societies in human prehistory have long been linked to burgeoning trade in essential raw materials such as copper and iron ore, or in luxuries of all types. But claiming that a dramatic increase in trading was a primary cause of civilization grossly oversimplifies a complex proceeding. Trade is two things: a helpful indicator of new social developments and a factor in the rise of civilization. Many commodities and goods are preserved in the archaeological record: gold and glass beads, seashells, obsidian mirrors, and many others. These finds have enabled archaeologists to trace trade routes over the Near East, Europe, and other regions. With the many analytic methods for looking at the sources of obsidian, stone ax blanks, and metals, people now realize that prehistoric trade was much more complex than a few itinerant tradespeople passing objects from village to village.[12]

Prehistoric trade is frequently thought of as a variable that developed at the same time that sociopolitical organization was becoming more complex. This notion goes back to the long-established hierarchy of bands, tribes, chiefdoms, and states and to a linear, evolutionary way of looking at civilization's origins. It has been assumed that trade proceeded from simple reciprocal exchange to the more complex redistribution of goods.

Trade and Exchange networks

Trade as an institution could have begun when people sought to acquire goods from a distance for prestige and for individual profit.

The decision to acquire any commodity from afar depends both on how urgent the need for the goods is and on the difficulties in acquiring and transporting the materials. Much early trade was based on acquiring specific commodities, such as copper ore or salt, that had peculiar and characteristic problems of acquisition and transport. There was no such thing as trading in general. Trade in any one commodity was specific, and almost a special branch on its own. Clearly such items as cattle or slaves are more easily transported than tons of iron ore or cakes of salt; the former move on their own, but metals require human or animal carriers or wheeled carts. To ignore these differences is to oversimplify the study of prehistoric trade.

In more complex societies the ruler and his immediate followers were generally entitled to trade and to initiate the steps leading to acquisition of goods from a distance. The king might employ merchants or traders to do the work for him, but the trade was in his name. The lowerclass traders of Mesopotamian society were more menial people, often bound by guilds or castes. These people were carriers, loan administrators, dealers — people who kept the machinery of trade going, with a carefully regulated place in society. Both the royal merchant and the lowerclass trader were distinct from trading peoples such as the Phoenicians, who relied on trade as a continuous activity and a major form of livelihood.

Trade before markets were developed can never be looked at as the one cause of civilization, or even as an unifying factor. It was far more than just a demand for obsidian or copper, for the causes of trading were infinitely varied and the policing of trade routes was a complex and unending task. It is significant that most early Mesopotamian and Egyptian trade was river-based, where policing was easier. With the great caravan routes opened, the political and military issues — tribute, control of trade routes, and tolls — became paramount. The caravan predates the great empires, a form of organized trading that kept to carefully defined routes set up and armed by state authorities for their specific tasks. The travelers moved along set routes, looking neither left nor right, bent only on delivering and exchanging imports and exports. These caravans were a far cry from the huge economic complex that accompanied Alexander the Great's army across Asia, or the Grand Mogul's annual summer progress from the heat of Delhi in India to the mountains, moving half a million people including the entire Delhi bazaar.

Trade itself has been analyzed intensively by both economists and anthropologists.[13] They distinguish between internal trade between neighboring communities in the same tribal area or state, and external trade with other peoples, states, or areas. They examine trade in the form of gifts, like that probably conducted by the Hopewell people of the Midwest (Chapter 13), which is really barter; and they consider trade by treaty, trading that results from political agreement. Formally administered trade is another important category, normally conducted from a port of trade — a place than can offer military security, commercial and loading facilities, and a safe haven for foreign traders.

There has been much debate about the origins of the market — both a place and a style of trading administration and organization. The market encourages people to develop one place for trading and relatively stable, almost fixed, prices for staple commodities. This does not mean regulated prices. The trade market is a network of market sites (marketplaces) at which the exchange of commodities from an area where supplies are abundant to one where demand for the same materials is high is regulated to some degree, especially the *mechanisms* of the exchange relationship.

This emphasis on mechanisms had led Johnson, Lamberg-Karlovsky, Rathje,[14] and others to study market networks and the mechanisms by which supplies are channeled down well-defined routes, profits are regulated and fed back to the source, providing further incentive for more supplies, and so on. There may or may not be a marketplace; it is the state of affairs surrounding the trade that forms the focus of the trading system and the mechanisms by means of which trade interacts with other parts of the culture. Taking a systems approach to trading activity means regarding archaeological finds as the material expressions of interdependent factors. These include the need for goods, which prompts a search for supplies, themselves the product of production above local needs, created to satisfy external demands. Other variables are the logistics of transportation and the extent of the trading network, as well as the social and political environments. With all these variables, no one aspect of trade is an overriding cause of cultural change, or of evolution in trading practices. Hitherto, archaeologists have concentrated on trade in the context of objects or as an abstraction — trade as a cause of civilization — but have had no profound knowledge about even one trading network from which to build more theoretical abstractions.

Systems approach

The study of prehistoric trade, especially in Mesopotamia, the Aegean, and the Mesoamerican area, is much in vogue. To quote only one example, people now realize that many phenomena were operating within the broad idea (almost a platitude) of a change from reciprocity to redistribution in Mesopotamia about 3000 B.C.* Long distance trade was carefully melded with fluctuating demands and availabilities of supplies. And there was room for private dealing, specialist merchants, perhaps even smuggling and tax evasion. That this intensification of reciprocal exchange and the development of methods for redistributive exchange was integral in the evolution of social and economic behavior in Mesopotamia is beyond question. But until there is much more systematic study of the data for early trade, no one will fully understand trade's influence on nascent civilization in Mesopotamia or, for that matter, anywhere.

---

* Up to this point we have used dates in years before present (B.P.) as the chronological framework for our narrative. Part 5 brings us into historical times, and straddles the last two millennia. It is at this point that we change our dating from years before present to years A.D. and B.C. (Anno Domini and Before Christ). The reason for the change is that most people are familiar with A.D./B.C. dates for early civilizations and there is less confusion if we use this convention for the remainder of this book.

To convert to years B.P.: *add* 1950 years to B.C. dates and *subtract* A.D. dates from 1950.

$$430 \text{ B.C.} = 2380 \text{ B.P.}$$
$$\text{A.D. } 760 = 1290 \text{ B.P.}$$

Warfare

There is an attractive simplicity in the idea that the early city was a mighty fortress to which the surrounding tribes would run in times of stress. Thus, goes the argument, they came to depend on one another and their city as a fundamental part of society. But warfare can be rejected as a prime cause of civilization without much discussion, for large military conflicts appear to have been a result of civilization, not a direct cause of it. For one thing, the earliest ceremonial centers apparently were not fortified. For another, in earlier times, the diffuse social organization of village communities had not yet led to the institutional warfare that resulted from the concentration of wealth and power in monopolistic hands. Only as absolute and secular monarchs arose did warfare become endemic, with raiding and military campaigns designed to gain control of important resources or to solve political questions. This type of warfare is a far cry from the tribal conflict common to many peasant societies. It presupposes authority.

Religion

Religion has been ignored by many writers in favor of trade and production as a major force in civilization's beginnings. Yet shrines and sacred places are common in agricultural settlements of great antiquity, like Jericho, Çatal Hüyük, and Las Haldas (Peru).[15] These religious shrines were predecessors of the great ceremonial centers of Mesopotamia and Egypt, Mesoamerica and Peru. In each part of the world where civilization appeared, ceremonial centers were preceded by inconspicuous prototypes tended by priests or cult leaders. These people must have been among the first to be freed of the burden of having to produce food, supported by the communities they served. And in every region the ceremonial center was the initial focus of power and authority, an authority vested in religious symbolism and organized priesthoods.

Priesthoods

Priesthoods may have become powerful authorities as people worried more about the cycles of planting and harvest and the soil's continuing fertility. It was no coincidence that the Mesopotamians' earliest recorded gods were those of harvest and fertility, or that in Mexico Tlaloc was God of rain and life itself. These preoccupations may have become the focus of new and communal belief systems. Those who served the deities of fertility thus became people of authority, the individuals who controlled economic surpluses, offerings, and the redistribution of goods. The temple became a new instrument for organizing fresh political, social, and religious structures.

As society grew more complex, more sophisticated ethics and beliefs provided a means for sanctioning the society's new goals. The temple was an instrument for disseminating these new beliefs, a means for the new leaders to justify their acts and develop coherent policies. Symbolic statements describing society served as models not only of behavior and belief, but also for the layout and function of the ceremonial centers that perpetuated and formulated them.

The Ceremonial Center

The nucleus of the first cities was some form of temple or ceremonial center, the edifice around which the business of the state, whether secular or religious, went on.[16] These ceremonial centers were either very compact, like the Mesopotamian *ziggurat*, or dispersed, like Mayan examples. Those of the Mesopotamians and Chinese were relatively compact, with a reasonably dense population around them. Some Mayan centers, like Tikal in Guatemala, may have had dense populations, while others held few people but were surrounded by scattered village communities. The priestly elite and rulers who lived at the center were surrounded by retainers and craftsworkers. The rural population in the environs was probably bound to the ceremonial center both economically and by kinship. As a ceremonial center became a focus for a group of independent settlements, it supplied reassurance or what Chinese historian Paul Wheatley calls "cosmic certainty." It was "the sanctified terrain where" the common people were "guaranteed the seasonal renewal of cyclic time, and where the splendor, potency, and wealth of their rulers symbolized the well being of the whole community."[17] The rural population felt no alienation from those who lived at the center; the distinction was between ruler and ruled.

This classic interpretation of the ceremonial center is long-established, noticeably in writings by Mircea Eliade.[18] To this school of thought, the ceremonial center was not a prime mover of civilization, but an instrument of "orthogenetic transformation." The religious and moral models of society provided a sacred canon circumscribing economic institutions and laying out the social order. It ensured the continuity of cultural traditions and was recited in temples, where the Word of the Gods rang out in reassuring chants passed from generation to generation. The ceremonial center was a tangible expression of this continuity.

Eliade and the ceremonial center

Eventually the ceremonial center became secularized, transformed by the rising secular kings, who were sometimes installed by force. As the kingship's power grew, the ceremonial center's political power declined, although its religious functions were faithfully retained. In Mesopotamia, church and state separated when the power of the temple ruler, or *en*, was restricted to religious matters after 3000 B.C. The *lugal*, or king, assumed the secular and often the militaristic leadership of the state. A somewhat similar transformation to secular power occurred in the Valley of Mexico, we are led to believe, after the great city of Teotihuacán fell, with the rise of the militaristic Toltec and Aztec peoples.

We can detect secularization of the ceremonial center in the appearance of the palace, where the secular king resided. The king himself might enthusiastically believe in the state faith, but his functions were almost entirely secular, even if he used religion to justify his actions. He might assume a divine role himself. When the palace appears, we find the royal tombs standing as garish and splendid monuments to the awesome political and social power behind them.

The Development of Cilivization

Everyone seems to agree that urban life and civilization came into existence gradually, during a period of major social and economic change. The earlier linear explanations invoking irrigation, trade, or religion as a major "integrative" force are inadequate for our purposes.

Adams: Multiple causes

Robert Adams has been a pioneer in looking at multiple causes of state formation. Back in 1966 he argued that irrigation agriculture, increased warfare, and "local resource variability" were three factors vital in newly appearing civilization.[19] Each of these affected society and each other with positive feedback, helping them reinforce each other. The creation of food surpluses and the emergence of a stratified society were critical developments. Irrigation agriculture and more intensive horticulture could feed a bigger population. Larger populations and increased sedentariness, as well as trade with regular centers for redistributing goods, were all pressures for greater production and increased surpluses, actively fostered by dominant groups in society. The greatly enlarged surpluses enabled those who controlled them to employ large numbers of craftsworkers, and other specialists who did not themselves grow crops.

Adams develops his thesis further by arguing that some societies were better able to transform themselves into states because of the favorable variety of resources on which they were able to draw. Higher production and increased populations led to monopolies over strategic resources. These communities eventually were more powerful than their neighbors, expanding their territory by military campaigns and efficiently exploiting their advantages over other peoples. Such cities became the early centers of religious activities, technological and artistic innovations, and the development of writing (Figure 14.1).

Flannery: Systems

Kent V. Flannery has a more complex and somewhat abstract scheme further explaining the state's origins.[20] He and others see the state as a very complicated living system, whose complexity can theoretically be measured by the internal differentiation and specialization of its subsystems, such as those for agriculture, technology, religious beliefs, and so on. Vital are the ways in which these subsystems are linked, as well as the controls that society imposes on the system as a whole. Archaeologists of this way of thinking make a fundamental distinction between:

The *processes* of cultural change, the succession of changes by which the early states developed their new complexity.

The *mechanisms*, the actual ways in which the processes of increasing complexity occurred.

The socioenvironmental *stresses* that select for these mechanisms. Socioenvironmental stresses can include food shortages, warfare, and population growth, and are by no means common to all states.

"An explanation of the rise of the state then centers on the ways in which the processes . . . took place," writes Flannery.

A series of subsystems operate in human cultural systems, subsystems that interact with one another, just as the cultural system as a whole interacts with

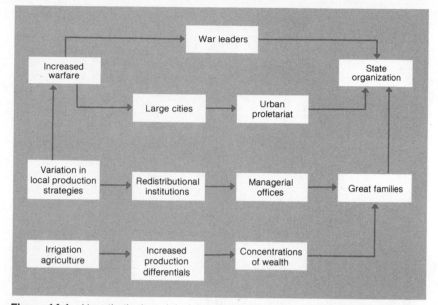

Figure 14.1 Hypothetical model of the state's beginnings, compiled from Adams. Compare with Figure 14.2

the natural environment. Each subsystem is regulated by a control apparatus that keeps all the variables in a system within bounds so that the survival of the system as a whole is not threatened. This apparatus of social control is vital, for it balances subsistence needs with religious, political, social, and other ideological values. There is a well-defined hierarchy of regulation and policy, ranging from those under the control of individuals to institutions within society with specialized functions (such as acquiring the information necessary to regulate the system), on up to the basic, highest-order propositions, which are those of societal policy. These abstract standards of values lie at the heart of any society's regulation of its cultural system. It is not only crops and domesticated animals that make up the basis of a civilization; it is all sorts of subtle relationships and regulatory measures as well (see Figure 14.2 for an example from Mesopotamia).

The management and regulation of a state is a far more elaborate and centralized undertaking than that of a hunter-gatherer band or a small chiefdom. Indeed, the most striking difference between states and less complicated societies is the degree of complexity in their ways of reaching decisions and in their hierarchic organizations, not their subsistence activities. Any living system is subjected to stress when one of the many variables exceeds the range of deviation that the system allows it. The stress may make the system evolve new institutions or policies. Such coping mechanisms may be triggered by warfare, population pressure, trade, environmental change, or other variables. These variables create what Flannery calls an "adaptive milieu" for evolutionary change. His specific mechanisms include "promotion" and "linearization," when an institution in a society may assume new powers or some aspect

Control apparatus

The Development of Cilivization

239

Figure 14.2 A systems diagram developed by Charles Redman that shows the interrelationships between cultural and environmental variables that led to increased stratification of class structure in early Mesopotamian urban society.

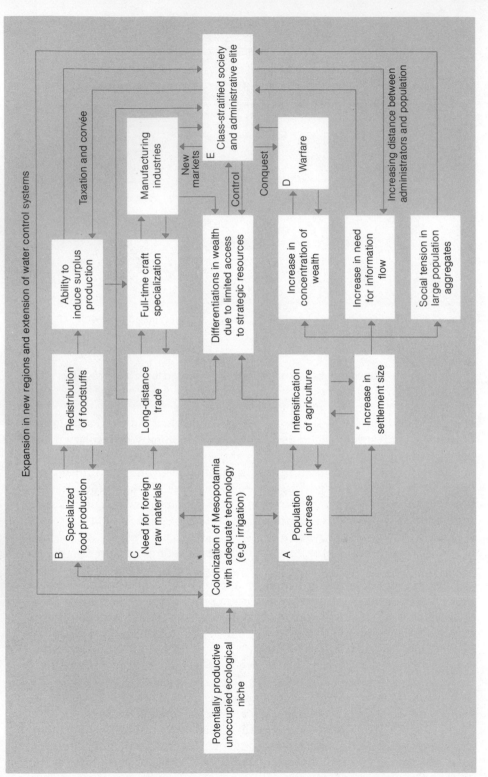

of life may become too complex for a few people to administer. Both mechanisms lead to greater centralization, caused by selective pressures on the variables that produced the response (coping) mechanisms.

The ultimate objective of a systems analysis of how a civilization began could be the establishing of rules by which the origins of a complex state could be simulated. But such rules are a goal for the future. Flannery lists fifteen beginning rules that could affect the cultural evolution of a simple human population forming part of a regional ecosystem. The rules can lead to new multivariate models for understanding the cultural evolution of civilization. Such models are certain to be most complex. We now have to be specific about the links between subsystems — distinguishing between the mechanisms and processes and the socioenvironmental pressures, which are peculiar to each civilization and have, until now, been the means by which we have sought to explain the origins of civilization.[21] Religious and informational factors now appear to be key elements in the regulation of environmental and economic variables in early civilizations and, indeed, in any human society. Although Flannery's notions enjoy widespread acceptance, it should be pointed out that he has not defined what either his mechanisms or processes actually were. In other words, his model needs testing in the field.

Chronological Table I

Dates A.D./B.C.	MESOPOTAMIA/IRAN	EGYPT	TROPICAL AFRICA	INDUS	SOUTHEAST ASIA
A.D. 1500 —			European contact		Historic times
			Zimbabwe		
A.D. 1000 —			⊥ Emergence of West African states		KAMBUJADESA
A.D. 500 —	Historic times	Historic times		Historic times	Mekong Delta city states
A.D. 1 —		Roman occupation Ptolemies	Bantu origins Ironworking		
	Alexander the Great		MEROE	King Darius invades India	Indigenous states?
	Cyrus ⊤ BABYLONIAN EMPIRE	LATE PERIOD			
1000 B.C. —	ASSYRIAN EMPIRE		Cattle herders in East Africa	Ironworking Painted gray wares	
		NEW KINGDOM	Early food production in West Africa		
2000 B.C. —	BABYLONIANS	MIDDLE ⊤ KINGDOM			
	Sargon of Agade			HARAPPAN CIVILIZATION	
	SUMERIAN ELAMITES CIVILIZATION	OLD KINGDOM	Hunter-gatherers		*Ban Chieng*
3000 B.C. —	Jemdet ⊤ Nasr ⏐ PROTO- ⏐ ELAMITES	ARCHAIC PERIOD			
	Uruk *Tepe Yahya*	UNIFICATION Naqada II			
		Amratian			
4000 B.C. —				Early food production	?
	Ubaid *Eridu*				
5000 B.C. —		Chapter 11 ⬆	Chapter 11 ⬆		
	Samarra HALAFIAN				
6000 B.C. —	Hassuna				Chapter 12 ⬆
	Chapter 10 ⬆				

Chapter Fifteen

MESOPOTAMIA AND THE FIRST CITIES

PREVIEW

- ☙ The Mesopotamian delta, home of the world's first literate civilization, is uncultivable without some form of irrigation agriculture.

- ☙ About 6000 B.C. highland peoples began to settle in northern Mesopotamia in areas where agriculture was possible using seasonal rainfall. These Hassuna people lived in close contact with other societies downstream who developed irrigation agriculture.

- ☙ About 5500 B.C. Halafian painted wares appeared over a wide area of northern Mesopotamia and Anatolia; they are thought to coincide with the emergence of chiefdoms in this area. Two hundred years later the first farmers settled in the Mesopotamian delta.

- ☙ A rapid evolution toward urban life ensued — marked by rapid growth of population, the congregation of people in cities, the development of long distance trade, the prospering of metallurgy, and the establishment of a literate civilization based on the comparatively recent invention of writing.

- ☙ The Sumerian civilization was in full swing by 2900 B.C. and depended heavily on trading with areas outside Mesopotamia. Its relationships with Proto-Elamites living in Khuzistan to the east were of critical importance. About 3000 B.C. the Proto-Elamites gained some degree of control over major trading centers on the Iranian plateau, centers that supplied obsidian, chlorite vessels, and other commodities and luxuries to Sumer.

- ☙ Sumerian civilization flourished until about 2000 B.C. when it was eclipsed by Babylonian power. In the late second millennium the city of Assur in the north nurtured the Assyrian Empire, which was extended by vigorous and despotic kings during the first half of the succeeding millennium. The Assyrian Empire at one time stretched from the Mediterranean to the Persian Gulf.

- ☙ The Assyrian Empire fell in 612 B.C. and the power vacuum was filled by the Babylonians, noticeably under Nebuchadnezzar. Babylon fell to Cyrus of Persia in 534 B.C. and Mesopotamia became part of the Persian Empire.

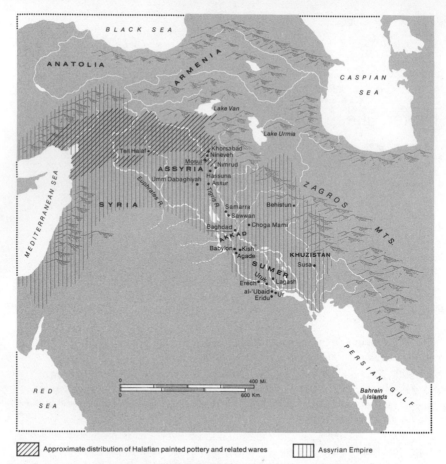

Approximate distribution of Halafian painted pottery and related wares   Assyrian Empire

Figure 15.1 Sites and culture distributions mentioned in Chapter 15.

Chronological
Table I

The delta regions and floodplain between the Tigris and Euphrates rivers form a hot, low-lying environment, much of it inhospitable sand, swamp, and dry mud flats. Yet this region, Mesopotamia, (Greek for "Land Between the Rivers") was the cradle of the world's earliest urban civilization.[1]* From north to south, Mesopotamia is approximately 600 miles (965 km) long and 250 miles (402 km) wide. (Figure 15.1 shows its location.) The plains are subject to long, intensely hot summers and harsh, cold winters. Before 5500 B.C. the floodplain was practically uninhabited, except by a few nomadic groups. Dry agriculture, which relied on seasonal rainfall, was totally impracticable; and the plants and animals of the highlands around Mesopotamia were unable to tolerate the climatic extremes of the delta.

There are few permanent water supplies away from the great rivers and their tributaries. Yet, once watered, the soils of Mesopotamia proved both fertile and potentially highly productive. The agricultural potential of the

* See page 386 for notes to Chapter 15.

Old World Civilizations

areas close to rivers and streams could be realized for the first time. By 5000 B.C. village farmers had settled on the delta and were diverting the waters of the rivers. Within two thousand years the urban civilization of the Sumerians was flourishing in Mesopotamia.

THE FIRST CITIES

With the continued improvement in the effectiveness of agriculture and the development of such technological innovations as pottery, the village communities of the Zagros foothills, east of Mesopotamia, achieved a more efficient subsistence base, which fed a gradually increasing farming population. These technological and economic changes were far from spectacular: some time in the sixth millennium B.C. the highland people moved out onto the Assyrian plains, at first into areas where they could rely on seasonal rainfall to water their crops; later, they settled by the rivers, with animals and crops that could tolerate the climate of the lowlands. There they developed simple irrigation methods to bring water to their crops.

The first farmers to settle in Assyria lived in areas where rainfall would water their crops. They were scattered over the undulating plains in small village settlements like Umm Dabaghiyah[2] that contained a few huts and storage bins made of packed mud. Commonly the houses, which were probably entered from the roof, consisted of two or three rooms with small doors. Ovens and chimneys were an integral part of the houses. The successive occupation layers of these sites are filled with pottery handmade of coarse clay and painted or incised with dots, circles, and other designs (Figure 15.2). Such wares — named Hassunan pottery, after Hassuna, the first village of this type excavated — is found over a wide area of the north, from the upper Tigris Valley to the plains west of the modern city of Mosul.

Hassuna
6000 B.C.

The regions between Mosul in the north and Baghdad in the south were inhabited by irrigation farmers by at least the middle of the sixth millennium B.C. We know this from discoveries of villages in the region of Samarra, on the fringes of the Mesopotamian delta. Samarran culture painted pottery (Figure 15.2) comes from such sites as Tell-es-Sawwan and Choga Mami, revealed early farming villages situated in areas where irrigation agriculture was the only viable means of food production.[3] The Samarran sites near Choga Mami are situated along low ridges parallel to nearby hills, located where irrigation could be practiced with the least effort. Traces of canals are found at Choga Mami, also wheat, barley and linseed, a crop that can be grown in this area only when irrigation is used. Choga Mami itself lies between two rivers where floodwaters could be diverted across the fields and then drained away to prevent salt build up. This is a relatively easy form of irrigation, one that was easy to adopt. Presumably, later refinements in irrigation technolgy enabled other farming settlements to move away from naturally flooded areas into regions where more extensive irrigation was necessary. There is every indication that the Samarrans were advanced farmers who lived in substantial villages which, in the case of Choga Mami, may have covered up to six hectares

Samarra
5500 B.C.

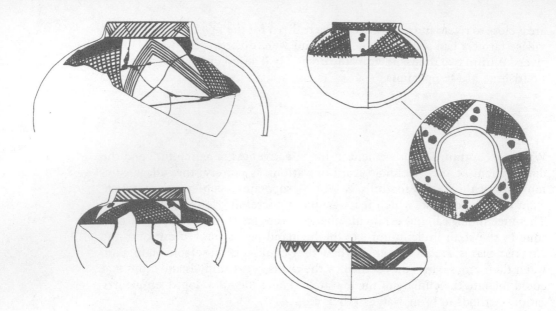

Figure 15.2 Early Mesopotamian painted pottery: above, vessels from Hassuna; below, Samarra-type vessels from Hassuna.

Old World Civilizations

Figure 15.3 Halafian vessel from Iraq.

and housed more than a thousand souls. The other excavated Samarran village, Tell es-Sawwan, was surrounded by a ditch and a wall, as if defense was a major consideration.

The Samarrans occupied relatively low-lying territory between the arid delta of the south and the dry-agriculture areas of the Hassunans to the north. Their newly developed irrigation techniques and heat-tolerant strains of wheat and barley enabled them to settle in areas that were hitherto inaccessible. Their sedentary and permanent settlements and great reliance on agriculture enabled them to forge community and external social and economic bonds that provided a catayst for more complex societies to develop in future millennia.

About 5500 B.C. many village farmers in the Near East began to make a characteristic style of painted pottery, abandoning the monochrome wares they had made before. The new fashion spread from southwestern Turkey around the shores of Lake Van, famous for its obsidian, and as far east as the Zagros Mountains. The most brilliantly painted pottery was made in northern Iraq by the inhabitants of Tell Halaf (Figure 15.3), whose enormous kilns produced bowls, dishes, and flasks adorned with elaborate, stylized patterns and representations of people and animals. The Halafian cultural tradition flourished in what had once been Hassunan territory, and the people maintained regular contact with the Samarrans to the south (see Figure 15.1).

Halafian
5500 B.C.

The Halafians still lived in much the same way as their predecessors and made no startling agricultural or technological innovations. But they developed new, far-flung contacts between villages hundreds of miles apart, trading such commodities as obsidian, semiprecious stones, and other luxury items. Their pottery is remarkably similar from one end of Halafian territory to the other, so much so that continuous and effective interaction over wide areas must have taken place. It has been suggested that this was the result of a major

Mesopotamia and the First Cities

change in social organization, where tribal villages of earlier times were now linked under chiefdoms.⁴ As with the Hopewell, these new elite groups required greater communication and the sharing of status goods such as painted pottery to reinforce their authority.⁵

5300 B.C.

About 5300 B.C. the first farmers to settle in the delta of the south moved onto the floodplains. They settled on river banks, where water could be used without digging huge ditches or carrying water long distances. At first the farmers do not seem to have done much more than clear out natural, clogged channels, occasionally digging small feeder canals for gardens already sited to take advantage of natural drainage. These simple irrigation works made it possible to grow vegetables in addition to cereal crops. Cattle probably were penned in lush pastures, conceivably on a communal basis. The abundant fish and waterfowl were important dietary supplements. Fruit of the date palm may have been a vital staple.

We do not know anything about how the first inhabitants of the Mesopotamian delta acquired or developed the skills needed to survive in their harsh environment. Mutual interdependence among members of the community was essential, because raw materials suitable for building houses had to be improvised from the plentiful sand, clay, palm trees, and reeds between the rivers. Digging even the smallest canal required at least a little political and social leadership to coordinate the activity. The annual backbreaking task of clearing silt from clogged river courses and canals can have been achieved only by communal effort. As both Adams and Flannery say, the relationship between developing a stratified society and creating food surpluses was close. Distinctive social changes came from the more efficient systems for producing food that were essential in the delta. As food surpluses developed and the

'Ubaid period
5300 to 3600 B.C.

specialized agricultural economies of these 'Ubaid villages grew successful, the trend toward sedentary settlement and higher population densities increased. Expanded trade networks and the redistribution of surpluses and trade goods also affected society, with dominant groups of 'Ubaid people becoming more active in producing surpluses, which eventually supported more and more

Al-'Ubaid

people who were not farmers. The Village of al-'Ubaid itself was built on a low mound, covering it with huts of mud brick and reeds, sometimes with roofs formed from bent sticks.⁶ The al-'Ubaid people relied on hunting and fishing as well as cereal crops, reaping their grain with sickles of clay, sometimes fitted with flint blades. Goats, sheep, and some cattle were herded on the floodplain.

Al-'Ubaid and similar small hamlets were clustered in groups, many with their own small ceremonial center. The villages were linked by kinship and clan, with one clan authority overseeing the villagers' affairs and, probably, the irrigation schemes that connected them. In time the small village ceremonial centers grew, like the one at Eridu (first settled around 4750 B.C., when the Tell Halaf people were still making their painted pottery in the north).

Eridu
4750 B.C.

Eridu consisted of a mud-brick temple with fairly substantial mud-brick houses around it, often with rectangular floor plan. The craftsworkers lived a short distance from the elite clustered around the temple, and still farther away were the dwellings of the farmers who grew the crops that supported everyone. By 3500 B.C. the Eridu temple had grown large, containing altars and offering places and a central room bounded by rows of smaller compartments. It has been estimated that the population of Eridu was as high as 5,000 at this time, but exact computations are impossible.

'Ubaid society was fully developed by 4350 B.C.; its institutions and material culture are found all over Mesopotamia. At every sizable 'Ubaid settlement the temple dominated the inhabitants' houses.

4350 B.C.

As Mesopotamian society grew in complexity, so too did the need for social, political, and religious institutions that would provide an integrative function for everyone. The settlement of Uruk epitomizes cultural developments just before Sumerian civilization began. Anyone approaching Uruk could see the great ziggurat, the stepped temple pyramid, for miles (Figure 15.4). Built with enormous expenditure of work as a community project, the ziggurat and its satellite temples were the center of Uruk life. The temples were not only storehouses and places of worship; they were also redistribution centers for surplus food. Hundreds of craftsworkers labored for the temple as stone masons, copperworkers, weavers, and at dozens of other specialized tasks. None of these people tilled the ground or worked on irrigation; they formed a distinctive class in a well-stratified society.[7]

Uruk period
3600
to 3000 B.C.

The entire life of Uruk, and its connections with cities, towns, merchants, and mines hundreds of miles away, revolved around the temple. The ruler of Uruk and the keeper of the temple was the *en*, both secular and religious leader of Uruk. His wishes and policies were carried out by his priests and by a complex hierarchy of bureaucrats, wealthy landowners, and merchants. Tradesmen and craftsworkers were a more lowly segment of society, and under them were the thousands of fishers, peasants, sailors, and slaves that formed the bulk of Uruk's burgeoning population.

In its heyday around 2800 B.C. Uruk was far more than a city. Satellite villages extended out for at least 6 miles (10 km), each with its own irrigation system. All provided food for those in the city, whether grain, fish, or meat. Each settlement depended on the others for survival, at first because each provided things essential for a well balanced existence; later they needed each other for protection from outsiders who would have plundered their goods. The Mesopotamian city had developed an elaborate system of management with a well-defined hierarchy of rulers and priests, landowners and bureaucrats, traders and peasants. This system organized and regulated society, meted out reward and punishment, and made policy decisions for the thousands of people who lived under it. So complex had society become that the temple records at Uruk were written on clay tablets as early as 3200 B.C. The earliest writing was pictographs (Figure 15.5), a style that soon evolved into cuneiform script. Temple records and accounts tell us much not only of economic and social organization, but also of Mesopotamian folklore and religion as well.

2800 B.C.

On the plateau to the north, copper tools and ornaments had been in use for centuries, first appearing as early as the fifth or sixth millennia B.C. Copper was intensively used in Iran during the fourth millennium, and was imported into the delta areas of Mesopotamia as early as 3500 B.C., probably earlier. It came into widespread use in the Jemdet Nasr period. Although many peasant societies were aware of the properties of native copper, and both the early Egyptians

Jemdet Nasr period
3100 to 2900 B.C.

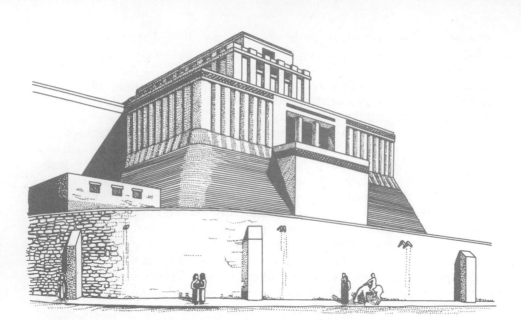

Figure 15.4 Reconstruction of an Uruk temple at Eridu. Notice the great platform supporting the temple and the drainage pipes in the walls. Below is a photograph of the great ziggurat (temple mound) of Ur, built around 2100 B.C.

Old World Civilizations

Earliest pictographs (3000 B.C.)	Denotation of pictographs	Pictographs in rotated position	Cuneiform signs c. 1900 B.C.	Basic logographic values Reading	Meaning
	Head and body of man			lu	Man
	Head with mouth indicated			ka	Mouth
	Bowl of food			ninda	Food, bread
	Mouth + food			kú	To eat
	Stream of water			a	Water
	Mouth + water			nag	To drink
	Fish			kua	Fish
	Bird			mušen	Bird
	Head of an ass			anše	Ass
	Ear of barley			še	Barley

Figure 15.5 The development of Sumerian writing, from a pictographic script to a cuneiform script, and then to a phonetic system. The word "cuneiform" is derived from the Latin word "cuneus," meaning a wedge, after the characteristic impression of the script.

and American Indians made hammered copper ornaments from it, the soft-ness of the metal limited the uses to which it could be put. Eventually, though, people familiar with kiln firing of pottery developed techniques for smelting copper ore. Copper is fine and lustrous and makes admirable ornaments. Its economic advantages (in terms of sharp cutting edges) were less obvious, until blacksmiths learned to alloy copper with tin or arsenic to produce bronze and other forms of tougher copper. Once alloying was understood, copper assumed a more important place in agriculture and warfare.

By 3000 B.C., copper specialists had begun to work in most Mesopotamian cities, smelting and casting weapons and ornaments of high quality. Some cities attempted to maintain a monopoly on copper weapons and tools by training specialist craftsworkers and controlling trade in ingots and artifacts. The later development of bronze weapons can be linked to the rise of warfare as a method of attaining political ends, for cities like Eridu and Uruk were not isolated from other centers. Indeed, they were only too aware of them. Ur of the Chaldees, a city much smaller than Uruk, is only 75 miles (120 km) away. The two were rivals for centuries, constantly bickering, competing in trading, and fighting with each other. Cities soon had walls, a sure sign that they needed protection against marauders. All the elements that made up Sumerian civilization were now in place.

SUMERIAN CIVILIZATION AND TRADE

Sumerian civilization
**c. 2900 to 2000
B.C.**
By 2900 B.C., Sumerian civilization was in full swing in the southern delta. Archaeologically this is reflected in increased wealth.[8] Metal tools became much more common and domestic tools as well as weapons proliferated. Technologically, they were far in advance of earlier tools. Smiths began to alloy copper with tin to produce bronze. Armies and farmers were equipped with wheeled chariots and wagons. With a shift in political power from priests to kings, Mesopotamian rulers became more despotic, concentrating the wealth ·of the state and controlling subjects by military strength, religious acumen, and taxation, as well as economic incentive.

The cities' power depended in part on intensive agriculture, which irriga-tion and fertile Mesopotamian soils had so encouraged that rural populations increased sharply. The plow was invented, depending on draft oxen trained to pull it through the soil for a deeper furrow, and increasing agricultural yields. Plows were not used in the New World, where draft animals were not domes-ticated, nor did the rice farmers of Asia have much use for such a tool. But it did permit higher yields of cereal crops and supported larger urban and rural populations in the Old World.

Trading was an integral part of Sumerian life, a many-faceted operation absorbing the energies of many people. The redistribution systems of the cities combined many activities, all controlled by the centralized authority that ruled the settlements. Food surpluses were redistributed and raw materials were obtained from far away for the manufacture of ornaments, weapons, and prestigious luxuries. We have every reason to believe that specialist merchants handled commodities like copper. If later historical records are any guide, there was wholesaling and contracting, loans were floated, and individual profit may have been a prime motivation.

Demands for raw materials appear to have risen steadily, spreading market networks into territories remote from the home state. For these long-distance routes to succeed, political stability at both ends of the route was essential. An intricate system of political, financial, and logistical checks and balances had to be kept in place, requiring an efficient and alert administrative organization to keep the pieces of the puzzle in place.

The raw materials traded by the Sumerians included metals, timber, skins, ivory, and precious stones like malachite. Many could be found only in the remote highlands to the north and east of Mesopotamia and were traded in bulk from the late third millennium onward. Wheeled vehicles and boats became vital in trade and warfare. Horses, asses, and oxen were put to drawing heavy loads.

Flourishing trade routes expanded along the delta waterways, especially up the placid Euphrates, which was easily navigable for long distances. This great river, whose ancient name Uruttu meant copper, transmitted raw materials from the north and trade goods from the Persian Gulf to the Mediterranean. Well before 3000 B.C., the Euphrates joined together many scattered towns, transmitting to all the products of Sumerian craftsworkers and a modicum of cultural unity.

Mesopotamia lacked the mineral and stone resources that were plentiful on the Iranian plateau to the east and in Anatolia. The Sumerians and their successors obtained them by trading their food surpluses in the form of grain, dried fish, textiles, and other perishable goods for basic raw materials. This capacity to produce surpluses was vital to Mesopotamian trading activities, for on the surpluses depended the viability of long distance commerce. This dependence on long distance trading made the Mesopotamians both vulnerable to, and dependent on, the activities of their neighbors, and even peoples living at a considerable distance from their own homeland.

THE PROTO-ELAMITES

While early farmers were settling the inhospitable Mesopotamian delta, other peoples were beginning to cultivate the area between the Zagros foothills and the Tigris and Euphrates.[9] During the sixth and early fifth millennia B.C. small farming villages flourished in the heart of Khuzistan. The people were irrigation farmers who herded goats, sheep, and cattle as well. So many of their sites are known that it seems certain that areas like the Deh Luran plain were intensively settled by this time. During the next thousand years or so Khuzistan was still densely settled and village settlements grew larger and larger. It was about this time that the famous archaeological site of Susa began to achieve special prominence.

The earliest occupation levels at Susa are broadly contemporary with the late 'Ubaid occupation of Mesopotamia. The first village on the site was about

6000 B.C.

Susa

25 to 30 hectares in area and was inhabited by metal-using farmers. Strong Mesopotamian influence can be detected in slightly later levels at Susa, as if there was at least some colonization of Khuzistan by Uruk people from the delta toward the end of the fourth millennium.

About 3200 B.C. a distinctive cultural tradition known as the "Proto-Elamite" appears at Susa and elsewhere in Khuzistan. The Proto-Elamite state seems to have evolved in what is now southwestern Iran. But within a short time its distinctive tablets, seals, and ceramic types are found on widely scattered sites on the Iranian highlands. Their clay tablets have been found on settlements in every corner of the Iranian plateau, in central Iran, and on the borders of Afghanistan.

The Proto-Elamite expansion took place over a very short time and appears to be connected with a desire of these people to control both key trade routes on the Iranian plateau and access to sources of key raw materials.

The most thoroughly excavated site on the plateau is Tepe Yahya, which was a prosperous rural community between 3400 and 3200 B.C.[10] The inhabitants were already importing such raw materials as obsidian and chlorite (steatite). After 3200 B.C. Tepe Yahya grew in size and was engaged in much more intensive trading activities. It is at this period that Proto-Elamite artifacts are found in the site, which seems to have served as a political center that coordinated trade by surrounding settlements. The Tepe Yahya area was a center of chlorite bowl production, for abundant deposits of this raw material are found nearby. The bowls produced at Tepe Yahya and elsewhere were definitely luxury items, so highly prized in Mesopotamia that they may have caused keen competition among those rich enough to be able to afford them.[11] Chlorite tools and ornaments were so popular that they occur over a very wide area of the Iranian plateau as well, on islands in the Persian Gulf, and at Moenjodaro, one of the major cities of the Harappan civilization of the Indus valley (Chapter 16).

The chlorite vessels produced near Tepe Yahya were made by local artisans perhaps working part-time or at certain seasons of the year. But the trade itself seems to have been managed by the Proto-Elamites, people who acted as middle agents in the long distance trade between Mesopotamia and the distant plateau. In a sense the Sumerians controlled the long distance trade through the laws of supply and demand. Their needs resulted in a degree of economic control of foreign areas without actual political control. But the Proto-Elamites seem to have recognized a political and economic opportunity which stemmed from their strategic position between Mesopotamia and Iran. So they expanded their sphere of interest onto the plateau. Their efforts at controlling trade and raw materials do not seem to have lasted very long. Perhaps their administrative and political system became overtaxed by the new demands made on it. Conceivably the benefits of political control did not justify the effort in terms of trade generated. In any event, Proto-Elamite artifacts vanish from the archaeological record within a few centuries.

Even if the Proto-Elamites (Elamite is a language) failed in their bid to control trade on the plateau, they certainly continued to flourish in Khuzistan. Susa itself grew into a great city, where the trade routes between Mesopotamia

and the East converged. The Elamite state emerged in all its complexity after
3000 B.C. and came under the domination of Akkadian kings from central Mesopotamia for a while. But by 2000 B.C. the Elamites were strong enough to attack and destroy Ur of the Chaldees in Sumer. Their power and importance depended on their geographical position at the center of a network of trade routes that led to the Iranian plateau, to the Persian Gulf, and to most city-states in the lowlands. Elamite history shows us how no great civilization can be considered in isolation, for no complex society flourishes without depending on political and economic factors outside its boundaries.

THE WIDENING OF POLITICAL AUTHORITY

In the early third millennium B.C. Mesopotamia held several important city- states, each headed by rulers who vied with the others for status and prestige. Political authority was most effective at the city level, with the temple priests as the primary authority for controlling trade, economic life, and political matters. Inevitably, as society became more complex the priests were increasingly concerned with secular matters such as the organization of irrigation systems that expanded as population densities rose and more and more prime agricultural land was taken under cultivation. As the Mesopotamian delta became an increasingly artificial environment controlled by human activities, the people began to concentrate in larger cities under secular leaders, abandoning many smaller towns. The motive for this shift was as much defense as population increase, for both Sumerian inscriptions and the archaeological record tell of warfare and constant quarreling between neighbors. Competition over natural resources intensified as each state raised an army to defend its water rights, trade routes, and city walls. The onerous tasks of defense and military organization passed to despotic secular kings supposedly appointed by the gods. As the wealth and power of the cities increased, so did internecine strife. Such states as Erech, Kish, and Ur of the Chaldees had periods of political strength and prosperity when they dominated their neighbors. Then, just as swiftly, the tide of their fortunes would change and they would sink into obscurity.

Some of these cities nurtured powerful and wealthy leaders. When Sir Leonard Woolley excavated a royal cemetery in Sumerian Ur of the Chaldees (Figure 15.6), he found a series of kings and queens who had been buried in huge graves accompanied by their entire retinue of followers.[12] One tomb contained the remains of fifty-nine people who were slaughtered to accompany the king, even courtiers and soldiers, as well as serving women. Each wore his or her official dress and insignia, and had lain down to die in their correct order of precedence, having taken poison.

The first Sumerian ruler to have ambitions wider than merely controlling a few city-states was Lugalzagesi (about 2360 to 2335 B.C.). Not content with
control of Uruk, Ur, Lagash, and several other cities, he boasted of overseeing the entire area from the Persian Gulf to the Mediterranean. The god Enlil, king of the lands, "made the people lie down in peaceful pastures like cattle and

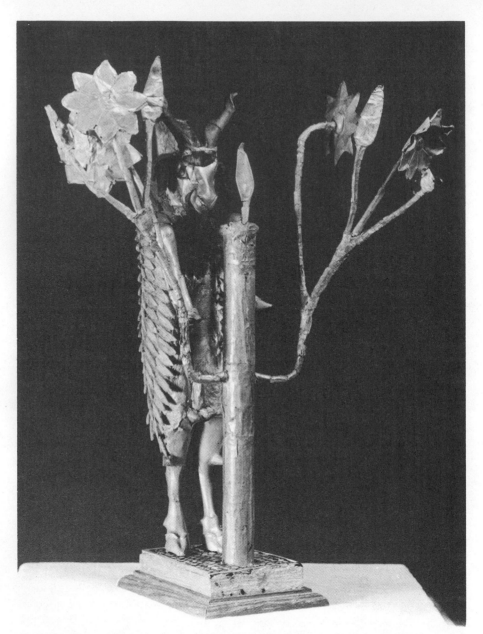

Figure 15.6 A famous ornament from the Royal Cemetery at Ur of the Chaldees, a goat in a tree. The wood figure was covered with gold leaf and lapis lazuli, the belly in silver leaf, and the fleece in shell.

supplied Sumer with water bringing joyful abundance."[13] Sumerian contacts with the outside world should not be judged in terms of conquering armies, but in the context of their constant trading, which was an integral part of their civilization. The people of Sumer traveled far and wide in search of raw materials and luxury imports. Life without trade was impossible. They carried their political and religious institutions with them as far as the shores of the Mediterranean and maintained at least tenuous contacts with dozens of city-states in the Near East.

THE ASSYRIANS

As Sumerian civilization prospered, so did urban centers spring up in northern Mesopotamia. Soon Assyrian cities began to compete with the delta city-states for trade and prestige. In about 2370 B.C., a Semitic-speaking leader, Sargon, founded a ruling dynasty at the town of Agade, south of Babylon. This northern house soon established its rule over Sumer and Assyria by military campaigns and skillful commercial ventures. After a short period of economic prosperity, the new kings were toppled by highland tribesmen from the north. Mesopotamia entered a time of political instability. But by 1990 B.C., the ancient city of Babylon was achieving prominence under Semitic rulers, culminating in the reign of the great king Hammurabi in 1790 B.C.

Sargon
2370 B.C.

Babylon
1990 B.C.

Hammurabi set up a powerful commercial empire reaching out from Mesopotamia as far as Assyria and Zagros. The unity of his empire depended on a common official language and a cuneiform writing system for its administration. Small city-states for the first time influenced world culture far more than their geographic territory appears to justify, an influence based on economic and political power maintained by despotic rule and harsh power politics. By this time, Mesopotamian influence was so great that weapon types used by Babylonian armies had spread to Russia, Europe, and western Mediterranean.

Hammurabi
1790 B.C.

One of the cities of the north that flourished for a long time was Assur on the Tigris, whose mounds contain the remains of Sumerian temples.[14] The merchants of Assur traded far to the east and west, as well as controlling the trade down the Tigris. Assur came into great prominence during the reign of King Assur-uballit I (1365 to 1330 B.C.), who incorporated the prime corn-growing lands of northern Assyria into a new empire that his successors extended over a vast territory from the Mediterranean to Egypt, and as far as the Persian Gulf. Great military kings like Shalmaneser, Assurnasirpal, Sargon, and Tiglath-Pileser were absolute despots, to whom warfare and prestige became veritable obsessions. When Assurnasirpal completed his palace at Nimrud he threw a party for the 16,000 inhabitants of the city, 1500 royal officials, "47,074 men and women from the length of my country," and 5000 foreign envoys.[15] The king fed this throng of over 69,000 people for ten days, during which time his guests ate 14,000 sheep and consumed over 10,000 skins of wine.

Assur

Assyrians
c. 1350 to 612 B.C.

The last of the great Assyrian kings was Assurbanipal, who died about 630 B.C. When he died, the Assyrian Empire entered a period of political chaos. The Babylonians achieved independence, and Assyrian power was finally broken in 612 B.C. when Nineveh was sacked by the Persians and Babylonians. For forty-three years the mighty Babylonian king Nebuchadnezzar ruled over Mesopotamia and turned his capital into one of the showpieces of the ancient

Babylonian Empire
612 to 534 B.C.

world. His double-walled city was adorned with magnificent mud-brick palaces with elaborate hanging gardens, a great processional way, and a huge ziggurat. It was to Babylon that a large contingent of Jews were taken as captives after Nebuchadnezzar's armies sacked Jerusalem, an exile immortalized by the lament: "By the waters of Babylon we sat down and wept."[16]

Cyrus
534 B.C.

The Babylonian Empire did not long survive the death of Nebuchadnezzar in 556 B.C. His successors were weak men, who were unable to resist the external forces that now pressed on Mesopotamia. The armies of Cyrus the Great of Persia took Babylon virtually without resistance in 534 B.C. and Mesopotamia became part of an empire even larger than that of the Assyrians. By this time the effects of constant political instability and of bad agricultural management were beginning to make themselves felt. The Mesopotamian delta was a totally artificial environment by 2000 B.C.; and poor drainage and badly maintained irrigation works in later centuries led to inexorable rises in the salt content of the soil and to drastic falls in crop yields. Nothing could be done to reverse this trend until modern soil science technology and irrigation techniques could be imported to the delta at vast expense.

Chapter Sixteen

PHARAOHS AND AFRICAN CHIEFS

PREVIEW

🌿 By 3600 B.C. the average Egyptian probably lived much as people do today in some Upper Egyptian villages.

🌿 These pre-Dynastic people lived at a time of gradual population growth and enrichment of the native culture, probably as a result of expanded trading contacts. The number of luxury goods increased, metallurgy was introduced from Mesopotamia, and social structure seems to have become more elaborate.

🌿 The acquisition of writing by the Egyptians was probably one of the catalytic events that led to the unification of Egypt and the emergence of civilization there. The process of unification culminated under a legendary pharaoh named Menes about 3000 B.C.

🌿 Ancient Egyptian Civilization is divided into four main periods: the Old, Middle, New and Late Kingdoms, the earlier of which were separated by brief intermediate periods of political chaos (Table 16.1).

🌿 The Old Kingdom is notable for its despotic pharaohs and the frenzy of pyramid construction, an activity that may be connected with pragmatic notions of fostering national unity.

🌿 The Middle Kingdom saw a shift of political and religious power to Thebes and Upper Egypt.

🌿 New Kingdom pharaohs made Egypt an imperial power with strong interests in Asia and Nubia. These pharaohs were buried in the Valley of Kings near Thebes. The cult of Amun was all powerful, except for a brief interlude when the heretic pharaoh Akenaten introduced the worship of the Sun God Aten.

🌿 Ancient Egyptian civilization began to decline after 1100 B.C., and the Nile eventually came under the rule of Assyrians, then the Persians, and finally the Greek pharaohs, the Ptolemies.

🌿 Egypt had few contacts with sub-Saharan Africa, which was widely settled by tropical farmers about two thousand years ago. The spread of farming coincided both with the introduction of ironworking and with the spread of the Bantu-speaking peoples from West Africa over much of east, central, and southern Africa.

ᴥ Indigenous African states developed on the southern fringes of the Sahara desert at the end of the first millennium A.D., owing their initial prosperity to the gold trade across the desert.

ᴥ The later prehistory of Africa is marked by continued contacts between Africans and societies living outside the continent. Complex states like that of the Karanga of southern Africa emerged in the last thousand years, several of them trading actively with foreign merchants and voyagers until Africa came into the purview of written history in recent times.

By 3600 B.C., the average Egyptian probably lived much as Upper Nile villagers do today.[1]* Wheat and barley were cultivated in riverside gardens and supplemented then by intensive gathering of wild vegetable foods. Cattle, goats, sheep, and pigs were herded. The meat from the herds was supplemented by the rich Nile game population and by fishing. These Amratian (or pre-Dynastic) people were the successors of the Badarians (Chapter 11).[2] Amratians derive their name from the archaeological site in Upper Egypt, El Amra. Amratian settlements apparently had a material culture somewhat similar to that which flourished in earlier centuries on the same sites of the Nile floodplain (Figure 16.1). The human population of the valley was growing slowly and there was some cultural fusion and increased interaction between more closely spaced settlements. Pottery was still being made but elegant stone vessels in alabaster and basalt were also used, probably shaped by specialist craftsworkers and traded widely through the valley. Amratian flintworkers created magnificent knives and daggers which were also prized possessions. A gradual enrichment of pre-Dynastic culture can be discerned over the centuries, an enrichment resulting in part from the introduction of copperworking from Asia. Soon metalworkers were making pins, flat axes, and daggers of the new material. The Amratians began to import copper from Sinai, while lead and silver came from Asia. The proportion of luxury goods to functional rose steadily; one of the locally manufactured items was faience, a form of glass widely traded in prehistoric times. Amratian settlements slowly became larger, and social structure became more elaborate. The archaeological record contains some signs of social classes, in the form of graves of varying opulence.

METALLURGY, WRITING, AND UNIFICATION

The increased volume of trade is reflected not only in the importation of copper, but in other exotic items found in pre-Dynastic sites. Many of them are of unmistakable west Asian or Mesopotamian origin. The Naqada site, for instance, yielded a cylinder seal of Mesopotamian form. Some of the late

* See pages 387–388 for notes to Chapter 16.

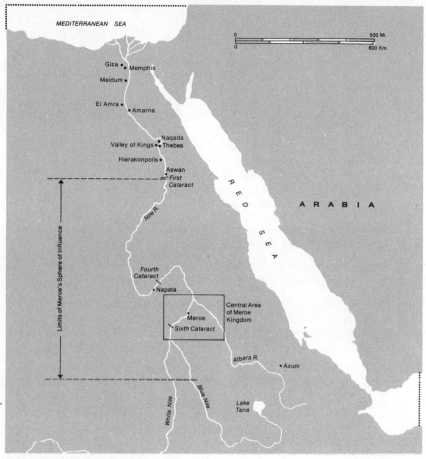

Figure 16.1 The Nile Valley.

pre-Dynastic pottery is painted with dark red colors on a buff background, in Asian style. There are depictions of Mesopotamian boat designs and of fabulous animals and creatures with intertwined necks and other motifs that derive from Asia.

But the most important innovation of all was the art of writing, which became fully developed in Egypt. Hieroglyphs (Greek for "sacred carving") are commonly thought to be a form of picture writing. In fact they comprise a combination pictographic (picture) and phonetic (representing vocal sounds) script which was not only written on papyrus but carved on public buildings, or painted on clay or wood. It seems most likely that writing was first developed in Mesopotamia, and that Egyptian priests developed their own script which was easier to produce with papyrus reed paper and ink rather than clay. Ultimately they developed a form of cursive (running on) hieroglyphic script that was a form of handwriting, much easier to use on documents and other less formal communications. Only the consonants were written in all forms of hieroglyphs; the vowel sounds were omitted, although both were pronounced.

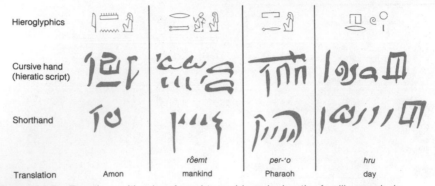

	Amon	rôemt mankind	per-'o Pharaoh	hru day
Hieroglyphics				
Cursive hand (hieratic script)				
Shorthand				
Translation				

Figure 16.2 Egyptian writing is referred to as hieroglyphs, the familiar symbols that appear on formal inscriptions and on tomb walls. In fact, Egyptian scribes developed cursive hands used in everyday life. These examples show formal hieroglyphic script (top line) and below it both the cursive style and the scribe's shorthand, which was used for rapid writing.

With practice, reading this form of script is easy enough, and a smple tst 'f ths srt shld shw ths qt wll (Figure 16.2).[3]

The acquisition of writing, with all its organizational possibilities, was probably one of the main catalysts of the unification of the whole of Egypt into a single political entity. Unity was not imposed on Egypt from Asia — despite the increase in Asian influences in the material culture of the pre-Dynastic cultures. Rather, it was the culmination of local social and political developments that resulted from centuries of gradual change in economic and social life. Pre-Dynastic villages were autonomous units, each with its local dieties. During the fourth millennium B.C. the more important villages became the focal points of different territories, which, in Dynastic times, became the *nomes*, or provinces, through which the pharaohs administered Egypt. The nomarchs (provincial leaders) were responsible for the gradual coalescence of Egypt into larger political and social units. Their deeds are recorded on ceremonial palettes that were used for moistening eye powder. Some of these palettes show alliances of local leaders dismantling conquered villages. Others commemorate the administrative skills of leaders who brought their villages through drought years by skillful management. The unification of Egypt was a gradual process of both voluntary and involuntary amalgamation. Voluntary unification resulted from common need and economic advantage. Perhaps it was only in the final stages of unification that military force came into play to bring larger and larger political units under single rulers.

The actual process of unification is badly documented, although there is reason to believe that Upper Egypt was unified under Narmer (Menes) Hierakonpolis in about 3100 B.C. In economic terms the unification of Egypt may have involved some intensification of agriculture as population densities rose. But, as Karl Butzer has pointed out, the technology for lifting water was so rudimentary that the early rulers of Egypt were unable to organize any elaborate forms of irrigation.[4] In all probability, most Ancient Egyptian agriculture involved irrigation schemes on a modest scale that merely extended the distribution of seasonal floodwaters from natural flood basins. But even these efforts must have involved a considerable degree of administrative organization. And, with a centralized form of administration, the divine leader, the pharaoh himself, was responsible for the success of the harvest. Since the Nile flood fluctuated considerably in cycles of abundant and lean years, and the pharaohs could do little to control the success or failure of irrigation without much more elaborate technology than they possessed, their political position could, theoretically at any rate, be threatened by famine years. If the divine leader could not provide, who could? A different leader, perhaps. Small wonder that some periods of political instability, which may have coincided with poor flood years, saw rapid successions of ineffective pharaohs.

PYRAMIDS AND THE OLD KINGDOM
(3100 TO 2181 B.C.)

Egyptologists conventionally divide Ancient Egyptian civilization into four broad periods, separated by at least two intermediate periods that were intervals of political change and instability (Table 16.1). The most striking feature of Ancient Egyptian civilization is its conservatism. Many of the artistic, religious, and technological features of early Egyptian civilization survived intact right into Roman times. The political and religious powers of the pharaohs changed somewhat through time, as later rulers became more imperialistic in their ambitions, or different gods assumed political supremacy. But the essential continuity was there, in the form of a civilization whose life was governed by the unchanging environment of the Nile Valley with its annual floods, narrow floodplain, and surrounding desert.

Archaic and old Kingdoms
3100 to 2181 B.C.

The Old Kingdom (c. 2700 to 2181 B.C.) saw four dynasties of pharaohs governing Egypt from a royal capital at Memphis near Cairo. Apparently the country's resources were well organized and controlled by a centralized government. Some of the pharaohs had a reputation as cruel despots, noticeably Cheops and Chephren, who built the pyramids of Giza. The building of pyramids is regarded as the mark of the Old Kingdom pharaohs.[5] The first royal pyramid was built by Djoser about 2680 B.C., a six-step pyramid that was surrounded by a veritable town of buildings and shrines. The Step Pyramid is a somewhat hesitant structure, but the great pyramids built over the next century show increasing confidence, culminating in the brilliant assurance of the pyramids of Giza with their perfect pyramid shape (Figure 16.3). The largest of these, the Great Pyramid, covers 13.1 acres and is 481 feet high. It dates to the Fourth Dynasty reign of Cheops, about 2600 B.C. Just under two centuries later, the pharaohs stopped building huge pyramids and diverted their organizational talents to other public works.

Giza
2600 B.C.

There is something megalomaniacal about the pyramids, built as they were with an enormous expenditure of labor and energy. They reflect the culmination of centuries of gradual evolution of the Egyptian state, during which the complexity of the state and the authority of the bureaucracy grew hand in hand. The pyramids were the houses and tombs for the pharaohs in eternity, symbols of the permanence of Egyptian civilization. They reflect the importance that the Egyptians placed on the life of the pharaoh in the afterworld, and in the notion of resurrection, a central belief in their religion for thousands of years.

Table 16.1   A much simplified chronology of Ancient Egyptian civilization.

Years B.C.	Period	Characteristics
30 B.C.	Roman occupation	Egypt an Imperial Province of Rome
332 to 30 B.C.	Ptolemaic Period	The Ptolemies bring Greek influence to Egypt, beginning with conquest of Egypt by Alexander the Great in 332 B.C.
1085 to 332 B.C.	Late Period	Gradual decline in Pharaonic authority culminating in Persian rule (525 to 404 B.C. and 343 to 332 B.C.).
1567 to 1085 B.C.	New Kingdom	Great imperial period of Egyptian history, with pharaohs buried in Valley of Kings. Pharaohs include Ramesses II, Seti I, and Tutankhamen, as well as Akhenaten, the heretic ruler.
1786 to 1567 B.C.	Second Intermediate Period	Hyksos rulers in the delta.
1991 to 1786 B.C.	Middle Kingdom	Thebes achieves prominence, also the priesthood of Amun.
c.2181 to 2173 B.C.	First Intermediate Period	Political chaos and disunity
2686 to 2181 B.C.	Old Kingdom	Despotic pharaohs build the pyramids and favor conspicuous funerary monuments. Institutions, economic strategies, and artistic traditions of Ancient Egypt established.
3100 to 2686 B.C.	Archaic Period	Consolidation of state (treated as part of Old Kingdom in this book)
3100 B.C.	Unification of Egypt under Narmer-Menes	

Figure 16.3 The pyramids of Giza.

Kurt Mendelssohn has argued that the pyramids were built over a relatively short period of time, during which the architects experimented with the pyramid shape. At least one pyramid collapsed during construction, before the builders mastered the correct 52-degree angles of the Great Pyramid. Every flood season when agriculture was at a standstill, the pharaohs organized thousands of peasants into construction teams who quarried, transported, and laid the dressed stones of the pyramids. The permanent (year-round) labor force was relatively small, mainly skilled artisans, the fruit of whose work was placed in position on the main structure once a year. As far as is known, the peasants were paid volunteers, fed by the state bureaucracy, whose loyalty to the divine pharaoh provided the motivation for the work. Mendelssohn feels the construction of the pyramids was a practical administrative device designed to organize and institutionalize the state. As construction proceeded from one generation to the next, the villagers became dependent on the central administration for food for three months a year, food obtained from surpluses contributed by the villages themselves in the form of taxation. After a while the pyramids fulfilled their purpose, and the state-directed labor forces could be diverted to other, less conspicuous state works. A new form of state organization had been created, one that both fostered and exploited the interdependence of Egyptian villages.

The Egyptian State

Egypt was the first state of its size in history. The pharaohs ruled by their own word, following no written laws, unlike the legislators of Mesopotamian city-states. The pharaoh had power over the Nile flood, rainfall, and all people, including foreigners. He was a god in his own right, respected by all people as a divine and tangible god whose being was the personification of *Ma'at*, or "rightness." Ma'at was far more than just rightness, it was a "right order," and stood for order and justice. The pharaoh embodied *ma'at* and dispensed justice. *Ma'at* was pharaonic status, and eternity itself — the very embodiment of the Egyptian state.[6]

The pharaoh's pronouncements were law, regulated by a massive background of precedent set by earlier pharaohs. Egyptian rulers lived a strictly ordered life. As one Greek writer tells us: "For there was a set time not only for his holding audience or rendering judgement, but even for his taking a walk, bathing, and sleeping with his wife; in short, every act of his life."

A massive, hereditary bureaucracy effectively ruled the kingdom, with rows of officials forming veritable dynasties. Their records tell us that much official energy was devoted to tax collection, harvest yields, and administering irrigation (Figure 16.4). An army of 20,000 men, many of them mercenaries, was maintained at the height of Egypt's prosperity. The Egyptian Empire was a literate one; that is to say, trained scribes who could read and write were an integral part of the state government. Special schools trained writers for careers in the army, the palace, the treasury, and numerous other callings.[7]

Despite the number of scribes and minor clerics, a vast gulf separated one who could read and write from the uneducated peasant worker. The life of a peasant, given good harvests, was easier than that of a Greek or a Syrian farmer, although the state required occasional bouts of forced labor to clear irrigation canals or to haul stone, both tasks being essential to maintain Egyptian agriculture. Minor craftsworkers and unskilled laborers lived more regimented lives, working on temples and pharaohs' tombs.[8] Many were organized in shifts under foremen. There were strikes, and absenteeism was common. A scale of rations and daily work was imposed. Like many early states, however, the Egyptians depended on slave labor for some public works and much domestic service. But foreign serfs and war prisoners could wield much influence in public affairs. They were allowed to rent and cultivate land.

Figure 16.4 A tomb painting from the tomb of Menena at Thebes showing the harvesting and measuring of fields near the Nile.

THE FIRST INTERMEDIATE PERIOD
AND MIDDLE KINGDOM (2181 to 1786 B.C.)

The Old Kingdom dynasties ended with the death of Pepi II in about 2200 B.C.[9] By this time the authority of the monarchy had been weakened by constant expenditure on lavish public works and, perhaps, by a cycle of bad harvest years which undermined the people's confidence in the abilities of the rulers to provide for them. A period of political instability now known as the First Intermediate ensued, during which there were Asian incursions into the fertile delta country and Egypt was ruled by the local nomarchs, even though there was nominal allegiance to a central government.

First Intermediate
Period
2181 to 2173 B.C.

About 2133 B.C. the city of Thebes in Upper Egypt became the center of rebel movements that eventually took over the country under pharaoh Mentuhotep II in 2040 B.C. The Middle Kingdom pharaohs who followed were

Middle Kingdom
1991 to 1786 B.C.

mostly energetic rulers who extended trading contacts throughout the Near East and conquered the desert lands of Nubia south of the First Cataract (see Figure 16.1). The pharaohs became somewhat less despotic and considered themselves more like shepherds of the people, who had some concern for the common welfare. It was during the Middle Kingdom that the city of Thebes came into prominence, especially as a center for the worship of the god Amun.

THE SECOND INTERMEDIATE PERIOD
(1786 to 1567 B.C.)

Second Intermediate
Period
1786 to 1567 B.C.

The Middle Kingdom lasted until about 1786 B.C. when another period of political instability and economic disorder ensued. Disputes over the royal succession at Thebes led to a whole procession of pharaohs who reigned for short periods. Pharaonic control of the Nile Valley as a whole weakened, and Asian intruders managed to penetrate the fertile lands of the delta downstream. Their leaders became known as the Hyksos, and formed two dynasties that ruled over much of Egypt between 1675 and 1567 B.C. They were probably nomadic chiefs from the desert, who brought the horse and chariot to Egypt for the first time.

The Hyksos had little control over Upper Egypt, where the pharaohs of Thebes quarreled among themselves. But eventually the Thebans came to realize that they could never control the whole of the country again unless they threw out the Hyksos and paid careful attention to the political realities of Asia. From this point on, the Egyptian pharaohs took an active interest in their Asian neighbors and there was a constant flow of people and ideas with other nations.

THE NEW KINGDOM
(1567 to 1085 B.C.)

New Kingdom
1567 to 1085 B.C.

The New Kingdom began when a series of Theban pharaohs fought and won a war of independence from the Hyksos. It was Ahmose the Liberator who finally overcame the foreigners and established a firm hold on Egypt from the delta to Nubia. He was the first of a series of great rulers, whose names have become symbolic of the power of Ancient Egypt: Tutmosis, Amenophis, Seti, and Ramesses, the greatest of Egypt's pharaohs all extended the Egyptian Empire, into deepest Nubia and far into Palestine. The pharaohs campaigned against the Hittites in Syria and tried to keep their eastern boundary secure against raiding Mesopotamian armies. The spiritual center of the empire was at Thebes, where the great temples of Luxor and Karnak housed the priests of Amun. This priesthood was a formidable political force in New Kingdom Egypt.

The New Kingdom pharaohs adopted new burial customs and abandoned conspicuous sepulchres. Their mummies were buried in the desolate Valley of Kings on the west bank of the Nile at Thebes. An entire community of workmen did nothing else but prepare the rock-cut tombs of the pharaohs, their queens, and privileged nobles. To date, only one undisturbed royal tomb has come to light in the Valley of Kings, that of the obscure pharaoh Tutankhamen, who died in 1346 B.C.[10] The world was astounded when Howard Carter and Lord Carnarvon discovered and cleared the tomb of the young pharaoh in the 1920s (Figure 16.5). It gives us an impression of the incredible wealth of the New Kingdom pharaohs' court.

Tutankhamen died in his late teens, but was responsible for restoring religious order after a curious interlude of chaos during the reign of Akhenaten (1363 to 1350 B.C.).[11] Like many pharaohs before him, Akhenaten had been worried about the overriding power of the priests of Amun at Thebes. So he espoused the worship of the god Aten, the life-giving disk of the sun. Akhenaten took up the new religion with fanatical zeal, even founded a new capital downstream of Thebes called Akhetaten, near the modern village of el-Amarna. After his death in 1350 B.C., the regents for Tutankhamen worked hard to restore the power and prestige of Amun, a move apparently supported by the mass of the people, for Akhenaten had produced no viable alternatives for the established political and religious institutions he had abolished.

Figure 16.5 The antechamber of Tutankhamen's tomb with two wooden figures of the king guarding the sealed entrance to the Burial Chamber.

THE LATE PERIOD
(1085 to 30 B.C.)

With the death of Rameses III in 1085 B.C., Egypt entered on a period of political weakness, when local rulers exercised varying control over the Nile. The pharaohs were threatened by Nubian rulers, who actually ruled over Egypt for a short time in the eighth century B.C. The Assyrians were a constant hazard after 725 B.C. and actually occupied parts of the country and looted Thebes in 665. After the eclipse of Assyria, the Egyptians enjoyed a few centuries of independence before being conquered by the Persians in 343 B.C. and Alexander the Great in 332 B.C. He in turn was succeeded by the Ptolemies, pharaohs of Greek ancestry, who ruled Egypt until Roman times. It was they who brought much of Egyptian lore and learning into the mainstream of emerging Greek civilization, and who ensured that the Land of the Pharaohs made a critical contribution to Western Civilization.

THE EMERGENCE OF AFRICAN STATES

What were Egypt's relationships with the vast African continent that bordered the Nile? Her influence on southern and Saharan neighbors was surprisingly small, for her ties were closer to the Mediterranean world than to Black Africa. The pharaohs exercised political control only as far south as the First Cataract, near today's Aswan Dam. But the areas to the south were an important source of ivory for ornaments and of slaves for the divine rulers.

Meroe

Around 900 B.C., however, an unknown governor of the southernmost part of Egypt founded his own dynasty and ruled a string of small settlements extending far south into the area that is now the Sudan. His capital at Napata began to decline because the fragile grasslands by the Nile were overgrazed. The inhabitants moved south and founded a town called Meroe on a fertile

floodplain between the Nile and Atbara rivers (Figure 16.1). There they built their own thriving urban civilization, which was in contact with peoples living far to the west on the southern edge of the Sahara.[12] Meroe's inhabitants kept up at least sporadic contacts with the Classical World. They gained prosperity from extensive trading in such items as copper, gold, iron, ivory, and slaves. Some of Meroe's prosperity may have been based on ironworking, for deposits of this vital material were abundant near Napata. Iron artifacts are, however, fairly rare in the city itself.

In the early centuries after Christ, the empire declined, following raids from the kingdom of Axum centered on the Ethiopian highlands.[13] Meroe was abandoned and the stratified society that had ruled it collapsed. A scattered rural population continued to live along the banks of the Nile. The fertile grasslands that had surrounded Meroe were now overgrazed and the increasingly arid countryside made urban life difficult. A dispersed settlement pattern replaced the centralized city style of Meroe's heyday. Chiefdoms replaced divine kings.

North Africa

The North African coast had long been a staging post for maritime traders from the eastern Mediterranean. During the first millennium B.C., the Phoenicians set up ports.[14] The colonists came into contact with well-established barter networks that criss-crossed the Sahara.[15] The desert is rich in salt deposits that were controlled by the nomadic peoples who lived there. They came in touch with Negro tribesmen living to the south of the desert who bartered salt for copper, ivory, gold, and the other raw materials that Africa has traditionally given to the world. Soon, long trading routes connected North Africa with tropical regions, well-trodden highways that provided much of the Greek and Roman wealth during the height of their civilizations.

Most of the Saharan trade was in the hands of nomadic tribesmen, middlemen between Black Africa and the bustling markets of the Mediterranean. In Roman times the camel was introduced to the Sahara. These "ships of the desert" enabled merchants to organize sizable camel caravans that crossed the Sahara like clockwork, from the North African coast to West Africa; the caravans increased direct contact between the Mediterranean world and West Africa and built a much greater volume of trade.

Ironworking and African States

Ironworking had reached West Africa by the fourth century B.C., perhaps by the Saharan trade routes.[16] The new metallurgy, unlike that of copper, spread rapidly over sub-Saharan Africa in a few centuries. Its spread was connected in part with the dispersal of Bantu-speaking peoples over much of eastern, central, and southern Africa. Bantu languages are now spoken by many inhabitants of tropical Africa. The original area of Bantu tongues may have been north of the Zaire forest.[17]

This spread of the new language coincides with the arrival of negroid peoples both in the Zaire forest and on the savannah woodlands to the east and south of it. Ironworking farmers were living near the great East African lakes by the third century A.D., by the banks of the Zambezi River at approximately the same time, and crossing the Limpopo into South Africa during the first millennium A.D. They introduced farming and domestic animals into wide areas of Africa, absorbing, eliminating, or pushing out the indigenous San hunter-gatherers.[18]

The Bantu farmers used shifting agriculture and careful soil selection to produce a diet of sorghum, millet, and other cereal crops. They kept cattle and sheep or goats, and relied on hunting and gathering for much of their diet. Their architectural styles and pottery have a clear but indirect relationship with those of many present-day rural black Africans.

West African States

The past thousand years have seen the proliferation of prosperous African states ruled by leaders whose power was based on religious ability, entrepreneurial skill, and control of vital raw materials.[19] The West African states at the southern edges of the Sahara, such as Ghana, Mali, and Songhay, based their prosperity on the gold trade with North Africa (Figure 16.6). The Saharan trade passed into Islamic hands at the end of the first millennium A.D., and Arab authors began describing the remarkable African kingdoms flourishing south of the desert. The geographer al-Bakri drew a vivid picture of the kingdom of Ghana, whose gold was well known in northern latitudes by the eleventh century. "It is said," he wrote, "that the king owns a nugget as large as a big stone."

Ghana   The Kingdom of Ghana straddled the northern borders of the gold-bearing river valleys of the Upper Niger and Senegal.[20] No one knows when it first came into being, but the kingdom was described by Arab writers in the eighth century A.D. The Ghanians' prosperity depended on the gold trade and the constant demand for ivory in the north. Salt, kola nuts (used as a stimulant), slaves, and swords also crossed the desert, but gold, ivory, and salt were the foundations of their power. Islam was brought to Ghana sometime in the late first millennium, the religion linking the kingdom more closely to the desert trade. The king of Ghana was a powerful ruler who, wrote al-Bakri, "can put 200,000 men in the field, more than 40,000 of whom are bowmen."

Ghana was a prime target for Islamic reform movements, whose desert leaders longingly eyed the power and wealth of their southern neighbor. One such group, the Almoravids, attacked Ghana about A.D. 1062, but it was fourteen years before the invaders captured the Ghanian capital. The power of Ghana was fatally weakened, and the kingdom fell into its tribal parts soon after.

Mali   The kingdom of Mali appeared two centuries later, after many tribal squabbles.[21] A group of Kangaba people under the leadership of Sundiata came into prominence about A.D. 1230 and annexed their neighbors' lands. Sundiata built his new capital at Mali on the Niger River. He founded a vast empire that a century later extended over most of sub-Saharan West Africa. The fame of the Malian kings spread all over the Muslim world. Timbuktu became an important center of learning. Malian gold was valued everywhere. When the king of Mali went on a pilgrimage to Mecca in A.D. 1324, the price of gold in Egypt was reduced sharply by the king's liberal spending. Mali appeared on the earliest maps of West Africa as an outside frontier of the literate world, providing gold and other luxuries for Europe and North Africa.

The key to Mali's prosperity was the unifying effect of Islam. Islamic rulers governed with supreme powers granted by Allah, and ruled their conquered provinces through religious appointees or wealthy slaves. Islam provided a reservoir of thoroughly trained, literate administrators, too, who owed allegiance to peace, stability, and good trading practices.

A.D. 1062

A.D. 1230

A.D. 1324

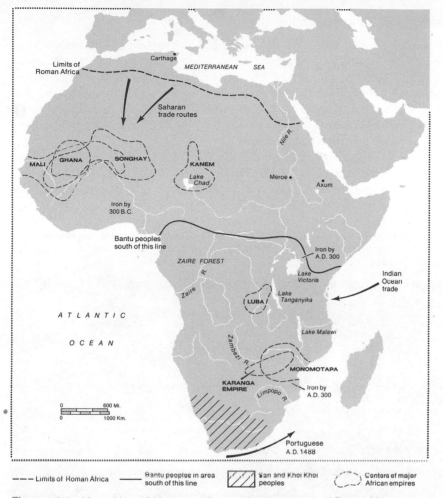

Figure 16.6 Map of later African prehistory, showing extent of Bantu Africa, and also indigenous states, as well as showing distribution of San and Khoi Khoi peoples.

Songhay About A.D. 1325 the greatest of the kings of Mali, Mansa Musa, brought the important trading center of Gao on the Niger under his sway.[22] Gao was the capital of the Dia kings, who shook off Mali's yoke around A.D. 1340 and founded the kingdom of Songhay. Their state prospered increasingly as Mali's power weakened. The great chieftain Sonni Ali led the Songhay to new conquests between A.D. 1464 and 1492, expanding the frontiers of his empire deep into Mali country and far north into the Sahara. He monopolized much of the Saharan trade, seeking to impose law and order with his vast armies to increase the volume of trade that passed through Songhay hands. Sonni Ali was followed by other competent rulers who further expanded Songhay. Its collapse came in the sixteenth century.

A.D. 1325

A.D. 1464 to 1492

A.D. 1550

Karanga and Zimbabwe

Powerful African kingdoms also developed in central and southern Africa. The Luba kingdom of the Congo and the Karanga empire between the Zambezi and Limpopo rivers were led by skilled priests and ivory traders who also handled such diverse raw materials as copper, gold, seashells, cloth, and porcelain. Their power came from highly centralized political organizations and effective religious powers, which channeled some of their subjects' energies into exploiting raw materials and long-distance trade.

The Karanga peoples lived between the Zambezi and Limpopo where Rhodesia is today, and developed a remarkable kingdom that built its viability on trade in gold, copper, and ivory and on its leaders' religious acumen.[23] The

Figure 16.7 The Zimbabwe ruins, Rhodesia: an important trading and religious center of the Karanga peoples of south-central Africa in the second millennium A.D. Most of the Great Enclosure, or Temple, was built by A.D. 1500.

Old World Civilizations

Karanga leaders founded their power on being intermediaries between the people and their ancestral spirits, upon whom the people believed the welfare of the nation depended. Around A.D. 1000, the Karanga began to build stone structures, the most famous of which is Zimbabwe, built at the foot of a sacred hill in southeastern Rhodesia. Zimbabwe became an important commercial and religious center. Its chiefs lived in seclusion on the sacred hill, known to archaeologists as "the Acropolis." In the valley below sprawled a complex of homesteads and stone enclosures, which were dominated in later centuries by the high, free-standing stone walls of the Great Enclosure, or Temple (Figure 16.7). A.D. 1000

At least five stages of occupation have been recognized at Zimbabwe, the first of them dating to the fourth century A.D., when a group of farmers camped at the site, but built no stone walls. They were followed by later occupants who constructed the Great Enclosure in stages and built retaining walls on the Acropolis. The heyday of Zimbabwe was between A.D. 1350 and 1450, when imported cloth, china, glass, and porcelain were traded to the site. Gold ornaments, copper, ivory, and elaborate iron tools were in common use. A.D. 1350 to 1450

Zimbabwe declined after A.D. 1450, probably because overpopulation impoverished the environment, where agricultural resources were relatively poor anyway.

Foreign Traders

Much of African history is about exploitation of the peoples and raw materials by foreign traders and explorers. The East African coast was visited by Arabs and Indian merchants who used the monsoon winds of the Indian Ocean to sail to Africa and back within twelve months on prosperous trading ventures. The Portuguese skirted Africa's western and southeastern coasts in the fifteenth century, establishing precarious colonies ruled from Portugal to exploit raw materials.[24] Some parts of Africa, however, had no contact with the outside world until Victorian explorers and missionaries met remote and exotic peoples as they strove toward elusive goals, including such prizes as the source of the Nile.[25] A.D. 1488 A.D. 1850

Chapter Seventeen

THE HARAPPAN CIVILIZATION AND SOUTHEAST ASIA

PREVIEW

⚜ The Harappan civilization of the Indus Valley (present-day Pakistan) is thought to have developed from indigenous roots sometime in the second millennium B.C.

⚜ The Harappans maintained extensive connections with areas to the north, especially Afghanistan, and are thought to have been in sporadic contact with the Iranian plateau and Mesopotamia.

⚜ Harappan civilization flourished from about 2800 to 1900 B.C. over an enormous area of the Indus Valley. Harappa and Moenjodaro were the largest cities, each laid out in an inflexible design, which was dominated by a great citadel. It is assumed that the civilization was ruled by priest-kings who controlled both religious and economic life.

⚜ After 1900 B.C. Harappan civilization declined, perhaps in part because of declining rainfall and deterioration of the environment. The period between the end of the Harappan culture and the beginnings of ironworking is obscure. Ironworking in India, by comparison, is associated with the period of Painted Grey wares, when the subcontinent was occupied by the Persian King Darius, in 516 B.C.

⚜ Southeast Asia is thought to have developed metallurgy at an early date, perhaps as early as the fourth millennium B.C. The process of local state formation is thought to have continued in the first millennium B.C., but the first historical records of complex states date to the fourth century A.D.

⚜ Later Southeast Asian prehistory was dominated by the changing fortunes of various empires ruled by divine kings who espoused a strongly centralized economic system, as secular and religious concerns were molded together in a single type of complex society.

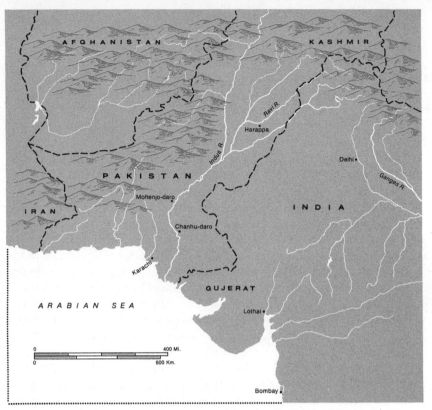

Figure 17.1 The Harappan civilization, showing sites mentioned in Chapter 17.

Chronological Table I

The earliest evidence for farming cultures in India comes from the Rajasthan desert of northwest India, where Gurdip Singh recovered clear signs of widespread burning of scrub around 7500 B.C., at about the same time that the counts for grass pollens rise sharply.[1]* Although similar pollen diagrams come from several localities, no one has excavated in the area. Singh considers it likely that people were modifying the local vegetational cover substantially, perhaps by simple cultivation. We have no reason to believe that he is wrong, for experiments with cereal crops and domestic animals undoubtedly took place in the general area.

Farming cultures were certainly widespread in northwestern Pakistan by 3500 B.C. (Figure 17.1).[2] Some of these people probably used simple copper implements and made painted pottery on slow, hand-turned wheels. By 3000 B.C. this type of farming culture was distributed over much of the present Pakistan. The general pottery tradition and other cultural traits have many links with regions to the west, and some distinctive pottery motifs are reminiscent of those found on Sumerian sites. The earliest farmers of northwestern India probably had much to do with diffusion of new inventions and forging of fresh trade links between India and western centers of urban civilization.

* See page 388 for notes to Chapter 17.

While we still do not know how the Harappan civilization arose, there seems to be general agreement that the societies among which it came into being were subject to prolonged influence and trading contacts with centers to the north and to the west in highland Iran and Mesopotamia.[3] Some people go as far as to think of the Harappans as a colonial offshoot of Sumerian civilization, citing parallels in ceremonial centers, trading and farming practices, and general features of city life — even though the Sumerians flourished much earlier than the Harappan cities. Others believe that the Harappan civilization is an indigenous development, coalescing numerous smaller villages into larger social and political units. The development of trade relationships with the Iranian plateau and the north served as a powerful integrative mechanism in forging the Harappan civilization, as did the development of irrigation agriculture and the emergence of a rigid class system and large cities in the Indus valley. The intensification of agriculture seems to have been particularly important, as a means of supporting rapidly growing urban populations of specialists, bureaucrats, and priests. Pollen analysis of numerous samples from the Indus region show a sharp rise in tree and scrub cover from about 3000 B.C., which must have resulted from a period of greater rainfall that lasted for at least two thousand years. This increased tree cover developed at a time when the people were beginning to clear the land by systematic burning of surface vegetation. The pollen diagrams for this period show a sharp increase in the proportions of cereal grass pollens, as the tree cover was replaced by the more open vegetational cover resulting from agriculture.

The earliest farming villages in the Indus Valley are thought to have practiced a form of mixed farming based on cereal cultivation and animal husbandry. Stone tools were augmented with a few copper artifacts. Usually the villages were sited close to streams and rivers swollen each year by runoff from the snow packs of mountains upstream. Precious river waters flooded the low plain providing natural irrigation for such crops as wheat, barley, and cotton. Nile-like, the rivers brought down copious amounts of silt deposited by the floodwaters on the gardens as a natural fertilizer.

The Harappan Civilization

3000 B.C.

The formative period of Harappan civilization began after 3000 B.C., when higher rainfall may have encouraged higher crop yields and intensified agriculture. The integrative forces that led to the emergence of this indigenous urban civilization were probably very similar to those in Mesopotamia.[4]

Harappan civilization
2800 to 1900 B.C.

The earliest levels of Harappan civilization are thought to date to about 2800 B.C., a date indicated by dated imported seals in Mesopotamian sites and by radiocarbon dates obtained on smaller Harappan villages where Harappan artifacts overlie earlier occupation. Unfortunately the excavation of the lowest levels of the great cities of the civilization is almost impossible on account of their great depth below the surface.

The scale of the Harappan civilization is almost mindboggling. At the height of its prosperity, Harappan territory extended 1000 miles (1610 km) from north to south, with an indented coastline 700 miles (1126 km) long. In recent years several cities have been excavated, including a port at Lothal in Gujerat and the important settlement of Chanhudaro. Both show a standardization of settlement layout and governance that is truly remarkable, for the area of Harappan civilization was far larger than that of patchwork city-states.

The Great Cities

The scale and standardization of the Harappan civilization is best illustrated by the great cities of Harappa (after which the civilization is named) and Moenjodaro. Both have a circumference of up to three miles (4.8 km) and, like Mesopotamian towns, are clustered around conspicuous ceremonial centers. Both towns are laid out on a rectangular grid, streets crossing each other with regularity (Figure 17.2). Drains and wells were part of city design.

The more prosperous inhabitants lived in houses with courtyards built of fired brick and complete sanitation facilities and storage rooms. The workers' quarters were humble, mud-brick cottages near brick kilns, smelting furnaces, and other work areas. Vast public granaries testify to a strongly centralized government, one that maintained rigid control over the cities and the surrounding countryside.

Harappa

Moenjodaro

Figure 17.2 A typical street in Moenjodaro, Pakistan, uncovered in Sir Mortimer Wheeler's excavations.

We know almost nothing of the political arrangements that enabled these cities and other similar but smaller settlements to flourish for so long. Both Harappa and Moenjodaro are laid out around a fortified citadel, the focus for the settlement. The citadel at Harappa was enclosed by brick walls adorned with defensive towers and encompassed an area 550 meters (600 yds) across. Each quarter of each city was well defined, and craftsworkers and laborers had their own quarters. The impression is of a hierarchic society divided into well-ordered classes or castes, whose rulers exercised great power. It is difficult to say whether leaders were priests, divine kings, or monks. We know little about them or their way of life, for no one has yet deciphered the Indus script.

Ever since the beginnings of recorded history, the Indian approach to governance and religion has interwoven temporal and spiritual considerations so closely that religious behavior and expectations strongly shaped political and social institutions. Perhaps the rulers of the Harappan cities were conceived of as religious leaders, whose piety and close relationship to the pantheon of gods provided a structure for society and the hierarchy of social classes that served the rulers. The sameness and monotony about Harappa and Moenjodaro is almost numbing to the onlooker, as if the entire society was circumscribed by beliefs and rules defining everyone's place in society. The notion that the people served the king seems an attractive hypothesis for understanding the structure of Harappan life, but it cannot be tested.

As with all early civilizations, huge food surpluses lay at the core of city life. The economy of the Indus Valley cities was built on cultivating wheat, barley, cotton, and secondary crops. Cattle, water buffalo, asses, horses, and camels were already domesticated, as we know by pictures on clay seals. Both domestic animals and cereal cultivation had been staples of economic life for millennia. Presumably irrigation was important in surplus food production, a state-controlled activity on the vast Indus floodplain.

Trading Practices

Though subsistence for the Harappan civilization was firmly based on mixed farming, trade was also important in the life of the cities. Harappan trade was far-flung, although many details of the long distance networks are imperfectly understood. Exotic raw materials such as gold, tin, copper, silver, and alabaster were obtained from the north, from Afghanistan, Kashmir, and Iran. Trading contacts between Mesopotamia and the Indus Valley have been much debated. Older interpretations of the Harappan civilization favored regular interaction. Scattered Harappan seals, pots, beads, and other trinkets have been discovered in Mesopotamian tells (mounds) as early as the time of Sargon, around 2370 B.C., but no Mesopotamian objects have yet come to light at Harappa or Moenjodaro. Harappan contacts with Mesopotamia seem to have been casual and probably indirect.

The unknown rulers who presided over the affairs of the Harappan cities had just as complex a recordkeeping problem as did the Sumerians and Egyptians. They divised a pictographic writing on clay seals, again presumably in response to a need for accounting devices. It has yet to be deciphered.

Old World Civilizations

AFTER THE HARAPPANS —
LATER PREHISTORY

The closing centuries of the Harappan civilization, from about 1900 B.C., show the cities declining in prosperity, culminating in the abandonment of Moenjodaro in the eighteenth century B.C. No one is sure why this decline took place.

1900 B.C.

One school claims the Harappan civilization was destroyed by Aryan invaders from the north. Skeletons found unburied in the streets of the latest levels of the city are said to be signs of warfare. Other theorists, among them Robert Raikes, a hydrologist, hypothesize that the Indus River was blocked by earthquake downstream of Moenjodaro.[5] The blockage formed a huge lake that periodically flooded the city until it was abandoned. Like the invasion theory, this hypothesis lacks supporting data. Pollen researcher Gurdip Singh has found signs that the lakes of the Indus region began to dry up around 1800 B.C., as a period of drier climate set in.[6] At about this time the Harappan civilization began its gradual decline, perhaps accelerated by the arid conditions and overgrazing and cultivation of the floodplains. Whether or not this gradual decline was terminated by a violent alien incursion we do not know.

From the archaeological point of view the period between the breakdown of the Harappan cities and the beginning of ironworking is the most obscure in India's later prehistory. Despite the abandonment of the cities, there were no major disruptions in economy or material culture. Iron tools appear in India in the late second millennium B.C. and are associated with Painted Grey Wares, made on a wheel and adorned with simple, black painted designs. The advent of iron tools enabled farmers to break up the hard, calcareous soils of the Ganges plain, an area that was to become the heartland of later empires.

Painted Grey Wares
1000 B.C.

Meanwhile, King Darius of Persia invaded the subcontinent in 516 B.C. and incorporated part of India into the Persian Empire. Two centuries later Alexander the Great ventured to the Indus River and brought Greek culture to the area. His incursion also provided a stimulus for cultural developments in the Ganges that culminated in a nationalistic revolt headed by the priest Chandragupta. This leader founded an empire which linked the Indus and the Ganges in a single administrative unit that traded as far afield as Malaya and the Near East. The period between about 200 B.C. and A.D. 300 saw India linked with lands far to the east and west by regular trading links that persisted more or less independently of political developments. By this time the influence of Indian religion in the form of Buddhism and Hinduism was being felt over enormous areas of Asia.

516 B.C.

010 B.C.

SOUTHEAST ASIAN CIVILIZATIONS

The emergence of complex states in Southeast Asia is probably closely connected with the spread of rice cultivation and bronze metallurgy. As we saw in Chapter 12, the early history of rice cultivation is still inadequately documented. But we do know that the spread of rice agriculture throughout Southeast Asia may prove some day to be connected with the Langshanoid peoples of China. Pottery that shows influence of their widespread traditions has been found in Thailand and possibly Malaya. The genesis of copper and bronze metallurgy in Southeast Asia is even less well documented than the genesis of rice cultivation. Solheim claims that bronze artifacts have been found at Non Nok Tha as early as 4000 B.C. Chester Gorman's excavations at Ban Chieng are claimed to document bronze artifacts in levels as early as 3600 to 2000 B.C., but few details of the site have yet been published.[7] If these early dates are substantiated, then Southeast Asia was indeed a very early center of metallurgy.

Ban Chieng
3600 to 2000 B.C.

Foreign Influences

Although archaeological evidence is still largely lacking, it seems likely that state forms of society were evolving in Southeast Asia from the second millennium B.C. What is uncertain is the extent to which foreign influences played a part in the dissemination of more complex state organizations. Perhaps it is significant that much of our information on early Southeast Asian states comes from Chinese and Indian archives.[8]

Trading systems are established   For centuries Southeast Asia was dominated, at least tangentially, by two foreign presences. To the north the Chinese imposed their political will on the Lăc peoples of the Tong-king lowlands and extended their tribute systems into the Red River Valley. This was an arbitrary imposition of an entirely different economic system onto trading systems based on reciprocity. It was quite different from the cultural changes going on in the southerly parts of Southeast Asia.

A.D. 1

About two thousand years ago, the busy sea-trading networks of Southeast Asia were being incorporated into the vast, oceanic trade routes stretching from China in the east to the shores of the Red Sea and the east coast of Africa in the west. No one people controlled the whole of this vast trade. Most of the Indian Ocean commerce was in the hands of Arabs, who used monsoon winds to traverse the long sea lanes from India to Africa and from Arabia to both continents. The trade carried raw materials and luxury goods such as glass beads and cloth. During the heyday of the Roman Empire the Greeks and Egyptians of Alexandria took some interest in the Indian Ocean trade, but rarely ventured farther than the Red Sea.

Beyond India the trade was held by Indian merchants who penetrated deep into the numerous islands and channels of Southeast Asia. The traders themselves were an entirely maritime people, called *Mwani* or *barbarians* by the Chinese of the time. They spoke a polyglot of tongues and were of many lands, some Malays, some Indians, true wanderers who ventured as far east as the South China Sea. The Gulf of Tonkin and South China were served by *Jiwet*, Chinese mariners who brought luxuries to the coast, from whence they were transported overland to the Chinese capital.

Indian merchants were certainly active on Southeast Asian coasts by the early centuries of the Christian era. They were actively trading with the tribal societies of both mainland and islands. Voyaging was now accelerated by

- *Extensive worldwide clinical experience in 117 countries with over 17 million patients.*

changing circumstances. First came larger cargo vessels with a more efficient rig that enabled them to sail closer to the wind. No one knows how large these vessels were, but they must have been substantial. The Chinese are known to have transported horses by sea to Indonesia in the third century A.D., and the monk Fa Hsien recorded his sailing trip from Ceylon to China with two hundred other passengers in A.D. 414.

Another factor influencing trade was a new demand for gold and other metals. The Roman Emperor Vespasian had prohibited exporting metals from the Roman Empire in about A.D. 70, a move that turned the Indian merchants' eyes to the southeast, particularly because the Siberian gold mines had been closed to them by nomadic raids on Asian caravans. And metals were not the only attraction; spices could be obtained in abundance. Trade was expanded entirely for commercial profit.

Imported religions   Buddhism had made great strides in India since it appeared in the fourth century B.C. The older religion, Brahmanism, had placed severe and authoritarian restraints on foreign voyages. But Buddhism and Jainism, a form of Hinduism, rejected the notion of racial purity espoused by the predecessor religion. Travel was encouraged; the merchant became a respected part of Buddhist belief. As voyaging increased, especially from southern India to Southeast Asia, a strong cultural influence emanated from the former to the latter. The tribal societies of Southeast Asia were introduced to many alien products and some of the foreigners' philosophical, social, and religious beliefs. In a few centuries kingdoms appeared with governments run according to Hindu or Buddhist ideas of social order.

Chieftains become divine kings   The initial but regular contacts between merchants and tribal societies were seasonal, dictated by the monsoon winds. The chieftains who represented the people of the tribes would have acted as intermediaries between the foreigners and the indigenous people. All exchanges and transactions having to do with the trade were channeled through them. Inevitably, argues Sinologist Paul Wheatley, the chieftains would learn a new way of seeing society and the world, perhaps organizing the collection of commodities for trade, acquiring new organizational skills alien to their own societies. As principal beneficiaries of the trade, they would acquire status, many more possessions, and strong interest in seeing the trade maintained. But the authority and powers needed to expand and maintain the commerce were not part of the kin-linked society in which the chieftains had lived all their lives. In time, they might come to feel closer sympathy with their visitors, the people who gave them their power and prestige. Philosophically they would come to feel closer to Indian models of authority and leadership. They would become familiar with the Brahman and Buddhist conceptions of divine kingship. There was even a brahmanic rite by which chieftains could be inducted into the ruling class, a group whose authority was vested in an assumption of divine kingship. Wheatley hypothesizes that regular trading contacts, combined with changes in beliefs about the legitimizing of authority, led to the birth of states in Southeast Asia.

Divine kingship was a cultural borrowing from India that revolutionized social and political organization in Southeast Asia. Numerous city-states arose in strategic parts of this huge region. Many were served by Brahman priests, who, among other functions, consecrated divine kings as they started their reigns. Some of these states became very powerful, with extensive trading connections and large Brahman communities. As early as the third century A.D., Chinese envoys to Southeast Asia reported on a state in the northern part of the Malay peninsula that enjoyed regular trading contacts with Parthia and India as well as with southern China.

The New City-States

The new states were headed by divine kings whose religious and secular authority was bolstered by a class of priests who also provided secular services and sometimes engaged in commerce. Royal authority had to have control over both labor forces necessary to perform community works and the surplus food needed to feed the growing number of specialists who were serving king and priesthood. Soon the *nagara* or city-state came to be, a political and economic unit whose authority was focused on the temple. The city-state was the last social and political transmutation converting the tribal chieftain into the divine king and the shaman into the priest. The village farmers were now bound to the temple by an obligation to provide grain to feed nonproductive mouths.

The "Indianization" of Southeast Asia was not a conquest but an adoption of new administrative and philosophical models, while the city-states themselves maintained political autonomy from the Indian continent. Wheatley points out that Indian thought and culture was flexible enough to absorb alien ideas and elements without losing its own identity. In any case, Indian cultural patterns, despite their sophisticated formulation in India itself, shared many beliefs and customs with much of tropical Southeast Asia. The temple of each city-state focused the new philosophies and religious inconography, enabling the rulers to command impressive public authority, even if the minutiae of religious dogma never entered the consciousness of the peasant farmers tilling their fields.

A.D. 400

There are historical records of complex states by the middle of the third century A.D. in the Mekong Valley, in central Vietnam, and in the Malayan peninsula. The original city-states were, without exception, on the main sea trade routes between India and China. In later centuries states expanded over the lowlands of Southeast Asia, with a royal city and temple at the center of each state. The entire state economy was organized to appease the gods of the Indian pantheon.

Kambujadeśa
A.D. 1181

Extravagance in Cambodia Some idea of the power these exchange systems had can be gained from a brief look at the ancient kingdom of Kambujadeśa in Cambodia. The architectural and religious achievements of its great king Jayavarman VII (A.D. 1181–1218) were quite extraordinary. The king and his nobles dedicated hundreds of elaborate shrines and temples

Figure 17.3 Guardian lion and causeway leading to the famous Angkor Wat temple in Cambodia.

throughout the kingdom. The shrine of Ta Prohm alone had as many as 3140 settlements and 79,000 people living in relationship with it. There were 18 high priests and at least 2740 officials, to say nothing of 615 female dancers. The property inventory included gold dishes weighing more than 500 kilograms, 512 sets of silk bedding, and thousands of sets of clothing for the temple statues.

Earlier kings had built the world-famous shrine at Angkor Wat (Figure 17.3); Jayavarman merely built 121 rest houses for pilgrims making their way to the sacred temple. His culminating architectural achievement was his own capital, now known as Angkor Thom. The new city was built on the foundations of an earlier but imposing settlement, almost a map of the Khmer kingdom in conception. A wall and ditch 10 miles (6 km) long surrounded the ceremonial precincts of the city. His palace and other parts of the ceremonial complex were connected by raised terraces, of which one, the Terrace of the Elephants, was 300 yards (274 m) long. Jayavarman created artificial lakes and ingenious hydraulic innovations that added to agricultural production and connected the ceremonial landscaping to pragmatic agronomic functions. The massive centralizing of products and services was brilliantly bound to both religious and day-to-day functions. The pace of economic growth was frightening, and, without doubt, led to the decline of the Khmer kingdom after Jayavarman's death.

Some have thought of Southeast Asia as an Indian colony; early European accounts of the region encouraged this idea, leading people to think of Southeast Asia as an area colonized and settled by foreigners hunting commercial profit. Reality suggests much more subtle cultural workings: the indigenous development of power and diverse city-states, which owed much to the pervasive beliefs and values of Indian administrative and religious philosophy.

Chronological Table J

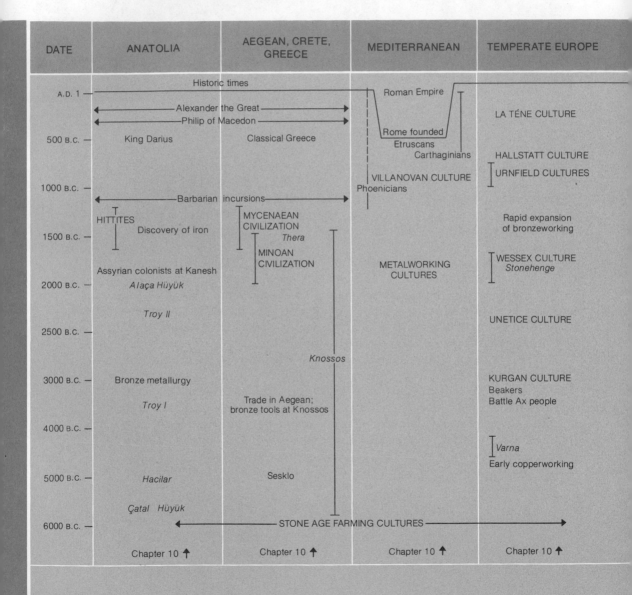

DATE	ANATOLIA	AEGEAN, CRETE, GREECE	MEDITERRANEAN	TEMPERATE EUROPE
		Historic times	Roman Empire	
A.D. 1 —				LA TÉNE CULTURE
	←——— Alexander the Great ———→			
	←——— Philip of Macedon ———→			
500 B.C. —	King Darius	Classical Greece	Rome founded	
			Etruscans	
			Carthaginians	HALLSTATT CULTURE
			VILLANOVAN CULTURE	URNFIELD CULTURES
1000 B.C. —			Phoenicians	
	←——— Barbarian incursions ———→			
	HITTITES	MYCENAEAN CIVILIZATION		Rapid expansion of bronzeworking
1500 B.C. —	Discovery of iron	*Thera*		
		MINOAN CIVILIZATION		WESSEX CULTURE *Stonehenge*
	Assyrian colonists at Kanesh		METALWORKING CULTURES	
2000 B.C. —	*Alaça Hüyük*			
	Troy II			UNETICE CULTURE
2500 B.C. —				
		Knossos		
3000 B.C. —	Bronze metallurgy			KURGAN CULTURE Beakers
	Troy I	Trade in Aegean; bronze tools at Knossos		Battle Ax people
4000 B.C. —				
				Varna Early copperworking
5000 B.C. —	*Hacilar*	Sesklo		
	Çatal Hüyük			
6000 B.C. —	←——————— STONE AGE FARMING CULTURES ———————→			
	Chapter 10 ↑	Chapter 10 ↑	Chapter 10 ↑	Chapter 10 ↑

Chapter Eighteen

ANATOLIA, GREECE, AND ITALY

PREVIEW

⚜ Anatolia was a major locale for the development of early farming villages — one of which, Çatal Hüyük, became a small town in the sixth millennium B.C. Strangely, however, Çatal Hüyük failed to develop the necessary administrative and social mechanisms to cope with the increased complexity of the settlement and its trading activities; the town failed, and Anatolians of the fifth millennium reverted to village life.

⚜ Small fortified villages, like the one preserved in the later levels of Hacilar, flourished in the fourth millennium. One of them, Troy I, dates to just after 3500 B.C. Troy II, founded in about 2300 B.C. was a fortified town with more elaborate architecture and fine gold and bronze metallurgy. By this time the Anatolians were trading widely over the highlands and into the Aegean, and chieftaincies were scattered over mineral-rich areas. In 1900 B.C. the Assyrians set up a trading colony at Kanesh in central Anatolia that was similar to those set up by the Mesopotamians elsewhere.

⚜ The Hittites were a small group of leaders who originated in the north and assumed power in Anatolia about 1650 B.C. They held a vital place in contemporary history, for they played the Assyrians off against the Egyptians. Hittite power was based on diplomatic and trading skills and lasted until about 1200 B.C. They were associated with the discovery of iron smelting.

⚜ The Aegean and the Greek mainland were settled by sedentary farming villages well before 5000 B.C. Painted pottery styles came into widespread use about that time.

⚜ There were radical changes after 3500 B.C. when the cultivation of the olive and the vine became widespread; and trading of minerals, stone wares, and other products expanded rapidly. Numerous small towns were flourishing throughout the Aegean and eastern Greece by 2500 B.C., linked by regular trading routes.

⚜ The Minoan civilization of Crete developed as a result of these cultural routes about 2000 B.C. and lasted until about 1400 B.C. The development of this civilization is known from the ruins of the Palace of Knossos. The Minoans traded as far afield as Egypt and the eastern Mediterranean and were expert metalworkers and potters, with a lively artistic tradition.

⚓ Minoan power was apparently weakened by the great explosion of its satellite island, Thera, in 1500 B.C. The center of civilization passed to the mainland, where the Mycenaeans flourished until 1150 B.C. The Mycenaeans were able to develop useful trading connections with temperate Europe as well as continuing many Minoan trade routes. They were overthrown by Phrygian peoples at the end of the second millennium.

⚓ Trading activities continued to expand in the Aegean after the decline of Mycenae. Small city-states flourished, unifying only in the face of a common danger like the Persian invasions of the fifth century B.C. The Athenians enjoyed a long period of supremacy among city-states, the period of Classical Greek civilization in the fifth century B.C.

⚓ Alexander the Great built an enormous empire over the Near East, of which Greece was part, in the late fourth century B.C. The Roman Empire which followed marks the entry of the entire Mediterranean area into historic times. Developed from Villanovan and Etruscan roots in Italy, the Roman Imperial power was based on the ruins of Alexander's empire.

Chronological
Table J

This chapter begins with a disclaimer: The prehistory of Anatolia, Europe, and the Mediterranean Basin is so complicated, and our knowledge so spotty, that we can only touch the highlights here.[1]* Interested readers should consult the references included in the Bibliography of Archaeology for more information on these areas.

ANATOLIA

Catal Hüyük
5600 B.C.

During the height of its prosperity in the sixth millennium B.C., the town of Çatal Hüyük controlled trade over huge areas of central Anatolia (Figure 18.1), so much so that it was the focus for villages hundreds of miles around.[2] This complex settlement was organized by creating ritual and other mechanisms that attempted to retain the close kinship ties of village life while adapting to the new complexities of long distance trading and growing population. Unlike Mesopotamia, where new mechanisms and organizations evolved to handle social change, the system at Çatal Hüyük broke down. Anatolia's first and largest town was abandoned and people went back to living in small villages.[3]

The entire plateau of Anatolia seems to have experienced a subsequent, gradual population increase during the fifth millennium B.C., as long distance trading with Mesopotamia in minerals and other materials picked up. The evidence for the concentration of power and wealth in major Anatolian set-

* See pages 388–389 for notes to Chapter 18.

Old World Civilizations

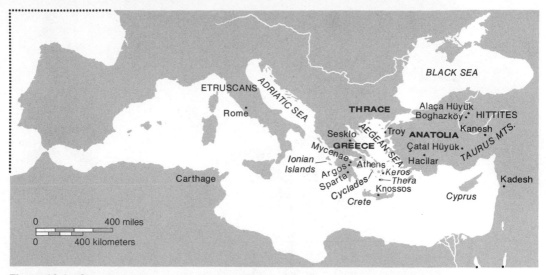

Figure 18.1 Sites and cultures mentioned in Chapter 18.

tlements is found after 3000 B.C. in the walled fortresses of Hissarlik (Troy) and Kultepe (ancient Kadesh).[4]

Hissarlik was first occupied about 3500 B.C., when a small fortress was built on bedrock. Its foundations show it contained a rectangular hall of a basic design that had been in use for centuries. The structure was to become the standard palace design of later centuries and perhaps a prototype for the Classical Greek temple. About 2300 B.C. a new settlement known to archaeologists as Troy II flourished at Hissarlik. This fortified town boasted of more elaborate buildings and yielded valuable hoards of gold and bronze ornaments — a clear sign that the rulers of the settlement were supporting skilled craftspeople who designed and executed fine ornaments of rank.

Thirteen royal tombs were found at the site of the town of Alaça Hüyük in central Anatolia, dating to the end of the third millennium B.C. The tombs contain the bodies of men and their wives accompanied by domestic vessels, weapons, and many metal items.[5] The ornaments include copper figurines with gold breasts, and finely wrought cast bronze stags inlaid with silver which were perhaps mounted on the ends of poles (Figure 18.2).

Both the Alaça Hüyük and Hissarlik finds testify to widespread trade in gold, copper, tin, and other raw materials by 2000 B.C. Major centers like these maintained long distance trading contacts throughout the Near East. These, along with trading offshore to Cyprus and the Aegean islands could well have influenced social and political developments.

Toward the end of the third millennium, Indo-European-speaking peoples seem to have infiltrated Anatolia from the northwest, causing considerable political unrest. By this time, central Anatolia was coming into much closer contact with Mesopotamia. By 1900 B.C. there was a sizable Assyrian merchant colony outside the city of Kanesh, one of several important trading centers or *karums* that were staging posts for long distance commerce in minerals and

Troy I (Hissarlik)
3500 B.C.

Troy II
2300 B.C.

Alaça Hüyük
2000 B.C.

Kanesh
1900 B.C.

Figure 18.2 Bronze stag from Alaça Hüyük, inlaid with silver (left), and miniature gold figure of a Hittite king.

other commodities.[6] The karums served as marketplaces and termini for caravans, neutral entrepots (commercial centers, sometimes warehouses) where prices for goods were regulated. Local rulers levied taxes on the caravans, which brought important Assyrian ideas to Anatolia and reinforced the political and economic power of Anatolian kings.

THE HITTITES

Hittites
1650 to 1200 B.C.

The Hittites appear to have been a group of able Indo-European people from the vast steppes north of Anatolia, who infiltrated the plateau and seized power from the leaders of Kanesh and other cities, probably just before the seventeenth century B.C.[7]

No historian would be taken in by the Hittites' own extravagant claims for their glorious history. The Hittites seem, in practice, to have been a foreign minority who rose to political power by judiciously melding conquest and astute political maneuvering. The minority soon became acculturated into their new milieu, even though they seem to have preserved their traditional values and outlook on life.

The Hittites were a down-to-earth people, with talent for political and military administration. They were not intellectuals, but religion was important to them. The king was not deified until after his death, if then. His duties were well defined: to ensure the state's welfare, wage war, and act as high priest under clearly defined circumstances. A hierarchy of officials supported the king. One unusual institution was the *pankush*, a form of assembly that may have had a restricted membership, perhaps open only to those of pure Hittite stock. But we see no sign that this institution, with its undertones of racial superiority, ever wielded much power.

The Hittites exercised enormous political influence in the Near East from their vast capital at Boghazköy with its four miles of city walls. They used their wealth and diplomatic skill to play Assyria and Egypt against one another. But they were hardened warriors as well, who campaigned as far south as Babylon and fought Ramesses II on the outskirts of Kadesh. Their objectives were simple enough: to acquire new spheres of political influence and to control trade routes.

Boghazköy

One major achievement of the Hittites was the systematic use of iron, thought to have been smelted first in the middle of the second millennium B.C., in the highlands immediately south of the Black Sea. The military advantages of this metal lay in its relative abundance in a natural state, even if it was harder to smelt. The Hittites seem to have guarded the secrets of ironworking for some time, but eventually foreign mercenaries in their armies carried the new techniques to their homelands. Iron tools soon became commonplace over a wide area of Europe and the Near East, although it was some time before domestic artifacts like axes and hoes were invariably made of the new metal.

Ironworking

Hittite rule did not last long in Anatolia. About 1200 B.C., repeated migrations of foreigners flowed into Anatolia from the northwest — whence the Hittites had come only four centuries earlier. These population movements came to a head when the Phrygian peoples from Thrace (see Figure 18.1) ravaged the plateau as far as the Taurus mountains. Anatolia became the homeland of dozens of small city-states, each striving to maintain its independence. Only a few Hittite communities survived, in small states in northern Syria that lasted until they were engulfed in the vast Persian Empire.

1200 B.C.
Phrygians

THE AEGEAN AND GREECE

Parts of mainland Greece and the Aegean were settled by farming peoples as early as 6500 B.C., but more intensive settlement of western Greece, the islands, and Crete did not occur until much later.

6500 B.C.

The Sesklo village in Thessaly, northern Greece, was occupied about 5000 B.C. and is typical of northern Greek sites of the time.[8] The people lived in stone and mud houses connected by courtyards and passages. Their mixed farming economy depended heavily on cereal cultivation. Somewhat similar villages are found on Crete where farming settlement dates back to at least 5500 B.C.

Sesklo
5000 B.C.

There were radical changes in the settlement pattern after 3500 B.C. when villages were established in the Cyclades, throughout Crete, and on the Ionian islands of the west. In contrast, northern Greece seems to have lagged behind.

3500 B.C.

Figure 18.3 Harpist in
marble, executed by a
craftsworker on the island of
Keros in the Aegean.

The reason may have been agriculture, for southern Greece and the islands are
ideal environments for the cultivation of olives and vines, with cereal crops
interspersed between them. There was a veritable explosion in village crafts as
well, in the manufacture of fine painted pottery, marble vessels, and magnificent stone axes. Stone vases and fine seals were made by Cretan workers
(Figure 18.3); the seals were used to mark ownership of prized possessions or
pots full of oil or other commodities. By 3500 B.C. the peoples of the Aegean
and Greece were smelting copper and making bronze artifacts as well as ornaments in gold and silver. These included exquisite gold and silver drinking
cups and the elaborate ornaments found at Troy II, which included over 8,700
gold beads, wire ornaments, chain links, and objects of fine gold sheet. The
achievements of the Aegean metallurgists were in part due to the rapid expansion of trading throughout the Aegean, far into Anatolia, and to Cyprus, with
its rich copper outcrops.

The Aegean is well endowed with comfortable ports and alternative trading
routes that provided easy communication from island to island for most of the
year. Even relatively primitive vessels could coast from one end of the Aegean
to the other in easy stages. Sailing vessels are depicted on Cretan seals dating to
about 2000 B.C. The Aegean trade flourished on olive oil and wine, metal tools
and ores, marble vessels and figurines, and pottery. The success of the trade led
to a constant infusion of new products and ideas to Greece and the Aegean. By
2500 B.C. numerous small towns housed farmers, traders, and skilled craftsworkers on the mainland and the islands.

The beginnings of town life created considerable cultural diversity in the
Aegean, a diversity fostered by constant trading connections and increased
complexity in social and political organization. Nowhere is this better docu-

2500 B.C.

mented than in Crete, where a brilliant civilization flourished at towns and palaces throughout the island. In contrast, mainland Greece lagged somewhat behind, its many small towns having only occasional contact with the Aegean islands and Crete.

THE MINOANS

The development of the Minoan civilization of Crete was almost certainly the result of many local factors, among them the intensive cultivation of the olive and the vine. Its development is best documented at the famous Palace of Knossos near Heraklion in northern Crete (Figure 18.4).[9]

The first prehistoric inhabitants of Knossos settled there in about 6100 B.C.[10] No less than 7 meters (23 feet) of early farming occupation underlie the Minoan civilization. The first Knossos settlement was founded at about the time that Çatal Hüyük was first occupied in Anatolia. The Knossos farmers lived in sun-dried mud and brick huts of a rectangular ground plan that provided for storage bins and sleeping platforms. By 3730 B.C. signs of long distance trading increase in the form of exotic imports such as stone bowls. The first palace at Knossos was built in about 1930 B.C., a large building with many rooms grouped around a rectangular central court.

At least nine periods of Minoan civilization have been distinguished by

Knossos
6100 to 1400 B.C.

3730 B.C.

Minoan Civilization
c. 2000 to 1400 B.C.

Figure 18.4   General view of the Palace of Minos at Knossos.

pottery styles found in the later levels of the Knossos site. Even during the earlier periods of the civilization, the Minoans were trading regularly with Egypt, for their pottery and metal objects have been found in burials there. In 1700 B.C. the earlier palaces were destroyed by an earthquake.

The high point of Minoan civilization followed that destruction, occurring between 1700 and 1450 B.C., when the Palace of Knossos reached its greatest size. This remarkable structure was made mainly of mud brick and timber beams with occasional limestone blocks and wood columns. Some buildings had two stories; the plaster walls and floors of the palace were usually painted dark red. Many walls and even the floors were decorated, initially with geometric designs, and after 1700 B.C. with vivid scenes or individual pictures of varying size. Sometimes the decorations were executed in relief; in other cases, colors were applied to the damp plaster (Figure 18.5).

Artistic themes included formal landscapes, dolphins and other sea creatures, and scenes of Minoan life. The most remarkable art depicted dances and religious ceremonies, including acrobats leaping vigorously along the backs of bulls (Figure 18.6). The writer Mary Renault has vividly reconstructed Cretan life at Knossos in novels that bring Minoan culture to life.[11]

At the height of its prosperity, Crete was self-supporting in food and basic raw materials, exporting foodstuffs, cloth, and painted pottery all over the eastern Mediterranean. The Cretans were renowned mariners. Their large ships transported gold, silver, obsidian, ivory, and ornaments from central Europe, the Aegean, and the Near East, and ostrich eggs were probably traded from North Africa.

Figure 18.5 Reconstruction of the Throne Room at Knossos, Crete. The wall paintings are modern reconstructions from fragments found at the site; details may be inaccurate.

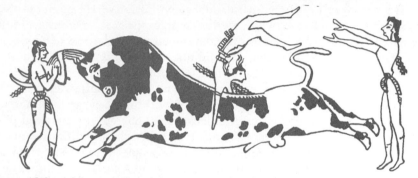

Figure 18.6 A Minoan bull and dancers, as painted on the walls of the Palace of Knossos. The ox, a domesticated form, has a piebald coat. This very fragmentary scene has been reconstructed from rather inadequate original pieces, and is somewhat controversial. After Evans.

In 1500 B.C. a volcano on the island of Thera, 70 miles (113 km) from Crete, exploded with such violence that it certainly caused catastrophic destruction on the north coast of the Minoan kingdom. This event is equated by some people with the eternal legend of Atlantis, the mysterious continent said to have sunk to the ocean bottom after one holocaust thousands of years ago.[12] The Thera eruption may have accelerated the decline of the Minoan civilization, which was already showing signs of weakness. Fifty years later many Minoan sites were destroyed and abandoned. Warrior farmers, perhaps from mainland Greece, established sway over the empire and decorated the walls of Knossos with military scenes. Seventy-five years later the palace was finally destroyed by fire, thought to have been the work of Mycenaeans who razed it. By this time the center of the Aegean world had shifted to the Greek mainland, where Mycenae reached the height of its power.

(margin) Thera
1500 B.C.

(margin) **?1400 B.C.**

(margin) **1375–1350 B.C.**

The dramatic flowering of Minoan civilization stemmed from the intensified trading contacts and the impact of olive and vine cultivation on hundreds of Greek and Aegean villages. As agricultural economies became more diversified and local food surpluses could be exchanged both locally and over longer distances, a far-reaching economic interdependence resulted. Eventually this led to redistribution systems for luxuries and basic commodities, systems that were organized and controlled by Minoan palaces and elsewhere in the Aegean where there were major centers of olive production.

The redistribution networks carried metal objects and other luxury products the length and breadth of the Aegean as the self-sufficiency of earlier farming communities was replaced by mutual interdependence. Interest in long distance trading brought about some cultural homogeneity from trade, gift exchange, and perhaps piracy. The skills of specialist craftsworkers were highly valued in village and palace alike. Specialized artisans practiced their crafts in the major palaces; they lived well, in stone buildings with well-designed drainage systems, and had wooden furniture.

Colin Renfrew describes both Minoan society and that of their successors, the Mycenaeans of the Greek mainland, as civilizations.[13] He points to their sophisticated art and metalwork, to the complex palaces organized around specialized craftsworkers, and to their developed redistribution networks for foods. The Minoans and Mycenaeans did not build vast temples like those at Tikal in Guatemala (Chapter 21) or those in Egypt. Nor did they live in cities. Palaces and elaborate tombs were the major monuments. Renfrew looks for the origins of Minoan and Mycenaean civilization within Greece and the Aegean, and considers them to be the result of local social change and material progress, not external population movements. His theory sharply differs from earlier hypotheses that called for migration of new peoples into Greece from the north or for diffusion of new culture traits from Anatolia or the eastern Mediterranean.

THE MYCENAEANS

Mycenaeans
1600 to 1200 B.C.

The Mycenaean civilization, centered on the fertile plain of Argos on the Greek mainland, began to flourish during the sixteenth century B.C.[14] The chieftains who ruled over the walled fortress of Mycenae (Figure 18.7) were buried in spectacular shaft graves that contained weapons adorned with copper and gold, as well as fine gold face masks modeled in the likeness of their owners (Figure 18.8). Their wealth and economic power came from far-flung trading contacts as well as from their warrior skills (Figure 18.9). The kings were skilled charioteers and horsemen, whose material culture and lifeway are

Figure 18.7 The Lion Gate at Mycenae.

Figure 18.8 Gold mask of a bearded man, from Shaft Grave V at Mycenae, Greece, sixteenth century B.C.

immortalized in the Homeric epics. These epics, however, were written many centuries after the Mycenaeans themselves had become folk memories.

Mycenaean commerce took over where Minoan left off. Much of the rulers' prestige was based on their contacts in the metal trade. Minerals were in constant demand in the central and eastern Mediterranean, especially tin for alloying copper to make bronze. Both copper and tin were abundant in central Europe and Cyprus, and the Mycenaeans developed the necessary contacts to obtain regular supplies.

Anatolia, Greece, and Italy

Figure 18.9 Impression of a warrior fighting an enemy with a dagger, from an engraved gold ring, Shaft Graves, Mycenae, Greece.

They also took an active interest in another long established trade, that in Baltic amber, a yellow-brown fossil resin that when rubbed seems to be "electric." Amber was being passed southward to the Mediterranean by the time the Mycenaeans came to power.[15] They capitalized on the magic properties that amber was believed to possess and made sure they had regular supplies for their own enjoyment. Amber was found in the royal graves at Mycenae. Amber traveled a well-established trade route that carried both metals and other commodities across the Brenner Pass in Switzerland toward the Elbe River, then from the Adriatic to Greece by sea (see the trade routes map, Figure 19.5, in the next chapter).

So complex did Mycenaean trading transactions become that the Mycenaeans found it necessary to establish a writing system. They refined one that had first been developed by the Minoans. The Mycenaeans used a form of script written in the Greek language, known now as Linear B.[16] Eighty-nine characters make up Linear B, forty-eight of which can be traced back to Minoan writing, Linear A. Linear A probably originated in the simple pictographic script of the earliest Minoans (Figure 18.10). The terms "Linear A" and "Linear B" were coined by Sir Arthur Evans when he first studied Minoan writing. Linear B was in more widespread use than A, partly because the Mycenaeans exerted greater political and economic power than their Cretan neighbors.

1150 B.C.

Mycenae continued to dominate eastern Mediterranean trade until the twelfth century B.C., when its power was destroyed by warrior peoples from the north. In the same century, other northern barbarians destroyed the Hittite kingdom in Anatolia. These incursions into the Mediterranean world were caused by unsettled political conditions in Europe, at least partly the result of population pressures and tribal warfare (Chapter 19).

THE MEDITERRANEAN AFTER MYCENAE

After Mycenae fell in 1200 B.C., small-town merchants on the Greek mainland continued to trade as their Mycenaean predecessors had, monopolizing commerce in the Aegean and the Black seas. By the seventh and eighth centuries B.C., small colonies of Greek settlers lived on the northern and western shores of the Black Sea and along the north coast of Anatolia, and developed trade in gold, copper, iron, salt, and other commodities. Other Greeks voyaged westward and settled in southern France; they soon made a brisk trade in wine and other commodities with central Europe.

1200 B.C.

600–700 B.C.

The Greek City-States

In Greece many fertile agricultural areas are separated by ranges of mountains. Traders and seamen of the Aegean islands and the Greek mainland therefore formed a network of small city-states that competed with each other for trade and political power. Athens was one of the larger and more prosperous states. The island of Sifnos in the Aegean was another, famous for its gold and silver. Paros marble was known all over the eastern Mediterranean, while Milos provided obsidian for many centuries.

Greek states unified only in times of grave political stress, as when the Persian King Xerxes sought to add Greece to his possessions. Xerxes' defeats at Marathon (490 B.C.) and ten years later in a naval battle at Salamis ensured the security of Greece and made Classical Greek civilization possible. Athens was foremost among the Greek states,[17] becoming head of a league of maritime cities, which was soon turned into an empire. This was the Athens that

490 B.C.

Athens

attracted wealthy immigrants, built the Parthenon, and boasted of Aeschylus, Sophocles, and other mighty playwrights. Classical Greek civilization flourished for fifty glorious years.

450 B.C.

But throughout the brilliant decades of Athenian supremacy, bickering rivalry with the city of Sparta in Peloponnesus never abated. A deep animosity between the two cities had its roots in radically different social systems. Sparta's government was based on military discipline and a rigid class structure. Athenians enjoyed a more mobile society and a democratic government.

430 B.C.

The long rivalry culminated in the disastrous Peloponnesian War from 431 to 404 B.C. that left Sparta a dominant political force on the mainland. The contemporary historian Thucydides documented the war, which was followed by disarray.[18] Greece soon fell under the sway of Philip of Macedonia, whose rule between 359 and 336 B.C. began to develop political unity. His son Alexander the Great then embarked on a campaign of imperial conquest that took him from Macedonia into Persia and then to Mesopotamia. Alexander was welcomed as a hero and a god in Egypt, where he paused long enough to sacrifice to local deities and have himself proclaimed pharaoh. His continued quests took him as far east as the Indus Valley and back to Babylon, where he died of fever in 323 B.C. By the time of his death, Alexander had united an enormous area of the ancient world under at least nominal Greek rule. His extraordinary empire fell apart within a generation, but his conquests paved the way for the uniform government of Imperial Rome.

359 B.C.

323 B.C.

The Phoenicians

Phoenicians

While the Greeks were developing their trading endeavors in the Aegean and Black seas, other maritime peoples too had turned into vigorous traders. The Phoenicians of Lebanon first rose to prosperity by acting as middlemen in the growing trade in raw materials and manufactured products.[19] Phoenician ships carried Lebanese cedarwood and dye to Cyprus and the Aegean area as well as to Egypt. After Mycenae declined they took over much of the copper and iron ore trade of the Mediterranean. Their trading networks later extended far to the west, as they ventured to Spain in search of copper, tin, and the purple dye extracted from seashells and much used for expensive fabrics. By 800 B.C. Phoenician merchants were everywhere. They were using a fully alphabetical script by the tenth century B.C.

1200 B.C.

800 B.C.

Phoenicians not only traded widely but also set up small colonies that served as their vassals and were marketplaces for the hinterland of Spain and North Africa. Some settlements won independence from home rule. The greatest was the North African city Carthage, which challenged the power of the Roman Empire.

The Etruscans

The Greeks and Phoenicians were expanding maritime activities at the same time as skilled bronze workers and copper miners in northern Italy were developing a distinctive but short-lived urban civilization.

In about 1000 B.C., some Urnfield peoples from central Europe (Chapter 19) had settled south of the Alps in the Po Valley. They developed a skilled bronzeworking tradition, whose products were traded far into central Europe and throughout Italy. This people evolved into the Villanovan culture, which appeared in the ninth century B.C. and was soon in touch with Greek colonies in southern Italy and perhaps with the Phoenicians.[20] Ironworking was introduced to the Villanovans about the ninth century. Iron tools and extensive trading contacts got the Villanovans political control over much of northern and western Italy. They established colonies on the islands of Elba and Corsica. Several centuries of trade and other contacts culminated in a literate Etruscan civilization.

Like Classical Greece, Etruscan civilization was more a unity of cultural tradition and trade than a political reality.[21] The Etruscans traded widely in the central Mediterranean and with warrior peoples in central Europe. Etruscan culture was derived from the Villanovan, but it owed much to eastern immigrants and trading contacts that brought oriental influence to Italian towns.

Etruscan territory was settled by city-states with much independence, each with substantial public buildings and fortifications. Their decentralized political organization made them vulnerable to foreign raiders. Warrior bands from central Europe overran some Etruscan cities in the centuries after 450 B.C. Etruscan prosperity began to crumble.

By the time of Etruscan decline, however, the Mediterranean was a civilized lake. Phoenician colonists had founded Carthage and other cities in North Africa and Spain and controlled the western Mediterranean. The rulers of Greece and Egypt and later Philip of Macedon controlled the east, and the Etruscans were in control of most of Italy and many central European trade routes.

The Romans

The Etruscans had been the first people to fortify the seven famed hills of Rome. In 509 B.C., a foreign dynasty of rulers was evicted by these native Romans, who began to develop their own distinctive city-state. The next few centuries saw the emergence of Rome from a cluster of simple villages by the Tiber River to the leadership of the Mediterranean and far beyond. The Romans inherited the mantle of Classical Greece and added their own distinctive culture to this foundation. They then carried Greco-Roman civilization to many parts of the world that were still inhabited by preliterate peasant societies. Roman legions campaigned not only in Egypt and Mesopotamia, and as far as India, but in central and western Europe and in Britain. If it were not for the Romans the administrative and linguistic face of Europe would be very different today.[22]

By 295 B.C. the power of Rome dominated the whole of Italy. At this time Rome was a form of democracy, governed by a delicate balance of aristocratic and popular authority. This type of governance was appropriate for a large city-state, but was helplessly inadequate for the complexities of governing a huge empire. Eventually, civil strife led to autocratic rule of the empire under the emperors, the first of whom was Julius Caesar, familiar to every student of Roman history for his epic conquest of Gaul (France). (His son Augustus was the first ruler to actually claim the title of emperor.)

200 B.C. to 133 B.C. After two vicious wars with their rich rival, Carthage, the Romans achieved mastery over the western Mediterranean by 200 B.C. By 133 B.C. much of Asia was under uneasy Roman domination. Unfortunately the Romans lacked the mechanisms to administer their empire successfully until the Emperor Augustus reorganized the civil service and established the Pax Romana over his vast domains. There ensued a period of great material prosperity and political stability — at the price of political freedom of speech.

The stresses that led to the collapse of the Roman Empire first began to appear on the European frontiers in the second and third centuries A.D. Roman power began to decline as ambition and sophistication grew among the Iron Age tribes living on the fringes of Roman territory. The "barbarians" on the fringes of the Empire were mainly peasant farmers who had obtained iron by trading and intermarriage with La Tène peoples (Chapter 19). Many served as mercenaries in the Roman armies, acquiring wealth and sophistication, and perhaps most important of all, an insight into Roman military tactics.

Shortage of farming land and increasing disrespect for Rome caused many Germanic tribes to raid Rome's European provinces. The raids were so successful that the imperial armies were constantly campaigning in the north. In A.D. 395 A.D. 395, after Emperor Theodosius died, the Roman Empire was split into eastern and western divisions. Large barbarian invasions from northern Europe A.D. 410 ensued. Fifteen years later a horde of Germanic tribesmen from central Europe sacked Rome itself; then the European provinces were completely overrun by warrior peoples. Other Germanic hordes disturbed North Africa and crossed much of Asia Minor, but left little lasting mark on history there.

What was the legacy of Rome? Their material legacy can be seen in their road system, which still provides a basis for many of Europe and the Near East's communications, and in their towns, like London, which are still flourishing modern cities. In cultural terms, their principal legacy was their legal system, which lies at the core of most western law codes. Roman literature and art dominated European culture for centuries after the Renaissance. Their spoken and written language, Latin, survived for centuries as the language of the educated person, and as the principal means of business communication between nations. Latin lies at the base of many modern European languages and was only recently abandoned as the liturgical language of the Roman Catholic Church. The Romans and their culture lie at the foundations of our own Western Civilization.

Chapter Nineteen

TEMPERATE EUROPE BEFORE THE EUROPEANS

PREVIEW

☙ In contrast to earlier hypotheses, archaeologists now believe that copperworking was developed independently in southeastern Europe in the fifth millennium. The Varna cemetery in Bulgaria shows just how elaborate the gold and copper metallurgy of the area became. The industry flourished because of a demand for fine metal ornaments. Copperworking also developed early in southern Spain and northern Italy.

☙ The spread of copperworking throughout Europe is associated in part with the Battle Ax and Beaker peoples who flourished around 3000 B.C.

☙ Bronzeworking began at an unknown date but was widespread in what is now Czechoslovakia by 2500 B.C., as part of the Unetice culture. The trading networks of earlier times expanded to meet increased indigenous demand for metal artifacts during a period of rapid technological change after 1700 B.C. Some rich chieftaincies developed in the temperate zones, among them the Wessex culture of southern Britain.

☙ The Urnfield peoples of central Europe began to expand from their homeland about 800 B.C. Armed with new, slashing, swords, they settled all over Europe, bringing their new and more effective agricultural techniques with them. Their economic organization probably included specialist smiths and traders.

☙ After 1000 B.C. ironworking techniques diffused into temperate Europe and spread through the Hallstatt and La Tène cultural traditions during the first millennium B.C. The La Tène people were the Celtic-speaking warriors encountered by Julius Caesar and his Roman legionaries in the first century B.C.

☙ After the Roman conquest of central and western Europe, much of the temperate zone became at least superficially Romanized. The ultimate downfall of the Roman Empire was due not only to internal weaknesses in the system but to the independence of the subjugated European peasants. Living on the frontiers of the Empire, they were able to use their military skills finally to overthrow Roman rule in the West.

The fundamental question about the emergence of complex societies in temperate Europe is simple: did they emerge as a result of indigenous cultural evolution, or because of diffusion of people and ideas from the Near East?

Gordon Childe, Stuart Piggott, and others have argued that the constant demands by Near Eastern societies for copper, tin, and other metals led to cultural development in the backwater that was temperate Europe.[1]* But this traditional viewpoint has been challenged by the new calibrated radiocarbon chronologies that place the appearance of copperworking in the Balkans earlier than in Greece or the Aegean. Many people now believe that Europeans were just as innovative as their eastern neighbors.

EARLY COPPERWORKING

Colin Renfrew and Ruth Tringham have argued that the farmers of southeastern Europe developed copper smelting independently, partly because they already used improved pottery firing techniques that were very suitable for copper smelting (Figure 19.1).[2] They cite as proof of the early development the finds at the Varna cemetery near the Black Sea in Bulgaria.

* See page 389 for notes to Chapter 19.

Figure 19.1 Major centers of early metallurgy in temperate Europe and the distribution of Battle Ax cultures.

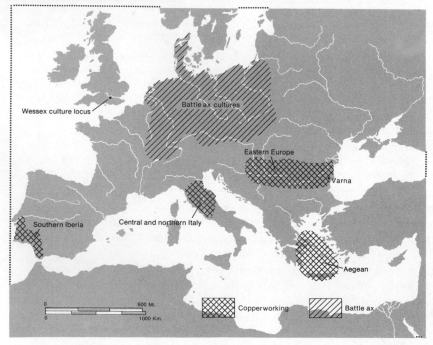

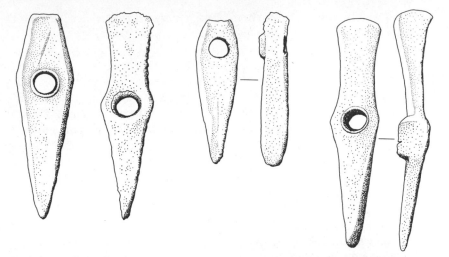

Figure 19.2 Copper ax heads from Czechoslovakia (one-third actual size).

The Varna Cemetery

At the Varna cemetery, over 130 richly decorated graves have yielded dozens of fine copper and gold tools and ornaments. Colin Renfrew has described the Varna finds as "the earliest major assemblage of gold artifacts to be unearthed anywhere in the world", for they date to about 4600 to 4200 B.C.[3] Both the copper and the gold are of Balkan origin, indeed both metals were being worked here earlier than they were in the Near East. (Such a statement reflects findings thus far; it does not preclude future discoveries of earlier metals in the Near East.) The Balkan copper industry was quite sophisticated and was organized to serve trading networks over a wide area. At Rudna Glava in Yugoslavia deep fissures mark the places where early miners followed ore veins deep into the ground. One mine in Bulgaria has ancient shafts over ten meters deep. These copper mines are the earliest so far discovered in the world and show that metallurgy developed rapidly into a considerable industry in the Balkans during the fifth millennium B.C.

The Varna burials provide striking evidence for differential wealth, for some of the graves are richly decorated with gold ornaments, while others contain few artifacts. Unfortunately the settlement associated with the Varna cemetery has yet to be found, but Renfrew has suggested that the users of the burial ground were part of a chiefdom, whose leaders used gold and copper ornaments to fulfil the social need for conspicuous display. As he points out, the problem with explaining the rise of metallurgy is not a technical one, but a social one — defining the social conditions under which metal objects first came into widespread use. The earliest copper artifacts had few practical advantages over stone axes. Both copper and gold were mainly used for ornamental purposes (Figure 19.2). Perhaps it was no coincidence that the first metallurgists in temperate Europe developed a wide range of ornaments, lux-

Varna
4000 to 4200 B.C.

Temperate Europe Before the Europeans

ury items widely traded through exchange networks that accelerated the spread of copperworking to other parts of temperate Europe.

Other Copperworking Sites in Europe

Two other possible areas of indigenous copperworking have been identified in southern Europe, both near copper outcrops. One is in southern Spain (Iberia) (Figure 19.1), the other in northern Italy. In both, the copperworkers started smelting in about the first half of the third millennium B.C. Their metalworking activities, carried out in the context of the local farming cultures, were probably indigenous developments, although some scholars prefer to think copper was introduced from Aegean trading sources. The controversy is much debated.[4]

3500 to 2300 B.C.

In the Aegean steady development followed from this early threshold of metalworking to complex state organizations, but Europe remained settled by small village societies. There were some cultural changes, which, as far as we can tell, included more stock breeding, more trading activity, and possibly increased bellicosity. The archaeological record of this period (between 3500 and 2300 B.C.) is incredibly complicated. But we can discern two broad groupings of societies, the Battle Ax and Beaker peoples, groups that ultimately mingled.

Kurgan culture
3000 B.C.

In eastern Europe, settled farming societies had lived on the edge of the huge Russian steppe for hundreds of years. Like the peoples of Anatolia and Greece, they had sporadic contacts with the nomads who roamed the plains to the east; about these we know little. In the southern Russian region a widespread population of copper-using agriculturalists lived in rectangular, thatched huts, cultivated many crops, and also tamed domestic animals, possibly including the horse. This loosely defined Kurgan culture was remarkable for its burial customs, depositing each corpse under a small mound.[5] The Kurgans used wheeled vehicles and made the copper or stone battle ax a very important part of their armory. Peoples with these culture traits spread rapidly over central and parts of northern Europe, reaching Holland by about 3000 B.C. Their globular vessels, many bearing characteristic cord-impressed decoration, are found at hundreds of sites. Their artifacts are also known from megalithic tombs and settlements of earlier inhabitants with whom they intermarried after first interrupting old cultural traditions. As in Anatolia, the arrival of newcomers with exotic customs and new values does not seem to have interrupted the gradual evolution of European ideas and cultural traditions. The new philosophies and cultural traits were absorbed and added to the European tradition.

Battle Ax people

These Battle Ax or Corded Ware peoples introduced copperworking to many peoples who had not met this soft and lustrous metal. The newcomers had wheeled carts and probably horses as well. Many linguistic experts feel that the Battle Ax peoples brought Indo-European language to Europe.[6] (Indo-European speech is thought to have originated in the region between the Carpathian and Caucasus mountains.) They did bring new, eastern European

Figure 19.3 Beaker vessels and other artifacts, including arrowheads, from various localities in south-central Britain.

ideas, cultural traditions, even settlement patterns to the West. These included replacing the Danubian long house with smaller, timber dwellings just big enough to house one family. The warriors, buried with their battle axes under small mounds, reflect some cultural traditions that were to persist in Europe for thousands of years. One of these was the notion of the warrior caste and the warrior leader. This was the kind of leader the Romans encountered on the frontiers of their European empire.

Around 3000 B.C. a second, important complex of copperworking peoples was spread over a massive region: coastal Spain, southern France, Sardinia, northern Italy, eastern and central Europe, the Low Countries, and Britain.[7] These were the Beaker people, named after the characteristic vessels found throughout this enormous area. The Beaker makers were expert archers with flint-tipped arrows (Figure 19.3). Many of these people, too, were buried under small mounds. The origins of the Beaker culture are disputed; people claim Spanish origin, but others consider eastern Europe a more likely homeland. In the Low Countries the Beaker tradition is mingled with that of the Battle Ax people from the northeast, and a mixture of the two traditions is common in the British Isles.

Beakers
3000 B.C.

BRONZE METALLURGY

Although the first occurrence of bronze may one day be shown to date to the fourth millennium in southeast Europe, the earliest widespread use of tin-copper alloys was about 2500 B.C. in what is now Czechoslovakia. The new bronze implements with tougher working edges (Figure 19.4) were initially in short supply, but their use spread gradually as new trade routes were opened across central and western Europe. The earliest bronzeworking was centered around Unetice, an industry manufacturing axes, knife blades, halberds, and many types of ornament.[8] The bronzeworkers themselves obviously belong to cultural traditions long established in the area, for their burial customs are identical to those of earlier centuries. Some believe that the art of alloying tin with copper, as well as casting techniques, came to Europe from Syria. Most people now argue, however, that bronzeworking developed independently in Europe, for the calibrated C14 dates for the Unetice industry are earlier than

Unetice culture
2400 B.C.

Figure 19.4 Copper and bronze implements from Britain: simple flat axes and flanged and socketed axes (left, one-third actual size), a dagger and sword blades (right, one-fourth actual size).

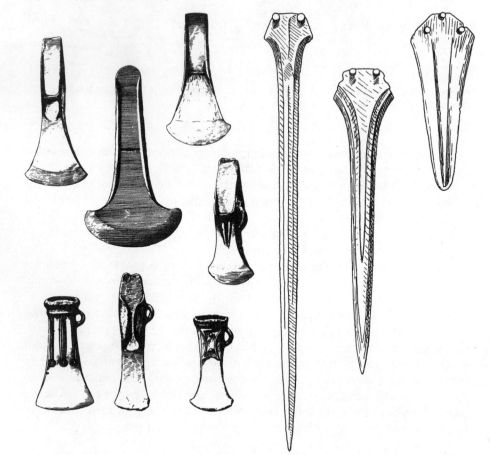

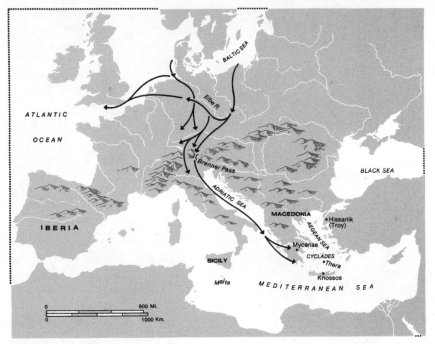

Figure 19.5 Amber trade routes in Europe and to Mycenae. The northern coastlines were the primary sources of amber.

those for the Near Eastern prototypes from which the other school of thought assumes Unetice to have evolved.

Bronzeworking soon appeared in southern Germany and Switzerland as well, where deposits of copper and tin were to be found. Other places with copper outcrops were soon using the new methods, including Brittany, the British Isles, and northern Italy, all more remote from the initial centers of bronzeworking. The trading networks that carried both raw ores and finished bronze artifacts from major centers to areas where there were no metals were expanded both by local demand and by demand from Greece, the Aegean, and the eastern Mediterranean. The period between about 1700 and 1300 B.C. was one of rapid technological progress and considerable social change, generated in large part by the reinforcing effects on the local centers of bronzeworking of persistent demand for critical raw materials and finished tools. **1700–1300 B.C.**

The trading networks carried far more than bronze artifacts and metal ores. The amber trade went from the shores of the Baltic to the Mediterranean, following well-established routes (Figure 19.5).[9] Seashells, perhaps faience (glass) beads, and other exotic luxuries were dispersed northward into the temperate zones in exchange for raw materials. Some centers of bronze production became major places for redistributing other goods as well. The salt mines of Austria were also very active in the long-distance trade.

By 1300 B.C., even societies remote from metal outcrops were engaged in metallurgy, supporting more and more people in the craft. But the archaeolog- **1300 B.C.**

Figure 19.6 Stonehenge from the air.

ical record tells little of increased specialization, although many richly adorned burials testify that the trade was concentrated among wealthy chieftains. The surplus food and energy were not devoted to generating additional surpluses and extra production, but, in some societies, were channelled into erecting majestic religious monuments, of which Stonehenge in southern Britain is probably the most celebrated (Figure 19.6).

Stonehenge

Shrouded in fantasy and speculation, associated by many people with the ancient Druids' cult, Stonehenge is in fact a fantastically old religious temple.[10] It began as a simple circle of ritual pits around 2000 B.C., and went through vigorous reconstructions, reaching the zenith of its expansion in the late second millennium B.C. That Stonehenge was associated with some form of

Old World Civilizations

astronomical activity seems unquestionable, although the details are much debated.

Stonehenge was the center of the so-called Wessex culture, named after richly adorned chieftains' graves from the heartland of the ancient British province of Wessex. Stuart Piggott characterizes the culture as a Bronze Age society dominated by small numbers of Breton warriors from northern France. The presence of these chieftains is marked by occasional richly adorned graves containing elegant stone battle axes, metal daggers with wooden handles decorated in gold, and many other gold ornaments.

The inhabitants of southern Britain also erected enormous earthwork enclosures and huge circles of timber uprights known as "henges." Doubtless special priests were needed to maintain these spectacular monuments and to perform the rituals in their precincts. Religious activity was supported by the food surplus, not the increased productivity that generated spectacular social evolution in the Near East. Thus, during the third and part of the second millennia B.C., little social evolution went on in Europe; political power and wealth belonged to the chieftains and warriors, not to divine kings and a hierarchic society.

Bronze Age Warrior Tribes

Eventually, bronze tools became more plentiful as trading connections with the Mediterranean expanded. Intensified trade inevitably led to trading monopolies and wealth concentrated in the hands of comparatively few individuals. Warlike tribes ruled by minor chiefs began to assert their authority, as population growth and possibly climatic deterioration put new pressure on agricultural land.[11]

Rivalries between petty chiefs and warrior bands brought much political instability to central Europe. New alliances of small tribes were created under the leadership of powerful and ambitious chiefs, themselves once minor chieftains. Some warrior groups began to strike the fringes of the Mediterranean, destroying Mycenae and the Hittite empire.   **1150 B.C.**

After 1200 B.C., the copper and amber trade with the Aegean declined because Mycenae had fallen. Many more copper and bronze artifacts became available for domestic consumption. Some new tool forms were introduced by central European smiths, including socketed axes, varied woodworking tools, and the ard (a scraping plow drawn by oxen). The ard was a particularly important innovation, for it allowed deeper plowing, more advanced agricultural methods, and higher productivity. The new farming techniques were vital to feed the many new mouths, and prime farming land was harder to find than ever before.

The pattern of European trade changed to fill greater demands for metal tools. Itinerant smiths and merchants peddled bronze weapons and axes all over Europe. Sometimes traders were caught in tribal raids or local wars, and buried their valuable merchandise for safety. Some never returned to collect their precious stock-in-trade, and their hoards, recovered by archaeologists, tell a clear story of unsettled political conditions.

Temperate Europe Before the Europeans

Between 1200 and 800 B.C. the population movements associated with central European peoples introduced a more consolidated system of agriculture to much of Europe, which allowed exploitation of much heavier soils, as well as stock breeding.[12] For the first time, stock were fully integrated into the food-producing economy, and cattle were used for meat, milk, and draught work, though sheep were bred as much for wool as for their flesh. Improved technology for new implements of tillage was fully exploited to achieve a truly effective economic symbiosis between flora and fauna, carefully balancing forest clearance with cultivation and pasturage.

Urnfield culture
?1000 B.C.

One powerful group of warrior tribes in western Hungary is known to archaeologists as the Urnfield people because of their burial customs: their dead were cremated and their ashes deposited in urns; huge cemeteries of urn burials are associated with fortified villages, sometimes built near lakes. Urnfield people began to make full use of horse-drawn vehicles and new weaponry. Skilled bronzesmiths produced sheet metal helmets and shields. The Urnfield people also used the slashing sword, a devastating weapon far more effective than the cutting swords of earlier times.

800 B.C.

750 B.C.

Around 800 B.C., the Urnfield people began to expand from their Hungarian homelands. Within a couple of centuries, characteristic slashing swords and other central European tools had been deposited in sites in Italy, the Balkans, and the Aegean. By 750 B.C., Urnfield peoples had settled in southern France and moved from there into Spain (Figure 19.7). Soon Urnfield miners were exploiting the rich copper mines of the Tyrol in Austria. Bands of miners used bronze-tipped picks to dig deep in the ground for copper ore. Their efforts increased the supplies of copper and tin available to central Europeans.[13]

The Scythians and Other Steppe Peoples

The vast rolling grasslands and steppes from China to the Ukraine were not settled by farming peoples until they had a culture enabling them to survive in an environment with extreme contrasts of climate and relatively infertile soils. The carrying capacity of the land is such that only a vast territory can support herds of domestic stock. The prehistory of this huge area is obscure until the first millennium B.C., when the Scythians (from Scythia, an area in southeastern Europe) and other steppe peoples first appear in the historical record.

Scythians
c. 500 B.C.

No one should doubt, however, the importance of nomads in the prehistory of Europe in earlier millennia.[14] The Battle Ax people and other possible Indo-European speakers were familiar with the vast open spaces of the steppes, where domestication of the horse ultimately made the nomadic life a potent force in frontier politics. For centuries before the Scythians came out of history's shadows, people had roamed the steppes relying on the horse and wagon for mobility, living in stout felt tents, and subsisting mostly on horse's milk and cheese, as well as on food from hunting and fishing. The nomadic life, though, leaves few traces in the archaeological record, except when permafrost preserves burials in a refrigerated state.

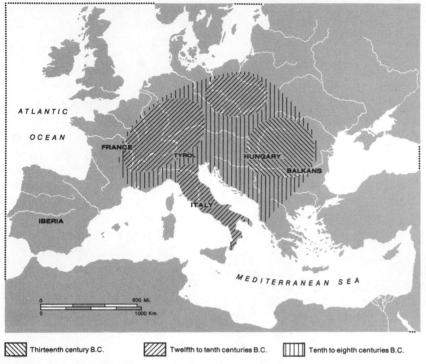

Figure 19.7 Approximate distribution of Urnfield cultures in Europe.

Thirteenth century B.C.   Twelfth to tenth centuries B.C.   Tenth to eighth centuries B.C.

We are fortunate in having extensive data about the vigorous society of nomad peoples from the spectacular frozen tombs of Siberia. Russian archaeologist Sergei Rudenko has excavated several nomad burial mounds at Pazyryk in northeastern Siberia.[15] The chiefs of Pazyryk were elaborately tattooed, wore woollen and leather clothes, and employed skillful artists to adorn their horse trappings and harnesses with exuberant, elaborate, stylized animal art. A powerful chief was accompanied to the next world by his wife and servants, horses and chariots, and many of his smaller possessions. The Pazyryk burials contain fragments of woven rugs, the earliest examples of such art in the world.

    The steppe peoples lived to the north of the well-traveled trade routes of Greek merchants, but their territory was constantly being explored and sometimes colonized by farmers, whose lands were becoming overpopulated or overgrazed. Enormous areas of steppe were needed to support even a small band of horsemen, for just a slight increase in population could drastically affect the food supplies of the original inhabitants. The result was constant displacement of populations as the nomads sought to expand their shrinking territory to accommodate their own population pressures. The nomads menaced the northern frontiers of the Mediterranean world throughout Classical and more recent times.

    The Eurasian nomad populations flourished during the closing millennia of

400 B.C.

prehistory. The Pazyryk finds let us see into a prehistoric way of life that in some areas survived unchanged right into historic times.

THE EMERGENCE OF IRONWORKING

The Urnfield people were effective agriculturalists as well as traders and metallurgists, capable of exploiting Europe's forested environment far more efficiently than their predecessors could. They lived amid a complicated network of trade that carried not only metals, but also salt, grain, gold, pottery, and many other commodities. Their economic organization probably included community smiths, specialists supported by the community, but still no centralized state system of the Near Eastern type.

Ironworking
1000 B.C.

The secrets of ironworking, guarded carefully by Hittite kings, were slow to reach Europe. But some time after 1000 B.C., ironworking techniques were

Figure 19.8 Bronze ritual cart from a Hallstatt grave in Austria (about 1 ft. long).

Old World Civilizations

introduced into temperate Europe, presumably down existing trade routes. Ironworking is much more difficult than bronzeworking, for the technology is harder to acquire and takes much longer. But once it is learned, the advantages of the new metal are obvious. Because the ore is found in many more places, the metal is much cheaper and could be used for weapons and for utilitarian artifacts as well. These would, of course, include both axes and hoes, as well as plowshares, all of which contributed much to agricultural efficiency, higher crop yields, and greater food surpluses. The population increases and intensified trading activities of the centuries immediately preceding the Roman Empire are partly attributable to the success of iron technology in changing European agriculture and craftsmanship. As iron technology spread into the country north of the Alps, new societies arose whose leaders exploited the new metal's artistic and economic potentials. The tribal chieftaincy was the structure of governance; the most coherent broader political unit, a loose confederacy of tribes formed in time of war or temporarily under the aegis of a charismatic chieftain. Despite the onslaught of Roman colonization and exploitation, European culture beyond the frontiers retained its essential "European" cast, an indigenous slant to cultural traditions that began when farming did.

The Hallstatt Culture

One strong culture was the Hallstatt, named after a site near Salzburg, Austria.[16] Hallstatt culture began in the seventh and sixth centuries B.C., and owed much to Urnfield practices, for the skillful bronzeworking of earlier times was still practiced. But some immigrants from the east may have achieved political dominance over earlier inhabitants. Bronze, however, was still the dominant metal for horse trappings, weapons, and ornaments. Chiefs were buried in large mounds within wooden chambers, some in wagons (Figure 19.8).

The Hallstatt people and their culture spread through former Urnfield territories as far north as Belgium and the Netherlands and into France and parts of Spain (Figure 19.9). Many Hallstatt sites are particularly notable for their fortifications. The Hallstatt people traded with the Mediterraneans, along well-traveled routes up the Rhone River and through the Alps into central Europe. A significant import was the serving vessel for wine; containers of Mediterranean wine were carried far into central Europe, as Hallstatt chieftains discovered the joys of wine drinking.

The La Tène People

By the last quarter of the fifth century B.C., a new and highly distinctive technology, La Tène, had developed in the Rhine and Danube valleys.[17] An aristocratic clique of chieftains in the Danube Valley enjoyed implements and

Hallstatt
730 B.C.

La Tène
450 B.C.

Temperate Europe Before the Europeans

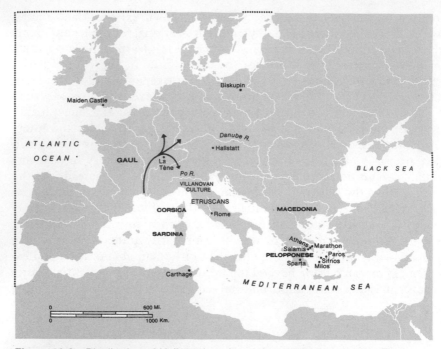

Figure 19.9 Distribution of Hallstatt Iron Age cultures (shaded area) in Europe during the seventh to fifth centuries B.C. The trade routes in southern France and the Mediterranean sites mentioned in this chapter are also shown, but Pazyryk is not on the map.

weapons elaborately worked in bronze and gold. Much of their sophisticated art had roots in Classical Greek and Mediterranean traditions, for La Tène craftsworkers were quick to adopt new motifs and ideas from the centers of higher civilization to the south (Figure 19.10). The La Tène people spoke Celtic, a language that spread widely through Europe from perhaps as early as the ninth century B.C. Greek and Roman writers referred to these people as Celts, a term that has survived in their linguistic label.

350 B.C.

La Tène technology was a specific adaptation of ironworking to woodland Europe. The culture extended north into the Low Countries and Britain in the fourth century. La Tène art is justly famous, and the hill forts and defensive settlements of this Iron Age culture are widespread in western Europe. The superior military tactics introduced the Romans to the short sword, for La

Roman conquest
55 B.C.

Tène peoples survived long after France and southern Britain had been conquered by Rome.[18] Much territory in the temperate zones came under Roman domination, an uneasy frontier province that eventually crumbled before the inexorable pressure of the warlike tribes on its boundaries. The illiterate peoples who eventually sacked Rome and ravaged its provinces were the descendants of prehistoric Europeans whose cultural traditions had been evolving ever since the first farming cultures developed north of the Mediterranean basin.

Old World Civilizations

Figure 19.10 Iron Age helmet from the bed of the River Thames in London (20.5 cm at base).

Chronological Table K

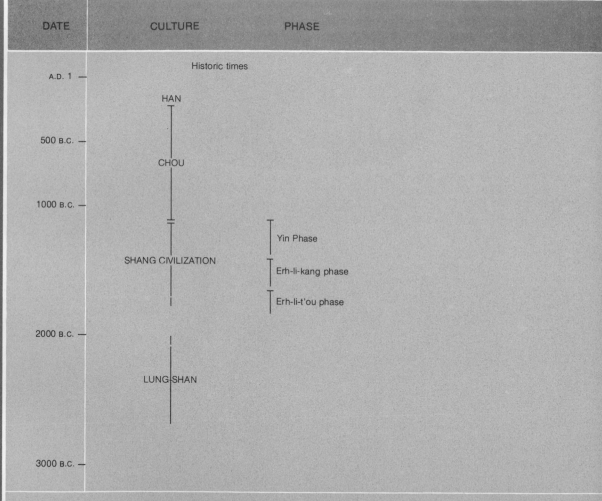

DATE	CULTURE	PHASE
	Historic times	
A.D. 1 —		
	HAN	
500 B.C. —		
	CHOU	
1000 B.C. —		
		Yin Phase
	SHANG CIVILIZATION	Erh-li-kang phase
		Erh-li-t'ou phase
2000 B.C. —		
	LUNG-SHAN	
3000 B.C. —		

Chapter 12 ↑

Chapter Twenty

SHANG CULTURE IN EAST ASIA

PREVIEW

🌱 Early Chinese civilization, which emerged somewhat later than urban civilization in the Near East, is generally agreed to have developed independently of similar developments in the West.

🌱 The roots of Chinese civilization lie in the Lungshanoid and Lung-shan cultures, which are associated with the spread of rice cultivation thorughout much of China, after 3200 B.C.

🌱 The Shang civilization of the Huangho Valley is the best-known early Chinese state, flourishing from about 1766 to 1122 B.C. It was probably the dominant state among several that flourished throughout northern China. Shang origins are partly from Lung-shan roots and partly from influences that came to the Shang from the east.

🌱 There are at least three stages of Shang civilization, associated with distinctive writing and bronze metallurgy. Shang society was organized along class lines, with the rulers and nobles living in segregated precincts while the mass of the people were scattered in townships and villages in the surrounding countryside.

🌱 Shang civilization ended with the overthrow of the Shang dynasty by Chou rulers, who reigned over a wide area of northern China from 1122 to 221 B.C.

The origins of Chinese civilization were known only from legend until the late 1920s, when Tung Tso-pin and, later, Li Chi began digging in the Anyang area of Honan province in northern China. Their excavations resulted in the discovery of the Shang civilization that flourished in the Huangho Valley over 3500 years ago.[1]*

Chronological Table K

* See page 390 for notes to Chapter 20.

CIVILIZATION EMERGES
FROM THE LUNGSHANOID TRADITION

Almost everyone agrees that Shang civilization developed from indigenous roots, but the details of its origins are little understood.[2] Chinese traditions speak of a dynasty of Hsia rulers from western Honan, whose religious beliefs and customs were adopted by the Shang in eastern Honan.[3] Recent excavations have shown that these legends may have some basis in historical fact, but details remain sketchy.

In Chapter 12 we recounted how the Lungshanoid cultures spread widely over northern, central, and southern China. Many regional variations of Lungshanoid developed, but most of them were associated with rice cultivation. In the interior, local Lung-shan ceramic styles developed from the Lungshanoid traditions often found underlying Shang levels (Figure 20.1). Radiocarbon dates for Lung-shan are in the 2680 to 2160 B.C. range.[4]

A number of Lung-shan elements foreshadowed Shang civilization. Lungshan peasants were already living in permanent settlements far larger than the villages of earlier millennia. This clustering of population was partly in self-

Figure 20.1 Distribution of Lung-shan cultures in China (left map). Each shaded area represents a different regional variant of Lung-shan (not discussed in detail in the text). Compare with the second map, which shows the approximate distribution of Shang culture. (Erh-li-kang and Hsiao-t'un are near Anyang.)

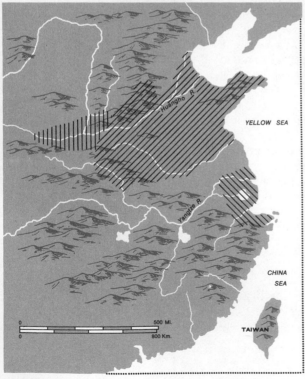
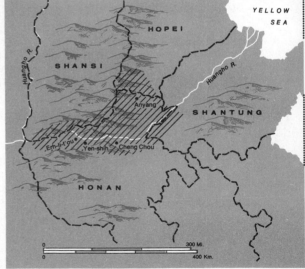

defense, for fortifications were common, a clear sign of warfare and raiding parties. Lung-shan villages sheltered some specialized craftsworkers, for fine pots and jade ornaments are found in occupation levels of the period. There is also evidence of social ranking and trade.

The time of the transition to full Shang civilization has not yet been precisely identified, but archaeologically it is marked by continuity of both economic strategies and such ritual practices as divination.

THE SHANG CIVILIZATION

Shang-type remains are found stratified on top of Lung-shan remains at many places in North China, and represent a dramatic increase in the complexity of material culture and social organization. The same trends toward increasing complexity are thought to have occurred elsewhere in China at about the same time, for literate states may have emerged from a Lung-shan base not only in the north, but in the south and east as well. In form they all probably resembled the Shang closely, but few details of the others are known. It seems likely that the Shang civilization was dominant from about 1766 to 1122 B.C., but that the other states continued to grow at the same time. The larger area of early Chinese civilization ultimately extended from the north into the middle and lower courses of the Huangho and Yangtze rivers. The several states within this large area were eventually unified under the Chou rulers, starting in 1122 B.C.

Shang
**c. 1766 to 1122
B.C.**

The Shang civilization saw the development of a number of distinctive innovations and ritual practices.

Writing was an important Shang innovation, an activity that has a remarkable history in China, for the analytic system of Chinese scribes has been used for at least 3500 years.[5] According to experts, the Shang inscriptions are in a script that had already undergone long development. They argue that earlier writing either has not survived because it was written on perishable materials or that it still awaits discovery. Other scholars think it was an artificially created script, possibly influenced by cuneiform, accounting for the transitional nature of Shang writing. We have no means of checking these theories. Most Shang writings consist of archaic Chinese characters found on oracle bones and bronzes at Anyang. Some inscriptions are little more than proper names or religious labels. The oracle texts, which are a bit longer, are thought to contain both the questions posed by clients and the priests' responses.

Writing

Bronzeworking is a remarkable attribute of Shang civilization. Sophisticated techniques such as casting were used from the earliest centuries of the Shang. For this reason, some scholars claim that metallurgy was introduced to China from the West, where it had flourished for some time. But whatever the influences from outside, native Chinese style, design, and technique are strongly developed from the first appearance of bronze technology. Some knife and dagger forms as well as socketed axes do recall similar types widely distributed over the central Russian plains; and detailed analogies between pieces

Bronzeworking

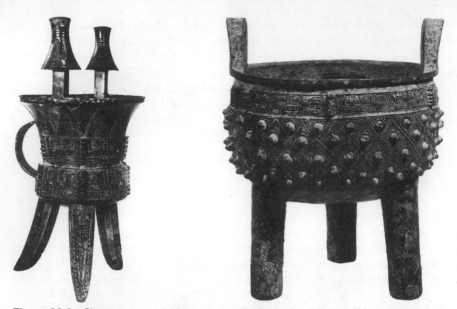

Figure 20.2 Shang ceremonial bronze vessels, from about the twelfth century B.C.

of Shang art and Russian finds may indicate extensive cultural contact and trade between the eleventh and fifteenth centuries B.C.

The well-known sinologist Noel Barnard is convinced, however, that Shang bronze metallurgy shows little similarity to Western practices and was invented in China.[6] Abundant deposits of copper and tin occur in North China and were readily available to innovative craftsworkers eager to copy traditional art forms and artifacts in a new medium. Shang bronzeworkers are justly famous for their intricate vessels and fine casting technique, the finest examples of the art appearing in later sites (Figure 20.2).

Scapulimancy

Shang writing is closely associated with another distinctive practice, that of scapulimancy — divination on animal shoulder blades (Figure 20.3). Scapulimancy first appears among Lung-shan villagers. When asked for a divination, the priest would apply a very hot object to a thin piece of sheep or deer shoulder blade. The heat would produce a crack, an irregular line that formed at an angle to the long axis of the bone. The diviner then read the significance of the crack, whose formation may have been at least partially predictable. The Shang people refined these techniques and also used turtle shells for the same purpose. Most of the Shang oracle bones found at Anyang were used to make prophecies for the royal family. Sometimes both the question and answer were recorded on the surface of the bone.

Shang Life

Both the oracle bones and later written records agree that Shang society was organized in classes.[7] Society was pyramidal, with the king at the summit. The

Old World Civilizations

royal lineages that surrounded him were supported by a large bureaucracy of officials and military officers. Below them was the huge mass of the peasantry. The gulf between the aristocracy and the masses is abundantly documented by the graves and dwellings of the Shang. Those of noble birth lived in imposing timber structures with carefully prepared foundations and gabled roofs. Peasants lived in small semisubterranean dwellings averaging about 4 meters across.

The Shang royal graves and cemeteries were discovered at Hsi-pei-kang, north of Hsiao-t'un.[8] Eleven highly elaborate tombs are thought to coincide

Figure 20.3 Oracle bone of the Shang dynasty, from Hsaio-t'un, Honan Province, China.

Shang Culture in East Asia

with the eleven Shang rulers who resided at Anyang at the height of its prosperity.[9] The bodies were laid in huge tomblike structures up to 9 meters (30 ft) deep, which were entered by long ramps on two or more sides. A wooden chamber inside each pit contained the royal coffin, surrounded by human sacrifices, and elaborate ornaments — bronze castings, remarkable stone sculptures of stylized beasts in a distinctive Chinese style, fine clay vessels, jade, and bone objects. Chariots and horses were buried with the dead (Figure 20.4). Sacrificial victims were placed both in the pit and on the ramps leading to the grave. Some were decapitated before burial, their heads buried separately from their trunks.

Shang civilization is epitomized by the organization of the settlements at Cheng Chou and Anyang. The aristocracy lived in their own compounds, which had ceremonial altars, temples, imposing palaces, and elaborate royal

Cheng Chou and Anyang

Figure 20.4 Chariot burial from the royal Shang tombs. The wooden parts of the chariot were excavated by following discolorations made by the decaying wood in the ground.

Old World Civilizations

tombs. Administrative powers were exercised from the aristocracy's secure precincts, where they had all the paraphernalia of economic, political, and religious prestige.

The royal seats were surrounded by extensive networks of villages whose economic and administrative structures made them depend on one another for specialist services. The peasant farmers supported the state by intensive agriculture, for which they used large digging sticks, stone hoes, spades, and sickles. Fishing was economically important; hunting perhaps was a royal sport, not a subsistence activity.

Chinese-American scholar Kwang-chih Chang stresses the contrast between the large urban populations of Mesopotamia and the scattered village networks around a Shang capital.[10] The Shang civilization was a definite break with earlier settlement traditions, but its foci were the royal compounds. The royal capitals supported the aristocracy and priesthood, employed craftsworkers, and were the nucleus of political and religious life. Scribes recorded official business, and stores of food were maintained. In these senses the capitals performed all the essential functions of the Mesopotamian city-states. Crafts-workers were especially important in Shang society. They lived not only in the royal capitals but in rural villages as well, often in special quarters.

Shang religious life was controlled by a regular calendar of events. The clannish aristocracy was much occupied with elaborate ancestor worship. A supreme being, Shang Ti, presided over gods, controlling all human affairs. The royal ancestors were intermediaries between the Shang rulers and Shang Ti, with scapulimancy and other rites providing communication with the dead. Shang art is remarkable for its animal motifs and human images, sculpted in stone and bronze, as well as in clay, jade, bone, and ivory. This artistic tradition was at least partly dictated by ceremonial specifications connected with burial and other ritual events.

Religion and art

Stages of Shang Civilization

At least three broad chronological stages of the Shang civilization have been identified; it is likely that this basic sequence will be much elaborated in the future.

Early Shang (Erh-li-t'ou phase), c. 1850 to 1650 B.C. Most Early Shang sites come from Honan and Shansi, especially from the Yen-shih area of Honan, a low-lying basin surrounded by mountain ranges and drained by tributaries of the Huangho (Figure 20.1).[11] Erh-li-t'ou yielded traces of a complex society with class divisions and a large labor force that used intensive agriculture. Some people believe that T'ang, legendary founder of the Shang dynasty in 1766 B.C., made his capital, Po, at Erh-li-t'ou. The settlement was of impressive size, dominated by a large T-shaped house with foundations of stone and walls of mud and sticks. Smaller rectangular houses, pottery kilns, wells, and numerous burials adorned with pottery and ornaments have come from the site. Other bodies were deposited in storage pits or occupation levels, often with hands tied or partially dismembered — perhaps deliberate sacrifices.

*Erh-li-t'ou
?1850 to 1650 B.C.*

Specialized craftsworkers turned out bronze arrowheads, fishhooks, and spearheads. Jade, stone, and turquoise ornaments are found in graves and houses. The pottery bears stylized animal motifs, including dragons, fish, and snakes. Specialized cooking vessels are common, as are wine-drinking pots, typically found in the graves of the more prosperous. Cord-impressed pottery is also abundant, much of it showing stylistic connections with earlier Lung-shan traditions.

Erh-li-kang
1650 to 1400 B.C.

Middle Shang (Erh-li-kang phase), 1650 to 1400 B.C. The Erh-li-kang phase follows Erh-li-t'ou around 1650 B.C., lasting until 1400 B.C. By then, Shang towns were distributed over a large area on both banks of the Huangho River. Literary sources tell us that the Shang kings changed their capital several times before finally settling at Anyang after 1400 B.C. One such early capital was at the modern city of Cheng Chou, a major center of Shang civilization during the Erh-li-kang phase.

Cheng Chou was a very large populated area with a central ceremonial and administrative area that lies under the modern town. A walled rectangular enclosure, 1.3 miles (2.1 km) from north to south and a mile (1.6 km) across, surrounded the ceremonial area. An Chin-huai, a Chinese scholar, estimates that the earth wall around Cheng Chou was more than 9 meters (30 ft) high, with an average width of 18 meters (60 ft). His experiments in earthmoving with Shang tools produced a rough calculation that 10,000 men would have taken at least eighteen years to build the walls.

Most workers and peasant farmers who supported this vast ceremonial complex lived around Cheng Chou in small villages scattered through the countryside. Bronze foundries and pottery kilns have been located outside the walls. Some craftsworkers lived in substantial houses, with floors of pounded-down earth, but most people lived in humble, semisubterranean huts and used vessels far less intricate than the skillfully cast ceremonial bronzes of the Shang kings.

Yin
1400 to 1100 B.C.

Late Shang (Yin phase), 1400 to 1100 B.C. By 1400 B.C., the center of Shang civilization had shifted north of the Huangho River, but the kingdom remained confined to northern Honan and parts of Hopei and Shantung. The Yin phase of Shang civilization, lasting until 1100 B.C., is best known from the great capital city of Anyang, seat of twelve Shang kings over nearly 300 years.

A huge ceremonial district at Hsiao-t'un near Anyang was built on the banks of the Huan River.[12] The north end of Hsiao-t'un was occupied by fifteen large rectangular structures (Figure 20.5). Other rectangular or square structures were built in the middle of this settlement. Many burials were found in their vicinity; included also were the foundations of five gates. A further complex of buildings at the southern end of the precinct may have been a ceremonial area. Hsiao-t'un houses were built with pounded-down earth foundations and a timber framework set on stone pillars. The walls of wattle and daub were topped with thatched roofs (Figure 20.5). Semisubterranean huts nestled near the larger structures, some of them bronze workshops or potters' areas. Others were presumably servants' quarters. Several of the

Figure 20.5 Reconstruction of a structure from the ceremonial area at Hsiao-t'un, Anyang, Honan Province, China.

temple structures had been consecrated with human sacrifices found huddled in pits near the foundations.

Near the imposing structures of the gods and their servants were "service areas": more than six hundred semisubterranean dwellings of servants and menial laborers, workshops, and storage pits, and pottery kilns or bronze foundries were uncovered.

THE CHOU DYNASTY SEIZES POWER

About 1122 B.C. the capital of the Shang Empire was plundered by the Chou people, who lived on the frontiers of the Shensi.[13] The basic features of Shang civilization were common to the Chou, who maintained the long-established social and cultural practices. Soon the Chinese acquired many of the customs and philosophical tenets that have survived until modern times. Ironworking was invented, apparently independently from the West, in the mid-first millennium B.C. Cast iron tools were used for cultivation, the earliest occurrence of such technology anywhere in the world. The innovation further increased the productivity of Chinese farmers.

Chou
1122 B.C.

500 B.C.

The Chou dynasty divided its territory into various, almost independent, provinces. Not until the last few centuries before Christ was China unified under the Ch'in and Han emperors, who shifted the political power base from Huangho in northern China to the Yangtze River area. During this time, the Chinese came into contact with the Roman Empire and began extensive trading with India. By Roman times, Chinese civilization had been flourishing for more than 2000 years, a distinctive and highly nationalistic culture that survives today.

Han
221 B.C.

PART SIX

NEW WORLD CIVILIZATIONS

(1550 B.C. to A.D. 1530)

What, then, must have been the emotions of the
Spaniards, when, after working their toilsome way into
the open air, the cloudy tabernacle parted before their
eyes, and they beheld these fair scenes in all their
pristine magnificence and beauty. It was like the
spectacle which greeted the eyes of Moses from the
summit of Pisgah, and, in the warm glow of their feelings,
they cried out, "It is the promised land!"
— W.H. Prescott, *The Conquest of Mexico,* 1843

Part 6 contains descriptions of the great and complex states of the New World.
The theoretical literature surrounding the emergence of states in Mesoamerica and
Peru is enormous, and interested readers are referred to Chapter 14 for some of
the principal arguments surrounding the subject.

Chronological Table L

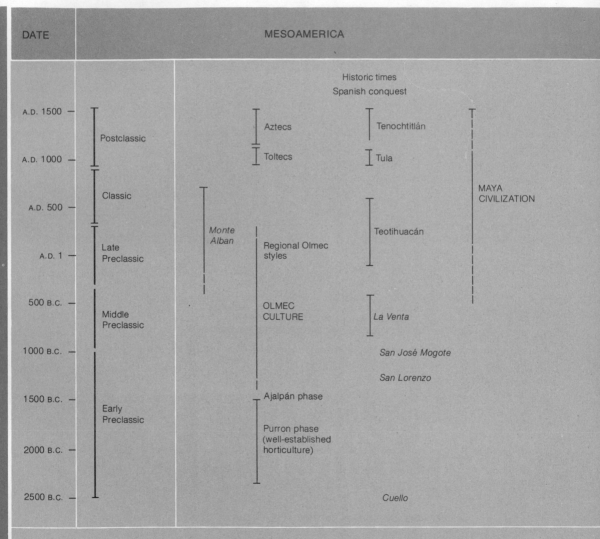

DATE	MESOAMERICA			
			Historic times	
			Spanish conquest	
A.D. 1500	Postclassic	Aztecs	Tenochtitlán	MAYA CIVILIZATION
A.D. 1000		Toltecs	Tula	
A.D. 500	Classic	*Monte Alban*	Teotihuacán	
A.D. 1	Late Preclassic	Regional Olmec styles		
500 B.C.	Middle Preclassic	OLMEC CULTURE	*La Venta*	
1000 B.C.			San José Mogote	
			San Lorenzo	
1500 B.C.	Early Preclassic	Ajalpán phase		
2000 B.C.		Purron phase (well-established horticulture)		
2500 B.C.			*Cuello*	

Chapter Twenty-One

MESOAMERICAN CIVILIZATIONS

PREVIEW

⚓ The Preclassic period of Mesoamerican prehistory lasted from about 2500 to 1000 B.C., a period of major cultural change in both lowlands and highlands. Sedentary villages traded with each other in raw materials and exotic objects. These exchange networks became increasingly complex and eventually came under the monopolistic control of larger villages. Increasing social complexity went hand in hand with the appearance of the first public buildings and evidence of social stratification.

⚓ These developments are well chronicled in the Valley of Oaxaca and in the Olmec culture of the lowlands, which flourished from about 1500 to 500 B.C. Olmec art styles and religious beliefs were among those that spread widely over lowlands and highlands during the late Preclassic.

⚓ The Preclassic cultural developments culminated on the highlands in a number of great cities, among them Monte Albán and Teotihuacán. The latter housed over 120,000 people, and covered over eight square miles at the height of its prosperity. Teotihuacán collapsed about A.D. 700, probably as a result of warfare with other, rival states in the highlands.

⚓ Maya civilization rose in the lowlands in a relatively uniform environment where trading activities may have been of prime importance in the development of a complex society. Classic Maya civilization flourished from A.D. 300 to 900, and was remarkable for its sophisticated trade networks, great ceremonial centers, and elaborate ceremonies, known through sculptures and hieroglyphs. Maya civilization was far from uniform and was unified more by religious doctrine than by political and economic interests.

⚓ Maya civilization collapsed suddenly in the Yucatán after A.D. 900; the reasons for the collapse are still uncertain, but pressure on the labor force and possible food shortages were doubtless among them.

⚓ Teotihuacán's collapse on the highlands resulted in a political vacuum for some centuries which was eventually filled by the Toltecs and then the Aztec, whose bloodthirsty civilization was dominant in the Valley of Mexico at the time of Spanish conquest in A.D. 1519.

⬇ Aztec civilization was unable to resist the Spanish and collapsed rapidly, partly as a result of serious internal stresses and rebellion by subject tribes.

Chronological
Table L

Who was responsible for American civilizations? Were they of indigenous development, or did they result from massive migrations of Egyptians and others across the Atlantic to the New World? Although there can be little doubt that some Old World visitors did reach America before Columbus, whether their existence here was culturally significant is another matter; and debate on the question is intense.[1]* Most serious scholars consider that the New World civilizations developed from local roots.

PRECLASSIC PEOPLES IN MESOAMERICA

Preclassic
2500 B.C. to A.D. 300

By 2000 B.C., sedentary farming villages were common in most of Mesoamerica.[2] In their agriculture people relied on many plant species, and slash-and-burn farming methods were in wide use in the lowlands. With such methods people could clear small gardens in the forest by cutting tree trunks and brush, carefully burning branches to fertilize the soil with a layer of wood ash. Then, using pointed digging sticks, they planted maize and other crops. A few seasons later they abandoned the land, planting less important crops on older plots or leaving them to the forest. The search for new lands was constant, even when slash-and-burn was combined with irrigation or riverside agriculture.

Early Preclassic

Many centuries elapsed between the beginnings of village life and that of Mesoamerican civilization. Mesoamericans began to live in larger settlements and to build elaborate ceremonial centers at the beginning of an era named the Preclassic or "Formative" period, approximately 2500 B.C. to A.D. 300. The earliest centuries of the Preclassic witnessed the appearance of pottery and the first ceremonial centers. One such site is Cuello in lowland northern Belize, which is radiocarbon dated to between 2600 and 2000 B.C.[3] The inhabitants of this site were cultivating maize and probably relied heavily on wild swamp plants for their diet (Figure 21.1). The Middle Preclassic is known for the Olmec culture, appearing from 1200 to 300 B.C. The Late Preclassic has various regional centers, some with Olmec-like artistic and cultural characteristics.[4]

Cuello
2600 to 2000 B.C.

* See pages 390–391 for notes to Chapter 21.

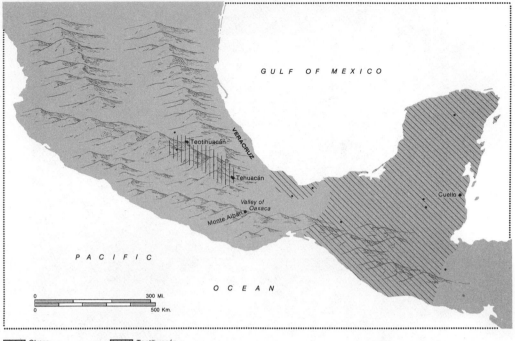

	Olmec			Teotihuacán
	1500–500 B.C.			100 B.C.–A.D. 700

Figure 21.1 Mesoamerican archaeological sites mentioned in Chapter 21. Approximate distributions of various traditions are shown.

Middle Preclassic — the Olmecs

The first really major ceremonial centers appear in the Middle Preclassic, marking the transformation of village society into a wider social order with more complex social and economic organizations.[5] Signs of social stratification begin to appear at the time when food surpluses were achieved; the extra food was used to support certain individuals, probably religious leaders, whose contribution to the society was to organize the production and distribution of food on a new scale. The first ceremonial centers probably developed as a response to population increase and the desire to maintain and symbolize kinship and religious unity. These revered centers became the foci of political and religious power, as their new priest-leaders engaged in trading, employed increasing numbers of specialized craftspeople, and manipulated labor forces and food surpluses.

The best-known Preclassic culture is that of the Olmec, centered in the lowland regions of southern Veracruz and western Tabasco.[6] There, ceremonial centers achieved remarkable complexity at an early date. *Olmec* means "rubber people," and the region was long important for rubber production. Although the Olmec homeland is low-lying, tropical, and humid, its soil is fertile, and the swamps, lakes, and rivers are rich in fish, birds, and other

Olmec
1500 to 500 B.C.

Figure 21.2 Giant stone head from San Lorenzo made from basalt, approximately 2.4 meters (8 ft) high. Michael Coe has suggested that these heads are portraits of rulers, while David Grove has identified what he thinks are name glyphs on the "helmets" of the heads.

animals. Olmec societies prospered in this region for a thousand years from about 1500 B.C., and created a highly distinctive art style.

San Lorenzo The earliest traces of Olmec occupation are best documented at San Lorenzo, where Olmec people lived on a platform in the midst of frequently inundated woodland plains. They erected ridges and mounds around their platform, upon which they built pyramids and possibly ball courts, and placed elaborate monumental carvings overlooking the site. The earliest occupation of San Lorenzo shows few Olmec features, but by 1250 B.C., the inhabitants were beginning to build some raised fields, a task that required enormous organized labor forces. By that time, too, distinctive Olmec sculpture began to appear. A century later, magnificent monumental carvings adorned San Lorenzo (Figure 21.2), distinctive, and often mutilated by the Olmec themselves.

One archaeologist has estimated the population of San Lorenzo at 2500. The inhabitants enjoyed extensive trade, especially in obsidian and other semi-precious materials obtained from many parts of Mesoamerica. San Lorenzo fell into decline after 900 B.C. and was surpassed in importance by La Venta, the most famous Olmec site, nearer the Gulf of Mexico.

San Lorenzo
1250 B.C.

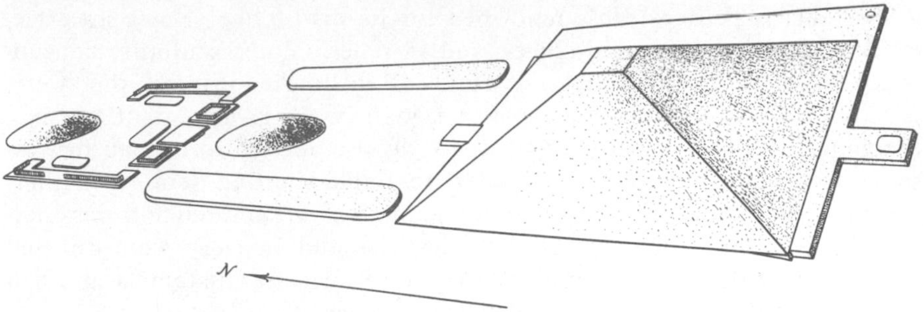

Figure 21.3 La Venta, site 4: layout of the major structures.

La Venta   The La Venta ceremonial center was built on a small island in the middle of a swamp.[7] A rectangular earth mound, 120 meters long by 70 meters wide and 32 meters high (393 ft by 229 ft and 105 ft high), dominates the island. Long, low mounds surround a rectangular plaza in front of the large mound, faced by walls and terraced mounds at the other end of the plaza (Figure 21.3). Vast monumental stone sculptures litter the site, including some Olmec heads bearing expressions of contempt and savagery; caches of jade objects, figurines, and a dull green rock (serpentine) are common, too (Figure 21.4). Every stone for sculptures and temples had to be brought from at least 60 miles (96 km) away, a vast undertaking, for some sculptured blocks weigh over forty tons. La Venta flourished for about four hundred years from 800 B.C. After about 400 B.C., the site was probably destroyed, which we deduce from signs that many of its finest monuments were intentionally defaced.

La Venta
800 to 400 B.C.

Figure 21.4 An Olmec altar or throne sculpture from La Venta. The sculpture is 3.4 meters (about 11 ft) high. At least one of these thrones shows the ruler in front connected to his parents on the side by umbilical cords.

La Venta is perhaps most renowned for its distinctive Olmec art style, executed both as sculptured objects and in relief. Olmec sculpture concentrated on natural and supernatural beings and its dominant motif, the "were-jaguar," or human-like jaguar. Many jaguars were given infantile faces, drooping lips, and large, swollen eyes, a style also applied to human figures; some have almost negroid faces; others resemble snarling demons in their ferocity. The Olmec contribution to Mesoamerican art and religion was enormously significant. Elements of their art style and imagery were diffused widely during the first millennium B.C., southward to Guatemala and San Salvador and northward into the Valley of Mexico.

Late Preclassic

Late Preclassic
300 B.C. to A.D. 300

We believe that the spread of the Olmec art style and the beginning of the Late Preclassic in about 500 to 300 B.C. signals the period during which a common religious system and ideology began to unify large areas of Mesoamerica. A powerful priesthood congregated in spectacular ceremonial centers, commemorating potent and widely recognized deities. Distinctive art and architecture went with the new religion, whose practice required precise measurements of calendar years and of longer cycles of time. Writing and mathematical calculations were developed to affirm religious practices, a unifying political force in the sense that they welded scattered village communities into larger political units. By the time the Classic Mesoamerican civilizations arose, dynasties of priests and aristocrats had been ruling parts of Mesoamerica along well-established lines for nearly a thousand years.

THE RISE OF COMPLEX SOCIETY IN OAXACA: MONTE ALBÁN

The Preclassic cultures of the Valley of Oaxaca have been studied intensively by Kent Flannery and his students, using highly sophisticated systems approaches to document changing settlement patterns, and economic and demographic trends.[8] Something like ninety percent of the Preclassic Oaxaca villages were little more than small hamlets of 50 to 60 people, while the remainder were much larger settlements of 1000 to 1200 souls, with populations of priests and craftspeople.

The evolution of larger settlements in Oaxaca and elsewhere was closely connected with the development of long distance trade in obsidian and other luxuries such as seashells and stingray spines from the Gulf of Mexico. The simple barter networks for obsidian of earlier times evolved into sophisticated regional trading organizations where village leaders controlled monopolies over sources of obsidian and its distribution. Magnetite mirrors, sea shells, feathers, and ceramics were all traded on the highlands, and from the highlands to the lowlands as well. Olmec pottery and other ritual objects began to appear in highland settlements between 1150 and 650 B.C., many of them

Figure 21.5 Four clay figurines shaped and posed deliberately to form a scene, buried beneath an Early Preclassic house at San José Mogote, Oaxaca, Mexico.

bearing the distinctive were-jaguar motif of the lowlands, which had an important place in Olmec cosmology.

Public buildings began to appear in villages like San José Magote between 1400 and 1150 B.C., many of them oriented eight degrees west of north; they were built on adobe and earth platforms. Conch shell trumpets and turtle shell drums from the Gulf of Mexico are associated with these buildings, as are clay figurines of dancers wearing costumes and masks (Figure 21.5). There were marine fish spines, too, probably used in personal bloodletting ceremonies that were still practiced even in Aztec times. (The Spanish described how Aztec nobles would gash themselves with knives or with the spines of fish or sting ray in acts of mutilation before the gods, penances required of the devout.[9]) It has been suggested that the sudden diffusion of the Olmec art style through Mesoamerica resulted from the increased need for religious rituals to bring the various elements of society closer together. This diffusion took place after long distance trading had been in existence for centuries, and probably signaled an increase in public ceremonies using communal temples or shrines that were situated in larger villages like San José Magote.

Monte Albán

By 400 B.C. there were at least seven small states in the Valley of Oaxaca, of which the one centered on Monte Albán soon became dominant in the area. Although massive population increases and increased economic power were among the interacting factors that aided in the rise of Monte Albán, the special terrain of Monte Albán may have been of vital importance in its ascendancy.[10] Richard Blanton has surveyed over 2000 terraces on the slopes of Monte Albán, terraces used for agriculture and housing areas. Monte Albán commanded the best terrain in the valley, sloping land that was organized for agriculture and dense settlement by a population of several thousand people, far larger than that of most major settlements in Mesoamerica at the time. Even as early as 400 B.C., some of the terraces were already in use by a highly organized population whose leaders resided in a ceremonial and civic center built on the summit of the Monte Albán ridge. Although the large-scale buildings of later times have contoured the summit of Monte Albán beyond recognition, it is clear that the first leaders to live there undertook major public works, many of them wood and thatch buildings, which had incised sculptures of what may be dead and tortured enemies set into the walls.

Monte Albán went on to develop into a vast ceremonial center with splendid public architecture; its settlement area included public buildings, terraces, and housing zones that extended over about fifteen square miles (40 square

Figure 21.6 Monte Albán: The center building, dating to c. A.D. 1300.

kilometers) (Figure 21.6). The more than 2000 terraces all held one or two houses, while small ravines were dammed to pond valuable water supplies. Blanton suggests that between 30 and 50,000 people lived at Monte Albán between A.D. 200 and 700. Many very large villages and smaller hamlets lay within easy distance of the city. The enormous platforms on the ridge of Monte Albán supported complex layouts of temples and pyramid-temples, palaces, patios, and tombs. A hereditary elite seems to have ruled Monte Albán, the leaders of a state that had emerged in the Valley of Oaxaca by A.D. 200. Their religious power was based on ancestor worship, a pantheon of at least thirty-nine gods, grouped around major themes of ritual life. The rain-god and lightning were associated with the jaguar motif; another group of deities are linked with the maize god Pitao Cozabi. Nearly all these gods were still worshipped at the time of Spanish contact, although Monte Albán itself was abandoned after A.D. 700, at about the same time as another great ceremonial center, Teotihuacán, in the Valley of Mexico, went into eclipse.

Mesoamerican States Are Shaped by Agricultural Techniques

Everyone agrees that the emergence of unifying artistic traditions (like the Olmec), religious ideologies, ritual organization, and extensive trading networks were key factors in the development of Mesoamerican civilization.[11] But it is only in recent years that people have begun to study early Mesoamerican agriculture in an attempt to understand how the Maya and other peoples were able to support the enormous urban populations that built and organized the ceremonial centers of both highland and lowland Mesoamerica.

There are sharp contrasts in subsistence patterns between lowlands and highlands. The former is a much more uniform environment where there is far less diversity of soils and resources than on the highlands. The traditional views of early Mesoamerican agriculture have been highly colored by hypotheses about lowland practices which do not apply to the highlands at all.

Long-held views of Mesoamerican agriculture, specifically those concerning the Maya, have always assumed that the populations lived in dispersed villages and used only slash-and-burn agriculture, which, as we have seen, cannot support a high population density.[12] This viewpoint is now discarded, for it has been shown that raised fields and terracing were important in lowland cultivation, not only of maize, but of other subsistence crops as well. There is good reason to believe that the lowland Maya relied heavily on tree culture, noticeably that of the ramon tree (Brosimum alicastrum), a species that produces a highly nutritious nut that can be stored up to 18 months and requires little care. As valuable as maize as a protein source, the ramon may have permitted much higher carrying capacities in the lowlands, of up to 400 to 600 people per square kilometer.

The lowland forest environment tends to be a uniform one, but those of the highlands are much more diverse, as we have seen in the case of Tehuacán (Chapter 13). The earliest farming villages in Oaxaca are concentrated in the valley floors, in areas where water is available within easy reach of the surface. Modern farmers choose similar villages for simple "pot" irrigation, where they plant their maize and other crops near small, shallow wells. They simply water the plants by dipping pots into the wells and watering surrounding plants from the shallow water table before moving on to the next well. Flannery has argued that the Oaxacans used the same technique in prehistoric times.[13]

Pot irrigation

Pot irrigation does not require large numbers of people or complex social organization to support it. From about 1300 B.C. to 350 B.C., Oaxaca was inhabited by widely spaced larger villages with small villages dependent on them. The changing settlement pattern was accompanied by population growth that led to the taking up of less desirable agricultural land on slopes and the devel-

Agriculture on the slopes

opment of new agricultural techniques to work this land. The Oaxaca environment was so diverse that the people were able to build on their simple and highly effective original techniques, which still remained part of their repertoire; they expanded to the slopes, then even cultivated the arid lands as populations grew. Eventually the economic power generated by these rising populations gave highland areas like Oaxaca a decided edge in cultural evolution.

Similar diversity of agricultural techniques is found in the Valley of Mexico, where slash-and-burn methods, dry farming, and irrigation agriculture were all in use. Irrigation used both floodwaters and canals to bring water to dry gardens. The most famous of all irrigation techniques, however, is the

Chinampas

most extraordinary *chinampa* or floating garden technique, a highly intensive and productive agricultural system based on the reclaiming of swamps. The farmers made use of standing water and built up marshy areas by piling up natural vegetation and lake mud to form huge grids of naturally irrigated gardens. The chinampas were used very systematically to grow a variety of crops, so timed that different crops came into harvest throughout the year.[14] This system is amazingly productive, and is estimated to have supported about 100,000 people from 25,000 acres in 1519, at the time of Spanish contact. But each chinampa produced large food surpluses that could be used to support thousands of nonagricultural workers and specialists. Sanders has argued that the 25,000 acres of chinampas referred to above could actually have supported about 180,000 people. That this highly effective agricultural system was the basis of early civilization and urban life in the Valley of Mexico is beyond question.

The agricultural system of the Valley of Mexico may seem complicated, but it supported, and was part of, a far more elaborate system of food marketing, which provided not only tribute for taxes, but opportunities for the trading of specialist foodstuffs from one area of the highlands to another. The highland

Market Economy

peoples relied on elaborate markets that were strictly regulated by the state, and conducted on a barter system. The Valley of Mexico was an economic unit before Teotihuacán made it a political one as well. It was the great agricultural productivity of the Valley, and the sophisticated market economy of the emerging city that made the prodigious social and religious, as well as material, developments of later centuries possible. This economic system fostered the development of specialist crafts that were sold in the markets of the cities and exported over wide areas.

The sequence of events in the highlands may have begun with the buildup of agricultural populations in diverse environments like the Valley of Oaxaca in the first and second millennia B.C. This population buildup led to the development of more intensive agricultural methods, including both irrigation and chinampa systems. At the same time different areas were linked by increasingly sophisticated trading networks and by an emerging market economy, with, perhaps, some specialized merchants.

Religious activity was stimulated by the introduction of religious beliefs and sacred objects from the lowlands. Trade in exotic luxuries increased as ceremonial centers and stratified societies were founded. By 200 B.C. the effects of increased religious activity, intensified trading, and the production of huge food surpluses from the diverse environment had led to the founding of at least two major cities in the Valley of Mexico, of which one, Teotihuacán, reached an enormous size and enjoyed vast political, economic, and religious power in the centuries that followed. In the Valley of Oaxaca, Monte Albán achieved a similar dominance. The two great states probably enjoyed an uneasy alliance.

Teotihuacán

Teotihuacán lies northeast of Mexico City and is now one of the great archaeological tourist attractions of the world. It was one of the dominant political and cultural centers of all Mesoamerica around A.D. 500, the culmination of centuries of vigorous cultural development in the Valley of Mexico.[15]

The first buildings appear at Teotihuacán in about 200 B.C., a handful of villages at least one of which may have specialized in obsidian manufacture. By 100 B.C. Teotihuacán had begun to expand rapidly and the scattered villages became a settlement covering more than 3½ square miles. Much of this early settlement is covered by the vast structures of later times. It is estimated that six thousand people inhabited this early town. There were several public buildings.

Teotihuacán
200 B.C. to A.D. 700

René Millon, who carried out a systematic survey of Teotihuacán, found that by A.D. 150 the city extended over 5 square miles and housed more than 20,000 people. Obsidian trade and manufacture were expanding fast. There were two major religious complexes for which, among other structures, the Pyramids of the Sun and Moon were first built at this time.

Between A.D. 150 and 750, Teotihuacán exploded in size. Anyone passing through the Valley of Mexico had to pass through the city with its diverse population of priests, merchants, craftspeople, and other specialists. The rulers of the city erected hundreds of standardized apartment complexes and continued a master plan that laid out the city on a north-south axis, centered on the Avenue of the Dead (Figure 21.7), with another great avenue oriented east-west. The eight square miles of Teotihuacán consisted of avenues and plazas, markets, temples, palaces, apartment buildings, and complex drainage and agricultural works. The entire city was dominated by the "Pyramid of the Sun" (a modern name), a vast structure of earth, adobe, and piled rubble. The pyramid, faced with stone, is 64 meters (210 ft) high and 198 meters (650 ft) square. A wooden temple probably sat on the summit of the terraced pyramid.

City layout

Figure 21.7 Aerial view of the ceremonial precincts at Teotihuacán, Mexico, with the Pyramid of the Moon in the foreground. At left in the background (to the left of the Avenue of the Dead) is the Pyramid of the Sun. (From *Urbanization at Teotihuacán, Mexico*, vol. 1, pt. 1. *The Teotihuacán Map: Text,* by René Millon, copyright © 1973 by René Millon, by permission of the author.)

The long "Avenue of the Dead" passes the west face of the pyramid, leading to the "Pyramid of the Moon," the second largest structure at the site (Figure 21.7). The avenue is lined with civic, palace, and religious buildings, and the side streets lead to residential areas. A large palace and temple complex dedicated to the Plumed Serpent (Quetzalcóatl), with platform and stairways around a central court, lies south of the middle of Teotihuacán, across from a central marketplace.

The Avenue of the Dead and the pyramids lie amid a sprawling mass of small houses. Priests and craftsworkers lived in dwellings around small courtyards; the less privileged lived in large compounds of rooms connected by narrow alleyways and patios. By any standard, Teotihuacán was a city, and once housed up to 120,000 people. Although some farmers probably lived within the city, we know that rural villages flourished nearby. These villages were compact, expertly planned, and administered by city rulers.

The comprehensive settlement pattern data from the Millon survey enables us to say something about the structure of Teotihuacán society. The food surpluses to support the city were produced by farmers who lived both in the city and in satellite villages nearby. Tribute from neighboring states also helped feed the city, and control of large areas of the plateau made sure that adequate food supplies came to Teotihuacán's huge market. But most of the people lived in the city. It is not known how important chinampa agriculture was for Teotihuacán, but irrigation farming was a key element in subsistence. Craftspeople accounted for perhaps twenty-five percent of the urban population, people who lived in compounds of apartments near the over 500 workshops that produced everything from obsidian tools to clay vessels. Merchants were probably an important class in the city, as were civil servants who carried out the routine administration of Teotihuacán. There were even foreign quarters, one of which housed Oaxacans. The elite included priests, warriors, and secular leaders, who controlled the vast city and its many dealings through a strictly class society. Religious beliefs continued the rituals of earlier times, but it appears that cannibalism and human sacrifice became increasingly important in later centuries, as the leaders of the city became more and more militaristic in their outlook, a trend that was to continue into Aztec times.

Teotihuacán ruled the Valley of Mexico and parts of Puebla, but its influence through alliance, tribute, and warfare, as well as trading, extended over a far larger area of Mesoamerica. As in later times, the rulers of Teotihuacán probably controlled some highly strategic and economically important zones, but there were large areas where their influence was minimal. The final analysis is this: Teotihuacán was probably a huge city-state bound to other city-states by uneasy alliances and tribute exchanges.

By A.D. 600 Teotihuacán was probably ruled by a secular ruler who was a divine king of some kind, a person with formidable military powers. A class of nobles controlled the kinship groups that organized the bulk of the city's huge population. In about A.D. 650 Teotihuacán was deliberately burnt down. Only fifty years later its urban population was scattered in a few villages. Much of the former urban population settled in neighboring regions, which thereby reaped the benefit of Teotihuacán's misfortunes. No one knows exactly why this great city collapsed so suddenly. The rapid development of the city may have resulted in serious internal weaknesses which made Teotihuacán vulnerable to easy overthrow. Conceivably a drought may have also weakened the city and provided an opportunity for jealous rivals to attempt an attack.

The very success of Teotihuacán may have accelerated its downfall. The new orders of society and politics spawned by the city may have been copied by other leaders, perhaps more aggressive and less tradition-bound than the mother city. Teotihuacán was not the only sophisticated city-state in the highlands between A.D. 500 and 700. Sanders has argued that Teotihuacán was overthrown by a coalition of city-states that included Tula to the northwest, Xochicalco in the southwest, and Cholula to the southeast.[16] All these states expanded after the downfall of Teotihuacán, all had been powerful regional states at the time of the former's collapse. Whatever the causes of Teotihuacán's downfall, its end resulted in a dispersal of specialist craftsworkers, priests, and other functionaries throughout Mesoamerica, as a period of political and military competition among rival states ensued.

The Maya civilization is probably the best known of all early American civilizations, one that has excited the imagination of scholars for over a century. Maya civilization took shape slowly. It was centered on lowland rain forest areas that provided a relatively uniform environment in which people grew both maize and other crops, as well as relying heavily on the harvesting of trees like the ramon. Traces of primordial Maya culture are discernible in the Yucatán and Belize many centuries before the brilliant Maya civilization flourished in the lowlands. Norman Hammond has found platforms and other structures at Cuello in Belize that date to the second millennium B.C.[17] The associated pottery styles can be traced through the first millennium B.C. and appear to be ancestral to Classic Maya ceramics.

Although the roots of Maya civilization go far back into the Preclassic, considerable debate surrounds the origins of Maya civilization. The initial Maya settlement pattern was a dispersed one, with villages scattered through the rain forest, in situations that seem to militate against political or economic unity. Their civilization was based on great ceremonial centers that often supported considerable urban populations and generated huge food surpluses. The earliest Maya settlements flourished in a fundamentally empty landscape, where there was plenty of space for slash-and-burn agriculture and little incentive for cooperation between neighboring communities. Debate about the origins of the Maya civilization centers around population growth and the factors that led these dispersed villages into closer economic and social cooperation.[18]

William Rathje has provided one possible explanation. He suggests that the Maya environment was very deficient in many vital resources, including stone for grinding maize, salt (always vital for agriculturalists), obsidian for knives and weapons, and many luxury materials.[19] All these could be obtained from the highlands in the north, from the Valley of Mexico as well as from Guatemala and other regions, if the necessary long distance trading networks and mechanisms could be set up. Such connections, and the trading expeditions to maintain them, could not be organized by individual villages alone. The Maya lived in a uniform environment where the rain forest provided smilarly deficient resources for every settlement. Long networks therefore were developed through the authority of the ceremonial centers and their leaders. The integrative organization needed must have been considerable, for communications in the rain forest, especially in areas remote from the highlands, were extremely difficult to maintain.

Rathje carries his argument a stage further. Obviously peoples living on the border between the lowlands and the highlands had the best opportunities for trade. Those who lived farther away, like the Maya, were at a disadvantage. They offered the same agricultural commodities and craft exports as their more fortunate border neighbors but were farther from markets. They had one competitive advantage, however — a complex and properly functioning state organization, and the knowledge to keep it going. This knowledge itself was very exportable. Along with pottery, feathers, specialized stone materials, and

Figure 21.8 Temple I at Tikal, Guatemala, which dates to about A.D. 700.

lime plaster, they exported their political and social organization, and their religious beliefs as well.

The Rathje hypothesis probably explains part of the complex processes of state formation during the early Classic period. Long trading networks did connect the lowlands and the highlands. A well-defined cosmology with roots in Olmec beliefs, a strongly centralized economic and religious system based on ceremonial centers, and sophisticated and highly competitive commercial opportunities all contributed to a complex system that caused the dramatic rise of Classic Mesoamerican civilization. It should be pointed out, however, that Rathje's hypothesis suffers from the objection that suitable alternative raw materials for metates (grindstones) and other imported objects do exist in the lowlands. It could be, too, that warfare became a competitive response to population growth and the increasing scarcity of prime agricultural land.

The Classic Maya civilization was in full swing by A.D. 300, centered around ceremonial centers such as Tikal and Copán, whose earth-filled pyramids were topped with temples carefully ornamented with sculptured stucco (Figure 21.8).[20] The pyramids were faced with cemented stone blocks and covered with a high quality plaster against the rains. The large temples on top

Classic Maya civilization **A.D. 300 to 900**

Mesoamerican Civilizations   345

had small, dark rooms because the builders did not know how to construct arches and were forced to corbel their roofs, supporting them with external braces. Tikal was an important trade center and, like others, attracted specialized craftsworkers who served the priests and the gods.

Astronomy

Maya rulers constantly sought to appease their numerous gods (some benevolent, some evil) at the correct moments in the elaborate sacred calendar. Each sacred year, as well as each cycle of years, had its destiny controlled by a different deity. The state's continued survival was ensured by pleasing the gods with sacrificial offerings, some of them human.

The Maya were remarkable astronomers who predicted most astronomical events, including eclipses of the sun and moon (Figure 21.9). Religious events were regulated according to a sacred year (tzolkin) with thirteen months of twenty days each. The 260 days of the sacred year were unrelated to any astronomical phenomenon, being closely tied to ritual and divination. The length of the sacred year was arbitrary and probably established by long tradition. Tzolkins were, however, closely intermeshed with a secular year (haab) of 365 days, an astronomical calendar based on the solar cycle. The haab was used to regulate state affairs, but the connections between sacred and secular years were of great importance in Mayan life. Every fifty-two years a complete cycle of all the variations of the day and month names of the two calendars occurred, an occasion for intense religious activity.

The Maya developed a hieroglyphic script used for calculating calendars and regulating religious observances.[21] The script was much used for recording genealogies, king lists, conquests, and dynastic histories. Partly thanks to the Spanish bishop Diego de Landa, who recorded Maya dialects surviving in the mid-sixteenth century, scholars have been able to decipher part of the script that was written on temple walls and modeled in stucco. The symbols are fantastically grotesque, mostly humans, monsters, or gods' heads (Figure 21.9).

Copán

Copán, founded in the fifth century A.D., was one of the major astronomical centers of Mesoamerica. Its pyramids, temples, and pillars are a remarkable monument to Maya skill. Copán, like Tikal, preserves the essential architectural features of Maya ceremonial centers. These include platforms, pyramids, and causeways, grouped around open concourses and plazas presumably for religious effect and also to handle the large numbers of spectators who flocked to the religious ceremonies.

Ball courts were built at some late centers. They were used for an elaborate ceremonial contest, perhaps connected with the fertility of crops, between competing teams using a solid rubber ball. The details of the game remain obscure, but it is known that the players hit the balls so as to strike stone markers shaped like parrot heads.

Maya civilization was far from uniform; each major center kept its political identity and ruled a network of lesser religious complexes and small villages. The calendar and hieroglyphic script were common to all, essential in regulating religious life and worshiping Maya gods. Architectural and artistic styles in ceramics and small artifacts varied from center to center as each developed its own characteristics and cultural traditions.[22] The Maya were unified more by religious doctrine than by political or economic interests, in much the same

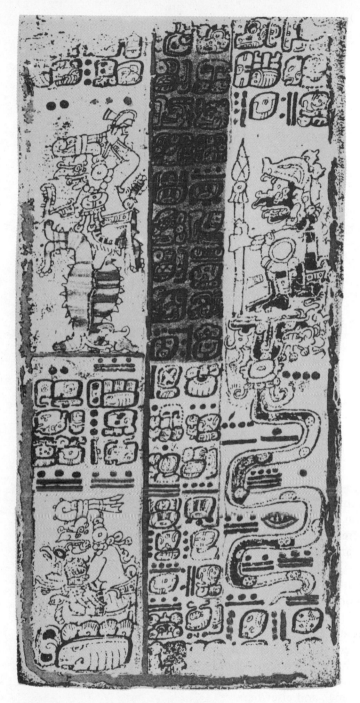

Figure 21.9 Only three certain, and one perhaps doubtful, Maya codices (books of picture writing) are known to have survived destruction by the Spanish. Here is a page from the so-called Dresden Codex, which records astronomical calculations, ritual detail, and tables of eclipses.

Figure 21.10 A richly clad Maya priest wears the mask of the long-nosed god. His name is Bird-Jaguar. Three people, probably prisoners about to be sacrificed, kneel before him — from Yaxchilán, C.A.D. 75. (From *The Rise and Fall of Maya Civilization*, by J. Eric S. Thompson. Copyright 1954, 1966, by the University of Oklahoma Press.)

way, perhaps, as the spread of Islam unified diverse cultures with a common religious belief (Figure 21.10).

Although religious power may have been a strong unifying force, both trade and the state's increased secularization were very important. The explosive population growth among the Maya is reflected in an orgy of temple-building and by increasing signs of changes in social structure. Hitherto only priests lived at the ceremonial centers, but now there are signs that elite families and large urban populations settled at such monumental sites at Tikal and Palenque. The aristocratic families were buried there, an elite of great wealth and secular power. There seems to have been a classic separation of religious and secular powers, accelerating the transformation Eliade suggested, making the ceremonial center more and more a secular precinct, with palaces rivaling temples in architectural splendor. And this change seems to have occurred at Tikal, Palenque, Uxmal, and elsewhere.

With increased secular authority, militarism reappeared. It may always have been a part of Mesoamerican civilization, but during the Late Classic it seems more pronounced. Palace and temple art have military scenes. Rathje and others speculate that new emphasis on warfare may have had several causes: loss of competitive edge in trading as Maya culture spread out, degraded agricultural land in the Maya homeland as population pressures mounted, and the need both for more territory and to force people to trade as they had for centuries, even if they were now fully competitive with the Maya and therefore in a position to exclude the Maya from their trading networks. We can only speculate on the reasons for more war, but one thing is certain. About A.D. 900, Maya civilization collapsed.

COLLAPSE OF THE CLASSIC MAYA CIVILIZATION

Maya civilization reached its greatest extent after A.D. 600. Then, at the end of the eighth century, the great ceremonial centers of the Peten and the southern lowlands were abandoned, the calendar was discontinued, and the structure of religious life and the state decayed. No one has been able to explain this sudden and dramatic collapse of Maya civilization, the subject of a prolonged debate in American archaeology.

The Classic Maya collapse has varied traditional explanations, most of them unilineal and monocausal. They have included catastrophes, such as earthquakes, hurricanes, and disease. Ecological theories mention exhausted soils, water loss, and erosion. Internal social revolt might have led the peasants to rebel against cruel rule by their elitist overlords. Each of these hypotheses has been rejected because either the evidence is insufficient or the explanations are oversimplified. Another hypothesis is popular: a disruptive invasion of Maya territory by peoples from the highlands. Certainly evidence reports Toltec intrusions into the lowlands, although it is hard to say how broad the effects of the invasions were, or what damage they did to the fabric of Maya society.

Invasion and the limited evidence for population stress and ecological stress do not by themselves provide an explanation for the Classic Maya collapse. Most people now agree that invasion, ecological stress, and social disruption had something to do with the collapse. But how do we interpret the evidence, and how widely can we extrapolate over Maya country the parts of the archaeological picture?

A multifactor approach is now universally accepted as the only valid avenue of inquiry. Important studies of the problem have recently been published in book form.[23] The interested reader is urged to consult this volume, for only a summary of the multivariate model for the Maya collapse is possible here. In this model, the collapse of Teotihuacán placed the Maya in a position to enlarge their managerial functions in Mesoamerican trade. Competition between ceremonial centers was intensified as the elite became increasingly involved in warfare, trade and competition between regions, and prestige activities, many of them secular. This competition for prestige and wealth grew during the Late Classic. The result was a frenzy of prestige-building projects and increased pressure on the labor force that resulted in lower agricultural productivity. Malnutrition and disease increased during the Late Classic Maya, the latter perhaps reached endemic or pandemic proportions under circumstances of warfare or crop failure. Population loss may have been so severe that recovery was impossible and productivity reduced to grossly inadequate levels. If the elite failed to make social or economic adjustments to the drastically changed situation, then collapse of the system was inevitable, for they recruited their numbers from a very small segment of the population.

The Maya were but a small part of the Mesoamerican scene. The highland peoples from central Mexico encroached on the Maya lowlands more and more during the Late Classic, with what effect it is still uncertain. But trade networks to the west must have gone through some disruption. This trade was critical to the prestige and survival of the Maya elite. Because of all these internal and external stresses and strains, the Maya society in the lowlands, at least five million souls, partly urbanized and living with much sociocultural integration, was no longer structurally viable. At some time between A.D. 771 and 790, these pressures came together and quickly collapsed the sociocultural system over much of the lowlands. And the system could not recover from the shock.

The model has, of course, many gaps, especially in not showing how the collapse affected the lowland population and why the Maya did not simply adopt several useful technological devices known to them that could have dramatically enhanced agricultural productivity. But we can be fairly sure that varied, interacting pressures helped throw down the Maya civilization. To test all the hypotheses in this comprehensive model will require large quantities of new field data and many new excavations.

The collapse was by no means universal, for the Maya elite continued to flourish on a reduced scale in northern Yucatán. We do not know how much of the population from the collapsed area moved north to this region.

THE TOLTECS

Although by A.D. 900 the Classic period had ended, Maya religious and social orders continued in northern Yucatán (Figure 21.11). The continuity of the ancient Mesoamerican tradition survived unscathed. Basic economic patterns and technological traditions were retained, although religious and ideological patterns and priorities were disarranged. New ceremonial centers were built, but war and violence became primary as militaristic rulers achieved dominance in Mesoamerica.

Postclassic
A.D. 900 to 1521

We have mentioned the unsettled Postclassic political conditions caused by population movements and tribal warfare. Many groups of invaders vied for political power in central Mexico until the Toltecs achieved dominance in the tenth century. The oral legends of the Aztec rulers, who followed the Toltecs, describe how the Toltecs came into Mesoamerica from the northwest frontiers beyond the civilized world. They settled at Tula, 37 miles (57 km) north of the Valley of Mexico, where they built a ceremonial center dedicated to their serpent god, Quetzalcóatl (Figure 21.12).[24] Tula is notable for its animal sculpture and pottery styles but it did not have a long life, for around A.D. 1160 some

Toltec

Tula
A.D. 900

A.D. 1160

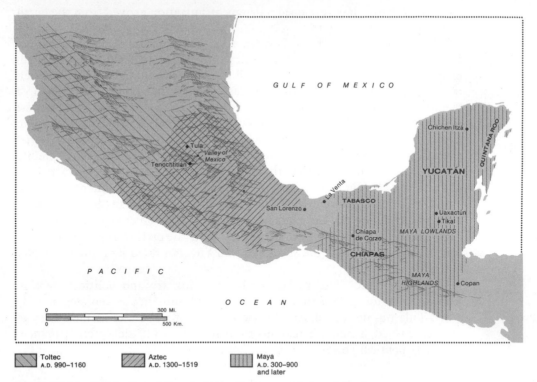

Toltec
A.D. 990–1160

Aztec
A.D. 1300–1519

Maya
A.D. 300–900
and later

Figure 21.11 Distribution of Classic Maya, Toltec, and Aztec civilizations.

Figure 21.12 The Toltec site at Tula is dominated by a stepped platform with giant columns modeled like warriors.

newcomers with a less developed religious organization arrived from the north and destroyed the temples.

Chichén Itzá

Chichén Itzá in northern Yucatán was an important Maya ceremonial center in Postclassic times. In the tenth century A.D., Chichén Itzá was occupied and enlarged by Toltec warriors.[25] It became the colonial capital by which the Toltec controlled the two great resources of the northern Yucatán: a talented, well-organized population, and the massive salt fields along the coast (Figure 21.13). The invaders introduced no new architectural elements to Chichén Itzá, but still used Maya hieroglyphs. Chichén Itzá boasted a sacred pool or *cenote* into which numerous sacrificial offerings were thrown. The site

Mayapán

was abandoned in the thirteenth century. But the city of Mayapán rose to prominence elsewhere in northern Yucatán, a walled settlement clustered around a ceremonial center. At least 12,000 people lived in this Maya city, which was ruled by the Cocom family. Maya civilization enjoyed a resurgence in this area, although Mayapán declined during the civil wars of the fifteenth century. A century later the Spanish found Yucatán ruled by numerous petty chiefs.

The militaristic Toltecs were the leading military and political force in Mesoamerica for such a short time that their influence evaporated rapidly when Tula was destroyed. Another period of political chaos in the Valley of Mexico ensued, as more barbarians from the north ("Chichimecs") maneuvered for political power.

Figure 21.13 Chichén Itzá, Temple of the Warriors.

When the first Spanish conquistadores arrived in highland Mexico in 1519, they were astounded by the rich civilization they found there. The capital city of Tenochtitlán was the headquarters of a series of militaristic Aztec kings, who ruled over a wide area by religious decree, constant human sacrifice, and bloodthirsty campaigning. Within a few years of Spanish contact Aztec civilization literally ceased to exist. Tenochtitlán was reduced to rubble after a siege that lasted ninety-one days.

The Aztec were one of the seven Chichimec tribes who sought power in the Valley of Mexico after the Toltec fell.[26] They seem to have arrived in the area about 1193, a politically weak but aggressive group who barely retained their own identity. Eventually an Aztec city was founded on Lake Texoco, a remarkable settlement reclaimed from swamp that became Tenochtitlán. The Aztec attempted to live peaceably with their neighbors, and their city flourished as an important market for the Valley. In the early fifteenth century, however, the Aztec quarreled with their neighbors and embarked on a ferocious campaign of military conquest that made them an independent city-state in their own right. Their remarkable leader was a counselor and general named Tlacaelel, who was the adviser to a whole series of Aztec kings, and the real ruler of the Aztec in everything but name. It was he who encouraged the use of terror and human sacrifice as a means of controlling conquered territory. The rich tribute from conquered states and cities enabled Aztec society to expand dramatically. Their conquests took them to the Pacific Coast and as far south as Guatemala.

Tenochtitlán was a spectacular sight in the sixteenth century, with enormous markets where more than sixty thousand people are said to have assembled every day.[27] The market sold every form of foodstuff and provided every luxury and service. The principal streets of Tenochtitlán were of beaten earth, there were at least forty pyramids adorned with fine decorated stonework. Tenochtitlán was certainly larger, and probably cleaner, than many European cities of the time (Figure 21.14).

Large residential areas surrounded the central precincts, while houses with chinampa gardens lay on the outskirts of the city. Six major canals ran through Tenochtitlán and there were three causeways that connected the city with the mainland. At least 200,000 canoes provided convenient transport for the people of the city, which was divided into sixty or seventy well-organized wards. Tenochtitlán was a magnificent city set in a green swath of country and a clear lake, with a superb backdrop of snow-capped volcanoes.

Aztec society was moving closer and closer to a rigid aristocratic class system at the time of Spanish contact. No commoner was allowed to enter a waiting room in the palace used by nobles. The king was revered as a semigod and had virtually despotic powers. A highly stratified class system supported the king's power. The king was elected from a limited class group of *pipiltin*, or nobles. There were full time professional merchants called *pochteca*, also a class of warriors whose ranks were determined by the numbers of people they had killed in battle. Groups of lineages called *calpulli* (big house) were the

Figure 21.14 The central plaza of Tenochtitlán, with a large temple at left — an artist's impression.

most significant factor in most peoples' religious, social, and political life. Many of them coincided with wards in the city. The great mass of the people were free people or *macehualtin*, while serfs, landless peasants, and slaves made up the bottom strata of society.

Much of Aztec society's efforts went toward placating the formidable war and rain gods, Huitzilpochtli and Tlaloc, deities whose benevolence was assured by constant human sacrifices. These sacrifices reached their peak at the end of each fifty-two-year cycle like those of the Maya when the continuity of the world would be secured by bloodthirsty rites.

By the time of Spanish contact in 1519, Aztec society seems to have been functioning in a world of frenetic and bloody terrorism that flourished at the behest of the imperial rulers. On one memorable occasion — the dedication of the enlarged portion of the great temple of Huitzilopochtli — the ruler sacrificed 80,000 victims. Most of the victims were either captured slaves or prisoners of war. The nobles consumed so much human flesh in preference to animal meat that military campaigns were virtually essential to provide a steady stream of captives. The aristocracy grew in numbers very sharply, for they were allowed to marry commoners and their children became nobles as well. So the demands for tribute both from subject states and from the free people of the city grew ever larger and more exacting. The internal and external strains on the Aztec state grew more and more intense, especially since the rulers could never trust the loyalty of their vassal states, a factor that became important during the Spanish conquest of the Aztec.

The Aztec were one of the most important groups in Mesoamerica when the Spaniards first explored the New World. From coastal villagers in the lowlands they heard stories of the fabled rich kingdoms in the high interior. Soon the conquistadores pressed inland to check on these stories of gold and other marvelous riches. Hernando Cortes was the first Spaniard to come into contact with the Aztec, now ruled by Moteczuma II, a despotic ruler who assassinated most of his predecessor's counselors and had himself deified. Moteczuma's reign was disturbed by constant unfavorable omens of impending doom, and predictions that the god Quetzalcoatl would return one day to reclaim his homeland. The king was deeply alarmed by the reports of Spanish ships on the coast. There were, then, considerable internal psychological stresses on Moteczuma and his followers before the Spaniards even arrived.

It took Cortes only two years to reduce the Aztec to slaves, and their marvelous capital to rubble. A handful of explorers on horses (imported), armed with a few muskets, were able to overthrow one of the most powerful tribute states in the history of America. Without question Cortes's task was made easier by both rebellious subjects of the Aztec and the extraordinary stresses the Aztec had placed on themselves.

In the next 160 years (by 1680), the Indian population of the Aztec heartland was reduced from about 1.2 million to some 70,000 — a decimation resulting from war, slavery, disease, overwork and exploitation, famine, and malnutrition. Mesoamerica as a whole lost between 85 and 95 percent of its indigenous population during that 160-year period. Only a few fragments of the fabulous Mesoamerican cultural tradition survived into modern times, as the Indian population faced a new and uncertain chapter in their long history.

Chronological Table M

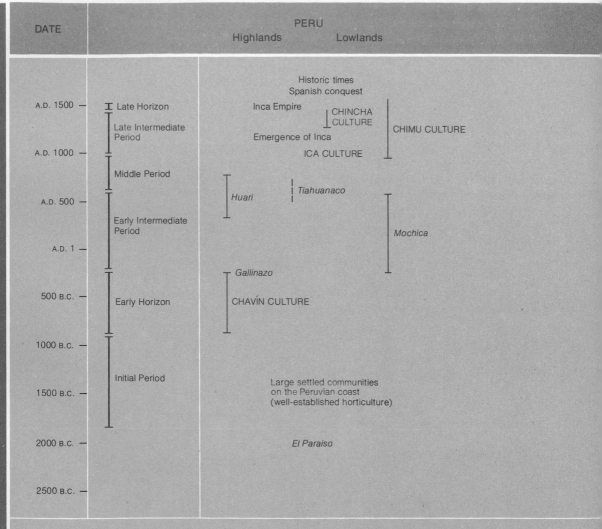

DATE		PERU	
		Highlands	Lowlands

Historic times
Spanish conquest

A.D. 1500 — ⫶ Late Horizon   Inca Empire   ⌐ CHINCHA
                                              ⌐ CULTURE   ⌐ CHIMU CULTURE
              Late Intermediate   Emergence of Inca
              Period
A.D. 1000 —   ICA CULTURE   ⌐

              Middle Period   Tiahuanaco
A.D. 500 —   Huari
              Early Intermediate   Mochica
              Period
A.D. 1 —

                                    Gallinazo
500 B.C. —   Early Horizon   CHAVÍN CULTURE

1000 B.C. —

              Initial Period   Large settled communities
1500 B.C. —   on the Peruvian coast
                                    (well-established horticulture)

2000 B.C. —   El Paraiso

2500 B.C. —

Chapter Twenty-Two

EARLY CIVILIZATION IN PERU

PREVIEW

🌿 The early civilizations of coastal Peru developed where people had flourished in sedentary settlements based on intensive exploitation of coastal resources. About 2500 B.C. cotton was introduced to the coast, at a time when much larger sites with public works begin to appear in the archaeological record.

🌿 During the so-called Initial Period of Peruvian prehistory, the coastal peoples began to move inland and to practice irrigation in river valleys, but fishing remained important on the coast. The level of material culture throughout Peru continued to be almost startlingly simple, despite the fact that large settled communities enjoyed political autonomy and erected large complexes of public buildings.

🌿 New cultural developments came to the coast as the Chavín art style and the religious beliefs associated with it spread widely over Peru between 900 and 200 B.C. Settlements like Chavín de Huántar became important ceremonial centers unifying many villages with a common religious belief. Chavín provided a vital basis for the spectacular cultural developments of later centuries.

🌿 After the Chavín style disappeared, a series of coastal kingdoms developed, whose political and economic influence spread beyond their immediate valley homelands. These empires included the Mochica, Lima, and Nazca, which were remarkable for their fine pottery styles and expert copper and gold metallurgy. They flourished in the first millennium A.D.

🌿 The Middle Period of later Peruvian prehistory lasted from A.D. 600 to 1000, and saw the rise of numerous small states that traded with one another and depended heavily on irrigation agriculture. We describe the highland kingdoms of Huari and Tiahuanaco, which saw an acceleration of the process of broader unification and an emergent militarism; one state followed another in supremacy in a volatile succession.

🌿 Around A.D. 1000, Chimu, with its great capital at Chan Chan on the northern coast, dominated a wide area of the lowlands. Its compounds reflect a stratified state, with many expert craftspeople and a complex material culture.

⚓ The Late Horizon of Peruvian prehistory sees the unification of highlands and lowlands under the Inca Empire, which may have emerged as early as A.D. 1200 and lasted until the Spanish Conquest in A.D. 1534. The Inca rulers were masters of bureaucracy and military organization and governed a highly structured state — one, however, that was so weakened by civil war that it fell easily to the conquistadore Francisco Pizarro and his small army of adventurers.

Chronological
Table M

The coastal foundations of Peruvian civilization began to develop after 2500 B.C., when the people of the coast adopted more sedentary settlement patterns and population densities rose more rapidly.[1*]

COASTAL FOUNDATIONS

In time, more permanent settlements, like El Paraiso, were sited at the mouths of rivers where they could draw on both maritime and littoral resources (Figure 22.1).[2] Such sites were large enough to have public works, El Paraiso boasting of complexes of stone-built rooms that took much labor to construct.

2000 B.C.

Coastal settlements like El Paraiso were settled by complex societies with well-established social orders.[3] Yet, with the exception of fine fabrics, the inhabitants had but the simplest of material possessions.[4]

Initial Period
1900 to 1800 B.C.

The *Initial Period* of Peruvian prehistory begins with the appearance of pottery on the coast, and with the tendency for large settlements to move inland, probably a sign that intensive agriculture, involving irrigation, had begun. Ceremonial centers built of adobe begin to appear at sites like Las Haldas on the northern coast, headquarters for a dense farming population. Food surpluses were devoted to canal and road building as well as the support of the craft production. An aristocracy with totalitarian powers gradually grew from generations of priest leaders. Although the larger settlements shared a common cultural tradition, they were still autonomous political units holding sway over a relatively small area.

THE EARLY HORIZON: CHAVÍN

Most cultural developments on the coast came from small societies achieving more social and political unity over wider areas. Not until about 900 B.C. did a semblance of greater cultural unity begin to appear in Peru. At about this time a distinctive art style in stone and precious metals appeared in northern Peru.

* See page 392 for notes to Chapter 22.

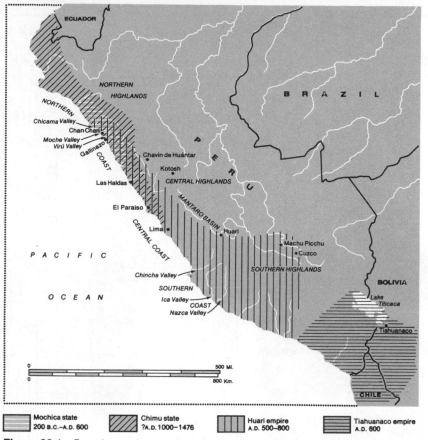

| | Mochica state
200 B.C.–A.D. 600 | | Chimu state
?A.D. 1000–1476 | | Huari empire
A.D. 500–800 | | Tiahuanaco empire
A.D. 600 |

Figure 22.1 Peruvian archaeological sites mentioned in this chapter. Approximate distributions of various traditions are also shown.

Within a century this Chavín style had spread far over the coast and highlands, forming an *Early Horizon* in Peruvian prehistory. The Chavín style takes its name from remarkable sculptures at Chavín de Huántar in the northern highlands.[5] The site lies in a fertile valley 3300 meters (10,000 ft) above sea level, its elaborate stone platforms decorated with sculptures and clay reliefs. Galleries and small rooms were built inside the platforms. The original temple housed a remarkable carving of a jaguar-like human with hair in the form of serpents (Figure 22.2).

Chavín art is dominated by animal and human forms, with jaguar motifs predominating. Humans, gods, and animals are given jaguar-like fangs or limbs. Snakes flow from the bodies of many figures. The art has a grace that is grotesque and slightly sinister. Many figures were carved in stone, others in clay or bone.

The Chavín style is so widely distributed that it must represent more than merely art for art's sake. Settlements like Chavín de Huántar were important ceremonial centers unifying surrounding farming villages with a common

Early Horizon
900 to 200 B.C.

Early Civilization in Peru   359

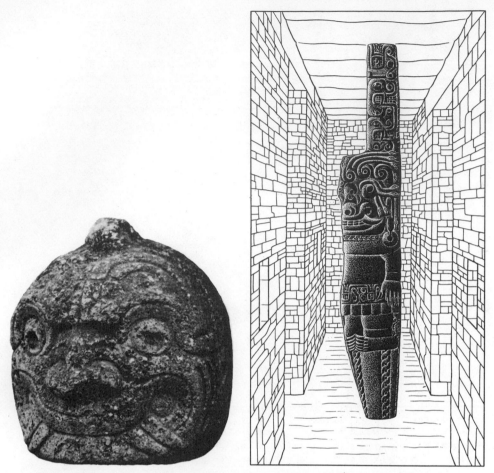

Figure 22.2 A Chavín wall insert (approximately 20 cm high) showing feline features, from Chavín de Huántar and a Chavín carving on a pillar in the temple interior at Chavín de Huántar. Stone insets such as these are common on the walls of the Chavín ceremonial buildings.

religious concern. Thus, a tradition of settled life was reinforced by a religious philosophy shared by most Peruvians. Chavín flourished for 700 years. It **200 B.C.** disappeared around 200 B.C., although some stylistic themes (and, presumably, religious philosophies) survived into later times. Chavín's influence extended into southern Peru. It provided a vital basis for the spectacular cultural developments of the first Peruvian kingdoms, which flourished after A.D. 200.

Some people believe that there are connections between the Olmec art tradition of Mesoamerica and the Chavín. Radiocarbon dates show that the two traditions are contemporary: the connections between them are, however, unproven. Nor do many authorities accept the notion that Chinese voyagers to South America provided the inspiration for Chavín art.[6]

THE EARLY INTERMEDIATE PERIOD: EARLY KINGDOMS

After the Chavín style disappeared, cultural and economic transition ensued in northern Peru, but its sociopolitical meaning is not clear. Sedentary life was now common, and the Chavín style with its religious philosophy may have provided a symbolic catalyst for larger political and economic units based on ceremonial centers and priestly leaders. Certainly substantial public works, foreshadowed in earlier centuries, were undertaken in the north. One settlement, Gallinazo, was built on the plains of the Virú Valley as a complex of ceremonial adobe buildings and pyramids, covering at least 1.3 square miles (2 sq km).[7] Approximately 5000 people lived at Gallinazo, and many more farmers dwelled elsewhere in Virú. Large irrigation works were begun in this and other coastal valleys. The population expanded rapidly and more villages and towns were constructed near the field systems and canals. The upper reaches of Virú were guarded by four great forts, a sign of warfare and competition.

Early Intermediate Period
200 B.C. to A.D. 600

By 200 B.C., the Mochica state had begun in northern coastal Peru. It continued to flourish for 800 years. Its origins lay in the Chicama and Moche valleys, with great ceremonial centers.[8] At Moche itself, two massive terraced pyramids dominate the landscape, one a temple and burial place, the other probably headquarters of the Mochica rulers. The Mochica people are best known for their beautiful pottery, especially their "stirrup-handled jars." These drinking vessels were created by craftsworkers who modeled human portraits, plants, and animals (Figure 22.3). Other Mochica were skillful smiths, casting gold into fine ornaments and making simple copper tools and weapons. Metallurgy, already practiced simply in Chavín times, reached extraordinary heights of sophistication in these cultures. Goldworkers produced fine hammered ornaments and trappings for the aristocracy that reveal an intimate and expert knowledge of the potentials of the metal.

Mochica
200 B.C. to A.D. 600

The central and southern coasts of Peru were experiencing somewhat similar development while the Mochica state flourished.[9] The valleys of the central coast supported fewer large settlements or towns. Some pyramids were erected at fairly substantial ceremonial centers; burials attest to important leaders who journeyed to the next world accompanied by fine ornaments and human sacrifices. A common pottery style (the Lima), adorned with painted geometric designs, is found in several valleys, possibly indicating common political and economic leadership.

Lima

The southern coast was dominated by another pottery style, the Nazca. Nazca vessels (Figure 22.3), bearing elaborate multicolored patterns, had their origins in earlier local pottery traditions. As on the northern coast, valley populations were drawn toward large ceremonial centers, whose adobe temples and platforms served as burial places and were surrounded by dwellings.

Nazca

These coastal states often influenced neighboring valleys or a territory wider than the local sphere of governance reflected in their own sources of food and other resources. In part this was due to the development of longer

Figure 22.3 Mochica portrait vessel about 29 centimeters (11.4 in) high (left) and a Nazca vessel about 18 centimeters (7 in).

trading networks, barter mechanisms that, as in Maya country, brought neighboring societies and ceremonial centers into closer contact and competition, as the Virú forts show. The usual complicated multiplier effects gradually moved Peruvian society toward larger social units and greater complexity.

THE MIDDLE PERIOD: STATES BEGIN UNIFICATION

Middle Period
A.D. 600 to 1000

By the Middle Period, Peruvian societies benefited from extensive irrigation and terrace agriculture, the latter based on systematic exploitation of hillside gardens. Agricultural populations concentrated around urban centers, the larger of which ruled regional kingdoms. Each small state had its own government and artistic tradition. The states competed for land and food resources; their leaders vied for power and prestige. Times were ripe for wider economic, political, and social initiatives. The rulers of Tiahuanaco and Huari in highland Peru were ambitious enough to try.

Huari

Huari
A.D. 500 to 800

An important ceremonial center had been built at Huari in the Manteco basin before Tiahuanaco achieved importance.[10] Huari lies on a hill, with huge stone walls and many dwellings that cover several square miles. Its inhabitants enjoyed wide trade, particularly with the southern coast of Peru. Eventually,

Huari power extended over a far larger tract of territory than any earlier Peruvian state. It embraced not only much of the Peruvian Andes but an enormous span of the coast, as far north as former Mochica country. Its frontiers were probably expanded by religious conversion, trade, and especially warfare. Storehouses and roads were probably maintained by the state, as the organized control of food and labor became essential to the power structure. The Huari empire was a political, social, and religious turning point for the Peruvians. Small, regional states were replaced by much larger political units. Common religious cults unified hundreds of ceremonial centers. As urban living and planning became more important, the government led the way in agricultural life, especially in northern Peru.

Huari itself was abandoned around A.D. 800, perhaps after being destroyed by enemies, but we have no clear evidence. The empire also collapsed. But the influence of this state did not disappear with it: the widespread Huari art styles were used for another 200 years, and the leaders of Huari had created administrative and social precedents that reemerged in later centuries.

Tiahuanaco

During the first millennium A.D., the highlands supported many small states. Tiahuanaco, at the southern end of Lake Titicaca, was one of the greatest population centers during the Middle Period.[11] The arid lands in which it lies were irrigated, supporting a population of perhaps 20,000 near the monumental structures at the center of Tiahuanaco. A large earth platform faced with stones dominates the site (Figure 22.4). Nearby, a rectangular enclosure is bounded with a row of upright stones entered by a doorway carved with an anthropomorphic god. Smaller buildings, enclosures, and huge statues are also near the ceremonial structures.

Tiahuanaco was flourishing around A.D. 600, acquiring much of its prosperity from trade around the lake's southern shores. Copperworking was especially important; it probably developed independently of the copper technology on the northern coast. The art styles of Tiahuanaco are distinctive and widespread. Such motifs as jaguars and eagles occur over much of southern Peru, as do the anthropomorphic gods depicted at Tiahuanaco, attended by lesser deities or messengers. The influence of Tiahuanaco art and culture is also found in Bolivia, the southern Andes, and perhaps as far afield as northwestern Argentina.

Tiahuanaco
A.D. 600

THE LATE INTERMEDIATE PERIOD:
LATE COASTAL STATES

Around A.D. 1000, new kingdoms arose to replace the political vacuum left by Huari. At least four states thrived in the coastal valleys, dimly recalled in Inca legends.

Late Intermediate Period
A.D. 1000 to 1476

The northern coast was dominated by Chimú, with a great capital at Chan Chan in the Moche Valley.[12] The ruins of Chan Chan cover at least 10 square

Chimú
A.D. 1000? to 1476

miles (26 sq km). Ten great quadrangles of ground were enclosed by thick adobe walls over 12 meters (40 ft) high (Figure 22.5). Courtyards, dwellings, and richly furnished graves occur inside the quadrangles. Some dwellings were lavishly decorated, obviously the homes of Chimú nobles. The great enclosure walls perhaps demarcated living areas for distinct kinship, craft, or religious groups. Each leader seems to have built his own compound, which was subdivided into distinct areas for different functions.

Chan Chan was an important center of Chimú religious and political life. Large rural populations lived nearby in the Moche Valley, occupying enclosures and houses that lacked the fine architecture of Chan Chan. The centers were probably linked by state-maintained highways, themselves used in later times by the Incas. Major irrigation systems ensured agricultural surpluses to support craftsworkers and the aristocratic superstructure of the state. Skillful Chimú copperworkers alloyed arsenic and copper to make bronze, while other artisans produced magnificent gold ornaments for the elite.[13]

The southern coastal peoples of the early second millennium A.D. did not live in large cities like their northern neighbors. They are named after two

Figure 22.4 Gateway of the Sun at Tiahuanaco, made from one block of lava. The central figure is known as the Gateway God; notice its jaguar mouth and serpent-ray headdress. The running figures flanking the god are often called messengers.

Figure 22.5 Chan Chan: oblique air photograph of a walled enclosure or compound.

dominant pottery styles: the Ica and Chincha.[14] The two pottery styles mingled, as local leaders jockeyed for military and political supremacy on the southern coast. Chincha was dominant after A.D. 1425, perhaps because of increased military power which enabled its users to raid far outside their home valley.

THE LATE HORIZON: THE INCA STATE

The Late Horizon of Peruvian archaeology is also the shortest, dating from A.D. 1476 to 1534. It is the period of the Inca empire, when those mighty Andean rulers held sway over an enormous area of highland and lowland country.[15] The Inca empire began in the Cuzco Valley of the Andes foothills, where humble peasants lived in stone huts.

Oral traditions speak of at least eight Inca rulers who reigned between A.D. 1200 and 1438, but these genealogies are hardly reliable. The ninth Inca king, Pachacuti Inca Yupanqui (1438–1471), was the first leader well known to us. He gained control of the southern Peruvian highlands and laid the foundations of Inca power in military campaigns. His successor, Topa Inca Yupanqui (1471–1493), expanded the Inca empire into Ecuador, northern Argentina, parts of Bolivia, and Chile. His armies also conquered the Chimú state, whose

Early Civilization in Peru   365

water supplies Topa already controlled. The best Chimú craftsworkers were carried off to work for the court of the Incas. Another king, Huayna Capac, ruled for thirty-four years after Topa Inca and pushed the empire deeper into Ecuador.

At the height of its prosperity, the Inca state was the culmination of earlier cultural traditions and empire-building efforts. Inca rulers were masters of bureaucracy and military organization, governing a highly structured state. The king, or Inca, was considered divine and ruled with great ceremony; he was surrounded by an elite aristocracy of blood relatives as well as able administrators, who achieved status by ability. An elaborate civil service controlled every aspect of Inca life by a large and apparently effective bureaucracy of civil servants.

Military service, farming, road building, and other activities were supported by a ruthless system of taxation, mostly in the form of forced labor. All corners of the empire were connected by well-maintained roads constantly traversed by messengers moving on foot or with llamas. A highly efficient army was armed with spears, slings, and clubs. The Inca used his soldiers to maintain his power. The official road system enabled him to move army units from one end of his kingdom to the other very rapidly. Conquered territories were incorporated into the communications network. Often the defeated ruler would be offered the governorship of his former domains within the empire. Revolts were prevented by moving entire conquered populations from their homelands into new areas.

Inca religion had a supreme creator figure, Viracocha, but the Sun God was more actively worshipped. Ritual and divination had much importance. A lunar calendar was maintained by the priests, but no writing was used for the state's business. The Inca relied on the *quipu*, knotted strings, for computing state accounts and inventories; the *quipu* seems to have been a highly effective accounting system that more than made up for the lack of writing.

THE SPANISH CONQUEST

At the time of the Spanish Conquest, 6,000,000 people may have been living under Inca rule, most of them in small villages dispersed around religious and political centers. Some of these settlements, like Cuzco in the Andes, did, however, reach considerable size. In these urban complexes, the ceremonial centers were built of carefully laid stones. Military, religious, and government buildings were large, as in the Cuzco area. Such urban centers as Machu Picchu, high in the Andes (Figure 22.6), are famous for their fine masonry structures.

The fact that they worked in villages rather than cities did not prevent craftsworkers from producing major works of art in silver and gold. Bronze was widely used also, mostly for agricultural implements and weapons. Inca pottery is distinctive, brightly painted in black, white, and red geometric designs. But despite the wide distribution of Inca pots and artifacts, regional pottery

Cuzco

Machu Picchu

Figure 22.6 Machu Picchu. Forgotten for 400 years after the Spanish Conquest, it was rediscovered by the American explorer Hiram Bingham in 1912.

styles flourished because the village potters, many of whom were conquered subjects rather than Inca, continued the cultural traditions of earlier centuries.

The Inca state was the culminating achievement of prehistoric Peruvians, a society that reached extraordinary heights despite a simple technology and an illiterate bureaucracy. It was the result of centuries of gradual cultural evolution, which accelerated rapidly after the first complex societies arose in the Initial Period.

The Spanish conquistadores stopped these traditions dead when they landed in Peru in 1532. When Francisco Pizarro arrived, the Inca state was in some political chaos. Inca Huayna Capac had died in an epidemic in A.D. 1525.

Spanish Conquest
A.D. 1532

The empire was plunged into a civil war between his son Huascar and another son, Atahuallpa, half-brother to Huascar. Atahuallpa eventually prevailed, but, as he moved south from Ecuador to consolidate his territory, he learned that Pizarro had landed in Peru.

The Spaniards had vowed to make Peru part of Spain and were bent on plunder and conquest. Pizarro arrived in the guise of a diplomat, captured Atahuallpa by treachery, ransomed him for a huge quantity of gold, and then brutally murdered him. A year later the Spaniards captured the Inca capital with a tiny army. They took over the state bureaucracy and appointed Manco Capac as puppet ruler. Three years later, Manco Capac turned on his masters in a bloody revolt. Its suppression finally destroyed the greatest of the Peruvian empires.

A.D. 1533

A.D. 1536

NOTES

1 ARCHAEOLOGY

1. Glyn Daniel's *A Hundred and Fifty Years of Archaeology*, Duckworth, London, 1975, chap. 1, contains a useful summary of archaeology's early development.

2. Margaret T. Hodgen, *Early Anthropology in the Sixteenth and Seventeenth Centuries*, University of Pennsylvania Press, Philadelphia, 1964, summarizes the events described in this paragraph.

3. For the history of anthropology see: T. K. Penniman, *A Hundred Years of Anthropology*, Humanities Press, New York, 1965. The nature and scope of anthropology is covered by Peter J. Pelto, *The Nature of Anthropology*, Charles Merrill Books, Columbus, Ohio, 1966.

4. A good basic text on physical anthropology: Mark L. Weiss and Alan E. Mann, *Human Biology and Behavior: An Anthropological Perspective*, 2nd ed., Little, Brown, Boston, 1978.

5. The best treatment of this complex subject: A. L. Kroeber and Clyde Kluckhohn, *Culture: A Critical Review of Concepts and Definitions*, Papers of the Peabody Museum of Archaeology and Ethnology, vol. 147, no. 1, Cambridge, Mass., 1952.

6. James Deetz, *Invitation to Archaeology*, Natural History Press, New York, 1967, p. 77.

7. J. G. D. Clark, *Archaeology and Society*, Methuen, London, and Barnes & Noble, New York, 1965, pp. 94–95.

8. Howard Carter, *The Tomb of Tut-ankh-amun*, Macmillan, London, 1923–1933.

9. Robert C. Dunnell, *Systematics in Prehistory*, Free Press, New York, 1971. This volume is a fundamental source on basic definitions.

10. For this and other basic concepts, see Brian M. Fagan, *In the Beginning*, 3rd ed., Little, Brown, Boston, 1978.

11. Dunnell, *Systematics in Prehistory*, p. 4.

12. Mary D. Leakey, *Olduvai Gorge*, vol. 3, Cambridge University Press, New York, 1971.

13. Leonard Woolley, *Excavations at Ur*, Barnes and Noble, New York, 1954.

14. Kent V. Flannery's *The Early Mesoamerican Village* (Academic Press, New York, 1976) contains invaluable essays and experiments in settlement archaeology.

15. Seriation has generated an enormous literature. James Deetz, *Invitation to Archaeology*, Natural History Press, Garden City, N.J., 1967, has an admirable introductory account.

16. Richard MacNeish, ed. *Prehistory of the Tehuacán Valley*, vol. 3, University of Texas Press, Austin, 1970.

17. V. G. Childe, *Piecing Together the Past*, Routledge and Kegan Paul, London, 1956, has a very fine account.

18. Joseph W. Michels, *Dating Methods in Archaeology*, Seminar Press, New York, 1973.

19. G. Brent Dalrymple and Mason Lamphere, *Potassium Argon Dating: Principles, Techniques and Applications in Geochronology*, W. H. Freeman, San Francisco, 1970.

20. Fagan, *In the Beginning*, pp. 134–138. Frank Hole and Robert F. Heizer, *An Introduction to Prehistoric Archaeology*, Holt, Rinehart and Winston, New York, 1973, chaps. 10–13.

21. A popular summary of this subject: Colin Renfrew, *Before Civilization*, Knopf, New York, 1973.

22. Bryant Bannister and William J. Robinson, "Tree-Ring Dating in Archaeology," *World Archaeology*, 1975 (7,2), 210–225. Also Bryant Bannister's "Dendrochronology" in Don Brothwell and Eric Higgs, eds., *Science in Archaeology*, 2nd ed., Thames and Hudson, London, 1969, pp. 191–205.

23. Samuel Kramer, *The Sumerians*, University of Chicago Press, Chicago, 1963.

24. Robert L. Fleischer, "Advances in Fission Track Dating, "*World Archaeology*, 1975 (7:2), pp. 136–150.

25. Jeffrey L. Bada and Patricia Masters Helfman, "Amino Acid Racemization Dating of Fossil Bones," *World Archaeology*, 1975 (7:2), pp. 160–173. On thermoluminescence, see Mark Aitken, "Thermoluminescence and the Archaeologist," *Antiquity*, 1977 (51), 11–19.

26. For some techniques, see O. G. S. Crawford, *Archaeology in the Field*, Praeger, New York, 1953, and Michael Schiffer and John House, *The Cache River Archaeological Project*, Arkansas Archaeological Survey, Fayetteville, 1977.

27. Gordon Willey, *Prehistoric Settlement in the Virú Valley, Peru*, Bureau of American Ethnology, Washington, D.C., 1953.

28. Lewis Binford, "A Consideration of Archaeological Research Design," *American Antiquity*, 1964 (29), pp. 425–441. Also James W. Meuller, ed., *Sampling in Archaeology*, University of Arizona Press, Tucson, 1975.

29. The classic source on excavation: Sir Mortimer Wheeler, *Archaeology from the Earth*, Clarendon Press, Oxford, 1954. See also: Philip Barker, *Techniques of Archaeological Excavation*, Batsford, London, 1977; Thomas R. Hester, Robert F. Heizer, and John A. Graham, *Field Methods in Archaeology*, Mayfield, Palo Alto, 1975.

30. Mary D. Leakey, *Olduvai Gorge*.

31. River gravels were much studied by archaeologists of the 1930s and 1940s. The subject is highly complex; a glimpse of its difficulties can be obtained from K. P. Oakley, *Frameworks for Dating Fossil Man*, Aldine, Chicago, 1964, chap. 7.

32. Two typical cave excavations are described in Jesse D. Jennings, *Danger Cave*, University of Utah Anthropological Papers no. 27, 1957, and C. B. M. McBurney, *The Haua Fteah (Cyrenaica)*, Cambridge University Press, Cambridge, 1967.

33. Joe Ben Wheat, *The Olsen-Chubbock Site*, Society for American Archaeology, Washington, D.C., 1972.

34. An enormous literature is available. For Mesoamerican sites: Murial Porter Weaver, *The Aztecs, Maya, and Their Predecessors*, Seminar Press, New York, 1972. Two other famous ceremonial complexes are covered in: I. E. S. Edwards, *The Pyramids*, Viking Press, New York, 1973; and R. J. C. Atkinson, *Stonehenge*, Pelican Books, Baltimore, 1960.

35. D. R. Brothwell, *Digging Up Bones*, British Museum, London, 1965.

36. Sir. Leonard Woolley, *Ur Excavations*, vol 2: *The Royal Cemetery*, Publications of the Joint Expedition of the British Museum and of the Museum of the University of Pennsylvania to Mesopotamia, British Museum, London, 1934, pp. 38–39, 41–42.

37. Kwang-chih Chang, *The Archaeology of Ancient China*, 2nd ed., Yale University Press, New Haven, 1968.

38. Sergei I. Rudenko, *The Frozen Tombs of Siberia: The Pazyryk Burials of Iron Age Horsemen*, trans. M. W. Thompson, University of California Press, Berkeley, 1970.

39. Patti Jo Watson, Steven A. LeBlanc, and Charles L. Redman, *Explanation in Archaeology*, Columbia University Press, New York, 1971.

40. Charles L. Redman, ed., *Research and Theory in Current Archaeology*, John Wiley Interscience, New York, 1973, gives guidance to the major controversies; while Lewis R. Binford, *An Archaeological Perspective*, Seminar Press, New York, 1972, is a highly personal account of the "new" archaeology.

41. For the history of the new archaeology see: Lewis R. Binford, *An Archaeological Perspective*, Academic Press, New York, 1972. Also: Charles Redman, ed., *Research and Theory in Modern Archaeology*, John Wiley, New York, 1973.

2 APPROACHES TO WORLD PREHISTORY

1. For an excellent account of human evolution, see Bernard Campbell, *Humankind Emerging*, 2nd ed., Little, Brown, Boston, 1979.

2. Bernard Campbell, *Human Evolution*, 2nd ed., Aldine, Chicago, 1974.

3. For a detailed account of these developments, see Brian M. Fagan, *In the Beginning*, 3rd ed., Little, Brown, Boston, 1978, or Lewis R. Binford, *An Archaeological Perspective*, Seminar Press, New York, 1972.

4. Glyn Daniel, *One Hundred and Fifty Years of Archaeology*, Duckworth, London, 1975, covers these developments.

5. Herbert Spencer, *Social Statistics*, Macmillan, London, 1855.

6. Edward Tylor is well described by Elvin Hatch, *Theories of Man and Culture*, Columbia University Press, New York, 1973.

7. Lewis Morgan, *Ancient Society*, Holt, Rinehart and Winston, New York, 1877.

8. Worsaae was an important figure in nineteenth-century archaeology. His most famous work is *The Primeval Antiquities of Denmark*, Murray, London, 1849.

9. Bruce Trigger, *Before Prehistory*, Holt, Rinehart and Winston, New York, 1968, is the best account of these processes for the beginning reader.

10. Richard MacNeish, ed. *The Prehistory of the Tehuacán Valley*, University of Texas Press, Austin, 1970.

11. Michael Moseley, *The Maritime Foundations of Andean Civilization*, Cummings Publishing, Menlo Park, 1973.

12. One account: James B. Griffin, "The Midlands and the Northeastern United States," in Jesse D. Jennings, ed., *Ancient Native Americans*, W. H. Freeman, San Francisco, 1978, chap. 6.

13. Peter Bellwood, *The Polynesians*, Thames and Hudson, London, 1978.

14. For Boas, see Elvin Hatch, *Theories*.

15. Julian Steward, *A Theory of Culture Change*, University of Illinois Press, Urbana, 1970, p. 1.

16. Leslie White, *The Science of Culture*, Grove Press, New York, 1949.

17. There is a scattered literature on this subject; the beginner is advised to turn to the references given in Brian M. Fagan, *In the Beginning*, or R. F. Hole and Frank Heizer, *An Introduction to Prehistoric Archaeology*, 3rd ed., Holt, Rinehart and Winston, 1973.

18. J. G. D. Clark, *Star Carr*, Cambridge University Press, Cambridge, 1954.

19. Childe wrote a highly fascinating account of his own career, see his "Retrospect," *Antiquity*, 1958, 32, pp. 69–74.

20. Quotation from V. G. Childe, *What Happened in History*, Penguin, Harmondsworth, 1942, p. 22.

21. For an account, see Gordon R. Willey and Jeremy A. Sabloff, *A History of American Archaeology*, W. H. Freeman, San Francisco, 1976.

22. The classic pioneer work is W. J. Sollas, *Ancient Hunters*, Macmillan, London, 1910, which compared entire prehistoric societies with living hunter-gatherers.

23. Two standard references are: Richard Lee and Irven DeVore, *Kalahari Hunter-Gatherers*, Harvard University Press, Cambridge, 1976; and Richard Gould, ed., *Explorations in Ethnoarchaeology*, University of New Mexico Press, Albuquerque, 1978.

24. Marshall Sahlins and Elman Service, eds., *Evolution and Culture*, University of Michigan Press, Ann Arbor, 1960.

25. Elman Service, *Primitive Social Organization*, Random House, New York, 1962, is the standard text.

26. Charles L. Redman, ed., *Research and Theory in Current Archaeology*, Wiley Interscience, New York, 1973.

27. Anatol Rapoport, "Foreword," in W. Buckley, ed., *Modern Systems Research for the Behavioral Sciences*, Aldine, Chicago, 1968, p. xvii.

28. Kent V. Flannery, "Archaeological Systems Theory and Early Mesoamerica," in Betty Meggers, ed., *Anthropological Archaeology in the Americas*, Anthropological Society of Washington, Washington, D.C., 1968, pp. 67–87.

29. Kent V. Flannery, "The Cultural Evolution of Civilizations," *Annual Review of Ecology and Systematics*, 1972, pp. 399–426.

3   THE PLEISTOCENE EPOCH

1. In writing this chapter I have drawn extensively on Richard F. Flint, *Glacial and Quaternary Geology*, John Wiley, New York, 1971, and Karl W. Butzer, *Environment and Archaeology: An Introduction to Pleistocene Geography*, 2nd ed., Aldine-Atherton, Chicago, 1971. An elaborate but somewhat outdated work on the Pleistocene is J. K. Charlesworth, *The Quaternary Era*, Edward Arnold, London, 1957. F. E. Zeuner, *The Pleistocene Period*, Hutchinson, London, 1959,

is another classic. The beginner is better advised to read I. W. Cornwall, *Ice Ages: Their Nature and Effect*, John Baker, London, and Humanities Press, New York, 1970.

2. Extended discussion in R. F. Flint, "The Pliocene-Pleistocene Boundary," in H. E. Wright and D. G. Frey, eds., *International Studies on the Quaternary*, Geological Society of America, Special Paper no. 84, 1965, pp. 497–533. Anyone deeply interested in this problem should read major portions of Glynn Isaac and Elizabeth R. McCown, eds., *Human Origins: Louis Leakey and the East African Evidence*, W. A. Benjamin, Menlo Park, Calif., 1976. This volume contains authoritative essays on all aspects of the problem.

3. The analysis of animal bones is described by Raymond E. Chaplin, *The Study of Animal Bones from Archaeological Sites*, Seminar Press, New York, 1971; also Björn Kurtén, *Pleistocene Mammals of Europe*, Aldine, Chicago, 1968. On extinctions, see Paul Martin and H. E. Wright, eds., *Pleistocene Extinctions: The Search for a Cause*, Yale University Press, New Haven, 1967.

4. Elephants are well described by Kurtén, *Pleistocene Mammals*, chap. 11.

5. Albrecht Penck and Edward Brückner, *Die Alpen im Eiszeitalter*, Tauchnitz, Leipzig, 1909. Their glacial terms have now been replaced by Scandinavian labels in general use: Würm = Weichsel, Ris = Saale, Mindel = Elster. Gunz has no equivalent. The interglacial sites described here are typified by the Swanscombe quarry near London, famous for its human remains and thousands of stone tools. See C. D. Ovey, ed., *The Swanscombe Skull: A Survey of Research on a Pleistocene Site*, Occasional Paper of the Royal Anthropological Institute no. 20, 1964.

6. For details of these complexities, see Karl Butzer and Glynn Isaac, eds., *After the Australopithecines: Stratigraphy, Ecology, and Culture Change in the Middle Pleistocene*, Aldine, Chicago, 1975.

7. See Flint, *Glacial and Quaternary Geology*, chap. 16.

8. Ibid., chap. 24.

9. Kurtén, *Pleistocene Mammals of Europe*, chap. 2.

10. In writing this description of Pleistocene glaciation, I have drawn heavily on Flint's *Glacial and Quaternary Geology*. Many of the details of the glacial stages and interglacials still remain more uncertain than I imply here.

11. Full references are given in chapter 4 of this book, but F. Clark Howell, *Early Man*, Time-Life Books, New York, 1974, has a popular account.

12. For discussion, see Flint, *Glacial and Quaternary Geology*, pp. 382–384.

13. Dramatic evidence for the flooding of the North Sea came with the discovery of a Stone Age harpoon dredged up in a lump of peat from the bed of the Dogger Bank in 1932; see M. C. Burkitt, "A Maglemose Harpoon Dredged up Recently from the North Sea," *Man*, 1932, no. 138, p. 132.

14. For discussion, see W. W. Bishop, "Pliocene Problems Relating to Human Evolution," in Isaac and McCown, eds., *Human Origins*, pp. 139–157.

15. Richard L. Hay, *Geology of the Olduvai Gorge*, University of California Press, Berkeley and Los Angeles, 1975, is a fine example of this type of study.

4 HUMAN ORIGINS

1. Thomas Huxley, *Man's Place in Nature and Other Anthropological Essays* (1911 ed.), Macmillan, London, 1863, p. 77. Huxley's elegant prose is worth reading for sheer pleasure.

2. These controversies are well summarized by: Bernard Campbell, *Humankind Emerging*, 2nd ed., Little, Brown, Boston, 1979; and David Pilbeam, *The Ascent of Man*, Macmillan, New York, 1972. See also John Pfeiffer, *The Emergence of Man*, 3rd ed., Harper & Row, New York, 1978.

3. The tarsier, in north-central Indonesia, is a tree-loving animal thought to be a surviving genus of the oldest primates. Its limbs are adapted to tree life, yet it has features such as a fully swiveling neck that bring it closer to the higher primates. See W. E. Le Gros Clark, *History of the Primates*, 4th ed., British Museum, London, 1954.

4. Elwyn L. Symons, *Primate Evolution*, Macmillan, New York, 1972, summarizes the evidence for this theory.

5. *Ramapithecus* is discussed by Pilbeam, *Ascent of Man*, pp. 91–98. See also Glynn Isaac and Elizabeth McCown, eds., *Human Origins: Louis Leakey and the East African Evidence*, W. A. Benjamin, Menlo Park, Calif., 1976. See also : Elwyn Symons, *Ramapithecus, Scientific American*, May 1977.

6. The literature is complex, controversial, and highly technical. An easily accessible sum-

mary is in Vincent Sarich, "A Molecular Approach to the Question of Human Origins," in Phyllis Dolhinow and Vincent M. Sarich, eds., *Background for Man*, Little, Brown, Boston, 1971, pp. 60–81.

7. These arguments are well covered by Sherwood Washburn and Ruth Moore, *Ape into Man*, Little, Brown, Boston, 1974.

8. Symons, *Primate Evolution*, chaps. 7–9.

9. Jane van Lawick Goodall, *In the Shadow of Man*, Houghton Mifflin, Boston, 1973, gives a popular account. In writing this part of the chapter, I have drawn heavily on the writings of Sherwood L. Washburn, including "The Study of Human Evolution," in Dolhinow and Sarich, *Background for Man*, pp. 82–117. See also S. L. Washburn, "Behavior and the Origin of Man," *Proceedings of the Royal Anthropological Institute*, 1967, pp. 21–27.

10. This is a controversial issue. Russell Tuttle has stated that there are no features in human hands that "give evidence for a history of knuckle-walking." See his "Knuckle-Walking and the Problem of Human Origins," *Science*, 1969, 166, p. 953. See also Tuttle's edited volume, *The Functional and Evolutionary Biology of Primates*, Aldine-Atherton, Chicago, 1972; J. R. Napier, "Fossil Hand Bones from Olduvai Gorge," *Nature*, 1962, 196, p. 409. For a general discussion, see Pilbeam, *Ascent of Man*, pp. 62–71.

11. George B. Schaller, *Serengeti: A Kingdom of Predators*, Knopf, New York, 1972, and *The Serengeti Lion*, University of Chicago Press, Chicago, 1972. An important paper is George B. Schaller and Gordon R. Lowther, "The Relevance of Carnivore Behavior to the Study of Early Hominids," *Southwestern Journal of Anthropology*, 25, 4, 1969.

12. There are many noteworthy arguments on either side of these issues. I would recommend consulting a physical anthropologist before reading about the issues in any detail.

13. Clifford Jolly, "The Seed-Eaters: A New Model of Hominid Differentiation Based on Baboon Analogy," *Man*, 1970, 5, pp. 5–26. See also the same author's *The Emergence of Man*, 2nd ed., Macmillan, New York, 1972.

14. Kay Martin and Barbara Voorhies, *The Female of the Species*, Columbia University Press, New York, 1975, changed a great deal of my thinking about prehistory. It should be compulsory reading for everyone interested in the evolution of humankind.

15. R. Allen Gardner and Beatrice A. Gardner, "Teaching Sign Language to a Chimpanzee," *Science*, August 1969, pp. 664–672.

16. Ann James Premack and David Premack, "Teaching Language to an Ape," *Scientific American*, October 1972, pp. 92–99.

17. C. F. Hockett and Robert Ascher, "The Human Revolution," *Current Anthropology*, 1964, 5, 3, pp. 135–168.

18. The literature on the Australopithecines is enormous. Raymond Dart's original Taung paper was "*Australopithecus africanus*: The Man-Ape of South Africa," *Nature*, 1925, 115, p. 195. Karl W. Butzer, *Environment and Archaeology*, 2nd ed., Aldine, Chicago, 1971, gives the geological background.

19. The most thorough study of an Australopithecine ever published is that of the original Bed I skull from Olduvai Gorge, Tanzania. See P. V. Tobias, *Olduvai Gorge*, vol. 2, Cambridge University Press, Cambridge and New York, 1967

20. F. Clark Howell, "Omo Research Expedition," *Nature*, August 10, 1968.

21. D. J. Johanson and M. Taieb, "Plio-Pleistocene Discoveries in Hadar, Ethiopia," *Nature*, March 25, 1976.

22. Mary Leakey, "Pliocene footprints at Laetolil, Northern Tanzania," *Antiquity*, LII, 205, 1978, p. 133.

23. The East Turkana finds are described in Richard Leakey and Glynn Isaac, "East Rudolf: An Introduction to the Abundance of New Evidence," in Isaac and McCown, eds., *Human Origins*, pp. 307–325 and in subsequent articles. See also Yves Coppens et al., *Earliest Men and Environments in the Lake Rudolf Basin*, University of Chicago Press, Chicago, 1976.

24. The earlier work at Olduvai was described by L. S. B. Leakey, *Olduvai Gorge*, Cambridge University Press, Cambridge, 1951. Three monographs on Olduvai have subsequently appeared, of which the third is the most significant from our point of view: Mary D. Leakey, *Olduvai Gorge*, vol. 3, Cambridge University Press, Cambridge and New York, 1971. This volume describes the finds in Beds I and II and includes complete accounts of the living floors there.

25. To embark on a survey of the complex literature on early human evolution is an act of temerity even for the expert. This section is written from a variety of sources, including: Campbell, *Humankind Emerging*; Mark L. Weiss and Alan E. Mann, *Human Biology and Behavior: An Anthropological Perspective*, 2nd ed., Little, Brown, Boston, 1978. See also the essay by Philip Tobias, "African Hominids: Dating and Phylogeny," in Isaac and McCown, eds., *Human Origins*, pp. 377–421.

26. Glynn Isaac, "The Food-sharing Behavior of Protohuman Hominids," *Scientific American*, April, 1978.

27. Leakey, *Olduvai Gorge*, vol 3.

28. Isaac, "The Food-sharing Behavior of Protohuman Hominids."

5 TOWARD MODERN HUMANITY

1. Described in Richard Leakey, *Origins*, Dutton, New York, 1977. This book is not very highly regarded by academic readers, but contains information of value for beginners.

2. Dubois and his discoveries have been summarized many times. An easily accessible first reference is Edmund White and Dale Brown, *The First Men*, Time-Life Books, New York, and Little, Brown, Boston, 1973. Another secondary reference is John Pfeiffer, *The Emergence of Man*, 3rd ed., Harper & Row, New York, 1978.

3. See M. Boule and H. V. Vallois, *Fossil Men*, Thames and Hudson, London, 1957, pp. 130–146; also Franz Weidenreich, *Apes, Giants, and Men*, University of Chicago Press, Chicago, 1946. About 45 individuals have been identified from cultural levels at Choukoutien, including a skullcap found in 1966.

4. John Pfeiffer, *The Emergence of Man*.

5. A good description of these finds occurs in Mark L. Weiss and Alan E. Mann, *Human Biology and Behavior*, 2nd ed., Little, Brown, Boston, 1978, chap. 7.

6. The classic descriptions of Olduvai hand axes are: L. S. B. Leakey, *Olduvai Gorge, 1931–1951*, Cambridge University Press, Cambridge, 1951, and Mary D. Leakey, *Olduvai Gorge*, vol. 3, Cambridge University Press, Cambridge, 1973.

7. An able account of African hand ax sites appears in J. Desmond Clark, *The Prehistory of Africa*, Thames and Hudson, London, and Praeger, New York, 1970, chap. 3. See also F. C. Howell and J. D. Clark, "Acheulian Hunter-Gatherers of Sub-Saharan Africa," *Viking Fund Publications in Anthropology*, 1963, 36, pp. 458–533. A new synthesis is Karl Butzer and Glynn Isaac, eds., *After the Australopithecines*, Aldine, Chicago, 1975.

8. The classic paper on the chopper tools of India and Asia was written soon after World War II; see H. L. Movius, "The Lower Paleolithic Cultures of Southern and Eastern Asia," *Transactions of the American Philosophical Society*, 1948, 38, pp. 329–420. A more recent but brief summary is J. M. Coles and E. S. Higgs, *The Archaeology of Early Man*, Faber and Faber, London, 1969, chaps. 18 and 19. Kwang-chih Chang, *The Archaeology of Ancient China*, rev. ed., Yale University Press, New Haven and London, 1968, has a brief account of the Chinese Paleolithic.

9. S. Hazzledine Warren, "The *Elephas antiquus* Bed of Clacton on Sea," *Quarterly Journal of the Geological Society*, 1923, 79, pp. 606–634, and his "The Clacton Flint Industry: A New Interpretation," *Proceedings of the Geologists' Association*, 1951, 62, pp. 107–135. A recent discussion of the Clactonian is in F. Bordes, *Old Stone Age*, McGraw-Hill, New York, 1968, pp. 83–97; see also Ronald Singer et al., "Clacton-on-Sea, Essex: Report on Excavations 1969–1970," *Proceedings of the Prehistoric Society*, 1973, 39, pp. 6–74.

10. Glynn Isaac, "Traces of Pleistocene Hunters: An East African Example," in Richard B. Lee and Irven De Vore, eds., *Man the Hunter*, Aldine, Chicago, 1968, pp. 253–261. The same author's *Olorgesailie*, University of Chicago Press, Chicago, 1977, is an admirable description of such adaptations.

11. F. Clark Howell, "Observations on the Earlier Phases of the European Lower Paleolithic," *American Anthropologist*, 1966, 68, 2, pp. 111–140.

12. For dating, see Butzer, *Environment and Archeology*, p. 466. For a site report, see Henry de Lumley, "Découverte d'habitats de l'Acheuléen ancien, dans des dépôts Mindéliens, sur le site de Terra Amata (Nice)," *Comptes Rendus de l'Académie des Sciences*, 1967, 264, pp. 801–804, and "A Paleolithic Camp at Nice," *Scientific American*, 1969, 220, pp. 42–50.

13. Kenneth P. Oakley, "Fire as a Palaeolithic Tool and Weapon," *Proceedings of the Prehistoric Society*, 1955, 21, pp. 36–48.

14. Arago is covered ably by Bernard Campbell, *Humankind Emerging*, 2nd ed., Little, Brown, Boston, 1979.

15. C. D. Ovey, ed., *The Swanscombe Skull: A Survey of Research on a Pleistocene Site*, Occasional Papers of the Royal Anthropological Institute, no. 24, 1964.

16. Bernard Campbell, *Humankind Emerging*, and *Human Evolution*, 2nd ed., Aldine, Chicago, 1974.

17. Thomas Huxley, *Man's Place in Nature*, Macmillan, London, 1863. See also Wilfred Le

Gros Clark, *The Fossil Evidence for Human Evolution*, 2nd ed., University of Chicago Press, Chicago, 1964.

18. Bordes, *The Old Stone Age*. For Le Moustier itself see Denis Peyrony, "Le Moustier: ses gisements, ses industries, ses couches géologiques," *Revue Anthropologique*, 1930, vol. 14. Nearly all the basic references to western European Stone Age sites are in French.

19. For Mount Carmel, see D. A. E. Garrod and Dorothy Bate, *The Stone Age of Mount Carmel*, Cambridge University Press, Cambridge, 1937.

20. Marcellin Boule and H. V. Vallois, *Fossil Men*.

21. F. Clark Howell, "Pleistocene Glacial Ecology and the Evolution of 'Classic' Neanderthal Man," *Southwestern Journal of Anthropology*, 1957, 8, pp. 377–410. Also the same author's "The Evolutionary Significance of Variation and Varieties of 'Neanderthal' Man," *Quarterly Review of Biology*, 1957, 32, pp. 330–347.

22. Bordes, *The Old Stone Age*.

23. Lewis R. Binford and Sally R. Binford, "A preliminary analysis of Functional Variability in the Mousterian of Levallois Facies," *American Anthropologist*, 1966, 68, 2, pp. 238–295, gives most of the arguments. Bordes, *Old Stone Age*, gives the French viewpoint. Paul Mellars, "The Character of the Middle–Upper Palaeolithic in Southwestern France," in Colin Renfrew, ed., *The Explanation of Culture Change*, Duckworth, London, 1973, pp. 255–276 and other essays in the same volume.

24. H. L. Movius, "The Mousterian Cave of Teshik-Tash, South Eastern Uzbekistan, Central Asia," *Bulletin of the American School of Prehistoric Research*, 1953, no. 17; also Richard G. Klein, "Open Air Mousterian Sites of South Russia," *Quaternaria*, 1967, 9, pp. 199–223.

25. On Shanidar, see Ralph S. Solecki, "Prehistory in Shanidar Valley, Northern Iraq," *Science*, 1963, 139, p. 179, and, by the same author, *Shanidar: The Humanity of Neanderthal Man*, Penguin Press, London, 1972.

26. Denis Peyrony, "La Ferrassie," *Préhistoire*, 1934, 3, pp. 1–54.

27. F. Clark Howell, *Early Man*, 2nd ed., Time-Life Books, New York, 1974.

28. Alberto C. Blanc, "Some evidence for the ideologies of Early Man," in S. L. Washburn, ed., *Social Life of Early Man*, Viking Fund Publications, New York, 1961, 31, pp. 119–136.

6   EUROPEANS AND NORTHERN ASIANS

1. Kay Martin and Barbara Voorhies, *The Female of the Species*, Columbia University Press, New York, 1975, chap. 7.

2. Richard Lee and Irven De Vore, eds., *Kalahari Hunter-Gatherers*, Harvard University Press, Cambridge, Mass., 1976.

3. David Pilbeam, *The Ascent of Man*, Macmillan, New York, 1972, chap. 8.

4. D. A. E. Garrod and Dorothea Bate, *The Stone Age of Mount Carmel*, Cambridge University Press, Cambridge, 1937.

5. François Bordes, *The Old Stone Age*, McGraw Hill, New York, 1968, chaps. 11, 12. Abri Pataud is described in Clark Howell's *Early Man*, Time-Life Books, New York, 1965, pp. 164–165; other sites and the basic cultural sequence are discussed by J. M. Coles and E. S. Higgs in *The Archaeology of Early Man*, Faber and Faber, London, 1968, chap 14. Radiocarbon chronologies for Europe have been summarized by H. L. Movius, "Radiocarbon Dates and Upper Paleolithic Archaeology in Central and Western Europe," *Current Anthropology*, 1960, 1, pp. 335–391. That account is, however, somewhat dated. Also see P. E. L. Smith, *Le Solutréen en France*, Publications de L'Institut de Préhistoire de L'Université de Bordeaux, Mémoire No. 5, Imprimeries Delmas, Bordeaux.

6. Some scholars have alleged that Upper Paleolithic hunters domesticated the reindeer. A recent fascinating paper on the reindeer problem is Ernest S. Burch, Jr., "The Caribou/Wild Reindeer as a Human Resource," *American Antiquity*, 1972, 37, 3, pp. 339–368.

7. The original monograph on La Madeleine itself is very rare today: L. Capitan and D. Peyrony, *La Madeleine, Son Gisement, Son Industrie, Ses Oeuvres d'Art*, Librairie Emile Nourry, Paris, 1928.

8. The finest books on Paleolithic art are: H. Leroi-Gourhan, *Treasures of Paleolithic Art*, Abrams, New York, 1968; Paolo Graziosi, *Paleolithic Art*, Faber and Faber, London, 1960. For a brief summary, try: Johannes Maringer and Hans-Georg Bandi, *Art in the Ice Age*, Praeger, New York, 1953. See also Peter J. Ucko and A. Rosenfeld, *Palaeolithic Cave Art*, World University Library, New York, 1968.

9. Ferdinand Windels, *The Lascaux Cave Paintings*, Faber and Faber, London, 1965.

10. No one should miss Henri Breuil, *La Caverne d'Altamira*, Payot, Paris, 1908, which is very rare today.

11. Marshack's work generates considerable controversy. His monograph, *The Roots of Civilization*, McGraw-Hill, New York, 1972, is a thought-provoking contribution. He has recently worked in Siberia and other areas. Space considerations make it impossible to summarize that work in this text.

12. Post Glacial cultures in northern Europe are best summarized by Grahame Clark, *The Earlier Stone Age Settlement of Scandinavia*, Cambridge University Press, Cambridge, 1975. The same author's *Star Carr* (Cambridge University Press, Cambridge, 1954) is a classic account of a postglacial hunter-gatherer encampment.

13. I have relied heavily on Richard Klein's admirable summary of Soviet archaeology: *Man and Culture in the Late Pleistocene*, Chandler, San Francisco, 1969. This book is heavily illustrated. For a summary account of the Russian Stone Age, try C. B. M. McBurney, *Early Man in the Soviet Union*, British Academy, London, 1976.

14. The English language literature on Siberia, realistically most readers' only source on the archaeology of this area, has proliferated rapidly in recent years. Try: Chester S. Chard, *Northeast Asia in Prehistory*, University of Wisconsin Press, Madison, 1974; Richard Klein, "The Pleistocene Prehistory of Siberia," *Quaternary Research*, 1971, 1, 2, pp. 131–161. See also McBurney's recent essay (note 13), and the essays by Soviet archaeologists in Alan Lyle Bryan, ed., *Early Man in America from a Circumpolar Perspective*, University of Alberta, Edmonton, 1978.

15. Diuktai is summarized by McBurney (note 13 above) and by Iuri A. Mochanov, "Stratigraphy and Chronology of the Paleolithic of Northeast Asia," in Bryan, *Early Man*, pp. 54–66.

16. M. M. Gerasimov, "The Paleolithic Site of Mal'ta (1956–57 excavations)"; this paper is in Russian and appeared in *Sovyetskayen etnografiya*, 1958, 3, pp. 28–52.

17. For Japanese Stone Age archaeology, start with Fumiko Ikawa-Smith, "Lithic Assemblages from the Early and Middle Upper Pleistocene Formations in Japan," in Bryan, *Early Man*, pp. 42–53.

7 THE FIRST AMERICANS

1. Anyone interested in the early exploration of North America should not miss Samuel Eliot Morison, *The European Discovery of America*, vol 1: *The Northern Voyages* A.D. *500 to 1600*, Oxford University Press, London and New York, 1971. This book is authoritative, entertaining, and crammed with interesting information.

2. The only comprehensive account is Gordon Willey and Jeremy A. Sabloff, *A History of American Archaeology*, W. H. Freeman, San Francisco, 1974. Recent, highly speculative volumes on New World origins are Cyrus H. Gordon, *Before Columbus*, Crown Publishers, New York, 1971, and Betty Bugbee Cusack, *Collectors' Luck: Giant Steps into Prehistory*, G. R. Barnstead Printing Company, Stonehaven, Mass., 1968. See also Brian M. Fagan, *Elusive Treasure*, Charles Scribners' Sons, New York, 1977.

3. Samuel Haven, *Archaeology of the United States*, Smithsonian Institution, Washington, D.C., 1856.

4. David Hopkins, ed., *The Bering Land Bridge*, Sanford University Press, Palo Alto, 1967.

5. The latest set of essays, which has the great advantage of being cheap, is Alan Lyle Bryan, ed., *Early Man in America from a Circum-Pacific Perspective*, University of Alberta, Edmonton, 1978. See also Jesse D. Jennings, ed., *Ancient Native Americans*, W. H. Freeman, San Francisco, 1978.

6. The best summary of Alaskan prehistory is Don E. Dumond, *The Eskimos and Aleuts*, Thames and Hudson, London, 1977.

7. Richard E. Morlan, "Early Man in Northern Yukon Territory: Perspectives as of 1977," in Bryan, *Early Man*, pp. 78–95.

8. For information on Dry Creek, see William R. Powers and Thomas D. Hamilton, "Dry Creek: A Late Pleistocene Human Occupation in Central Alaska," in Bryan, *Early Man*, pp. 72–78. On Onion Portage, read Douglas D. Anderson, "Akmak," *Acta Arctica*, 1970, 15.

9. The literature is complicated. For a start, read Fumiko Ikawa-Smith, "Lithic Assemblages from the Early and Middle Upper Pleistocene Formations in Japan," in Bryan, *Early Man*, pp. 42–53.

10. Jesse D. Jennings, "Origins," in Jennings, ed., *Ancient Native Americans*, pp. 1–42.

11. J. M. Adovasio et al.,"Meadowcroft Rockshelter," in Bryan, *Early Man*, pp. 140–180.

12. While this may be a simplification of the evidence, I feel it is best to take a conservative position on the issue. For discussion, see Alan L. Bryan, "An Overview of Paleo-American Prehistory from a Circum-Pacific Perspective," in Bryan, *Early Man*, pp. 306–327. The Bryan volume contains comprehensive references to all dated sites, including those mentioned in this chapter.

13. For this controversial material, try Jeffrey L. Bada and Patricia Masters Helfman, "Amino Acid Racemization Dating of Fossil Bones," *World Archaeology*, 1975 (7:2), pp. 160–173.

14. Described by Lorena Mirambell, "Tlapacoya: A Late Pleistocene Site in Central Mexico," in Bryan, *Early Man*, pp. 221–230.

15. MacNeish's excavations at Pikimachay are about to be published in full. In the meantime, his "Early Man in the Andes," *Scientific American*, 1971, 4, pp. 36–46 covers the ground.

16. Vance Haynes, "Fluted Projectile Points, Their Age and Dispersion," *Science*, 1964, 145, pp. 1408–1413; also H. J. Müller-Beck, "Paleo-Hunters in America: Origins and Diffusion," *Science*, 1966, 152, pp. 1191–1210. See also George Frison, *Prehistoric Hunters & the High Plains*, Academic Press, New York, 1978.

17. A vivid example is Joe Ben Wheat, "A Paleo-Indian Bison Kill," *Scientific American*, 1967, 1, pp. 44–52.

18. Clifford Jolly and Fred Plog (*Physical Anthropology and Archaeology*, Alfred A. Knopf, New York, 1976, pp. 206–207) have an outline account and cite an unpublished manuscript for their conclusion.

19. The issue of extinction of Pleistocene mammals in North America was discussed by Paul Martin and H. E. Wright, Jr., eds., *Pleistocene Extinctions: The Search for a Cause*, Yale University Press, New Haven, 1967. I have also relied on Jolly and Plog's account in *Physical Anthropology and Archaeology*, pp. 206–207. Here again they rely on unpublished materials.

20. A basic description is in Jesse D. Jennings, *The Prehistory of North America*, 2nd ed., McGraw-Hill, New York, 1975, chap. 4. For Danger Cave, see Jesse D. Jennings, *Danger Cave*, University of Utah Anthropological Papers no. 27, Salt Lake City, 1957. A summary of this site and of Lovelock and Gypsum caves appears in the same author's *Prehistory*, p. 157 ff. See also Claude Warren and Anthony Ranere, "Outside Danger Cave: A View of Early Men in the Great Basin," in Cynthia Irwin-Williams, *Early Man in Western North America*, Eastern New Mexico University Press, Portales, N.M., 1968, pp. 6–18. Another important site is Humboldt Cave; see Robert F. Heizer and Alex D. Krieger, *The Archaeology of Humboldt Cave, Churchill County, Nevada*, University of California Publications in American Archaeology and Ethnology, Berkeley, 1956, 47, 1, pp. 1–190.

21. Melvin C. Aikens, "Hogup Cave," *University of Utah Anthropological Papers*, 1970, 93.

22. A good description of the Archaic tradition is in Willey, *Introduction to American Archaeology*, vol. 1, pp. 60–64 and chap. 5; see also Jennings, *Prehistory*, chap. 4.

23. The Lake Superior copper trade is described by Tyler J. Bastian, *Prehistoric Copper Mining in Isle Royale National Park, Michigan*, Museum of Anthropology, University of Michigan, Ann Arbor, 1969.

24. For early contact between explorers and hunters see Morison's *Northern Voyages*.

25. For a discussion, see Thomas F. Lynch, "The South American Paleo-Indians," in Jennings, *Ancient Native Americans*, pp. 455–490.

26. Kent V. Flannery, "Archaeological Systems Theory and Early Mesoamerica," in Betty Meggers, ed., *Anthropological Archaeology in the Americas*, Anthropological Society of Washington, Washington, D.C., 1968, pp. 67–87.

27. I drew heavily on Don Dumond's *The Eskimos and Aleuts* for this section. But see also Willey's *Introduction to American Archaeology*, vol. 1, pp. 416–419, which contains references to W. N. Irving's important work on the Arctic small-tool tradition. Iyatayet is described by J. L. Giddings, *The Archaeology of Cape Denbigh*, Brown University Press, Providence, R.I., 1964. The same author's *Ancient Men of the Arctic*, Alfred A. Knopf, New York, 1967, is a popular account. Hans-Georg Bandi, *Eskimo Prehistory*, University of Washington Press, Seattle, 1968, summarizes Arctic archaeology and its complex literature.

28. W. S. Laughlin and G. H. Marsh, "The Lamellar Flake Manufacturing Site on Anangula Island in the Aleutians," *American Antiquity*, 1954, 20, 1, pp. 27–39. See also Jean S. Aigner, "The Unifacial, Core, and Blade Site on Anangula Island, Aleutians," *Arctic Anthropology*, 1970, 7, 2, pp. 59–88; and Douglas Anderson, "A Stone Age Campsite at the Gateway to America," *Scientific American*, 1968, 218, pp. 24–33.

29. Moreau S. Maxwell, ed., "Eastern Arctic Prehistory: Paleoeskimo Problems," *Memoirs of the Society for American Archaeology*, no. 31, 1976.

8 AFRICANS AND AUSTRALIANS

1. Bridget Allchin, *The Stone Tipped Arrow*, Barnes and Noble, New York, 1966.
2. George Peter Murdock, "The Current Status of the World's Hunting and Gathering Peoples," in Richard Lee and Irven De Vore, eds., *Man the Hunter*, Aldine, Chicago, 1968, pp. 13–20.
3. J. Desmond Clark, *The Prehistory of Africa*, Thames and Hudson, London, and Praeger, New York, 1970, is a useful synthesis of this period in African prehistory.
4. J. Desmond Clark, *The Prehistory of Southern Africa*, Pelican Books, Baltimore, 1959, contains a fascinating account of San daily life compiled from rock art. For the art itself, see: A. R. Wilcox, *The Rock Art of South Africa*, Thomas Nelson, Johannesburg, 1963.
5. Brian M. Fagan and Francis Van Noten, *The Hunter-Gatherers of Gwisho*, Musee Royal de l'Afrique Centrale, Tervuren, Belgium, 1971. See also Creighton Gabel, *Stone Age Hunters of the Kafue: the Gwisho A site*, Boston University African Research Studies, no. 6, 1965.
6. For the San and archaeology, see Richard Lee and Irven De Vore, Hunter-Gatherers of the Kalahari, Harvard University Press, Cambridge, Mass., 1976; see also John Yellen, *Archaeological Approaches to the Present*, Academic Press, New York, 1977.
7. Roland Oliver and Brian Fagan, *Africa in the Iron Age*, Cambridge University Press, New York, 1975.
8. Louis Peringuey, *The Stone Age in South Africa*, South African Museum, Capetown, 1911, gives fascinating insights into recent San culture. See also Isaac Schapera, *The Khoisan Peoples of South Africa*, Humanities Press, New York, 1930.
9. A basic source on Australian prehistory is D. J. Mulvaney, *The Prehistory of Australia*, 2nd ed., Pelican Books, Baltimore, 1975. See also: J. Peter White and James F. O'Connell, "Australian Prehistory: New Aspects of Antiquity," *Science*, 1979, vol. 205, pp. 21–28.
10. For a discussion of land bridges, see J. Allen, J. Golson, and Rhys Jones, eds., *Sunda and Sahel: Prehistoric Studies in Southeast Asia, Melanesia, and Australia*, Academic Press, New York, 1977.
11. Tom Harrisson, "The Great Cave of Niah," *Man*, 1957, article 211. Anyone interested in Borneo and Thailand should read *Asian Perspectives*, 1972, 13.
12. For discussion, see White and O'Connell, "Australian Prehistory." Also: Duncan Merrilees, "Man the Destroyer," *Journal of the Royal Society of Western Australia*, 1968, 51, pp. 1–24. For South Australia, read Ron Lampert, "Kangaroo Island and the Antiquity of the Australians," in *Archaeology and Physical Anthropology in Oceania*, 1973, 8, pp. 89–115. Also: D. R. Horton, "Extinction of the Australian Megafauna," *Australian Institute of Aboriginal Studies Newsletter*, 1978, 9, 72–75.
13. See White and O'Connell, "Australian Prehistory," and Sylvia Hallam, *Fire and Hearth*, Australian Institute of Aboriginal Studies, 1975.
14. J. M. Bowler, R. Jones, H. Allen, and A. G. Thorne, "Pleistocene Human Remains from Australia: A Living Site and Cremation from Lake Mungo, Western N.S.W., "*World Archaeology*, 1970, 2, pp. 39–60. The characteristics of the two groups have been discussed by Alan Thorne, "Mungo and Kow Swamp: Morphological Variation in Pleistocene Australians" *Mankind* 1971, 8, 85–89. See also the collection of papers in R. Kirk and A. Thorne, eds., *The Origin of the Australians*, Australian Institute of Aboriginal Studies, 1976.
15. Charles Dortch and Duncan Merrilees, "Human Occupation of Devil's Lair, Western Australia, during the Pleistocene," *Archaeology and Physical Anthropology in Oceania*, 1973, 8, 89–115. Also: J. Balme, D. Merrilees, and J. K. Porter, "Late Quaternary Mammal Remains, Spanning About 30,000 Years, from Excavations in Devil's Lair, Western Australia," *Journal of the Royal Society of Western Australia*, 1978, 61, 33–65. For prehistoric Australian artifacts, read: R. V. S. Wright, ed., *Stone Tools as Cultural Markers*, Australian Institute of Aboriginal Studies, Canberra, 1977.
16. Richard V. S. Wright, ed., *Archaeology of the Gallus site, Koonalda Cave*, Australian Institute of Aboriginal Studies, 1971.
17. The Tasmanians are a fascinating subject. The principal references are given by Rhys Jones in the edited volume *Sunda and Sahul*. See also: N. J. B. Plumley, "An Annotated Bibliography of the Tasmanian Aborigines," *Occasional Paper of the Royal Anthropological Institute*, no. 28, 1969.
18. See Sandra Bowdler's discussion "The Coastal Colonization of Australia," in the edited volume *Sunda and Sahul*.
19. Richard Gould, *Puntutjarpa Rockshelter and the Australian Desert Culture*, American Museum of Natural History, 1977.
20. For discussion and references: White and O'Connell, "Australian Prehistory," pp. 25–26.

1. Richard A. Watson and Patty Jo Watson, *Man and Nature: An Anthropological Essay in Human Ecology*, Harcourt, Brace and World, 1969, chap. 7. Many points touched in this chapter are covered more thoroughly in that work.

2. Probably the classic work on the consequences of food production is by V. Gordon Childe, whose popular volumes contain much uncontroversial material on the origins of agriculture. See his *Man Makes Himself*, Watts, London, 1936. Many of the papers referred to in this and later chapters have been collected in a most useful reader on prehistoric agriculture: Stuart Struever, ed., *Prehistoric Agriculture*, Natural History Press, Garden City, N.J., 1971.

3. William Allan, *The African Husbandman*, Oliver and Boyd, Edinburgh, 1965, is a mine of information on shifting cultivation.

4. This thesis has been expounded in part by Thayer Scudder, *Gathering among African Woodland Savannah Cultivators*, University of Zambia, Institute for African Studies Paper no. 5, Lusaka, 1971. For an idea of how complex a subsistence-level agricultural economy can be, try Thayer Scudder, *The Ecology of the Gwembe Tonga*, Manchester University Press, Manchester, England, 1962. This is about a people relying on their environment for supplementary foods.

5. Harold L. Roth, "On the Origins of Agriculture," *Journal of the Royal Anthropological Institute*, 1887, 16, pp. 102–136.

6. For a history of research into agricultural origins, see Gary A. Wright, "Origins of Food Production in Southwestern Asia: A Survey of Ideas," *Current Anthropology*, 1971, 12, 4–5, pp. 447–478.

7. The desiccation theory is well expressed by Childe himself in V. Gordon Childe, *New Light on the Most Ancient East*, 4th ed., Routledge and Kegan Paul, London, 1952. His revolutions are described in detail in his *Man Makes Himself*, Watts, London, 1936.

8. Harold Peake and Herbert J. Fleure, *Peasants and Potters*, Oxford University Press, London, 1927.

9. Robert J. Braidwood and Bruce Howe, "Southwestern Asia beyond the Lands of the Mediterranean Littoral," in Robert J. Braidwood and Gordon R. Willey, eds., *Courses toward Urban Life*, Viking Fund Publications in Anthropology, no. 32, New York, 1962, pp. 132–146.

10. Carl O. Sauer, *Agricultural Origins and Dispersals*, American Geographical Society, New York, 1952.

11. Lewis R. Binford, "Post-Pleistocene Adaptations," in Sally R. Binford and Lewis R. Binford, eds., *New Perspectives in Archaeology*, Aldine, Chicago, 1968, pp. 313–341.

12. Kent V. Flannery, "The Origins of Agriculture," *Biannual Review of Anthropology*, 1973, pp. 271–310, is a useful synthesis that is still relatively up to date.

13. Kent V. Flannery, "The Ecology of Early Food Production in Mesopotamia," *Science*, 1965, 147, pp. 1247–1256.

14. Frank Hole and Kent V. Flannery, "Excavations at Ali Kosh, Iran," *Iranica Antiqua*, 1962, 2, pp. 97–148. See also the final report on this important site: Frank Hole and others, "Prehistory and Human Ecology of the Deh Luran Plain," *Memoirs of the Museum of Anthropology*, Ann Arbor, 1969.

15. The rest of this section is based on Mark Cohen's *The Food Crisis in Prehistory*, Yale University Press, New Haven, 1977. This important essay on population and food production is bound to generate discussion for many years. Any serious student of early agriculture and domestication should read it thoroughly.

16. D. Harris, "Alternative Pathways toward Agriculture," in Charles A. Reed, ed., *The Origins of Agriculture*, Mouton, The Hague, 1978.

17. Kent V. Flannery, "Origins," note 12 above.

18. A fundamental reference is R. J. Berry, "The Genetical Implications of Domestication in Animals," in Peter J. Ucko and G. W. Dimbleby, eds., *The Domestication and Exploitation of Plants and Animals*, Duckworth, London, and Aldine, Chicago, 1969, pp. 207–218.

19. It is worth reading Kent V. Flannery, "Origins and Ecological Effects of Early Domestication in Iran and the Near East," in Ucko and Dimbleby, *Domestication and Exploitation*, pp. 73–100. But see Higgs and Jarman, "Origins of Agriculture," *Antiquity*, 1969, 43, pp. 31–41.

20. Dexter Perkins, "The Prehistoric Fauna from Shanidar, Iraq," *Science*, 1964, 144, pp. 1565–1566. Considerable progress has been made in recent years with the measurement of limb bones of domestic and wild animals as a basis for distinguishing tamed and game animals.

21. Kent V. Flannery, "Origins and Ecological Effects."

22. A useful summary can be found in David and Joan Oates, *The Rise of Civilization*, Phaidon, Oxford, 1976.

23. Carl O. Sauer, *Agricultural Origins and Dispersals*, American Geographical Society, New York, 1952.

24. Argued by, among others, Grahame Clark, *Aspects of Prehistory*, University of California Press, Berkeley, 1970, pp. 91–95.

25. Jack Harlan has experimented with the harvesting of wild grains, reported in "A Wild Wheat Harvest in Turkey," *Archaeology*, 1967, pp. 197–201.

26. The distribution of wild cereals has been studied by many scientists. A classic work is N. I. Vavilov, "Phytogeographic Basis of Plant Breeding," *Chronica Botanica*, 1951, 13, pp. 14–54. See also his "The Origin, Variation, Immunity, and Breeding of Cultivated Plants," ibid., pp. 1–6. For a survey of early crops in the Near East, see Daniel Zohary, "The Progenitors of Wheat and Barley in Relation to Domestication and Agricultural Dispersal in the Old World," in Ucko and Dimbleby, *Domestication and Exploitation*, pp. 47–66, 24. Childe, *Man Makes Himself*, pp. 67–72.

27. The early history of pottery in the Near East is described by James Mellaart, *The Earliest Civilizations of the Near East*, Thames and Hudson, London, 1975, chap. 4.

28. B. A. L. Cranstone, "The Tifalmin: A Neolithic People in New Guinea," *World Archaeology*, 1972, 3, 2, pp. 132–142.

29. A. C. Renfrew, J. E. Dixon, and J. R. Cann, "Obsidian and Early Cultural Contact in the Near East," *Proceedings of the Prehistoric Society*, London, 1966, 32, pp. 1–29 and subsequent articles.

10 ORIGINS OF FOOD PRODUCTION: EUROPE AND THE NEAR EAST

1. A survey of the relevant research of the past two centuries has been compiled by Gary A. Wright, "The Origins of Food Production in Southwestern Asia: A Survey of Ideas," *Current Anthropology*, 1971, 12, 4–5, pp. 447–478.

2. Such cultures as the Atlitian, Kebaran, and Zarzian belong in this time bracket. For one typical site, Palegawra, see Robert J. Braidwood and Bruce Howe, *Prehistoric Investigations in Kurdistan*, Oriental Institute, University of Chicago, Chicago, 1960.

3. The Natufian was originally described in Dorothy A. E. Garrod and Dorothea M. A. Bate, *The Stone Age of Mt. Carmel*, vol. 1, Oxford University Press, Oxford, 1937. A later review article is D. A. E. Garrod, "The Natufian Culture: The Life and Economy of a Mesolithic People in the Near East," *Proceedings of the British Academy*, 1957, 43, pp. 211–217. For a survey of the literature see James Mellaart, *The Neolithic of the Near East*, Thames and Hudson, London, 1975, pp. 37–42.

4. An introductory survey of Jericho can be found in Kathleen Kenyon, *Archaeology in the Holy Land*, Benn, London, 1961. See also James Mellaart, *The Earliest Civilizations of the Near East*, Thames and Hudson, London, and McGraw-Hill, New York, 1965.

5. For Beidha, see Diana Kirkbride, "Beidha: Early Neolithic Village Life South of the Dead Sea," *Antiquity*, 1968, 42, pp. 263–274.

6. Dexter Perkins, "Prehistoric Fauna from Shanidar, Iraq," *Science*, 1964, 144, pp. 1565–1566.

7. David and Joan Oates, *The Rise of Civilization*, Phaedon Press, Oxford, 1976, contains a description of Mureybet.

8. For Jarmo, see Braidwood and Howe, *Prehistoric Investigations*. See also Mellaart, *Neolithic*, pp. 80–82.

9. Frank Hole, Kent V. Flannery, and James A. Neely, *The Prehistory and Human Ecology of the Deh Luran Plain*, University of Michigan, Museum of Anthropology Memoir no. 1, Ann Arbor, 1969.

10. The domestic animals at Çayönü are described by B. Lawrence, "Evidences of Animal Domestication at Çayönü," *Bulletin of the Turkish Historical Society*, vol. no. 46, 1969.

11. For Hacilar, see Mellaart, *Neolithic*, pp. 111–119. Further references are given there.

12. James Mellaart, *Çatal Hüyük*, Thames and Hudson, London, and Praeger, New York, 1967.

13. A. C. Renfrew, J. E. Dixon, and J. R. Cann, "Obsidian and Early Cultural Contact in the Near East," *Proceedings of the Prehistoric Society*, 1966, vol. 32, pp. 1–29.

14. V. Gordon Childe, *The Dawn of European Civilization*, Routledge & Kegan Paul, London, 1925.

15. Colin Renfrew, "The Tree-Ring Calibration of Radiocarbon: An Archaeological Evaluation," *Proceedings of the Prehistoric Society*, 1970, 36, pp. 280–311; and Colin Renfrew, "New

Configurations in Old World Archaeology," *World Archaeology*, 1970, 2, 2, pp. 199–211. Another useful review is Euan MacKie and others, "Thoughts on Radiocarbon Dating," *Antiquity*, 1971, 45, 179, pp. 197–204. An outline description of the problem and further references are given in Brian M. Fagan, *In the Beginning*, 3rd ed., Little, Brown, Boston, 1978, pp. 136–138. See also H. L. Thomas, "Near Eastern, Mediterranean, and European Chronology," *Studies in Mediterranean Archaeology*, 1, 1967.

16. Karl W. Butzer, *Environment and Archaeology: An Ecological Approach to Prehistory*, Aldine-Atherton, Chicago, 171, chap. 33.

17. H. T. Waterbolk, "Food Production in Prehistoric Europe," *Science*, 1968, 162, pp. 1093–1102.

18. Reiner Protsch and Rainer Berger, "Earliest Radiocarbon Dates for Domesticated Animals," *Science*, 1973, 179, pp. 235–239. See also Robert J. Rodden, "Excavations at the Early Neolithic Site at Nea Nikomedeia, Greek Macedonia (1961 season)," *Proceedings of the Prehistoric Society*, 1962, 28, pp. 267–288.

19. Ruth Tringham, *Hunters, Fishers, and Farmers of Eastern Europe: 6000–3000 B.C.*, Hutchinson University Library, London, 1971, is an important synthesis of southeast European prehistory.

20. The basic summary of European prehistory to refer to throughout the later part of this chapter is Stuart Piggott, *Ancient Europe*, Edinburgh University Press, Edinburgh, and Aldine, Chicago, 1965. For up-to-date references, consult a specialist or specific notes in this book. For the Danubians, see ibid., pp. 50 ff., and chap. 2, note 53. See also Waterbolk, "Food Production."

21. Literature summarized in Piggott, *Ancient Europe*, p. 57, and note 58.

22. Ferdinand Keller published his finds in five memoirs presented to the Anthropological Society of Zurich. They were subsequently translated into English by J. E. Lee under the title *The Lake Dwellings of Switzerland and Other Parts of Europe*, Murray, London, 1866. See Glyn Daniel, *A Hundred and Fifty Years of Archaeology*, Duckworth, London, 1975, pp. 89–93; and Hansjürgen Muller-Beck, "Prehistoric Swiss Lake Dwellings," *Scientific American*, December 1961.

23. The literature on megaliths is enormous. A synthesis is given in Glyn Daniel, *Megaliths in History*, Thames and Hudson, London, 1973. See also Colin Renfrew, "Colonialism and Megalithismus," *Antiquity*, 1967, 4, 41, pp. 276–288 and the same author's *Before Civlization*, Knopf, New York, 1973.

24. J. G. D Clark, *The Earlier Stone Age Settlement of Scandinavia*, Cambridge University Press, Cambridge, 1975, is the best description of these cultures.

25. A basic description is in J. G. D. Clark, *Prehistoric Europe: The Economic Basis*, Methuen, London, 1952, chap. VII.

11 EARLY FARMERS OF AFRICA

1. A succinct account of the Nile environment appears in Cyril Aldred, *The Egyptians*, Thames and Hudson, London, and Praeger, New York, 1961, chaps 2 and 3. Another fascinating source of information on Egypt ancient and modern is Robin Feddon's *Egypt: Land of the Valley*, John Murray, London, 1977.

2. In writing the next section, I have referred constantly to J. Desmond Clark, "A Re-examination of the Evidence for Agricultural Origins in the Nile Valley," *Proceedings of the Prehistoric Society*, 1971, 37, 2, pp. 34–79.

3. For Qadan, see Fred Wendorf, ed., *The Prehistory of Nubia*, vol. 2, Southern Methodist University Press, Dallas, 1968, pp. 791–996. The cemetery is described by Fred Wendorf, "A Nubian Final Paleolithic Graveyard near Jebel Sahaba, Sudan," in ibid., pp. 954–995.

4. This complicated cultural sequence is described by Philip E. L. Smith, "The Late Paleolithic of North-East Africa in the Light of Recent Research," *American Anthropologist*, 1966, 68, 2, pp. 326–355. For the Kom Ombo environment, see Karl W. Butzer and C. L. Hansen, *Desert and River in Nubia*, Wisconsin University Press, Madison, 1968.

5. In writing this section, I made full use of Karl Butzer's *Early Hydraulic Civilization in Egypt*, University of Chicago Press, 1976.

6. Butzer, *Early Hydraulic Civilization*, p. 11.

7. G. Caton-Thompson and E. W. Gardner, *The Desert Fayum*, 2 vols., Royal Anthropological Institute, London, 1934.

8. Jacques Vendrier, *Manuel d'archéologie égyptienne*, vol. 1: *Les Epoques de formation: le*

préhistoire, Edition A. et J. Picard, Paris, 1952, is a fundamental source of Merimde and other early sites. See also Bruce G. Trigger, *Beyond History: The Methods of Prehistory*, Holt, Rinehart and Winston, 1968.

9. See Walter B. Emery, *Archaic Egypt*, Penguin Books, London, 1961; and Aldred, *Egyptians*, pp. 66–69.

10. Butzer, *Early Hydraulic Civilization*, corrects the old notion that the early farmers lived on higher ground overlooking the floodplain.

11. G. Hamdan, "Evolution of Irrigation Agriculture in Egypt," *Arid Zone Research*, 1961, 17, pp. 119–142.

12. A brief synthesis of Saharan archaeology appears in J. Desmond Clark, *The Prehistory of Africa*, Thames and Hudson, London, and Praeger, New York, 1970, chaps. 4–6.

13. For some discussion of dates, see J. Desmond Clark, "The Problem of Neolithic Culture in Sub-Saharan Africa," in W. W. Bishop and J. Desmond Clark, eds., *Background to Evolution in Africa*, University of Chicago Press, Chicago and London, 1967, pp. 601–628.

14. On the domestication of animals in the Sahara, see Clark, "Re-examination," pp. 52–74.

15. Saharan rock art is vividly described by Henri Lhote, *The Search for the Tassili Frescoes*, Hutchinson, London, 1959.

16. Roland Oliver and Brian Fagan, *Africa in the Iron Age*, Cambridge University Press, Cambridge, 1975, gives a basic account with key references.

17. On yams, see D. G. Coursey, *Yams in West Africa*, Institute of African Studies, Legon, Ghana, 1965. See also Thurston Shaw, "Early crops in Africa: a review of evidence," in J. R. Harlan (ed.), *Plant Domestication and Indigenous African Agriculture*, University of Chicago Press, Chicago, pp. 312–339, for a discussion of early agriculture near the forest.

18. Clark, "Problem of Neolithic Culture."

19. An interesting assessment of Africa in prehistory was made by Thurston Shaw in a long review of Grahame Clark's *World Prehistory*, rev. ed., Cambridge University Press, 1969: Thurston Shaw, "Africa in Prehistory: Leader or Laggard?" *Journal of African History*, 1971, 12, 1, pp. 143–154.

12 ASIA: RICE, ROOTS, AND OCEAN VOYAGES

1. Carl O. Sauer, *Agricultural Origins and Dispersals*, American Geographical Society, New York, 1952.

2. For a recent assessment of the Hoabhinian, see I. G. Glover, "The Hoabhinian: hunter-gatherers or early agriculturalists in South-East Asia?" in J. V. S. Megaw, ed., *Hunters, Gatherers, and First Farmers Beyond Europe*, Humanities Press, Atlantic Highlands, N.J., 1977, pp. 145–166.

3. Chester F. Gorman, "Hoabhinian: A Pebble-Tool Complex with Early Plant Associations in Southeast Asia," *Science*, 1969, 163, pp. 671–673. See also Chester F. Gorman, "Hoabhinian and After: Subsistence Patterns in Southeast Asia during the Late Pleistocene and Early Recent Periods," *World Archaeology*, 1971, 2, 3, pp. 300–320.

4. Douglas E. Yen, "Hoabhinian Horticulture: the evidence and the questions from northwest Thailand," in J. Allen, J. Golson, and R. Jones, eds., *Sunda and Sahel*, Academic Press, New York, 1977, pp. 567–600.

5. Wilhelm Solheim, "An Earlier Agricultural Revolution," *Scientific American*, 1972, 1, pp. 34–41.

6. See discussion in Yen, "Hoabhinian Horticulture."

7. Charles Higham, "Initial Model Formation in Terra Incognita," in David L. Clarke, ed., *Models in Prehistory*, Methuen, London, 1972, pp. 453–476.

8. Gorman, "Hoabhinian: A Pebble-Tool Complex."

9. Rice cultivation at Non Nok Tha and other sites is discussed by Yen, "Hoabhinian Horticulture," and by D. T. Bayard, "Excavations at Non Nok Tha, northeast Thailand, 1968: an interim report," *Asian Perspectives*, 1970, 13, pp. 109–144.

10. N. I. Vavilov, "The Origin, Variation, Immunity, and Breeding of Cultivated Plants," *Chronica Botanica*, 1949–50, p. 26.

11. Kwang-Chih Chang, *The Archaeology of Ancient China*, 3rd ed., Yale University Press, New Haven, 1977, is essential reading for anyone interested in early China. Unlike many regional syntheses, it has the merit of being revised at regular intervals. See also K. C. Chang, "The Continuing Quest for China's Origins: I. Early Farmers in China," *Archaeology*, 1977, 30, 2, pp. 116–123.

12. Throughout this section I have relied heavily on Chang's *Archaeology of Ancient China*. This contains details of the numerous regional cultures that can be distinguished in the Lungshanoid and other traditions. Another major source is Ho Ping-ti, *The Cradle of the East: An Inquiry into the Indigenous Origins of Techniques and Ideas of Neolithic and Early Historic China, 5000–1000 B.C.* Chinese University of Hong Kong, Chicago and London, 1975.

13. Ping-ti Ho, "Loess and the Origin of Chinese Agriculture," *American Historical Review*, October 1969, pp. 1–36.

14. Chang, *Archaeology of Ancient China*, chap. 3. The reference to early cord-marked pottery is from Kwang-Chih Chang, "The Beginnings of Agriculture in the Far East," *Antiquity*, 1970, 44, p. 177.

15. Some of the dates are discussed by Chang, both in *Archaeology of Ancient China*, pp. 105–120, and in "Beginnings of Agriculture," pp. 181–184. See also Richard Pearson, "Radiocarbon Dates from China," *Antiquity*, 1973, 47, 186, pp. 142–143, where a date of c. 4400 B.C. is quoted for early irrigation.

16. On Lungshanoid cultures, see Chang, *Archaeology of Ancient China*, chap. 4.

17. Alan Moorehead, *The Fatal Impact*, Hamish Hamilton, London, 1966.

18. Jack Golson, "No Room at the Top: Agricultural Intensification in the New Guinea Highlands," in J. Allen et al., eds., *Sunda and Sahel*, pp. 602–638. See also Jim Allen, "The hunting Neolithic: adaptations to the food quest in prehistoric Papua New Guinea," in Megaw, ed., *Hunters, Gatherers*, pp. 167–188. These two papers give most of the key references.

19. Bronislaw Malinowski, *Argonauts of the Western Pacific*, Routledge and Kegan Paul, London, 1922.

20. In writing this section I have drawn on Jim Allen, "Sea Traffic, Trade and Expanding Horizons," in J. Allen et al., eds., *Sunda and Sahel*, pp. 387–417.

21. Andrew Sharp, *Ancient Voyagers in the Pacific*, Penguin Books, Baltimore, 1957, is the classic but outdated reference.

22. The literature is complex, but see Andrew P. Vadya, "Polynesian Cultural Distribution in New Perspective," *American Anthropologist*, 1959, 61, 1, pp. 817–828.

23. Ben R. Finney, "New Perspectives on Polynesian Voyaging," in Highland et al., eds., *Polynesian Culture History*, Bishop Museum Press, Honolulu, 1967, pp. 141–166.

24. David Lewis, *We the Navigators*, University of Hawaii Press, Honolulu, 1972, is a fascinating book worth reading for sheer pleasure.

25. A. Pawley and R. C. Green, "Dating the dispersal of the Oceanic Languages," *Oceanic Linguistics*, 1976, 12, pp. 1–67.

26. The basic paper on this pottery is L. M. Groube, "Tonga, Lapita pottery and Polynesian Origins," *Journal of the Polynesian Society*, 1971, 80, pp. 278–316.

27. W. R. Ambrose, "Obsidian and its prehistoric distribution in Melanesia," in N. Barnard, ed., *Ancient Chinese bronzes and Southeast Asian metal and other archaeological artifacts*, National Museum of Victoria, Melbourne, 1976, pp. 351–378.

28. For Polynesian prehistory see Peter Bellwood, *The Polynesians*, Thames and Hudson, London, 1979.

29. Hawaiian archaeology is scattered in many articles. Fishhook typology is fundamental; see Kenneth Emory, William J. Bonk, and Yoshiko H. Sinoto, *Hawaiian Archaeology: Fishhooks*, Bishop Museum Special Publications, 1959, no. 47. For Easter island see Kenneth P. Emory, "Easter Island's Position in the prehistory of Polynesia," *Journal of the Polynesian Society*, 1972, 81, pp. 57–69. See also R. C. Green and M. Kelly, eds., *Studies in Oceanic Culture History*, Bishop Museum, Honolulu, 1970–71.

30. For the Polynesians before European contact, the basic source is Douglas Oliver, *Ancient Tahitian Society*, University of Hawaii Press, Honolulu, 1977.

31. New Zealand's archaeology is briefly surveyed by Wilfred Shawcross, "Archaeology with a Short, Isolated Time-Scale: New Zealand," *World Archaeology*, 1969, 1, 2, pp. 184–199. This useful paper contains a basic bibliography and is thoroughly provocative. Moa hunters are described by R. Duff, *The Moa-Hunter Period of Maori Culture*, Government Printer, Wellington, 1956.

32. A fundamental paper on New Zealand agriculture is Kathleen Shawcross, "Fern Root and 18th-Century Maori Food Production in Agricultural Areas," *Journal of the Polynesian Society*, 1967, 76, pp. 330–352. See also L. M. Groube, "The Origin and Development of Earthwork Fortifications in the Pacific," in Green and Kelly, eds., *Studies in Oceanic Culture History*, vol. 1, Pacific Anthropological Records no. 11, 1970, pp. 133–164. Another important paper is Peter L. Bellwood, "Fortifications and Economy in Prehistoric New Zealand," *Proceedings of the Prehistoric Society*, 1971, 37, 1, pp. 56–95.

Notes

1. No one should miss George Carter's fascinating essay on pre-Columbian chickens in America, arguing that they came from Southeast Asia, in Carroll L. Riley, et al., eds., *Man across the Sea*, University of Texas Press, Austin, 1971.

2. The archaeology of Tehuacán is described in a series of monographs: Richard S. MacNeish, *The Prehistory of the Tehuacán Valley*, University of Texas Press, Austin, 1967–76.

3. Paul C. Mangelsdorf has written many papers on the origins of maize. One of the best known is Paul C. Mangelsdorf, Richard S. MacNeish, and Walton C. Gallinat, "Domestication of Corn," *Science*, 1964, 143, pp. 538–545. See MacNeish, *Prehistory of the Tehuacán Valley*, vol. 1.

4. In writing this section, I used not only the Tehuacán monographs, but Richard MacNeish's *The Science of Archaeology?*, Duxbury Press, North Scituate, Mass., 1978.

5. See Kent V. Flannery's edited *The Early Mesoamerican Village*, Seminar Press, New York, 1976, which spells out the evolution of more complex Mesoamerican settlements in elegant detail. It is also a mine of information on new approaches to settlement archaeology.

6. Evidence summarized by Gordon Willey, *An Introduction to American Archaeology*, vol. I, Prentice-Hall, Englewood Cliffs, N.J., 1967.

7. Kent V. Flannery, "Archaeological Systems Theory and Early Mesoamerica," in B. J. Meggers, ed., *Anthropological Archaeology in the Americas*, Washington, D.C., 1968, pp. 67–87.

8. See Richard MacNeish, *The Science*, chap. 6; also Michael Moseley, *The Maritime Foundations of Andean Civilization*, Cummings, Menlo Park, Calif., 1975.

9. For Chilca, see Frederic Engel, *Geografia humana prehistórica y agricultura precolumbina de la Quebrada de Chilca*, vol. 1: *Informe preliminar*, Universidad Agraria, Lima, 1966.

10. For Huaca Prieta, see Junius B. Bird, "Preceramic Cultures in Chicama and Virú," in W. C. Bennett, ed., *A Reappraisal of Peruvian Archaeology*, Society for American Archaeology, Memoir no. 4, Madison, Wisc., 1948, pp. 21–28.

11. For Playa Culebras, see Frederic Engel, "Early Sites on the Peruvian Coast," *Southwestern Journal of Anthropology*, 1957, 13, pp. 54–68. The classic study of a Peruvian coastal valley is: Gordon R. Willey, "Prehistoric Settlement Patterns in the Viru Valley, Peru," Smithsonian Institution, *Bureau of American Ethnology Bulletin*, no. 155, Washington, D.C., 1953.

12. Richard MacNeish, *The Science*, chap. 6, was a source for this highland section, as were Richard S. MacNeish, Thomas C. Patterson, and David L. Browman, "The Central Peruvian Interaction Sphere," *Papers of the Robert S. Peabody Foundation for Archaeology*, vol. 7, Andover, Mass., 1975. See also Michael Moseley, "The Evolution of Andean Civilization," in Jesse D. Jennings, ed., *The Ancient Native Americans*, W. H. Freeman, San Francisco, 1978, pp. 491–542.

13. The archaeological literature on the Southwest is enormous. See especially Paul Martin and Fred Plog, *The Archaeology of Arizona*, Natural History Press, Garden City, N.J., 1973. I drew heavily on William D. Lipe, "The Southwest," in Jennings, ed., *Ancient Native Americans*, pp. 403–454.

14. Herbert W. Dick, *Bat Cave, School of American Research Monograph*, no. 27, Santa Fe, N.M., 1965. Also: Cynthia Irwin-Williams, "The Oshara Tradition: origins of Anasazi culture," *Eastern New Mexico University Contributions in Anthropology*, 1973, 4, 3.

15. Cynthia Irwin-Williams and Vance Haynes, "Climatic Change and Early Population Dynamics in the Southwestern United States," *Quaternary Research*, 1970, 1, 1, pp. 59–71.

16. See the discussion in Lipe, "The Southwest."

17. Michael Glassow, "Changes in the Adaptations of Southwestern Basketmakers," in Mark P. Leone, ed., *Contemporary Archaeology*, Southern Illinois University Press, Carbondale, 1972, pp. 289–302.

18. For a summary of Hohokam, Mogollon, and Anasazi, refer to either of the works cited in note 13 above. Also Emil Haury, *The Hohokam, Desert Farmers and Craftsmen: Excavations at Snaketown, 1964–65*, University of Arizona Press, Tucson, 1976.

19. Mogollon was first identified by Emil Haury, *The Mogollon Culture of Southwestern New Mexico*, Medallion Papers no. 20, Gila Pueblo, Globe, Arizona, 1936. The subsequent literature is summarized by Jesse Jennings, *The Prehistory of North America*, 2nd ed., McGraw-Hill, New York, pp. 291–298, which I have drawn on here.

20. Two important reports by Neil M. Judd describe the Pueblo Bonito site. See Neil M. Judd, *The Material Culture of Pueblo Bonito*, Smithsonian Miscellaneous Collections no. 124, 1954, and *The Architecture of Pueblo Bonito*, Smithsonian Miscellaneous Collections no. 147, vol. 1, 1964. For other references on the Anasazi, see Jennings, *Prehistory of North America*, pp. 297–315. On the general question of carrying capacities, try Ezra Zubrow, "Carrying Capacity and Dynamic Equilibrium in the Prehistoric Southwest," *American Antiquity*, 1971, 36, 2, pp. 127–138.

21. Again, there is an enormous literature. Try, for example: James B. Griffin, "The Midlands and Northeastern United States," and Jon D. Muller, "The Southeast," in Jennings, ed., *Ancient Native Americans*, note 12 above, chaps. 7 and 8. See also W. S. Webb, *The Indian Knoll, site Oh 2, Ohio County, Kentucky*, University of Kentucky Reports in Archaeology and Anthropology, 1046, pp. 11–365. The Woodland tradition is described by Willey, *Introduction to American Archaeology*, vol. 1, chap. 5. See also Stuart Struever, "Woodland Subsistence-Settlement Systems in the Lower Illinois Valley," in Sally R. Binford and Lewis R. Binford, eds., *New Perspectives in Archaeology*, Aldine, Chicago, 1968, pp. 285–312.

22. Adena is described by W. S. Webb and G. E. Snow, *The Adena People*, Reports in Anthropology and Archaeology, vol. 6, University of Kentucky, Lexington, 1945. A second report is W. S. Webb and R. S. Baby, *The Adena People, no. 2*, published for the Ohio Historical Society by the Ohio State University Press, 1957. For the Hopewell, see J. B. Griffin, *The Chronological Position of the Hopewellian Culture in the Eastern United States*, University of Michigan, Museum of Anthropology, Anthropological Papers no. 12, Ann Arbor, 1958.

23. The Mississippian is most ably described by Willey, *Introduction to American Archaeology*, vol. 1, pp. 292–310. Another important reference is Philip Phillips, James A. Ford, and James B. Griffin, *Archaeological Survey in the Lower Mississippi Alluvial Valley, 1940–47*, Peabody Museum Papers, 25, Harvard University, Cambridge, Mass., 1951.

24. Surprisingly little has been published on Cahokia. See W. K. Moorhead, *The Cahokia Mounds*, Bulletin, University of Illinois, Urbana, 1928, vol. 26, no. 4; Melville L. Fowler, ed., "Explorations into Cahokian Archaeology," *Illinois Archaeological Survey Bulletin*, no. 7, 1969. A recent synthesis is Melvin L. Fowler, "Cahokia, Ancient Capital of the Midwest," *Addison-Wesley Module in Anthropology*, 1974, 48.

25. See John R. Swanton's translation of Le Page du Pratz, *Histoire de la Louisiane*, Paris, 1758. Printed in Smithsonian Institution, *Bureau of American Ethnology Bulletin no. 43*, Washington, D.C., 1911, pp. 144–149. This important account has been reprinted in Jesse D. Jennings and E. Adamson Hoebel, eds., *Readings in Anthropology*, 2nd ed., McGraw-Hill, New York, 1966.

14   THE DEVELOPMENT OF CIVILIZATION

1. V. Gordon Childe, *The Prehistory of European Society*, Pelican Books, Harmondsworth, Eng., 1956, p. 78, and his *Man Makes Himself*, Watts, London, 1936.

2. In writing this section, I owe a great deal to Colin Renfrew's *The Emergence of Civilization*, Methuen, London, 1972, chaps. 1–3, also to Charles Redman, *The Rise of Civilization*, W. H. Freeman, San Francisco, 1978.

3. Robert M. Adams, *The Evolution of Urban Society*, Aldine, Chicago, 1966, p. 119.

4. Elman Service, *Primitive Social Organization*, Random House, New York, 1962, is a basic reference. The same author's *The Origins of the State and Civilization*, W. W. Norton, New York, 1975, is a development of this viewpoint.

5. In writing these sections, I have made much use of Paul Wheatley's *Pivot of the Four Quarters*, Aldine, Chicago, 1971, a fundamental source on the origins of civilization for anyone even vaguely interested in the subject.

6. Adams, *Evolution of Urban Society*.

7. For Ester Boserup and a series of critiques of her hypotheses, see Brian Spooner, ed., *Population Growth: An Anthropological Perspective*, MIT Press, Cambridge, Mass., 1972.

8. William Allan, *The African Husbandman*, Oliver and Boyd, Edinburgh, 1965, is a source neglected by those connected with this subject.

9. Karl W. Wittfogel, *Oriental Despotism: A Comparative Study of Total Power*, Yale University Press, New Haven, 1957. See also the contributions by Wittfogel and Julian Steward to Julian Steward and others (eds.), *Irrigation Civilizations: A Comparative Study*, Pan American Union, Washington, D.C., 1955.

10. Robert M. Adams, "Early Civilizations, Subsistence, and Environment," in Carl H. Kraeling and Robert M. Adams, eds., *City Invincible*, Oriental Institute, University of Chicago, 1960, pp. 269–295.

11. Robert M. Adams, "Developmental Stages in Ancient Mesopotamia," in Steward and others, *Irrigation Civilizations*.

12. Essays on trade are in J. A. Sabloff and C. C. Lamberg-Karlovsky, eds., *Ancient Civilizations and Trade*, University of New Mexico Press, Sante Fe, 1975.

13. Karl Polyani, "Traders and Trade," in Sabloff and Lamberg-Karlovsky, *Ancient Civilizations and Trade*, pp. 133–154.

14. See Sabloff and Lamberg-Karlovsky, *Ancient Civilizations and Trade*.

15. Wheatley, *Pivot of the Four Quarters*, was my source for this section.

16. In addition to the Wheatley volume, I consulted Mircea Eliade, *The Myth of the Eternal Return*, Pantheon Books, New York, 1954, and the same author's *The Sacred and the Profane*, Harcourt, Brace, New York, 1959.

17. Wheatley, *Pivot of the Four Quarters*, p. 346.

18. Eliade, *Sacred and Profane*.

19. Adams, *Evolution of Urban Society*.

20. Kent V. Flannery, "The Cultural Evolution of Civilizations," *Annual Review of Ecology and Systematics*, 1972, pp. 399–426.

21. Charles Redman, *Rise of Civilization*, pp. 229–243, discusses a systems-ecological model for the emergence of civilization and describes the difficulty of investigating complex societies in the archaeological record. Unfortunately, Norman Yoffee's "The Decline and Rise of Mesopotamian Civilization: An Ethnoarchaeological Perspective on the Evolution of Social Complexity," *American Antiquity*, 1979, 44, 1, pp. 5–35, was published too late for discussion in this edition.

15 MESOPOTAMIA AND THE FIRST CITIES

1. For the history of Mesopotamian archaeology, see Seton Lloyd, *Foundations in the Dust*, Oxford University Press, Oxford, 1947; see also Brian M. Fagan, *Return to Babylon*, Little, Brown, Boston, 1979. The word *tell* means mound or low hill in Arabic. For tell excavation, read Seton Lloyd, *Mounds of the Near East*, Edinburgh University Press, Edinburgh, and Aldine, Chicago, 1963.

2. For a general summary of Hassunan life, see David and Joan Oates, *The Rise of Civilization*. Phaedon Press, Oxford, 1976, chaps. 2, 3, 4. See also Charles Redman, *The Rise of Civilization*, W. H. Freeman, San Francisco, 1978, chap. 6. For general background on Mesopotamia, see Seton Lloyd, *The Archaeology of Mesopotamia*, Thames and Hudson, London, 1978; Diana Kirkbride, "Umm Dabaghiyah 1974: A Fourth Preliminary Report," *Iraq*, 1975, 37, pp. 3–10.

3. See note 2 above as well as Joan Oates, "The Background and Development of Early Farming Communities in Mesopotamia and the Zagros," *Proceedings of the Prehistoric Society*, 1973, 39, pp. 147–181.

4. See discussion in Redman, *Rise*, p. 199.

5. For references, see Redman, *Rise*, bibliography.

6. For 'Ubaid culture, see Redman, *Rise* pp. 247–252. Also Robert McC. Adams and Hans J. Nissen, *The Uruk Countryside*, University of Chicago Press, Chicago, 1972.

7. For Eridu, see Lloyd, *The Archaeology of Mesopotamia*.

8. The Sumerian civilization is brilliantly described by Samuel Kramer, *The Sumerians*, University of Chicago Press, Chicago, 1963. His essay is written from both archaeology and clay tablet perspectives, and throws valuable light on the beliefs and literature of the world's first civilization.

9. For this section I relied on C. C. Lamberg-Karlovsky, "The Proto-Elamites and the Iranian Plateau," *Antiquity*, 1978, 52, 205, pp. 114–120. Also see Henry T. Wright and others, "Early Fourth Millennium Developments in Southwestern Iran," *Iran*, 1975, 13, pp. 103–121; Henry Wright and G. Johnson, "Population, Exchange, and Early State Formation in Southwestern Iran," *American Anthropologist*, 1975, 77, pp. 267–289.

10. On Tepe Yahya see C. C. Lamberg-Karlovsky, "Urban Interaction on the Iranian Plateau: Excavations at Tepe Yahya 1967–1973," *Proceedings of the British Academy*, 1973, 59, pp. 5–43. See articles and comments by C. C. Lamberg-Karlovsky in Jeremy A. Sabloff and C. C. Lamberg-Karlovsky, eds., *Ancient Civilization and Trade*, University of New Mexico Press, Albuquerque, 1975.

11. P. L. Kohl, "Carved Chlorite Vessels: A Trade in Finished Commodities in the Mid-Third Millennium," *Expedition*, 1975, Fall, pp. 18–31.

12. Sir Leonard Woolley, *Ur Excavations*, vol. 2: *The Royal Cemetery*, Publications of the Joint Expedition of the British Museum and of the Museum of the University of Pennsylvania to Mesopotamia, British Museum, London, 1934, pp. 33–38, 41–44.

13. Samuel Kramer, *The Sumerians*, p. 56.

14. An outline summary of Assur, with references, will be found in Lloyd, *Mesopotamia*.

15. A good general description of the Assyrians is contained in Nicholas Postgate, *The First Empires*, Phaidon, Oxford, 1977. Quote from p. 121. For Mesopotamian epics, see Kramer, *The Sumerians*.

16. Robert Koldeway's excavations at Babylon are described in Fagan, *Return to Babylon*, Biblical quote: Psalm 137,1.

16 PHARAOHS AND AFRICAN CHIEFS

1. General works on Egypt have proliferated in recent years, so it is difficult to recommend the best. For the history of Egyptology and tomb robbing on the Nile, see Brian M. Fagan, *The Rape of the Nile*, Scribners, New York, 1975. For general accounts of Ancient Egypt, see John Ruffle, *Heritage of the Pharaohs*, Phaidon, Oxford, 1977; A. Rosalie David, *The Egyptian Kingdoms*, Phaidon, Oxford, 1975; and Paul Johnson, *The Civilization of Ancient Egypt*, Weidenfeld & Nicholson, London, 1978. Robin Feddon, *Egypt*, John Murray, London, 1976, is a marvelous introduction to Ancient and Modern Egyptians.
2. For Pre-Dynastic cultures, Bruce Trigger, *Beyond History: the Methods of Prehistory*, Holt, Rinehart and Winston, New York, 1968.
3. David Diringer, *Writing*, Thames and Hudson, London, and Praeger, New York, 1962, pp. 46–53, contains a summary of hieroglyphs. See also Michael Pope's *Decipherment*, Thames and Hudson, London, 1973.
4. Karl Butzer, *Early Hydraulic Civilization in Egypt*, University of Chicago Press, Chicago, 1976.
5. Kurt Mendelssohn, *The Riddle of the Pyramids*, Praeger, New York, 1974, is a basic source on theories about the pyramids. I. E. S. Edwards, *The Pyramids*, Viking Press, New York, 1973, is a classic.
6. Siegfried Morenz, *Egyptian Religion*, Macmillan, London, 1973, is the best survey of this complicated subject.
7. Cyril Aldred, *The Egyptians*, Thames and Hudson, London, and Praeger, New York, 1961, chaps. 9 and 10.
8. The Theban archives are a massive source of information on Egyptian workpeople. Try also George Steindorff and Keith C. Seele, *When Egypt Ruled the East*, University of Chicago Press, Chicago, 1957.
9. A brilliant account of Ancient Egyptian History is J. A. Wilson, *The Burden of Egypt*, University of Chicago Press, Chicago, 1951.
10. There is an enormous popular literature on Tutankhamun. The best account is still Howard Carter's *The Tomb of Tut-ankh-Amun*, Macmillan, London, 1923, 1927, 1933, in which Carter gives his blow by blow account of the discovery. Another reliable source: C. Desroches Noblecourt, *Tutankhamun*, New York Graphic Society, New York, 1963.
11. The most controversial incident in Egyptian history is well summarized by Cyril Aldred, *Akhenaten, Pharaoh of Egypt*, Thames and Hudson, London, 1968.
12. Peter Shinnie, *Meroe*, Thames and Hudson, London, and Praeger, New York, 1967, is an authoritative summary.
13. Roland Oliver and John Fage, *A Short History of Africa*, Pelican Books, Harmondsworth, Eng., 1963 and later editions.
14. N. K. Sanders, *The Sea Peoples*, Thames and Hudson, London, 1977.
15. A look at the Saharan trade in recent times can yield much information of value for prehistory; see E. W. Bovill, *The Golden Trade of the Moors*, Heinemann, London, 1968.
16. Thurstan Shaw, *Nigeria*, Thames and Hudson, London, 1978 summarizes the latest data.
17. For the most widely read synthesis of historical and archaeological data on Bantu origins, see Roland Oliver and Brian Fagan, *Africa in the Iron Age*, Cambridge University Press, Cambridge, 1975; for an update, see the same authors' chapter on the subject in Roland Oliver, ed., *Cambridge History of Africa*, vol. II, Cambridge University Press, Cambridge, 1979.
18. David Phillipson, *The Iron Age of Eastern and Southern Africa*, Heinemann, London, 1977 is the best general summary.
19. An attractive, illustrated account of African history is Basil Davidson, *Africa: History of a Continent*, Weidenfeld & Nicholson, London, 1966.
20. On Ghana, see Nehemia Levtzion, *Ancient Ghana and Mali*, Methuen, London, 1973.
21. The kingdom of Mali is covered not only by Levtzion, ibid., but also by Charles Monteil, "Les Empires du Mali: Étude d'histoire et de sociologie soudanais," *Bulletin de Commission d'Études Historiques et Scientifiques*, A.O.F., Paris, 1929, pp. 291–447.
22. John D. Hunwick, "Songhay, Bornu and Hausaland in the sixteenth century," in Jacob F. A. Ajayi and Michael Crowder, eds., *History of West Africa*, vol. 1, Longmans, 1971, pp. 120–157.

23. Peter Garlake, *Great Zimbabwe,* Thames and Hudson, London, 1973, is the best summary of the Karanga and Zimbabwe.

24. Try Edward A. Alpers, *Ivory and Slaves in East Central Africa,* University of California Press, Berkeley and Los Angeles, 1975, for this trade.

25. The writings of the early explorers make fascinating reading. An admirable starting point is Fawn Brodie's biography of Sir Richard Burton, *The Devil Drives,* Eyre and Spottiswoode, London, 1957.

17 THE HARAPPAN CIVILIZATION AND SOUTHEAST ASIA

1. Gurdip Singh, "The Indus Valley Culture," *Archaeology and Physical Anthropology in Oceania,* 1971, 1, 2, pp. 177–188.

2. Bridget Allchin, "Hunters, pastoralists, and early agriculturalists in South Asia," in J. V. S. Megaw, ed., *Hunters, Gatherers, and First Farmers Beyond Europe,* Leicester University Press, Leicester, 1977, pp. 127–144; J. P. Joshi, *Comparative Stratigraphy of the Protohistoric Cultures of the Indo-Pakistan Subcontinent,* Ethnographic and Folklore Society, Lucknow, 1963.

3. For discussion, see Sir Mortimer Wheeler, *Early India and Pakistan,* rev. ed., Thames and Hudson, London, and Praeger, New York, 1968, and references in note 4 below. For a recent collection of essays, see Norman Hammond, ed., *South Asian Archaeology,* Noyes Press, Park Ridge, N.J., 1973.

4. The Harappan civilization is described in Wheeler, *Early India,* chap. 5; Sir Mortimer Wheeler, *The Indus Civilization,* 3rd ed., Cambridge University Press, Cambridge, 1968; D. H. Gordon, *The Prehistoric Background of Indian Culture,* Bhulabhai Memorial Institute, Bombay, 1958; and Walter A. Fairservis, *The Roots of Ancient India: The Archaeology of Early Indian Civilization,* Macmillan, New York, 1971.

5. Robert L. Raikes, *Water, Weather, and Prehistory,* John Baker, London, 1967. For a lively account, see George F. Dales, "The Decline of the Harappans," *Scientific American,* May 1966. A more technical account is Robert L. Raikes, "The End of the Ancient Cities of the Indus," *American Anthropologist,* 1964, 66, 2, pp. 284–299.

6. Singh, "Indus Valley Culture."

7. For discussion, see Grahame Clark, *World Prehistory in New Perspective,* Cambridge University Press, Cambridge, 1977, p. 377.

8. Because of the pioneer state archaeology is in for Southeast Asia, this section is mainly theoretical. In writing it I have relied on Paul Wheatley's elegant article "Satȳarta in Suvarnadvīpa: from Reciprocity to Redistribution in Ancient South-East Asia," in Jeremy A. Sabloff and C. C. Lamberg-Karlovsky, eds., *Ancient Civilizations and Trade,* University of New Mexico Press, Albuquerque, 1977, pp. 227–284.

18 ANATOLIA, GREECE, AND ITALY

1. One Synthesis: Stuart Piggott, *Ancient Europe,* Aldine, Chicago, 1965.

2. James Mellaart, *Çatal Hüyük,* McGraw-Hill, New York, 1968.

3. James Mellaart, *The Neolithic of the Near East,* Thames and Hudson, London, 1975. For general discussion, read Charles Redman, *The Rise of Civilization,* W. H. Freeman, San Francisco, 1978.

4. Carl Blegan, *Troy,* Thames and Hudson, London, and Praeger, New York, 1961.

5. Piggott, *Ancient Europe.*

6. Seton Lloyd, *The Early Highland Peoples of Anatolia,* McGraw-Hill, New York, 1967, has an account of Kanesh written for the lay person.

7. Beyond Seton Lloyd's *Early Highland Peoples,* try O. R. Gurney, *The Hittites,* Pelican Books, Baltimore, 1961, and J. G. MacQueen, *The Hittites and Their Contemporaries in Asia Minor,* Thames and Hudson, London, 1975. Also, Johannes Lehmann, *The Hittites: People of the Thousand Gods,* Collins, London, 1977.

8. Peter Warren, *The Aegean Civilizations,* Phaidon Press, Oxford, 1975 is a good general account. See also Colin Renfrew, *The Emergence of Civilization,* Methuen, London, 1972.

9. See Warren, *Aegean Civilizations.*

10. Sinclair Hood, *The Minoans,* Thames and Hudson, London, and Praeger, New York, 1973, is a relatively up-to-date account. Arthur J. Evans, *The Palace of Minos at Knossos,* vols. 1 to 4, Clarendon Press, Oxford, is the classic account of the palace itself.

11. See especially Mary Renault, *The King Must Die,* Random House, New York, 1963.

12. J. V. Luce, *Atlantis,* McGraw-Hill, New York, 1973, is a convincing account of the legend.

13. Renfrew, *Emergence of Civilization*.

14. In addition to the Warren volume, note 8 above, try Lord William Taylour, *The Mycenaeans*, Thames and Hudson, London, and Praeger, New York, 1964.

15. Piggott, *Ancient Europe*, chap. 3, describes the amber trade.

16. David Diringer, *Writing*, Thames and Hudson, London, and Praeger, New York, 1962, pp. 54–63, and John Chadwick, *The Decipherment of Linear B*, Cambridge University Press, Cambridge, 1958.

17. Two fundamental books on Ancient Greece are: M. I. Kinley, *The Ancient Greeks*, Chatto and Windus, London, 1963; H. D. F. Kitto, *The Greeks*, Pelican Books, Harmondsworth, Eng., 1955.

18. Thucydides, *History of the Peloponnesian War*. A good translation is that by Sir R. Livingstone, Oxford University Press, Oxford, 1943.

19. Donald Harden, *The Phoenicians*, Thames and Hudson, London, and Praeger, New York, 1962. Also N. K. Sanders, *The Sea Peoples*, Thames and Hudson, London, 1978.

20. Piggott, *Ancient Europe*, p. 192.

21. The Etruscans are described by M. Pallotino, *The Etruscans*, trans. David Ridgeway, Alan Lane Press, Harmondsworth, Eng., 1977.

22. Apart from Pallotino, *The Etruscans*, try Michael Grant, *The Romans*, Weidenfeld & Nicholson, London, 1960. The best Roman source is Titus Livy, (59 B.C.–A.D. 17), *Early History of Rome*, bks. 1–4, Aubrey de Selincourt, Penguin Books, Harmondsworth, Eng., 1966. A new survey: Michael Vickers, *The Roman World*, Phaidon, Oxford, 1977.

19 TEMPERATE EUROPE BEFORE THE EUROPEANS*

1. V. Gordon Childe, *The Dawn of European Civilization*, Routledge and Kegan Paul, London, 1925. Also Stuart Piggott, *Ancient Europe*, Aldine, Chicago, 1965.

2. Colin Renfrew, "The Autonomy of the South-East European Copper Age," *Proceedings of the Prehistoric Society*, 1969, 35, pp. 12–47; see also Ruth Tringham, *Hunters, Fishers and Farmers of Eastern Europe*, Hutchinson University Library, London, 1971, chap. 4.

3. Colin Renfrew, "Varna and the Social Context of Early Metallurgy," *Antiquity*, 1978, 52, 206, pp. 199–203.

4. Piggott, *Ancient Europe*, was a basic source for this chapter and covers these controversies.

5. Piggott, *Ancient Europe*, pp. 81–84.

6. An extremely large literature takes up this problem. For a summary: R. A. Crossland, "Indo-Europeans: The Linguistic Evidence," *Past and Present*, 1957, XII, pp. 16–46.

7. Desmond Collins, Ruth Whitehouse, Martin Henig, and David Whitehouse, *Background to Archaeology*, Cambridge University Press, New York, 1973; chap. II has a summary.

8. Piggott, *Ancient Europe*, pp. 123–129.

9. Piggott, *Ancient Europe*, pp. 137–138, 161.

10. R. J. C. Atkinson, *Stonehenge*, Pelican Books, Baltimore, 1960, is the definitive account. Gerald Hawkins, *Stonehenge Decoded*, Souvenir Press, New York, 1965, is highly controversial, and Alexander Thom's papers on the astronomical significance of the site are fascinating: Alexander Thom and others, "Stonehenge," *Journal for the History of Astronomy*, 1974, 5, 2, 13, pp. 71–89.

11. Piggott, *Ancient Europe*, pp. 150–188.

12. J. G. D. Clark, *Prehistoric Europe: The Economic Basis*, Methuen, London, 1952, chap. 7.

13. J. G. D. Clark, *Prehistoric Europe*, chap. 5.

14. Piggott, *Ancient Europe*, pp. 176–185. See also E. D. Phillips, "The Scythian Domination in Western Asia," *World Archaeology*, 1972, 4, pp. 129–138.

15. Sergei I. Rudenko, *Frozen Tombs of Siberia: The Pazyryk Burials of Iron Age Horsemen*, trans. M. W. Thompson, University of California Press, Berkeley, 1970. This is also a basic reference on Scythian art. See also M. I. Artamonov, "Frozen Tombs of the Scythians," *Scientific American*, May, 1965.

16. Ralph Rowlett, "The Iron Age North of the Alps," *Science*, 1967, 161, pp. 123–134.

17. P. Jacobsthal, *Early Celtic Art*, Oxford University Press, Oxford, 1944, is still the classic work on La Tène art. Also: J. V. S. Megaw, *Art of the European Iron Age*, John Baker, Bath, Eng., 1970.

18. Julius Caesar, *Commentaries*, Pelican Books, Harmondsworth, Eng., 1947.

* European archaeological literature is so complicated and fast moving that you should consult a specialist for specific information before getting too deeply into the references listed above.

20 SHANG CULTURE IN EAST ASIA

1. I have drawn heavily on two basic sources by Kwang-Chih Chang when writing this chapter: *The Archaeology of Ancient China*, Yale University Press, New Haven, 1977; and *Early Chinese Civilization: Anthropological Perspectives*, Harvard University Press, Cambridge, Mass., 1976.

2. These theories are discussed by Glyn Daniel, *The First Civilizations*, Thames and Hudson, London, 1968, pp. 131–134.

3. Chang, *Archaeology of Ancient China*, chap. 6. See also the same author's "The Continuing Quest for China's Origins," *Archaeology*, 1977, 30, 3, pp. 186–193.

4. Lungshanoid and Lung-shan cultures are described by Chang, *Archaeology of Ancient China*, chaps. 4 and 5.

5. See David Diringer, *Writing*, Thames and Hudson, London, and Praeger, New York, 1962, chap. 3.

6. Noel Barnard, *Bronze Casting and Bronze Alloys in Ancient China*, Australian National University and Monumenta Sinica, Canberra, 1961.

7. Paul Wheatley, *Pivot of the Four Quarters: A Preliminary Inquiry into the Origins and Character of the Ancient Chinese City*, Edinburgh University Press, Edinburgh, and Aldine, Chicago, 1971, is the classic source on early Chinese urbanization.

8. Paul Wheatley, "The Archaeology and the Chinese City," *World Archaeology*, 1970, 2, 2, pp. 159–185. Also Chang, *Archaeology of Ancient China*, pp. 248–258.

9. The Shang royal graves are described by Cheng Te-k'un, *Archaeology in China, vol. 2: Shang China*, Heffers, Cambridge, 1960.

10. Chang, *Archaeology of Ancient China*, chap. 6; and Li Chi, *The Beginnings of Chinese Civilization*, University of Washington Press, Seattle, 1957. The site of Anyang is described by the same author in his *Anyang*, University of Washington Press, Seattle, 1976.

11. Here I have followed Chang's chronology and subdivisions of Shang civilization. See Chang, *Archaeology of Ancient China*, chap. 6.

12. See the references by Wheatley, note 7 above, and Li Chi's *Anyang* for details.

13. Chang, *Archaeology of Ancient China*, chap. 7 ff.

21 MESOAMERICAN CIVILIZATIONS

1. Anyone interested in the Spanish conquest of Mexico should begin with Hernando Cortés, *Five Letters of Cortés to the Emperor, 1519–26*, rev. ed., trans. J. Bayard Morris, Norton, New York, 1962. For pre-Columbian contacts, an authoritative and up-to-date summary of the issues is Carol L. Riley, J. Charles Kelley, Campbell W. Pennington, and Robert L. Rands, eds., *Man across the Sea*, University of Texas Press, Austin, 1971. For a review of recent literature, see Glyn Daniel, "The Second American," *Antiquity*, 1972, 46, 184, pp. 288–292.

2. Muriel Porter Weaver, *The Aztecs, Maya, and Their Predecessors*, Seminar Press, New York, 1972, is one basic source for this chapter. She includes some discussion of environmental topics. Another source is William T. Sanders and Barbara J. Price, *Mesoamerica: The Evolution of a Civilization*, Random House, New York, 1968.

3. Norman Hammond, "British Archaeology in Belize, 1976," *Antiquity,* 1977, 51, 202, pp. 61–64.

4. I have used the chronology and terminology employed by Gordon R. Willey, *An Introduction to American Archaeology, vol. 1: North and Middle America*, Prentice-Hall, Englewood Cliffs, N.J., 1966, chap. 3. This volume is a basic source on Mesoamerican archaeology.

5. Willey, *Introduction*, vol. 1, p. 98.

6. Ignacio Bernal, *The Olmec World*, University of California Press, Berkeley, 1969, and Michael D. Coe, *The Jaguar's Children*, Museum of Primitive Art, New York, 1965. Elizabeth Benson's edited volume, *Dumbarton Oaks Conference on the Olmec*, Dumbarton Oaks Research Library and Collection, Washington, D.C., 1968, includes important contributions to the subject. Michael D. Coe's *America's First Civilization: Discovering the Olmec*, American Heritage, New York, 1968, is a good starting point on the Olmec.

7. On La Venta, see Phillip Drucker, *La Venta, Tabasco: A Study of Olmec Ceramics and Art*, Smithsonian Institution, Bureau of American Ethnology Bulletin no. 170, Washington, D.C., 1959.

8. Kent V. Flannery, ed., *The Early Mesoamerican Village*, Academic Press, New York, 1976, is a modern classic, and formed the basis for writing this section.

9. G. C. Valliant, *Aztecs of Mexico*, Doubleday, New York, 1941.

10. Richard E. Blanton, *Monte Albán: Settlement Patterns at the Ancient Zapotec Capital*, Academic Press, New York, 1978, is a must for all students of Mesoamerican archaeology.

11. One of the classic arguments about Maya archaeology has been that rural populations supported the centers, without large urban populations at places like Tikal. This interpretation has been shown to be only partly correct. See William A. Haviland, "Tikal, Guatemala, and Mesoamerican Urbanism," *World Archaeology*, 1970, 2, 2, pp. 186–197.

12. I relied heavily on Richard E. W. Adams, *Prehistoric Mesoamerica*, Little, Brown, Boston, 1977, in this and other sections of this chapter.

13. Kent V. Flannery, "The Olmec and the Valley of Oaxaca: A Model for Interregional Interaction in Formative Times," in Benson, ed., *Dumbarton Oaks Conference*, pp. 79–110.

14. Adams, *Prehistoric Mesoamerica*, pp. 27–29. Also W. T. Sanders, and others, "The Natural Environment, Contemporary Occupation and 16th Century Population of the Valley," The Teotihuacán Valley Project, Final Report, vol. 1. *Occasional Papers in Anthropology*, No. 3, Department of Anthropology, Pennsylvania State University, 1970.

15. René Millon, R. Bruce Drewitt, and George L. Cowgill, *Urbanization at Teotihuacán, Mexico*, University of Texas Press, Austin, 1974 and later years, is a multivolume account of all aspects of this spectacular settlement. A fascinating account of trade at Teotihuacán has been written by Lee Parsons and Barbara Price, "Mesoamerican Trade and Its Role in the Emergence of Civilization," *Contributions of the University of California Archaeological Research Facility*, Berkeley, 1971, pp. 169–195.

16. W. T. Sanders, *Cultural Ecology of the Teotihuacán Valley*, Department of Sociology and Anthropology, Pennsylvania State University, 1965.

17. Norman Hammond, "Ex Oriente Lux: A View from Belize," in Richard E. W. Adams, *The Origins of Maya Civilization*, University of New Mexico Press, Albuquerque, 1977, pp. 45–77.

18. Many of the viewpoints are summarized in Adams, *Origins*, note 19 above.

19. William L. Rathje, "Praise the Gods and Pass the Metates, A Hypothesis of the Development of Lowland and Rainforest Civilizations in Mesoamerica," in Mark P. Leone, ed., *Contemporary Archaeology*, Southern Illinois University Press, Carbondale, 1972, pp. 365–392.

20. M. D. Coe, *The Maya*, Thames and Hudson, London, and Praeger, New York, 1966, is a fundamental reference for this civilization. See also J. E. S. Thompson, *The Rise and Fall of Maya Civilization*, University of Oklahoma Press, Norman, 1966. See also William L. Rathje, "The Origin and Development of Lowland Classic Maya Civilization," *American Antiquity*, 1971, 36, 3, pp. 275–285. See also T. P. Culbert, *The Lost Civilization: The Story of the Classic Maya*, Harper & Row, New York, 1974.

21. Maya script was described by J. E. S. Thompson, *Maya Hieroglyphic Writing: Introduction*, Carnegie Institution of Washington, Washington, D.C., and University of Oklahoma Press, Norman, 1950.

22. Willey, *Introduction*, vol. 1, p. 136, note 4 above.

23. The latest research is summarized in T. P. Culbert, ed., *The Classic Maya Collapse*, University of Mexico Press, Albuquerque, 1973. I made particular use of two articles in writing this section: Richard E. W. Adams, "The Collapse of Maya Civilization: A Review of Previous Theories," pp. 21–34 and Gordon R. Willey and Dimitri B. Shimkin, "The Maya Collapse: A Summary View," pp. 457–502. I also recommend the article by William Rathje in the same volume: "Classic Maya Development and Denouement: A Research Design," pp. 405–456.

24. On Toltecs and Tula, see Beatrice P. Dutton, "Tula of the Toltecs," *El Palacio*, 1955, 62, 7–8, pp. 195–251; also Eric Wolfe, *Sons of the Shaking Earth*, University of Chicago Press, Chicago, 1959. See also: Nigel Davis, *The Toltecs until the Fall of Tula*, University of Oklahoma Press, Norman, 1977.

25. On Chichen Itzá, see the Summary in Adams, *Prehistoric Mesoamerica*, pp. 237–240. Two key references are: R. Roys, "Native Empires in Yucatan: the Maya-Toltec Empire," *Sociedad Mexicana de Antropologia Revista*, 1966, 20, pp. 153–177, and the same author's *The Indian Background of Colonial Yucatan*, University of Oklahoma Press, Norman, 1972.

26. The Aztecs are well described by Bernal Diaz del Castillo, *The True History of the Conquest of New Spain*, trans. A. P. Maudslay, Hakluyt Society, London, 1908–1916. For archaeology, see Willey, *Introduction*, vol. 1, pp. 156–161; for social and economic structure, see Friedrich Kats, *Situación social y Económica de los Aztecas durante los siglos XV y XVI*, Universidad Nacional Autónoma de México, Mexico City, 1966.

27. Tenochtitlán is best visited in company with Hernando Cortés; see note 1. Also see Edward Calnek, "Settlement Patterns and Chinampa Agriculture at Tenochtitlán," *American Antiquity*, 1972, 37, 1, pp. 104–115.

1. In this chapter I have followed the long-used subdivisions of Peruvian prehistory, which are subdivisions of convenience rather than actual cultural reality. While it is more realistic to conceive of Peruvian prehistory in terms of a continuous development, the subdivision used here reflects common usage, and may aid understanding of the events described in this chapter. My primary source for the coastal sections of this chapter is Michael Edward Moseley, *The Maritime Foundations of Andean Civilization*, Cummings, Menlo Park, Calif., 1975. See also the same author's "The Evolution of Andean Civilization," in Jesse D. Jennings, ed., *Ancient Native Americans*, W. H. Freeman, San Francisco, 1978, pp. 491–542.

2. Frederic Engel, "Le Complexe Précéramique d'El Paraiso (Pérou), *Journal de la Société des Américanistes*, 1967, LV, pp. 43–96.

3. Moseley, *Maritime Foundations*, chap. 2.

4. For weaving, see A. H. Gayton, "The Cultural Significance of Peruvian Textiles: Production, Function, Aesthetics," in John H. Rowe and Dorothy Menzel, eds., *Peruvian Archaeology*, University of California Press, Berkeley, 1961, pp. 125–167.

5. The archaeology of Peru has been ably summarized by G. H. S. Bushnell, *Peru*, rev. ed., Thames and Hudson, London, and Praeger, New York, 1963. In writing this account, I have drawn both on this reference and on Gordon R. Willey, *Introduction to American Archaeology*, vol. 2: *South America*, Prentice-Hall, Englewood Cliffs, N.J., 1971. Throughout this part of the chapter, I have adopted Willey's terminology and dating. The reader can identify dating controversies by consulting the notes to Willey's chap. 3. See also J. H. Rowe and Dorothy Menzel (eds.), *Peruvian Archaeology: Selected Readings*, Peek, Palo Alto, 1967. A good analysis and description of the Chavín art style is John H. Rowe, *Chavín Art: An Inquiry into Its Form and Meaning*, Museum of Primitive Art, New York, 1962. In the interests of clarity I have omitted discussion of the Paracas culture of southern Peru (Willey, *Introduction to American Archaeology*, vol. 1, pp. 127 ff.). See also the basic sources under note 1 above.

6. For a discussion, see Stephen C. Jett, "Pre-Columbian Transoceanic Contacts," in Jennings, ed., *Ancient Native Americans*, pp. 593–650.

7. For Gallinazo, see Gordon R. Willey, *Prehistoric Settlement Patterns in the Virú Valley, Peru*, Smithsonian Institution, Bureau of American Ethnology Bulletin no. 155, Washington, D.C., 1953.

8. Mochica is described by G. H. S. Bushnell, *Peru*, Thames and Hudson, London, and Praeger, New York, rev. ed., 1963. See also Rafael Larco Hoyle, "A Culture Sequence for the North Coast of Peru," in Julian H. Steward, ed., *Handbook of South American Indians*, Smithsonian Institution, Bureau of American Ethnology Bulletin no. 143, Washington, D.C., 1946, vol. 2, pp. 149–175.

9. Summarized briefly by Willey, *Introduction to American Archaeology*, vol. 2, pp. 142–148.

10. For Huari, see John H. Rowe, Donald Collier, and Gordon R. Willey, "Reconnaissance Notes on the Site of Huari, near Ayacucho, Peru," *American Antiquity*, 1950, 16, 2, pp. 120–137. A highly complex study of the Huari problem is Dorothy Menzel, "Style and Time in the Middle Horizon," *Nawpa Pacha*, 1964, 2, pp. 1–106. Also: William H. Isbell and Katherina J. Schreiber, "Was Huari a State?" *American Antiquity*, 1978, 43, 3, pp. 372–389.

11. The Tiahuanaco site is described by E. P. Lanning, *Peru before the Incas*, Prentice-Hall, Englewood Cliffs, N.J., 1967, chap. 9. He also describes Huari.

12. Lanning, *Peru before the Incas*, chap. 10. A recent, vivid, popular account is Michael E. Moseley and Carol Mackey, "Chan Chan, Peru's Ancient City of Kings," *National Geographic*, March 1973, pp. 319–345. See also Michael Moseley, "Chan Chan: Andean alternative to the preindustrial city," *Science*, 1975, 187, pp. 219–225.

13. Garcilaso de la Vega (el Inca), *The First Part of the Royal Commentaries of the Incas*, trans. Clements R. Markham, Hakluyt Society, London, 1869–1871.

14. Chincha and Ica are discussed in Dorothy Menzel, "The Pottery of Chincha," *Nawpa Pacha*, 1966, 4, pp. 63–76.

15. The classic source on the Inca empire is W. H. Prescott, *History of the Conquest of Peru*, Everyman's Library, no. 301, London and New York, 1908. For archaeology, see John H. Rowe, "An Introduction to the Archaeology of Cuzco," *Peabody Museum Papers*, Harvard University, Cambridge, 1944, vol. 27, no. 2. The same author's *Inca Culture at the Time of the Spanish Conquest*, Smithsonian Institution, Bureau of American Ethnology Bulletin no. 143, Washington, D.C., 1946, vol. 2, pp. 183–331, is a key source, and the literature is summarized by Gordon R. Willey, *Introduction to American Archaeology*, vol. 2, pp. 175–183.

BIBLIOGRAPHY
OF ARCHAEOLOGY

The chapters on the basic methods and theory of archaeology in this book are necessarily sketchy. To supplement these, here is an annotated bibliography of primary sources on aspects of archaeology itself.

WORLD PREHISTORIES

It is fashionable but shamefully wasteful for textbook authors to ignore their competition, for all world prehistories have different things to offer. Grahame Clark's *World Prehistory, in New Perspective*, Cambridge University Press, Cambridge and New York, 1977, is the third edition of a global culture history that is strong on later prehistory and gives little consideration to theoretical controversies. Chester S. Chard, *Man in Prehistory*, 2nd ed., McGraw-Hill, New York, 1975 is a widely used text with attractive presentation and much coverage on Asia.

GENERAL BOOKS ON METHOD AND THEORY IN ARCHAEOLOGY

A good starting point is my own *Archaeology: A Brief Introduction*, Little, Brown, Boston, 1978, or, if you want a more detailed treatment, any of the following: Brian M. Fagan, *In the Beginning*, 3rd ed., Little, Brown, Boston, 1978; Frank Hole and Robert F. Heizer, *Prehistoric Archaeology: A Brief Introduction*, Holt, Rinehart and Winston, New York, 1977; S. J. Knudson, *Culture in Retrospect: An Introduction to Archaeology*, Rand McNally, Chicago, 1978. Frank Hole and Robert Heizer's *An Introduction to Prehistoric Archaeology*, 3rd ed., Holt, Rinehart and Winston, New York, 1973, has a heavy systems emphasis and an outstanding bibliography for the serious student. All these volumes will lead the interested reader towards the major controversies in the field.

HISTORY OF ARCHAEOLOGY

Glyn Daniel's *A Hundred and Fifty Years of Archaeology*. Duckworth, London, 1975, is a standard work, and the same author's *The Origins and Growth of Archaeology*, Pelican Books, Harmondsworth, Eng., 1967, is an invaluable anthology. American archaeology is described by Gordon R. Willey and Jeremy Sabloff in *A History of American Archaeology*, W. H. Freeman, San Francisco, 1974. The history of archaeological theory has been poorly served by archaeological writers, but Marvin Harris, *The Rise of Anthropological Theory*, Crowell, New York, 1968, is an invaluable if polemical source. W. W. Taylor, *A Study of Archaeology*, American Anthropological Association, Menasha, Wisconsin, 1948, is also a landmark monograph.

TIME

How archaeologists date their finds has been summarized by J. W. Michels, *Dating Methods in Archaeology*, Seminar Press, New York, 1973. H. N. Michael and E. K. Ralph, eds., *Dating Techniques for the Archaeologist*, MIT Press, Cambridge, 1971, is also useful. Karl Butzer's *Environment and Archaeology*, 2nd ed., Aldine, Chicago, 1972, is the best source on Pleistocene geochronology, to which K. P. Oakley's *Frameworks for Dating Fossil Man*, Aldine, Chicago, 1964, adds some detail. V. Gordon Childe's *Piecing Together the Past*, Routledge and Kegan Paul, London, 1956, contains an interesting and cogent section on chronology and dating. Stratigraphy is well summarized by Mortimer Wheeler, *Archaeology from the Earth*, Clarendon Press, Oxford, 1954, and Edward Pydokke, *Stratification for the Archaeologist*, Phoenix, London, 1961, is a useful source.

ARCHAEOLOGICAL SURVEY

A good survey of preservation conditions is to be found in J. G. D. Clark, *Archaeology and Society*, Methuen, London, 1939. S. J. de Laet, *Archaeology and Its Problems*, Macmillan, New York, 1957, is also useful. Electronic survey methods are summarized by John Coles, *Field Archaeology in Britain*, Methuen, London, 1972. Robert F. Heizer and J. Graham, *A Guide to Archaeological Field Methods*, 3rd ed., National Press, Palo Alto, 1966, includes valuable data on survey methods. O. G. S. Crawford, *Archaeology in the Field*, Praeger, New York, 1953, is a classic, old-fashioned essay on field archaeology.

EXCAVATION

The Directing of Archaeological Excavations by John Alexander, Humanities Press, New York, 1970, is a useful basic essay, especially when read in conjunction with R. J. C. Atkinson's classic *Field Archaeology*, Methuen, London, 1953, or Thomas R. Hester, Robert F. Heizer, and John A. Graham, *Field Methods in Archaeology*, 6th ed., Mayfield Press, Palo Alto, Calif., 1975. An up-to-date British manual: Phillip Barker, *The Techniques of Archaeological Excavation*, Batsford, London, 1977. Conservation is described by Elizabeth A. Dowman, *Conservation in Field Archaeology*, Methuen,

Bibliography of Archaeology

London, 1970, and photography by V. M. Conlon, *Camera Techniques in Archaeology*, John Baker, London, 1973.

Historical archaeology is most ably covered by Ivor Noël Hume, *Historical Archaeology*, Knopf, New York, 1968, and underwater archaeology is summarized by George Bass, *Archaeology Underwater*, Praeger, New York, 1966. The same author's *A History of Seafaring Based on Underwater Archaeology*, Thames and Hudson, London, 1972, is a beautiful summary of the results of underwater research. Paul L. MacKendrick, *The Greek Stones Speak*, St. Martin's Press, New York, 1962, and *The Mute Stones Speak*, St. Martin's Press, New York, 1961, are two surveys of Classical archaeology. Industrial archaeology: Kenneth Hudson, *World Industrial Archaeology*, Cambridge University Press, Cambridge and New York, 1979. Last, Warwick Bray and David Trump, *A Dictionary of Archaeology*, Penguin Press, London, 1970, is a useful tool.

ENVIRONMENT AND SUBSISTENCE

There is no definitive work on economic archaeology, although Creighton Gabel, in *Analysis of Prehistoric Economic Patterns*, Holt, Rinehart and Winston, New York, 1967, has attempted a survey of the literature. J. G. D. Clark, *Prehistoric Europe*, Methuen, London, 1952, is a classic account of economic prehistory. Animal bones are described by R. E. Chaplin, *The Study of Animal Bones from Archaeological Sites*, Seminar Press, New York, 1971, and by Ian Cornwall, *Bones for the Archaeologist*, Phoenix, London, 1956. A useful short work on the subject is S. J. Olsen, *Zooarchaeology: Animal Bones in Archaeology and Their Interpretation*, Addison-Wesley Modules in Anthropology, 1971. Seeds and vegetal remains are covered by Jane M. Renfrew, *Palaeoethnobotany: The Prehistoric Food Plants of the Near East*, Methuen, London, 1973. New methods of seed recovery are described in Eric Higgs, ed., *Papers in Economic Prehistory*, Cambridge University Press, Cambridge, 1972. One of the best monographs on economic archaeology is Frank Hole, K. V. Flannery, and J. A. Neely, *Prehistory and Human Ecology of the Deh Luran Plain*, University of Michigan Museum of Anthropology, Memoir No. 1, 1969. For New World examples, see Jesse D. Jennings, *The Prehistory of North America*, 2nd ed., McGraw-Hill, New York, 1974. Peter J. Ucko and G. W. Dimbleby, eds., *The Domestication and Exploitation of Plants and Animals*, Aldine, Chicago, 1969, contains many useful essays.

TECHNOLOGY

The literature on ancient technology is enormous, but the following are useful introductions. Stone technology is summarized by J. Bordaz, *Tools of the Old and New Stone Age*, American Museum of Natural History, New York, 1971. François Bordes, *The Old Stone Age*, McGraw-Hill, New York, 1968, contains much information on stone tool types. H. McWhinney, *A Manual for Neanderthals*, University of Texas Press, Austin, 1957, is a lighthearted look at the knapping (manufacture) of stone tools. Anna O. Shepard, *Ceramics for the Archaeologist*, Smithsonian Institution, Washington, D.C., 1956, is the definitive work on pottery, and R. F. Tylecote's *Metallurgy in Archaeology*, Edward Arnold, London, 1962, is a useful reference book on metals. David L. Clarke's *Analytical Archaeology*, Methuen, London, 1968, Chapters 11–14, has a lengthy analysis of advanced taxonomic methods.

ORDERING AND INTERPRETATION

Gordon R. Willey and Philip Phillips, *Method and Theory in American Archaeology*, University of Chicago Press, Chicago, 1958, contains fundamental reading on archaeological units. V. Gordon Childe, *Piecing Together the Past*, Routledge and Kegan Paul, London, 1956, is another thought-provoking source. The principles of diffusion, migration, and independent invention are well described by Bruce C. Trigger, *Beyond History: The Methods of Prehistory*, Holt, Rinehart and Winston, New York, 1968, and by V. Gordon Childe, *Piecing Together the Past*, Routledge and Kegan Paul, London, 1956. Colin Renfrew has edited a large volume of papers, *The Explanation of Culture Change: Models in Prehistory*, Duckworth, London, 1973, which contain much provocative and theoretical discussion on cultural process. See also W. W. Taylor, *A Study of Archaeology*, American Anthropological Association, Menasha, Wis., 1948. See also Fred Plog, *The Study of Prehistoric Change*, Academic Press, New York, 1974.

PROCESSUAL ARCHAEOLOGY

Patty Jo Watson, Steven A. LeBlanc, and Charles L. Redman, *Explanation in Archaeology*, Columbia University Press, New York, 1971, is a useful starting point. Then try Lewis R. Binford, *An Archaeological Perspective*, Seminar Press, New York, 1972, which has a very personal essay on the development of processual archaeology and reprints Binford's major papers. Sally and Lewis Binford, eds., *New Perspectives in Archaeology*, Aldine, Chicago, 1968, contains some early attempts at processual archaeology. Mark P. Leone, ed., *Contemporary Archaeology*, Southern Illinois Press, Carbondale, 1972, reprints many basic articles on processual archaeology and adds some new contributions. D. L. Clarke, ed., *Models in Prehistory*, Methuen, London, 1972, also has useful papers. Charles L. Redman, ed., *Research and Theory in Current Archaeology*, John Wiley Interscience, New York, 1973, has many valuable and thought-provoking articles on the latest developments in archaeology.

SETTLEMENT ARCHAEOLOGY

K. C. Chang, ed., *Settlement Archaeology*, National Press, Palo Alto, Calif., 1968, is a fundamental source. So is Kent V. Flannery's edited *The Early Mesoamerican Village*, Academic Press, New York, 1976, which talks more common sense about contemporary archaeology than any other source known to me. For trade in prehistory, see Jeremy Sabloff and C. C. Lamberg-Karlovsky, eds., *Early Civilization and Trade*, University of New Mexico Press, Albuquerque, 1975.

ETHNOARCHAEOLOGY (LIVING ARCHAEOLOGY)

This is probably the most fashionable field of archaeology at the moment. Try: Richard A. Gould, ed., *Explanations in Ethnoarchaeology*, University of New Mexico Press, Albuquerque, 1978. Also John E. Yellen, *Archaeological Approaches to the Present*, Academic Press, New York, 1977. Lewis Binford, *Nunamiut Ethnoarchae-*

ology, Academic Press, New York, 1978, is bound to become a much quoted case study. Another aspect of living archaeology is ably summarized by John Coles. *Archaeology by Experiment*, Hutchinson University Library, London, 1973. See also: D. Ingersoll and others, *Experimental Archeology*, Columbia University Press, New York, 1977.

THE DESTRUCTION OF ARCHAEOLOGICAL SITES

Karl Meyer, *The Plundered Past*, Atheneum Press, New York, 1973, is a fascinating and shocking account of the illegal traffic in antiquities. C. R. McGimsey, *Public Archaeology*, Seminar Press, New York, 1972, is fundamental reading for all American archaeologists. M. Pallotino, *The Meaning of Archaeology*, Thames and Hudson, London, 1968, is a thoughtful analysis of archaeology in the modern world. For the new and expanding field of cultural resource management, I would advise you to start with the chapter on this subject in my *In the Beginning*, 3rd ed., Little, Brown, Boston, 1978, simply because it is the only available beginning summary of the complex issues involved.

ATLAS OF ARCHAEOLOGY

Although several atlases of archaeology are on the market, by far the best tool is David and Ruth Whitehouse, *Archaeological Atlas of the World*, Thames and Hudson, London, and W. H. Freeman, San Francisco, 1975. This book belongs on every archaeologist's bookshelf.

CREDITS

(continued from page iv)

Perspective, 2nd Ed. Copyright © 1978, 1975 by Little, Brown and Company (Inc.). Reprinted by permission. *Figure 4.11:* Page 68 and Page 69, top: Redrawn from Lowell Hess in Life Nature Library/*Early Man*, © 1965 Time Inc., by permission of the publisher, Time-Life Books Inc. Page 69, bottom: Adapted by permission from *Olduvai Gorge*, Excavations in Beds I and II, by M. D. Leakey, © 1971 Cambridge University Press.

CHAPTER 5
Figure 5.1: Cambridge Museum of Archaeology and Anthropology. *Figure 5.3:* Page 78, top: Adapted by permission from *Olduvai Gorge*, Excavations in Beds I and II, by M. D. Leakey, © 1971 Cambridge University Press. Page 78, bottom: Adapted by permission of Doubleday & Company, Inc. from *Tools of the Old and New Stone Age* by Jacques Bordaz. Copyright © 1970 by Jacques Bordaz. Copyright © 1958, 1959 by The American Museum of Natural History. Page 79 top: Redrawn from Figure 26, *The Swanscombe Skull: A Survey of Research on a Pleistocene Site* (Occasional Paper no. 20, Royal Anthropological Institute of Great Britain and Ireland), by permission of the Society. Page 79, bottom left: From *The Distribution of Prehistoric Culture in Angola* by J. D. Clark, 1966, Companhia de Diamantes de Angola, Africa. Page 79, bottom right: Adapted from *Prehistory of Africa* by J. D. Clark, Thames and Hudson Ltd., London. *Figure 5.4:* From H. L. Movius, Jr., "The Lower Paleolithic Structures of Southern and Eastern Asia," *Transactions of the American Philosophical Society*, Vol. 38, Pt. 4 (1948). Reprinted by permission of the Society and the author. *Figure 5.5:* Top: From Grahame Clark, *Aspects of Prehistory*. Copyright © 1970 by The Regents of the University of California. Reprinted by permission of the University of California Press. Bottom: Redrawn by permission from Ronald Singer et al., "Excavation of the Clactonian Industry," *Proceedings of the Prehistoric Society*, by permission of the Society. *Figure 5.6:* Courtesy of F. Clark Howell. *Figure 5.7:* By permission of Henry de Lumley, Laboratoire de Paléontologie Humaine et de Préhistoire, Marseille. *Figures 5.8 and 5.9:* From *Mankind in the Making* by William Howells. Drawings by Janis Cirulis. Copyright © 1959, 1967 by William Howells. Reprinted by permission of Doubleday & Company, Inc. and Martin Secker & Warburg Ltd. *Figure 5.10:* Adapted by permission from Mark L. Weiss and Alan E. Mann, *Human Biology and Behavior: An Anthropological Perspective*, 2nd Ed. Copyright © 1978, 1975 by Little, Brown and Company (Inc.). *Figure 5.11:* Page 90, top: Adapted by permission of Doubleday & Company, Inc. from *Tools of the Old and New Stone Age* by Jacques Bordaz. Copyright © 1970 by Jacques Bordaz. Copyright © 1958, 1959 by The American Museum of Natural History. Page 90, bottom left and Page 91, bottom right: Redrawn from J. M. Coles and E. S. Higgs, *The Archaeology of Early Man* by permission of Faber and Faber Ltd. Page 90, bottom right: Redrawn from *Prehistory* by Derek Roe. Courtesy of the Trustees of the British Museum. Page 91, top, middle left and center, bottom center: Adapted from *The Old Stone Age* by F. Bordes. Copyright © 1968 by McGraw-Hill, Inc. Used by permission of McGraw-Hill Book Company and Weidenfeld & Nicolson Ltd. Page 91, middle right: Redrawn from *The Stone Age of Mt. Carmel* by D. A. E. Garrod and D. M. A. Bate by permission of Oxford University Press. Page 91, bottom left: Adapted from *Prehistory of Africa* by J. D. Clark, Thames and Hudson Ltd., London. *Figure 5.12:* Ralph S. Solecki. *Figure 5.13:* A. C. Blanc, 1958, "Torre in Pietra Saccopastore, Monte Circeo. On the Position of the Mousterian in the Pleistocene Sequence of the Rome Area," in *Hundert Jahre Neanderthaler*, Cologne: Bohlau Verlag.

CHAPTER 6
Figure 6.2: M. Shostak/Anthro-Photo. *Figure 6.3:* Left, top and bottom: Adapted from *The Old Stone Age* by F. Bordes. Copyright © 1968 by McGraw-Hill, Inc. Used with permission of McGraw-Hill Book Company and Weidenfeld & Nicolson Ltd. Top right: Adapted by permission of Doubleday & Company, Inc. from *Tools of the Old and New Stone Age* by Jacques Bordaz. Copyright © 1970 by Jacques Bordaz. Copyright © 1958, 1959 by The American Museum of Natural History. Bottom right: Adapted by permission from *Le Paléolithique Supérieur en Périgord* by Denise de Sonneville-Bordes, Directeur de recherches au Centre national de la Recherche scientifique, Institut du Quaternaire, Universite de Bordeaux I, France. *Table 6.1:* Page 104, bottom and Page 105, bottom left: H. Breuil. Page 105, top and middle left: Adapted by permission from *Le Paléolithique Supérieur en Périgord* by Denise de Sonneville-Bordes, Directeur de recherches au Centre national de la Recherche scientifique, Institut du Quaternaire, Université de Bordeaux I, France. Middle right: After Lowell Hess in Life Nature Library/*Early Man*, Time-Life Books Inc. Bottom right: Adapted from *The Old Stone Age* by F. Bordes. Copyright © 1968

by McGraw-Hill, Inc. Used with permission
of McGraw-Hill Book Company and
Weidenfeld & Nicolson Ltd. *Figure 6.4:*
Courtesy of Musée de l'Homme. *Figure 6.5:* ©
Alexander Marshack 1972. *Figure 6.6:* Top:
From Richard G. Klein, *Man and Culture in
the Late Pleistocene.* © 1969 by Chandler
Publishing Company. By permission of
Dun-Donnelly Publishing Corporation.
Bottom: From *The Archeology of the USSR*
by A. L. Mongait, Mir Publishers, Moscow.
Figure 6.7: From C. B. M. McBurney, *Early
Man in the Soviet Union* (Oxford University
Press, 1976). Reprinted by permission of the
British Academy. *Figure 6.8:* Reprinted by
permission of Faber and Faber Ltd. from J. M.
Coles and E. S. Higgs, *The Archeology of
Early Man.*

CHAPTER 7
Figure 7.2: Redrawn with permission of
the Glencoe Press from *Foundations of
Archaeology* by Jason W. Smith. Copyright ©
1976, Jason W. Smith. *Figure 7.3:* Redrawn
from Gordon R. Willey, *An Introduction to
American Archaeology,* Vol. I: *North and
Middle America,* © 1966, p. 65. Reprinted by
permission of Prentice-Hall, Inc., Englewood
Cliffs, N.J. *Figure 7.4:* Redrawn from G. H. S.
Bushnell, *The First Americans,* Thames and
Hudson Ltd. *Figure 7.5:* Joe Ben Wheat,
University of Colorado Museum. *Figure 7.6:*
Redrawn by permission of McGraw-Hill Book
Company from *Prehistory of North America*
by Jesse D. Jennings. Copyright © 1968 by
McGraw-Hill, Inc. *Figure 7.7:* Courtesy, Field
Museum of Natural History, Chicago. *Figure
7.8:* U. S. Information Agency No.
111-SC-33831 in National Archives Building.
Figure 7.9: University of Alaska Museum.

CHAPTER 8
Figure 8.1: Top: Redrawn by permission
of Doubleday & Company, Inc. from *Tools of
the Old and New Stone Age* by Jacques
Bordaz. Copyright © 1970 by Jacques Bordaz.
Copyright © 1958, 1959 by The American
Museum of Natural History. Bottom row and
right: Adapted from *The Old Stone Age* by F.
Bordes. Copyright © 1968 by McGraw-Hill,
Inc. Used by permission of McGraw-Hill
Book Company and Weidenfeld & Nicolson
Ltd. *Figure 8.2: South African Archeological
Bulletin* and Professor v. Riet Lowe. *Figure
8.3: South African Archeological Bulletin* and
Murray Schoonraal. *Figure 8.4:* F. Peron.
Figure 8.5: Courtesy Robert Edwards,
Aboriginal Arts Board. *Figure 8.6:* Redrawn
by permission from Richard A. Gould, "The
Archaeologist as Ethnographer," *World
Archaeology* 3, 2 (1971), pp. 143–177, Fig. 18.

CHAPTER 9
Figure 9.1: Adapted by permission from
*The Material Culture of the Peoples of the
Gwembe Valley* by Dr. Barrie Reynolds,
published by Manchester University Press for
the Livingstone Museum, Zambia. *Figure 9.2:*
S. von Heberstain. *Figure 9.3:* From Sonia
Coles, *The Neolithic Revolution,* by
permission of the Trustees of the British
Museum (Natural History). *Figure 9.4:* Maria
Martinez, photographer; courtesy, Museum
of New Mexico. *Figure 9.5:* Courtesy of the
Trustees of the British Museum.

CHAPTER 10
Figure 10.2: Left: Redrawn from D. A. E.
Garrod and D. M. A. Bate, *The Stone Age of
Mt. Carmel* by permission of Oxford
University Press. Right: From James Mellaart,
The Earliest Civilizations of the Near East.
Reprinted by permission of Thames and
Hudson Ltd. *Figure 10.3:* Jericho Excavation
Fund. *Figures 10.4 and 10.5:* Redrawn from
James Mellaart, *Çatal Hüyük* by permission
of Thames and Hudson Ltd. *Figure 10.6:* From
Proceedings of the Prehistoric Society by
permission of the Society. *Figure 10.8:* From
Prehistory by Derek Roe, with permission of
the Biologisch-Archaeologisch Instituut,
Groningen, The Netherlands. *Figure 10.9:*
Reprinted from *Archeology,* January 1976,
p. 35. By permission. *Figure 10.10:* From
Grahame Clark, *World Prehistory,* 3rd. ed.,
Fig. 68, p. 140; © 1977 Cambridge University
Press. *Figure 10.11:* From *Prehistory* by Derek
Roe with permission of Presses Universitaires
de France. *Figure 10.12:* Redrawn from
Ancient Europe by Stuart Piggott, with the
permission of the Edinburgh University Press.
Copyright © Stuart Piggott, 1965.

CHAPTER 12
Figures 12.3 and 12.4: From *The
Archeology of Ancient China* by Kwang-chih
Chang, Harvard University. *Figure 12.6:*
Reprinted by permission from *The
Archeology of Ancient China* by Kwang-chih
Chang (New Haven: Yale University Press,
1968). *Figure 12.8:* Courtesy, Professor R. C.
Green. *Figure 12.9:* From Grahame Clark,
World Prehistory (New York: Cambridge
University Press, 1977) with permission of the
publisher. *Figures 12.10 and 12.11:* Courtesy
of the Trustees of the British Museum.

CHAPTER 13
Figure 13.2: Redrawn from *Prehistory of
North America* by Jesse D. Jennings.
Copyright © 1968 by McGraw-Hill, Inc. Used
with permission of McGraw-Hill Book
Company. (After P. C. Manglesdorf, R. S.

MacNeish, and W. C. Galinat, *Harvard University Botanical Museum Leaflets*, vol. 17, no. 5, and J. Hawkes and Sir L. Woolley, *Prehistory and the Beginnings of Civilization*.) *Figure 13.3:* From Gordon R. Willey, *An Introduction to American Archaeology*, Vol. II: *South America*, © 1971. Reprinted by permission of Prentice-Hall, Inc., Englewood Cliffs, N.J. *Figure 13.4:* Drawing by Junius Bird. Courtesy of The American Museum of Natural History. *Figure 13.5:* Jonathan E. Reyman. *Figure 13.6:* Redrawn by permission of McGraw-Hill Book Company from *Prehistory of North America* by Jesse D. Jennings. Copyright © 1968 by McGraw-Hill, Inc. After W. S. Webb, *University of Kentucky Reports in Anthropology and Archeology*, vol. 5, no. 2. *Figure 13.7:* Werner Forman Archive and Courtesy of the Museum of the American Indian, Heye Foundation, N. Y. *Figure 13.8:* Artist reconstruction, J. W. Hodge. Photograph courtesy of Illinois State Museum. *Figure 13.9:* From *Cahokia: Ancient Capital of the Midwest* by Melvin L. Fowler (Reading, Mass.: Addison Wesley Publishing Company, Inc., 1974). Courtesy of Melvin L. Fowler.

CHAPTER 14
Figure 14.1: Adapted from *Physical Anthropology and Archaeology* by Clifford J. Jolly and Fred Plog. Copyright © 1976 by Alfred A. Knopf, Inc. Reprinted by permission of Alfred A. Knopf, Inc. *Figure 14.2:* From *The Rise of Civilization: From Early Farmers to Urban Society in the Ancient Near East* by Charles Redman. W. H. Freeman and Company. Copyright © 1978. Reprinted by permission.

CHAPTER 15
Figure 15.2: Courtesy of The Oriental Institute, University of Chicago. *Figure 15.3:* Hirmer Fotoarchiv München. *Figure 15.4:* From *Early Mesopotamia and Iran* by Max E. Mallowan. Thames and Hudson Ltd., London (top) and Hirmer Fotoarchiv München (bottom). *Figure 15.5:* From Samuel Noah Kramer, "The Sumerians," *Scientific American*, October 1957. Reprinted with permission of W. H. Freeman and Company. Copyright © 1957 by Scientific American, Inc. All rights reserved. *Figure 15.6:* Reproduced by permission of the University Museum, University of Pennsylvania.

CHAPTER 16
Figure 16.3: George Holton/Photo Researchers. *Figure 16.4:* Michael Holford, London. *Figure 16.5:* The Metropolitan

Museum of Art, N.Y. *Figure 16.7.:* Courtesy of the Rhodesian National Tourist Board.

CHAPTER 17
Figure 17.2: Roger Viollet Photo Agency, Paris. *Figure 17.3:* The Bettmann Archive.

CHAPTER 18
Figure 18.2: From *Ancient Europe* by Stuart Piggott, with permission of the Edinburgh University Press (left) and courtesy of the Trustees of the British Museum (right). *Figure 18.3:* Ekdotike Athenon S. A. Athens. *Figure 18.4:* Hirmer Fotoarchiv München. *Figure 18.5:* Peter Clayton. *Figures 18.7 and 18.8:* Hirmer Fotoarchiv München. *Figure 18.9:* From *Ancient Europe* by Stuart Piggott, with permission of the Edinburgh University Press. *Figure 18.10:* Adapted from *Writing* by David Diringer, with permission of Thames and Hudson Ltd. © David Diringer, 1962.

CHAPTER 19
Figures 19.1 and 19.2: From *Ancient Europe* by Stuart Piggott, with permission of the Edinburgh University Press. Copyright © Stuart Piggott, 1965. *Figure 19.3:* Ashmolean Museum. *Figure 19.4:* Courtesy of the Trustees of the British Museum. *Figure 19.6:* Dr. Georg Gerster/Photo Researchers. *Figure 19.8:* From *Ancient Europe* by Stuart Piggott with permission of the Edinburgh University Press. *Figure 19.10:* Courtesy of the Trustees of the British Museum.

CHAPTER 20
Figure 20.2: Courtesy of the Smithsonian Institution, Freer Gallery of Art, Washington, D.C. *Figure 20.3:* Courtesy of the Trustees of the British Museum. *Figure 20.4:* The China Friendship Society; from Grahame Clark, *World Prehistory*, 3rd. ed. p. 306; © 1977 Cambridge University Press.

CHAPTER 21
Figure 21.2: Courtesy of Franklin C. Graham. *Figures 21.3 and 21.4:* From Gordon R. Willey, *An Introduction to American Archaeology*, Vol. I: *North and Middle America*, © 1966. Reprinted by permission of the author and Prentice-Hall, Inc., Englewood Cliffs, N.J. *Figure 21.5:* Kent V. Flannery, "Contextual Analysis of Ritual Paraphenalia from Formative Oaxaca," Fig. 11.9 in *The Early Mesoamerican Village*, Kent V. Flannery (ed.), (New York: Academic Press, 1976). *Figure 21.6:* Lee Boltin. *Figure 21.7:* From *Urbanization at Teotihuacán, Mexico*, vol. 1, *The Teotihuacán Map*: text, by Rene Millon. Copyright © 1973 by Rene Millon. By

permission of the author. *Figure 21.8:* Carl Frank/Photo Researchers. *Figure 21.9:* Smithsonian Institution National Anthropological Archives. *Figure 21.11:* Smithsonian Institution. *Figure 21.12:* Courtesy of Franklin C. Graham. *Figure 21.14:* Lee Boltin. *Figure 21.15:* Specified illustration from p. 8 (bottom) in *Mysteries of the Mexican Pyramids* by Peter Tompkins and Hugh Harleston. Copyright © 1976 by Peter Tompkins. Reprinted by permission of Harper & Row, Publishers, Inc.

CHAPTER 22

Figure 22.2: Right: From Gordon R. Willey, *An Introduction to American Archaeology*, Vol. II: *South America*, © 1971. Reprinted by permission of the author and Prentice-Hall, Inc., Englewood Cliffs, N.J. Left: Courtesy of Franklin C. Graham. *Figure 22.3:* Left: Peabody Museum, Harvard University. Right: Courtesy of Franklin C. Graham. *Figure 22.4:* The Bettmann Archive. *Figure 22.5:* Michael Moseley/Anthro-Photo. *Figure 22.6:* George Holton/Photo Researchers.

Index

Art [cont.]
   Olmec, 334, 336, 337, 360
   in Peru, 213, 358–360, 361, 363, 366
   Shang, 321–322, 325
   Upper Paleolithic, 106–110
Artifacts, 7, 19, 28, 129, 130
Asia, 97–114, 187–196, 319–327. See also
      Southeast Asia
Association, law of, 8
Assur, 257
Assurbanipal, 257
Assurnasirpal, 257
Assyrians, 245, 257–258, 270, 290, 291
Astronomy, 346
Athens, 299–300
Atlantic period, 43
Atlantis, 295
Augustus, 302
Aurignacian, culture, 104–105
Australia, 140–145
Australian aborigines, 22, 31, 140, 141, 144,
      156
Australopithecus, 50–51, 57–58, 61, 62, 66
Australopithecus africanus, 57, 62, 65, 66
Australopithecus boisei, 62
Australopithecus robustus, 57, 58, 59, 65, 66
Axes, 4, 128, 150, 162, 201, 305
   hand, 75–76, 78–79, 80–81, 82, 92
   stone, 306, 308, 315
Ayacucho culture, 214
Aztec civilization, 229, 237, 337, 350, 351,
      353–355

Babylon, 257, 258
Badarian culture, 183, 260
Baikal, Lake, 112–113
Bakri, al-, 272
Ball games, 346
Ban Chieng, 282
Bands, 31
Bantu languages, 271
Banyon Valley Cave, 190–191
Barbarians, 282, 302, 352
Barnard, Noel, 322
Bat Cave, 215
Battle Ax culture, 304, 306–307, 312
Beaker culture, 306, 3–7
Bear cult, 93–94
Beidha, 169
Beringia glaciation, 120
Bering Strait Land Bridge, 112, 114, 119–120
Big game hunting, 82, 106, 124–127
Binford, Lewis, 32, 92, 152–153, 154
Binford, Sally, 92
Bipedalism, 52, 53, 54, 56
Bison, 18, 125, 126
Black, Davidson, 74
Blanton, Richard, 338, 339
Boas, Franz, 27, 30
Boghazköy, 291
Bordes, François, 92
Boserup, Ester, 231

Boule, Marcellin, 86–87
Bow and arrow, 101, 136, 182, 307
Brahmanism, 283
Braidwood, Robert J., 152–153
Brain size, 61
Bronze Age, 23, 29
Bronzeworking
   in China, 321–322, 326
   In Europe, 301, 308–314, 315
   in Mesopotamia, 252
   in Southeast Asia, 281–282
Bruckner, E., 38, 39
Buddhism, 281, 283
Burials
   in Africa, 138
   in the Americas, 128, 220–221
   in Anatolia, 289
   in Asia, 313
   in Egypt, 182, 183, 268–269
   in Europe, 178, 305, 306–307, 311, 312, 313,
      315
   Mycenean, 296
   origins of, 18, 92–94
   in Peru, 211, 361
   Shang, 323, 324, 324, 326
Burins, 102, 104
Bushmen, See !Kung San
Butchery sites. See Kill sites
Butzer, Karl, 262

Caesar, Julius, 302
Cahokia, 222, 223–224
Calendar, Mayan, 346
Cambodia, 284–285
Camels, 271
Canals, 233, 245, 353
Canines, 51, 55, 74, 143
Cannibalism, 94
Canoes, 199, 200, 203, 353
Capac, Atahuallpa, 368
Capac, Huascar, 368
Capac, Huayna, 366, 367
Capac, Manco, 368
Carbon 14 (C14), 172–173, 176n
Cardium-decorated wares, 177, 178
Carnarvon, Lord, 269
Carter, Howard, 269
Carthage, 300, 301, 302
Çatal Hüyük, 170, 171–172, 236, 288, 293
Caton-Thompson, Gertrude, 183
Cattle, 158, See also Domestication, animals
   in Europe, 174, 312
   in Mesopotamia, 230
   in the Sahara, 184
Cave Bay, 143
Cave paintings, 107, 108, 109, 137–138
Caves, 17, 19, 28, 103, 106, 109, 123, 128, 142,
      184
Çayönü, 170
Celts, 316
Cereal crops, 150, 159, 174, 182–183, 191, 195,
      271, 291

Green, R.C., 200
Guattari cave, *94*
Gunz glaciation, 38
Gwisho, 138, 139
Gypsum Cave, 128

Hacilar, 170–171
Hadar, 59
Halafian civilization, *244*, 247–248
Hallstatt culture, *314*, 315–316
Hammond, Norman, 344
Hammurabi, 257
Hand axes, 75–76, *78–79*, *80–81*, 82, 92
Harappan civilization, 227, 254, 277–281
Harris, David, 155
Hassuna, 245
Haury, Emil, 216
Haven, Samuel, 119
Hawaii, 27
Haynes, Vance, 215
Herds, 156–157
Hieroglyphic writing, 261–262, *346*, *347*, 352
Higham, Charles, 190
Hinduism, 281, 283
Hissarlik, 289
Historical archaeology, 3–4
Historical records, 14
Hittites, 268, 290–291, 298, 311, 314
Hoabinhian culture, 188
Hockett, Charles F., 56
Hogup Cave, 128
Hohokam culture, 216
Hole, Frank, 153
Holocene epoch, 43
Holstein interglacial, 40, *41*, 85
Hominidae, 22, 40, 48
Homo, 61, 62, 65, 66, 74
Homo erectus, 64, 74–75, 77, 80, 81, 82, 84, 85, 86, 87, 101, 112
Homo habilis, 62–63
Homo sapiens, 22, 85–92, *88*, 101, 112
Homo sapiens neanderthalensis, 86
Homo sapiens sapiens, 86, 98, 101, 142
Honan, 320, 325, 326
Hopewell culture, 26, 32, 221–222, 234
Hopi Indians, 217, 218–219
Horizontal excavation, 16
Houses
  in Africa, *150*, 160
  in the Americas, *212*, 216–218, *220*, 221, 353, 364
  in Asia, 110, 111, *193*, 279, 325, 326
  in Europe, 176, 177, 178, 307
  in the Near East, *170*, 173, 245
Howell, F. Clark, 82, 87, 88, 89
Hsiao-t'un, 326, 327
Hsia rulers, 320
Hsi-pei-kang, 323–324
Huaca Prieta, 212
Huangho Valley, *192*, 193, 195, 326
Huari, 362–363
Human behavior, 52–56

Human origins, theories, 49–52. *See also* *Homo sapiens*
Hunter-gatherers, 18, 70, 99, 149–151, 155, 160. *See also* Gathering; Hunting
  in Africa, 16, 75, 89, 137–140, 182–185
  in Asia, 89, 113, 114, 119, 154, 162, 188–191
  in Australia, 140–145
  in Central and South America, 130–131, 214
  in Europe, 84, 89, 101, 103–106, 179–180
  in the Near East, 166–167
  in North America, 30, 117–133, 215–216, 219
Hunting, 54–55. *See also* Hunter-gatherers
  in the Americas, 124–125, 133, 207–208
  in Asia, 77, 92–94, 190, 202
  in Australia, 141–143, 202
  in Europe, 82–84, 92–94, 106
  in the Near East, 157
  in the Nile Valley, 182, 183
Huxley, Thomas, 49
Hydraulic State, 232
Hyksos, 268

Ica pottery, 365
Ice Age, 119–120. *See also* Glaciations
Inca civilization, 229, 363, 365–368
India, 282. *See also* Harappan civilization
Indians (American), 14, 99, 119, 124–125, 132, 206, 315–319
Indus Valley, 227, 254, 277–281
Interglacials, 36, 38
Invention, 25
Iron Age, 23, 302, *316*, 317
Ironworking
  in Africa, 184, 270, 271
  in Anatolia, 291
  in Asia, 281
  in China, 327
  in Europe, 301, 314–317
Irrigation, 183, 193, 194, 216, 217, 228, 232–233, 245, 339–340, 343, 361, 362, 364
Irwin-Williams, Cynthia, 215
Isaac, Glynn, 61, 70
Islam, 272, 348
Italy, 300–302

Jainism, 283
Japan, 114
Jarmo, 169–170
Java, 74, 85
Jayavarman VII, 284–285
Jemdet Nasr, 249–252
Jericho 166–169, 236
Johanson, Don C., 59
Jolly, Clifford, 55
Jomon culture, 162

Kalahari desert, 138–139
Kambujadeśa, 284–285
Kanesh, 289, 290
Kansan glaciation, 40
Karanga culture, 274–275

Quetzalcóatl, 350–352, 355

Radiocarbon dating, 13, 29, 141, 176n
Raikes, Robert, 281
Ramapithecus, 50–51, 52
Rathje, William, 235, 344–345, 348
Regourdou, 94
Relative chronology, 9–10
Religion. *See also* Temples
   in Africa, 272
   in the Americas, 224, 360, 363
   in Anatolia, 171, 290
   in Àsia, 280, 281, 283, 284, 325
   and civilization, 236
   in Egypt, 269
   in Europe, 311
   in Mesoamerica, 336, 339, 341, 345–348, 354
   origins of 92–94
   in Peru, 366
Renault, Mary, 294
Renfrew, Colin, 172, 295–296, 304, 305
Research design, 16
Rice, 190–191, 196, 281–282, 320
Rift Valley, 44
Riss glaciation, 38
Ritual, 94, 220–221, 311, 354, 366
Roman Empire, 300, 301–302, 315
Romans, 5, 14
Root crops, 152, 158, 191, 192, 207
Rudenko, Sergei, 313
Rudna Glava, 305
Russia, 110–114

Saale glaciation, 40, 41, 85
Sahara, 39, 184, 271
Sahlins, Marshall, 31
Samarra, 245–247
San culture, 99, *100,* 138–140, *139,* 185, 271, 273
Sanders, 340, 343
San José Magote, 337
San Lorenzo, 334
Sargon of Agade, 257
Sarich, Vincent, 51
Sauer, Carl O., 152, 158
Scandinavia, 179
Scapulimancy, 322, 325
Schaller, George, 54
Scythians, 312–313
Sea levels, 39, 43, 119, 120, 140, 141, 143, 153, 191
Seals, 280, 292
Seed crops, 158
Seeds, 28, 34, 169, 188–189
Seriation, 9, *11*
Service, Elman, 31
Sesklo, 291
Settlement patterns, 16, 150, 217–219, 325, 336, 342, 344, 358
Sex, and social roles, 55
Shang civilization, 18, 319–327
Shang Ti, 325

Shanidar, 92, 101
Sheep, 157
Shelters. *See* Houses
Shrines. *See* Ceremonial centers; Temples
Siberia, 110–114, 120, 132
Simons, Elwyn, 50
Singh, Gurdip, 277, 281
Sites, 7
Siwalik Hills, 50
Skulls, 61, 74, 85, 87
Slaves, 266, 270
Snaketown, 216
Social organization, 228, 229, 233
   Adena, 220
   Anasazi, 218–219
   Aztec, 353–354
   Greek, 300
   Harappan, 280
   Mayan, 348, 349–350
   Mesopotamian, *240,* 248, 249
   Mississippian, 222, 224
   at Monte Albán, 339
   Olmec, 333
   Peruvian, 358
   Shang, 322–323, 325
   Southeast Asian, 283
   at Teotihuacán, 342–343
Social surplus, 230
Society, stages of, 31
Soil conditions, 6
Solheim, Wilhelm, 189, 282
Solutrean culture, *104–105*
Southeast Asia, 152, 154, 158, 188, *189,* 190–191, 192, 197, 281–285
Space and spatial relationships, 7–8
Spaniards, 26, 353–355, 366–368
Sparta, 300
Spencer, Herbert, 24
Spirit Cave, 188–189, 190
Star Carr, 28
State-organized societies, 32
States, 238, 239, 255, 345, 346
   African, 270–275
   Anatolian, 288–291
   Egyptian, 266–269
   European, 306
   Greek, 299
   Mesoamerican, 339–341, 345, 353
   Peruvian, 362
   Southeast Asian, 281–285
Steinheim, *85*
Steppe peoples, 312–314
Steward, Julian, 27, 31, 232
Stone Age, 23, 38, 106, 110, 113, 158, 180, 182, 184
Stonehenge, *310–311*
Stone technology. *See* Technology, stone
Storage, food, 153, 160, 167, 183, 203
Stratigraphy, *9–10*
Sumerian civilization, 245, 249, *251,* 252–253, 254, 255, 257, 278
Sumerian King Lists, 14

Sundiata, 272
Superposition, law of, 9, *10*
Susa, 253–254
Swanscombe, *85*
Swiss Lake cultures, 177–178
Systems theory, 32–34, 235, *240–241*

Tabon Cave, 140–141
Taieb, Maurice, 59
Taiwan, 191
T'ang, 325
Ta-p'en-k'eng culture, 191
Ta Prohm, 285
Taro, 197, 198
Tarsiers, 49
Tasmanian culture, 143–145
Technology, 23. *See also* Bronzeworking; Copperworking; Ironworking; Tools
  and agriculture, 231–233
  blade, 103, *104*, 122–213, 136
  bone, 143
  and civilization, 231–232
  and domestication, 160–163
  maritime, 199–200, 294
  of the plains, 111, 112
  stone,.68–69, *90–91*, *102*, 123, 136, 140–141, 143, 260
Teeth. *See* Canines
Tehuacán Valley, 9, 26, 28, 127, 130, 155–156, 207–210, *209*, 339
Tell Halaf, 247
Tells, 7, 18
Temples, 236. *See also* Ceremonial centers
  in Africa, 268, 274, 275
  in the Americas, 223–224, 339, 341–342, 345–348, 352, 359
  in Asia, 201, 284, 285
  Greek, 289
  in Mesopotamia, 249
Tenochtitlán, 353, *354*
Teotihuacán, 339, 340, 341–343, 349
Tepe Yahya, 254
Terra Amata, 82–84
Terracing, 338, 339, 362
Teshik-Tash, 92
Thailand, 188–190
Thebes, 267–268, 270
Thera, 295
Thermoluminescence dating, 15
Thomsen, Christian Jurgensen, 23–24
Thucydides, 300
Thule culture, 133
Tiahuanaco, 362, 363, *364*
Tierra del Fuego, 131
Tikal, 18, 237, *345–348*
Time, 8–15
Tlacaelel, 353
Tlapacoya, 123
Toi Ete'huatai, 202
Toltecs, 237, 349, 350–352, *351*, 353
Tombs. *See* Burials
Toolmaking

Acheulian, 77–81
  in the Americas, 122–123, 128
  in Asia, 190, 191, *201*
  in Australia, 140–142, 145
  evolution of, 66–70, 80
  of *Homo erectus*, 74–77
  in Middle-Paleolithic period, *90–91*, 92, 112–113
  Mousterian, 89–92
  Oldowan, *67*, *68–69*, 70, 80
  in Upper Paleolithic period, 101–*102*, *103*
Tools
  agricultural, 150, 160, 162–163, *167*, 170, 312, 315, 325, 327
  axes (*see* Axes)
  choppers, *69*, *76*, *77–81*, 143
  cleavers, 79, 82
  composite, 89, 101, *102*
  cores, 90, 123
  flakes, 70, 81, 89, *90–91*, 92, 114, 123, 143, 153, 182
  points, 78, 89, 91, 92, 122–123, *124*, 143
  projectile heads, 124
  scrapers, 77, 82, 89, 92, *102*, *104*, 143
  spears, *91*, 106
Torralba, 82, *83*, *84*
Trade, 233–235
  Aegean, 292–295, 297, 298, 299, 300
  African, 270–275
  Anatolian, 288–290
  Asian, 169, 278, 280, 281, 282–283, 327
  Egyptian, 234, 260, 268
  European, 180, 301, 309–310, 311, 314, 315
  Indian Ocean, 282
  Mediterranean, 177, 298, 299–302
  Mesoamerican, 334, 336, 337, 339, 344–345, 346, 349, 350
  Mesopotamian, 234, 252–255, 257, 280
  in the Near East, 289
  in North America, 128, 221, 222, 224
  Peruvian, 362
  Polynesian, 199, 200
Tribes, 32
Tringham, Ruth, 174, 304
Trinil, 74
Tripolye culture, 175, *177*
Troy I and II, 289, 292
Tula, 350, *351*, 352
Tung Tso-pin, 319
Turkana, Lake, 61, 66, 74
Tutankhamun, 5, *6*, 269
Tylor, Edward, 24–25, 27
Tzolkins, 346

'Ubaid, al-, 248
'Ubaid culture, 248–249, 253
Unetice, 308–309
United States. *See* Americas
Urban Revolution, 228–229
Urnfield cultures, 301, 312, *313*, 314, 315
Ur of the Chaldees, 18, *250*, 252, 255, *256*
Uruk, 249, *250*, 252, 254

van Lawick-Goodall, Jane, 52–53
Varna, 304–306
Vavilov, N.I., 191
Ventana cave, 123
Venus figurines, 107
Vertical excavation, 16
Vespasian, 283
Villafranchian, 40
Village farming
  in Europe, 177–178
  in India, 278
  in Mesoamerica, 332
  in the Near East, 169, 245–247, 253–254
  in Peru, 359–360
Villanovan culture, 301
Virú, 361, 362
Volcanic areas, 12
von Koenigswald, G.H.R., 74
Voorhies, Barbara, 55, 99
Voyaging, 282–283, 299

Warfare
  in Asia, 321
  Aztec, 353
  and civilization, 236
  in Europe, 311–312
  Incan, 365, 366
  Maori, 203
  Mayan, 345, 348–349, 350
  Mesopotamian, 253, 300
  Toltec, 350, 352
Washburn, Sherwood L., 52, 55
Weichsel glaciation, 39, 40, 42–43, 86, 87, 88, 98, 101, 110, 112, 136, 140, 142, 143
Wessex culture, 311

Wheat, Joe Ben, 125
Wheatley, Paul, 237, 283, 284
White, Leslie, 27, 31
White, Peter, 198
Wilson, Alan, 51
Wisconsin glaciation, 119
Wittfogel, Karl, 232
Wooden tools, 6
Woodland culture, 219–220
Woolley, Leonard, 255
Writing, 229, 300
  cuneiform, 257
  hieroglyphic, 261–262, 346, 347, 352
  linear, 298, 299
  Minoan, 298
  pictographic, 249, 251, 280, 298, 299
  Shang, 321, 322
Würm glaciation, 38

Xerxes, 299

Yams, 184, 188–189, 197, 198
Yangshao, 193–194, 195–196
Yen, D.E., 188
Yenesei Valley, 112–113
Yin, 326–327
Yucatán, 332–355
Yupanqui Pachacuti Inca, 365
Yupanqui Topa Inca, 365

Zagros Mountains, 92, 152, 157, 169, 245, 257
Zawi Chemi Shanidar, 157, 169
Ziggurats, 237, 250
Zimbabwe, 274–275
Zinjanthropus, 67